ISRAEL NOW:

PORTRAIT OF A TROUBLED LAND

ISRAEL NOW:

DELACORTE PRESS/NEW YORK

PORTRAIT OF A TROUBLED LAND

Lawrence Meyer

For Aviva

Published by
Delacorte Press
1 Dag Hammarskjold Plaza
New York, N.Y. 10017

Grateful acknowledgment is made for permission to reprint excerpts from the following publications:

Rebirth and Destiny of Israel by David Ben-Gurion: Translated by Pinchas Rimon. New York: Philosophical Library, Inc., 1953. Reprinted by permission of Philosophical Library.

My Talks with Arab Leaders by David Ben-Gurion. Keter Publishing House Jerusalem Ltd.

A History of Israel: From the Rise of Zionism to Our Time by Howard M. Sachar. Copyright © 1976 by Howard M. Sachar. Reprinted by permission of Alfred A. Knopf, Inc.

Tin Soldiers on Jerusalem Beach by Amia Lieblich. Copyright © 1978 by Amia Lieblich. Reprinted by permission of Pantheon Books, a division of Random House, Inc.

Manufactured in the United States of America

First printing

Designed by Rhea Braunstein

LIBRARY OF CONGRESS CATALOGING IN PUBLICATION DATA

Meyer, Lawrence, 1941–
  Israel now.

  Bibliography: p.
  Includes index.
  1. Israel. I. Title.
DS126.5.M485   956.94   81–22216
ISBN 0–440–04179–1   AACR2

CONTENTS

Preface   ix
1/   INTRODUCTION   1
2/   THE CHARACTER OF ISRAEL   45
3/   THE ECONOMY   96
4/   THE SECOND ISRAEL   152
5/   POLITICS   174
6/   ARABS IN ISRAEL   236
7/   SECURITY   296
8/   THE KIBBUTZ   327
9/   RELIGION   346
10/ CONCLUSION   387
Bibliography   395
Index   401

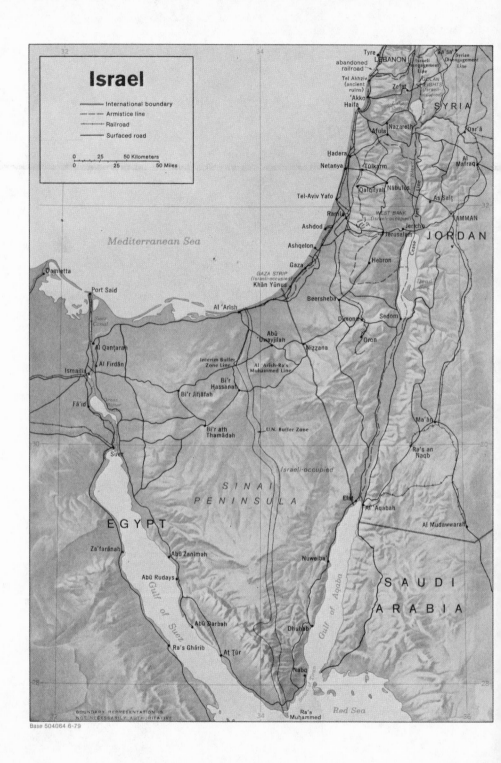

PREFACE

This book is designed to fill a gap in the literature about Israel. An enormous amount has been written about the Jewish state, but almost all of it has been on specialized, somewhat narrow topics. The reader, trying to find something that will provide useful background and explanations about Israel—her problems, her institutions, her basic characteristics and perspective—searches in vain for a serious but readable account. Five or six books taken together can serve that function, but no single work exists.

I set out four years ago to write such a book in order to make sense out of what is happening in Israel. This book is not a personal account of my stay in or my reactions to Israel. Occasionally I have chosen to share a personal experience I consider relevant to the point I am trying to make. For the most part, however, I have chosen to remain in the background, letting Israelis speak for and about themselves. I have tried throughout the book—and I ask the reader to do the same—to remember the unique circumstances of Israel, circumstances that are contradictory in nature and that make the problem of putting Israel into perspective extremely difficult: a country that is Western in orientation, though more than half of its population originated in non-Western countries; a country with no history prior to 1948, yet a national heritage that goes back thousands of years; a modern industrial state with a population dominated by citizens still making the transition from the traditional societies of their origin; a democracy with an electorate largely inexperienced until a generation ago as regards free speech, a free press, and the traditions of moderation and restraint so essential to maintaining democratic institutions.

The examples could be multiplied, but the point is simply that the perspective of a citizen from a modern industrial polyethnic democracy—like the United States—is not always apt for understanding Israel and her problems. I had to learn to step out of my own experience with its limitations, and try to enter the experience of the people I was writing about in order first to understand them. Having understood them, I could analyze and attempt an intelligent evaluation.

I lived in Israel with my wife, Aviva, and my three children, Ariel, Evan and Noah—for two years. We lived in two typical Jerusalem neighborhoods—the Greek Colony and Baka (Geulim). My children went to Israeli schools and learned Hebrew (as I did—my wife already was fluent). Our friends were mostly Israeli. Save for a one-week trip to Egypt, I did not leave Israel the entire time I was working on the book. We lived in Israel in much the same style as that of a middle-class Israeli family. I would not, however, presume to say that we lived like an Israeli family. Although we shared many of the experiences of Israelis, we remained an American family living in a foreign country.

My research was based on extensive reading, interviews, discussions, and conversations with literally hundreds of Israeli Jews and Arabs, and from firsthand observation of Israeli life.

No one, though, writes a book like this one without help. Although the responsibility for any errors of omission or commission is mine, I have been fortunate from the outset in finding assistance and encouragement. I am grateful to my editors at *The Washington Post*—Ben Bradlee, Howard Simons, and Bob Woodward—for giving me an extended leave to research and write this book. My agent, Charlotte Sheedy, pursued this project with the zeal of a true believer. Without her effort I would not have been able to write this book. Nahum Barnea, correspondent for *Davar*, offered advice and guidance to me in penetrating the maze of Israeli politics, history, and development. Laura Sachs graciously read my manuscript, editing and refining it. William Claiborne, Israeli correspondent for *The Washington Post*, was especially helpful and generous in smoothing my path and giving me his time. David Shipler, correspondent for *The New York Times* in Israel, read the manuscript and made helpful suggestions for improving it. My editor, Morgan Entrekin, refined the manuscript and prodded me to clarify my thinking.

I regret that I cannot thank everyone else who helped. Some prefer to remain anonymous. I would, however, like to mention those whose assistance was especially valuable. Robert Kaiser, Peter Osnos, Barry Sussman, and Richard Cohen, all colleagues at *The Washington Post*, offered me advice and moral support. Wolf Blitzer, Washington correspondent for *The Jerusalem Post*, and Sue Lehmann also provided me with useful suggestions.

In Israel, I had help and advice from a variety of friends and sources. Most prominent among those were Charles Wolfson, bureau chief for CBS, Gad Ranon, Tami Barnea, Yehiel Shemi, Kapai Pines, Dr. Clinton Bailey, Abraham Friedman, Nahum Astar, Zvi Sachs, Simcha Dinitz, Yehoshafat Harkabi, Yael and Abraham Katzir, Ronny and Miki Shtarkshal, Meron and Shoshana Benvenisti, Ehud Olmert, Yonathan Shimshoni, Sara Kestenbaum, Amnon Rubenstein, Stef Wertheimer, David Fields, Ze'ev Heffetz, Linda Rembaum, Dr. Mark Spivak, Prof. Michael Bruno, Yuval Elizur, Gideon Samet, Hirsch Goodman, Hillel Halkin, Shlomo Hillel, Yaron Ezrahi, Allan Shapiro, Dan Cohen, Charles Hill, Tamar Eldar, Amos Ettinger, Uri Freund, Edna Pe'er, Haim Margalit, and of my closest friends, Yosi Langotsky, David Harman, and Yoram Lehmann.

LAWRENCE MEYER

My parents, Fred and Gertrude Meyer, and my in-laws, Wolfe and Hadassah Sagalovitch, also were supportive during trying periods of this project, and I want to acknowledge their very substantial help.

Finally, I want to thank the person who served as my researcher, secretary, translator, typist, adviser, and source of solace—my severest critic, my best friend—my wife, Aviva. I simply could not have done it without her.

1 / INTRODUCTION

These are the words of the Lord God: When I gather the Israelites from among the peoples among whom they are scattered, I shall thereby prove my holiness in the sight of all nations. They shall live on native soil, which I gave to my servant Jacob. They shall live there in peace of mind, build houses and plant vineyards.

Ezekiel 28:25

We understand that a commonwealth must have an ideal, that this ideal is not merely beneficial but—why not say it—that it is indispensable.

Theodor Herzl

In the north, Israel begins on a chalk-white promontory overlooking the eastern edge of the Mediterranean. Before encountering Israel at this point, the coastline drops down from Turkey in a relatively straight line for four hundred miles, running along the western edge of Syria and Lebanon. Once known by the Arabic name, Ras-Nqura, the spot is now called Rosh HaNiqra in Hebrew. Rosh HaNiqra's slight bulge into the sea is the only natural demarcation between Israel and Lebanon. The coast continues its southerly direction in a generally smooth line past Acre—the only city Napoleon tried to conquer without success—past the modern port of Haifa, belching smoke and fire from its factories and refinery, past the concrete and stucco buildings of Tel Aviv and the ancient port of Jaffa directly south of it. Some twenty or so miles below Tel Aviv, near the biblical city of Ashqelon, the coast begins curving to the west, along the sands of Gaza, where the Philistines settled thousands of years ago, turning across the northern edge of the Sinai Peninsula where Moses and the Children of Israel wandered in the desert for forty years, and then, sweeping past the brown mud and marshes of the Nile delta, across North Africa and back to the Strait of Gibraltar.

To the east of Rosh HaNiqra lie the fertile fields of the western Galilee. Bananas hang in profusion directly below the promontory. In the distance are checkerboard fields of cotton, soybeans, and corn, grown through the elaborate irrigation and sprinkling systems that have been installed in the country wherever the sandy, brown soil shows promise of producing a crop.

Above Rosh HaNiqra, to the north, is Lebanon. What can be seen of it from Rosh HaNiqra is bleak and forbidding—barren landscape dotted with boulders and dried grass, a dusty panorama reflecting the sun. Farther east—as the northern border moves inland in a jagged line south, east, north, and then east again—the hills and mountains become verdant, reminding visitors, so green is the landscape, of Switzerland or Shangri-la. But all of that is to the east. Here from the coast the view of Lebanon is forbidding—rocky hills and scrub.

Directly below the promontory the Mediterranean penetrates into a blue-green grotto, a pocket of blissful relief from the scorching summer sun. Outside the entrance to the grotto, which Israelis proudly describe as more beautiful than the famed Blue Grotto of Capri, the railroad from Beirut once ran past on its way to Haifa. The tracks still come down from Lebanon, but they halt suddenly here at Israel's northern border. During Israel's War of Independence in 1948 Israeli engineers dynamited a small bridge at this point. A chain link fence now bars entry into the tunnel where the train used to run under Rosh HaNiqra. What little remains of the bridge serves as a stark reminder of Israel's isolation from her surrounding neighbors.

Back on top of Rosh HaNiqra, hard against the border, is a drab building painted in the muted browns and greens of camouflage. Radar turrets and antennae sprout from the building like electronic trees. Tourists stopping for a cold drink and a photograph rub shoulders with Israeli and United Nations soldiers. Rosh HaNiqra may be a tourist attraction but it is also a border area and Israel, after more than thirty years of independence, is still technically at war with all of her neighbors save Egypt.

This little sliver of land that is modern Israel, extending as far as Gaza to the south and east to the Jordan rift, is one of the most ferociously contested spots on earth. It is the birthplace of Judaism and Christianity and, through them, the fountain for much of Western thought and culture. From the Bible and historical research we know that the Hebrews first came to the land four thousand years ago when Abraham left his home near the Persian Gulf and traveled west. The land of Canaan, stretching from the Jordan to the Mediterranean was promised to Abraham. ("The Lord said: 'Raise your eyes and look into the distance from the place where you are, north and south, east and west. All the land you can see I will give to you and to your descendants for ever.' " Genesis: 13:14) Abraham, Isaac and Jacob lived on the plains and in the hills of Canaan until the Children of Israel were taken by Joseph to Egypt where the Israelites lived for more than 400 years before Moses and Joshua led them back to the land that God had promised Abraham.

What followed were the great days of the Jewish people in the Land of Israel—the defeat of the Philistines around 1010 B.C., the establishment of the kingdom of David, the defeat of the Jebusites and the conquest of Jerusalem in 1006 B.C. Over the next quarter of a century, David extended his empire from the Red Sea to the Euphrates and consolidated his rule, defeating the Ammonites, the Arameans, the Moabites, the Amalekites and the Edomites—all peoples who have faded into history. David died in 973 B.C. and was succeeded by his favorite son, Solomon, who built the Temple his father had started, some 900 years before Jesus. There is scarcely a square inch not in some way significant to Jewish or Christian history. The modern state of Israel has become the custodian of religious sites and shrines of three of the world's great religions and is full of remnants of past wars and civlizations that fought or settled in this tiny piece of land along the eastern edge of the Mediterranean basin. Over thousands of years of history the armies of Egypt, Babylonia, Assyria, Greece, and Rome, the Arabians, the Crusaders, the Mamluks, the Turks, the British, the Arabs and the Jews fought for control of this land. It is unlikely that any small portion of land anywhere else in the world has been so ardently sought after for so long by so many different armies and civilizations.

Why that should be so is not readily apparent. The country is minute. From its northernmost point in the northeast at Metulla to its southernmost point at Eilat, Israel is only 265 miles long. At its widest point—from the coastal plain to the eastern edge of the Negev, it is only 45 miles wide—and it is a parched, sandy type of land at that. Israel is roughly the same size as New Jersey—the Garden State—but unlike New Jersey, only twenty-five percent of Israel's land is suitable for farming. Much of the rest of Israel comprises rocky hills where trees have to search for crevices to fasten their roots. Without the aid of irrigation the land is capable of giving only one crop a year. The soil, rocky and brown rather than a rich black, must have yielded indifferent crops in ancient times. Water is not plentiful. Rain falls only four or five months during the year. Modern agriculture would be impossible without the painstaking construction of underground reservoirs and the development of innovative, highly sophisticated systems of irrigation. The land lacks natural resources. It has neither gold nor silver nor any other useful metals in commercial quantities, save for the potash deposits by the Dead Sea. Despite the abundance of oil in the region no significant quantities have yet been found here.

The chief attraction of Israel in ancient times derived from its central location, since it sits astride the main land-routes between Asia and Africa. History's great Western and Mideastern empires all have occupied this land at one time or another: the Egyptians, the Babylonians, the Greeks, the Romans, the Arabs—who swept out of the Arabian Peninsula and across North Africa—the Ottomans; and finally, the British, who saw it as an important strategic asset in the defense and protection of the Suez Canal to the west and, perhaps even more important, of India to the east.

Jews lived uninterruptedly in Israel as the dominant people of the country from approximately 1200 B.C until the conquest of Israel by Muslim Arab armies in the seventh century A.D. By that time Jewish communities—founded by Jews driven from Israel during the several wars and conquests—had been established in what are now Spain, France, Italy, Germany, Tunis, Morocco, Algeria, Libya, Turkey, Egypt, Greece, Iran, and Saudi Arabia. In 1099, when the Crusaders entered Jerusalem, Jewish and Muslim Arab defenders were slaughtered fighting side by side. Despite the Crusader conquests, Palestine, as the Romans called Israel (after the Philistines who had occupied the land before the Jews), had a Jewish population—large or small—for an unbroken span of time from the return of the Children of Israel from Egypt in 1180 B.C. until the present—a period of more than three thousand years.

Jews came and went from Palestine. In 1187 the Muslim conqueror, Saladin, drove the Crusaders from Jerusalem, and by 1291 the Mamluks had driven them completely out of Palestine. The Mamluks, Muslims who had been bought as slaves from poor peasant families in Georgia and the Caucasus, were brought to Egypt where they were raised as a special military class. In Palestine the Mamluks encouraged Jewish settlement at times. Jews, wandering from one country to another in search of a safe haven, sought refuge in Palestine. Jews continued to immigrate to—and emigrate from—Palestine after the Ottoman Turks defeated the Mamluks and incorporated Palestine into the Ottoman Empire in 1517.

Turkish rule over Palestine lasted four hundred years. In the last hundred years of that period Palestine suffered from the same atrophy and neglect that characterized the decadent, dying empire groaning under a succession of corrupt rulers. The Turkish occupiers stripped the land of its foliage. The already sensitive environment became wasted. Herman Melville, traveling through Palestine in the mid-1850s, described the landscape as "unleavened nakedness of desolation." Mark Twain, on a similar journey some years later, found little to extol in what he saw:

> Of all the lands there are for dismal scenery, I think Palestine must be the prince. The hills are barren, they are dull of color, they are unpicturesque in shape. The valleys are unsightly deserts fringed with a feeble vegetation that has an expression about it of being sorrowful and despon-

dent. . . . Every outline is harsh, every feature is distinct, there is no perspective—distance works no enchantment here. It is a hopeless, dreary, heartbroken land.

The Palestine Twain described one hundred years ago looked far different from the Israel we can see below us from our vantage point at Rosh HaNiqra. The flat lands of the coastal plain, a strip of land no more than ten or fifteen miles wide, now are green with crops winter and summer. The denuded hills have been reforested. Irrigation has made it possible to grow citrus in abundance. Mile after mile of orange, lemon, and grapefruit groves now line the roads of the coastal plain. Some of the familiar landmarks that Twain visited, fixtures on maps of the Holy Land since medieval times, have disappeared. Lake Hula, where volcanic ash once imprisoned the waters of the Jordan River to form a small lake and malarial swamp extending across the Hula valley, no longer exists. Groves of eucalyptus trees and extensive reterracing of the land by Jewish settlers have turned the former lake and swamp into a lush checkerboard of cultivated fields. The Jordan River itself, which once flowed through the great crack in the earth's surface that forms the Jordan rift from Lake Kinneret (the Sea of Galilee) to the Dead Sea, has been diverted by Israel and Jordan. The Dead Sea is slowly drying up. Beersheba, the desert well where Abraham swore an oath not to feud with Abimelech, now is the site of a city of more than one hundred thousand.

Modern technology and agricultural techniques, combined with the muscle and blood of four generations, have transformed the wasteland Twain saw into a sun-drenched cornucopia, the literal re-creation of the Land of Milk and Honey shown to Moses more than three thousand years before.

For more than one thousand years, however, the Jewish people had lived as a nation without territory. Dispersed first by the Babylonians, and later by the Romans, the Crusaders, and the Muslims, the Jews had settled in virtually every part of the world, on every continent where human beings established civilizations. For the most part, though, they settled in Europe, millions of them in the eastern part of Europe—in Poland, Russia, Lithuania, Latvia, Hungary, Bulgaria, and Romania.

In the age-old tradition of the Jews, they studied the Torah (the first five books of the Bible), and the rabbinical interpretations of it, the Talmud. They preserved their culture and followed the laws and commandments of their religion. Sometimes they survived. They did not prosper. Under the yoke of repressive laws—confined in some countries to carefully defined ghettos, towns, and areas; barred from entering certain occupations; often forbidden to own land—Jews lived outside the mainstream of European society.

Then, at the beginning of the nineteenth century, a new wave of self-determination and sensitivity to human rights swept across Europe. Jews were gradually freed from the restraints that had kept them separate. In England and western Europe discriminatory laws were eliminated and new opportunities for Jews opened, even if the old prejudices died more slowly.

Despite these gains, beneath the surface anti-Semitism continued to fester. "The Jews are our misfortune," a German intellectual wrote in 1879. In Germany, a country where Jews enjoyed enormous freedom and prosperity, anti-Semitic movements cropped up recurrently. These movements were not all disreputable collections of crackpot rabble. Some made elevated appeals founded on the philosophic and sociological reasoning of some of the best minds of Germany.

In France in 1894 mobs roamed the streets of Paris shouting, "Death to the Jews," as the trial of Captain Alfred Dreyfus proceeded.

In villages and hamlets of Russia, Jews continued to live in poverty, eking out a living under laws and traditions that continued to discriminate against them. Periodically, when the czar's government needed a scapegoat to release the tension mounting against the increasingly repressive regime, Jews were beaten and murdered in government-sanctioned pogroms. In 1882 the Russian government enacted laws forcing all Jews from smaller towns and villages to move to larger ones within the area of the Pale of

Settlement, generally an area in western Russia where Jews were permitted to live. Beaten down, living in constant fear and often on the edge of starvation, the Jews of Russia harbored a dream of returning to the homeland of their ancestors. Occasionally, a poor Jew was able to emigrate to Palestine to realize his dream to study Torah and to die in the Land of Israel.

By the mid-nineteenth century the Jewish communities of Europe were coming under pressure. The function that Jews had served as merchants and moneylenders was becoming obsolete with the rise of the modern state. Hostility to the Jews, ever present, grew as an indigenous Christian entrepreneurial class developed and became eager to take over the functions served by the alien Jewish communities.

In 1882 a Russian Jewish physician, Leo Pinsker, wrote *Auto-Emancipation*, arguing that Jews could overcome anti-Semitism only by having a state of their own. At about the same time in Russia, in the town of Kharkov, a group of Jews formed a group that eventually became known as Hovevei Zion, Lovers of Zion. Similar groups were formed in other towns of Russia and Poland. Between 1882 and 1903 some twenty thousand to thirty thousand Jews emigrated from eastern Europe to Palestine. Most left, finding the work too difficult, unable to adjust to squalid living conditions, and racked by malaria and other diseases. Some drifted back to Russia and Poland. Others set out for the New World, for the United States and Canada.

The idea of a return to the homeland and the creation of a Jewish state might have remained no more than an abstract idea had it not been for an assimilated Viennese Jew who was so struck by the anti-Semitism uncovered by the Dreyfus trial in Paris that he became obsessed with the problem. Without knowing that Pinsker had already plowed the same ground and come to the same conclusion, this urbane Jewish journalist in 1896 published *Der Judenstaat*. In Theodor Herzl, Zionism had found its Moses.

As Herzl surveyed the position of the Jew in the emerging world, he started with one premise: "We are a people—one people." Jews, he wrote, had attempted to merge into the social life of countries where they lived and to preserve only their religion.

We are not permitted to do so. In vain are we loyal patriots, our loyalty in some places running to extremes; in vain do we make the same sacrifices of life and property as our fellow citizens; in vain do we strive to increase the fame of our native land in science and art, or her wealth by trade and commerce. In countries where we have lived for centuries we are still cried down as strangers, and often by those whose ancestors were not yet domiciled in the land where Jews had already made experience of suffering. . . . It is useless, therefore, for us to be loyal patriots, as were the Huguenots who were forced to emigrate. If we could only be left in peace. But I think we shall not be left in peace.

Herzl's solution to the plight of the Jews was simple—almost too simple—the restoration of the Jewish state. At age thirty-six Herzl became a man possessed of a vision, the vision of

the promised land, where we may at last have hooked noses, black and red beards, bow legs, without being despised for it. . . . Where we can at last live as free men on our soil. . . . Where the offensive cry of "Jew" may become an honorable appellation like German, Englishman, Frenchman; in short, like all civilized people.

Herzl lived for eight years after the publication of *The Jewish State*. During those years he devoted his life and his small fortune to the cause of creating a Jewish state. When he died in 1904 at the age of forty-four, his goal was no closer to realization than it had been when he wrote his first pamphlet proposing the idea, except that hundreds of thousands of Jews, especially those of eastern Europe, had been ignited by the idea: "We shall not revert to a lower state, we shall rise to a higher one. We shall not dwell in mud huts; we shall build new and more beautiful and modern houses, and possess them in safety."

Unlike socialism or communism or other ideologies of the day, Zionism was not a comprehensive view of the world. Herzl did not attempt to do what Marx had done, to offer in his writings an explanation for any civilization other than that of the Jews. Rather he presented an analysis of the causes of anti-Semitism and a prescription to cure it, much as Pinsker had done before him. And unlike Marx, Herzl was also a political figure, who took an active role in implementing the program he had outlined in his pamphlet.

As a program political Zionism was directed at the liberation and revival of the Jewish *nation* and not the Jewish religion. Herzl was less concerned with the religious entity than with preserving the Jewish people. This focus of Zionism on nationalist rather than religious considerations aroused the enmity and opposition of ultrareligious Jewish leaders who were perfectly content to live in an intellectual and cultural backwater in a rapidly changing world, letting new ideas and trends pass them by while they concentrated on centuries-old commentaries that for them summed up the total wisdom and knowledge needed by Jews to cope with life. The nationalist emphasis also put Herzl and his followers at odds with Jewish assimilationists who were prepared to identify themselves *religiously* as Jews, but *nationally* as loyal German, French, British, or American citizens.

Herzl also made it clear at the outset that he was less concerned with the location of the Jewish state than with its creation. In *The Jewish State,* Herzl entertains the idea of using either Palestine or Argentina as the locus for a Jewish homeland. For Herzl the location was a matter of expediency. He favored a Jewish homeland wherever land was available for it, although he recognized that the wishes of the Jews who would do the settling would be controlling. Herzl created a furor within the Zionist movement in 1903 by bringing to it an offer of the British government to establish a Jewish colony in Uganda. Pinsker had been positively opposed to returning to Palestine. "We should above all not dream of a resurgence of ancient Judea," Pinsker had written.

We must not resume the connection with the place where our political life was formerly interrupted and shattered. Let our problem, if it is ever to be solved, be a modest one. It is difficult enough anyway. Not the "holy land" should be the aim of our endeavors, but a "land of our own."

Pinsker was touching on a pregnant issue, though at the time its full significance could not be realized. Pinsker, and later Herzl, were interested in a refuge, a "land of our own," for Jews so that they could become a normal people and thus become secure. Neither Herzl nor Pinsker appealed to any divine or historical right to a homeland, or to a particular piece of real estate. Herzl was perfectly willing to use land in Palestine—he understood the draw it had for Jews—but was not insistent. As it turned out, however, no other place but Palestine would do. The Zionists who rallied to Herzl's call, especially those from eastern Europe, thought only in terms of Palestine. And so the issue of choosing between a refuge, a "land of our own," and a return to the ancient homeland did not then arise. The Jewish state could be both. But the question was still there, beneath the surface, unresolved, ready to reappear—as it would periodically. What was the purpose of the Zionists in creating a state? Did they simply want a refuge in an increasingly threatening world, or did they want to restore their ancient homeland in all its former glory? The answer was that—in the best of all worlds—they wanted both. But faced with the necessity of choosing one or the other, of establishing priorities, which would it be—refuge or Land of Israel? The question still looms large even in an Israel established in Palestine, whenever the question of her national purpose is the issue.

For the Zionist movement, however, the matter was momentarily resolved with the rejection of Herzl's Uganda proposal and his death in 1904. Herzl's death was a blow to the Zionist movement, but not a fatal one. He had brought it to spectacular new heights, but he was not the only prophet of Zionism. An amorphous sort of movement existed before his pamphlet was published. The Jews who came to Palestine in the late nineteenth century and early twentieth century, and their children, were responding to a new vision of what the Jew should be in the modern world. They answered the call of a series of Jewish poets and prophets—Pinsker, Moses Hess, Chaim Nachman Bialik, Achad Ha'am (Asher Ginsburg) and A. D. Gordon.

Gordon, a Russian Jewish writer and philosopher, was concerned with different symptoms of the same disease that had attracted Herzl and Pinsker. Jews were not, Gordon conceded, a normal people. Years of wandering, persecution, and deprivation had transformed them. If Jews wanted to be a natural people again rather than a rarefied (and dying) religious species, they had, he argued, to relearn the skills of a normal people and to redevelop their culture:

A people that was completely divorced from nature, that during 2,000 years was imprisoned within walls, that became inured to all forms of life except to a life of labor, cannot become once again a living, natural working people without bending all its will-power toward that end. We lack the fundamental element; we lack labor, but labor by which a people becomes rooted in its soil and in its culture.

Labor, for Gordon, was the sine qua non of the establishment of a Jewish culture, and in the revitalization of the Jewish people:

A living people always possesses a great majority to whom labor is its second nature. Not so among us. We despise labor. Even among our workers there are those who work because of necessity and with the continual hope of some day escaping from it and leading "the good life." We must not deceive ourselves. We must realize how abnormal we are in this respect, how alien labor has become to our spirit, and not alone to the individual life, but also to the life of the nation. Quite characteristic of us is the Hebrew expression: "When Israel does the will of the Lord, its work is done by others." These with us are not mere words. The sentiment, whether we are aware of it or not, has become a subconscious attitude within us, a second nature to us.

Gordon's writing and his example were not without effect. He became an apostle of HaPoel HaZair (the Young Worker), one of many organizations that sprang up among the new, young Jewish settlers who began the long journey back to Palestine. Their insistence that *Jews* should do the work was not motivated by prejudice or the intent to discriminate against Arabs, but by a sincere desire to gain the spiritual as well as the material benefits of labor. Such a course was not, however, without opposition even within the growing Jewish community, or Yishuv, in Palestine. Earlier Jewish settlers from the late nineteenth century—or at least those who stayed—found it easier and more profitable to hire and supervise Arab labor. For ideological as well as practical reasons (they had to eat), the young Jews who started coming in the early years of the twentieth century insisted that they be given the work that needed doing.

These young settlers lived an ascetic life, shunning comfort and luxuries which were, in any case, in short supply. They took as their motto a simple slogan, which says, in translation from the Hebrew, "We came to build the land and to be built by it."

The life of the early pioneers was dangerous and exhausting. They faced attack from hostile Bedouin, were at the mercy of the elements and fell prey to malaria-carrying mosquitoes. One of the earliest settlers wrote years later of the hardships of his fellow pioneers:

> The land was badly neglected. Only a small part of the land was usable for agricultural purposes. It was also out of the way of other settlements and far from Gaza, its county seat. To reach there with a wagon was almost impossible in winter as the wadis were full of water, the country around was wild. They began to put up a barn for themselves and for their cattle, but, owing to the treachery of their Arab neighbors who reported to the government that they were building an arsenal, they were not allowed to complete the building. There were no trees, no houses and no wells, and the poor idealists were compelled to drink the water from stagnant

pools. . . . They proceeded with much deliberation, but unfortunately with little technical skill. At first some progress was made, but sickness, misfortune and want handicapped them. They did not possess sufficient land suitable for agriculture and when they were fortunate enough to have sowed the fields, their hostile neighbors drove their horses and cattle upon the fields and destroyed the crops. The yield of the crops was entirely inadequate to their needs. Skilled agriculturists could not be hired; the outlook became in all respects gloomy. Yet these idealists were not dismayed for they sought neither wealth nor luxuries.

Despite their simple tastes, many of the "young idealists" found the going too difficult and simply left. Some estimates place the number of emigrants at eighty-five percent or more of the total. But those who remained were often driven by a vision that neutralized the hardships. "I never felt so thoroughly contented as when my friend and I met together in our little stone hut after a hard day's toil," wrote another pioneer.

The settlement then was in a stage of transition between wilderness and so-called colony. . . . We were city dwellers used to city life and our removal to a wilderness meant more to us than all the hardships we endured. Yes! It was the idea that we were building a social structure for our brethren, meant to last for all time, and houses where we could at least hope to pass the years of our natural life that supported us constantly with frenetic energy to continue the work we started. It was the unselfish, deeply rooted idealism and intense love for the land that stimulated the desire in my friends to carry out the plan.

Zionism, according to the philosophy of the heralds who followed Herzl, had as its purpose the reconstitution of the Jewish people, the creation of a new Jew to replace the frail, cowering, pale city-dweller of eastern Europe with a strong, brave, bronzed creature whose hands plowed into Mother Earth.

"Zionism in its essence is a revolutionary movement," David Ben-Gurion, Israel's first prime minister, wrote.

One could hardly find a revolution that goes deeper than what Zionism wants to do to the life of the Hebrew people. This is not merely a revolution of the political and economic structure—but a revolution of the very foundations of the personal lives of the members of the people. . . . It is a revolt against a tradition of many centuries, a tradition of practically living in exile while in theory longing helplessly for redemption. Instead of rootless life in exile, we substitute an attempt at reconstruction and creativity on the soil of the homeland. Instead of a people dependent on others, instead of a minority living at the mercy of a majority—we call for a self-sufficient people, master of its own fate. Instead of a corrupt existence of middlemen, suspended in mid-air, we call for an independent existence of a working people, at home on the soil and in a creative economy.

In Russia and throughout the rest of Europe the miseries of dying feudalism and the excesses of the industrial revolution, combining with the optimism of the Enlightenment, were spawning new ideologies of social justice and reform. Young Russian and Polish Jews, many of them scorched by the abortive revolution of 1905, made their way to Palestine carrying with them the idea that they belonged to the working class but that they were *Jewish* workers. Despite the derision they suffered from other socialists, some of them also Jews, these émigrés believed that the principles of Zionism and socialism could be melded into a cohesive ideology that would serve as the intellectual framework of the new society they were building—founded on Jewish labor, on principles of equality and social justice.

The end result of Zionism would be not only the redemption of the Jewish people but also the creation of a society that would serve as an example for the rest of humanity. In this way the new society would fulfill the biblical prophecy that Israel would be "a light unto the nations."

15

"If the Jewish State is to become a fact," wrote the Labor Zionist Nahman Syrkin,

> there must be no place in it for the conflicts of modern life. The Jewish State must constantly have before it the ideals of justice and social wisdom if it wishes to attract modern man. And when the social and scientific foundations of the state are laid they will be followed by modern technical achievements. The Jewish State must be socialist, if it is to be at all. Zionism must of necessity merge with socialism, if it wishes to be the ideal of all Jews—the worker, proletariat, middle class, the intelligentsia and the Jewish ideologist.

But Zionism was not a monolithic movement. The Labor Zionists, who emerged as the dominant force, were on the left. The General Zionists, bourgeois Jews who often sided with the Labor Zionists, were in the center. A small minority of religious Zionists also were in the movement. And on the right stood the Zionist Revisionists. Led by Ze'ev Jabotinsky, a fiery orator and something of a romantic, the Revisionists were an antisocialist, ultranationalist group that believed in strength and force as the way to win what they believed was theirs by historical right. Jabotinsky ultimately led his followers out of the mainstream Zionist movement and the two streams remained in conflict—occasionally violent—throughout the period of the British Mandate from 1918 until 1948. The forces of the two movements narrowly averted civil war during the Israeli War of Independence and echoes of those past conflicts continue to reverberate in Israel today.

The universal characteristics of the Labor Zionist's socialism mollified, but did not entirely remove, the narrower and sometimes even chauvinistic elements of Zionism. Zionism, whether that of the socialists, the General Zionists, or the Revisionists, was above all a movement of national reawakening. Nowhere was this revival clearer than in the Herculean effort to overhaul a moribund language and put it into service as the tongue of the new Jew. Herzl, emerging from cosmopolitan *fin de siècle* Vienna, had underestimated the nationalist sentiments he was encouraging. Whatever the language the inhabitants of the Jewish state would speak, he was certain what it would *not* be.

"We cannot converse with one another in Hebrew," he wrote in *The Jewish State*. "Who amongst us has a sufficient acquaintance with Hebrew to ask for a railway-ticket in that language? Such a thing cannot be done." Herzl privately favored German (his own native language) as the lingua franca of the new country. Hebrew, after all, was a dead language and had not been used for everyday commerce for almost two thousand years. It was the language of the Torah, the Talmud, and the synagogue, reserved for holy occasions, and as a result, a language in which it was impossible to carry out the functions of normal life and commerce—unless, of course, someone undertook to revitalize the language and harness it for use in the modern age. The task was assumed by a slight Jew from Russia, Eliezer Perlman—later known to the world as Eliezer Ben-Yehuda—who emigrated to Palestine in 1881. According to legend Ben-Yehuda forbade his wife to speak to their infant son until she could speak to him in Hebrew. The couple's children were not permitted to play with other children lest they be exposed to a language other than Hebrew. Ben-Yehuda himself endured hardship and the violent hostility of the established Orthodox Jewish community in Palestine, which he vehemently attacked for opposing the use of Hebrew for everyday discourse.

Gradually, however, his efforts were successful. In 1904, the year Herzl died, Ben-Yehuda published the first volume of a new Hebrew dictionary. The use of Hebrew as the spoken language of the new Jewish community in Palestine increased—outside of the ultra-Othodox community—so that by 1916 forty percent of the Jewish population spoke Hebrew as their first language. A Hebrew Teachers Association was formed. The turning point in the struggle can probably be dated to 1913, when the board of governors of the newly established Technion, the Israel Institute of Technology, decided to make the language of instruction German rather than Hebrew. After a controversy that shook the growing Jewish community of Palestine, the decision was reversed. Hebrew was designated the language of instruction of the Technion and later of the newly established Hebrew University in Jerusalem.

As a movement of national revitalization Zionism concentrated on the situation of Jews without proclaiming any racial superiority. These new settlers were not coming, as the colonialists had come to Africa and Asia, to subdue the natives and to exploit the natural wealth of the land. In fact, the land had little natural wealth to exploit. To the extent that they thought about the Arabs at all in the early days of the movement, the young Jewish settlers assumed that their presence would benefit the Arabs, who would share in the increasing prosperity and welcome the Jews who were bringing it. That it worked out otherwise is a reflection of the naïveté of the Jewish settlers, rather than a manifestation of their ill will. As we shall see, neither Herzl nor the Jewish pioneers who went to settle in Palestine gave much early thought to the Arabs. The Zionists were too preoccupied with events in Europe and were too busy talking about and working for the world they wanted to create to pay close attention to the world that actually surrounded them in Palestine.

Herzl had exhausted himself in two principal endeavors: trying to find a patron to finance the new society he envisioned, and trying to find a friendly power that would give him a place to put it. Although Herzl had considered the idea of Argentina and even brought the Uganda proposal before the Zionist congress, Palestine emerged as the only place where a Jewish homeland could work in the same way that Hebrew, as we can see in retrospect, was the only language that a revived Jewish nation could speak. Throughout the centuries of exile Jews had never forgotten Jerusalem in their prayers. Jerusalem is mentioned continually in the Torah. The city figures as the spiritual locus of the Jewish religion, the people, and the state that had been. Palestine was the place to which the young pioneers journeyed. They had no interest in going anywhere else to create a Jewish state.

The issue was resolved finally on November 2, 1917, when the British cabinet authorized Arthur James Balfour to write to Lord Rothschild, president of the British Zionist Federation. Balfour's short letter informed Rothschild that the British cabinet ministers "view with favour the establishment in Palestine of a national home for the Jewish people, and will use their best endeavours to facilitate the achievement of this object."

The Balfour Declaration was carefully phrased. It referred, after much discussion, to "*a* national home" rather than "*the* national home" as had been proposed. And, the declaration noted in qualification, "it being clearly understood that nothing shall be done which may prejudice the civil and religious rights of existing non-Jewish communities in Palestine."

It was a momentous step forward toward the realization of Herzl's dream. Precisely why the British government chose the moment it did to respond to the efforts of the Zionist movement is not entirely clear. Balfour's own explanation, in his memoirs, was that the cabinet wanted to reward Chaim Weizmann, a Russian Jewish chemist and ardent Zionist, whose discovery of an alternative method for synthesizing acetone had immeasurably assisted the British war effort. More likely, however, it seems that the British hoped to secure the support of Russian Jews at a moment when Russian support for the Allied war effort was wavering. And no doubt, the British government saw a Jewish community in Palestine as a natural ally and buffer on the eastern flank of the Suez Canal, Britain's vital passage to India. Weizmann in his memoirs also credits the sincere Christian belief of Balfour; Lloyd George; Jan Christian Smuts, a South African; and other prominent Englishmen for their support of a Jewish homeland.

The Balfour Declaration has to be understood in the broader context of the victorious Allied powers carving up the former Ottoman Empire into spheres of interest. The Arabian Peninsula, Syria, Iraq, Lebanon, and Palestine all were part of that empire. France showed an interest in Syria and Lebanon, Britain in Palestine and the countries along the Arabian Sea.

As referred to in the Balfour Declaration, Palestine originally meant what is now Israel, the West Bank, and Jordan. Transjordan was separated by the British from the rest of Palestine in 1921 in an effort to placate King Abdullah, son of King Hussein ibn-

Ali, the Grand Sharif of Mecca and descendant of Muhammad the Prophet. This division of Palestine, largely unnoticed at the time it occurred, contributed to later difficulties in the region.

Within a few years the Balfour Declaration and the British government's support of a Jewish homeland with unlimited Jewish immigration to Palestine were a matter of controversy in the region and an issue for debate in the British Parliament. Pressured by the leaders of rising Arab nationalism on the one side and by prominent Jewish figures and supporters of Zionism on the other, subsequent British governments tacked back and forth between them, trying to appease first one and then the other—never successfully satisfying either. It was a classic case of rights—Arab and Jewish—in conflict. By the end of the 1930s England had virtually abrogated the Balfour Declaration in an effort to placate Arab nationalists and to quell riots in Palestine. Jews who had already settled there would be allowed to remain, but the British government restricted further Jewish immigration to Palestine.

By the 1930s Herzl's darkest visions were coming true in ways more horrible than he or anyone else had imagined. Nazism had seized Germany. German Jews, who had once considered themselves thoroughly assimilated—more German than Jewish—found themselves disfranchised, stripped of their civil rights and property, and hounded in the streets. A frightful night was descending on Europe, threatening, among its many victims, the Jewish people who lived there.

In 1939 almost nine million Jews lived in Europe—the largest grouping of Jews in the world. Although not so wealthy or so secure as their brothers and sisters in the United States, Europe's Jews were heirs to a rich heritage. In France a Jew had risen to prime minister. In Poland, where Jews had had a difficult time with anti-Semitism for centuries, Jews accounted for roughly ten percent of the country's population of thirty-three million. By 1939, however, only the most optimistic—perhaps foolhardy—did not believe that a terrible storm was about to break over their heads. Some of the more prescient of Europe's nine million Jews already had left. Many went to England, Argentina, Brazil, Cuba,

Australia, New Zealand, and the United States. A fraction came to Palestine.

As war grew closer, the civilized countries of the world took various measures to restrict the flow of Jewish immigrants across their borders. England refused the entreaties of the archbishop of Canterbury to abandon its quota system. Chile limited Jewish immigration to 300 persons a year. Cuba and the United States turned away 900 German Jewish refugees on the S.S. *St. Louis,* forcing them to return to Europe and the fate awaiting them there. In 1940 the Congress of the United States rejected a bill to open Alaska to Jewish refugees. In 1941 Congress *tightened* the quota system under which immigrants were admitted to the United States, making it *more* difficult for Jews to enter. An attempt to gain entry for 20,000 German Jewish children beyond the limit imposed by law was rejected by Congress.

Jews *were* wanted in one place. Those who could sneak into Palestine, past the picket ships and lookouts posted by the British to restrict their entry, were welcomed by the hundreds of thousands of Jews already settled there. Some ships were intercepted by the British and turned back. Two such ships sank, and most of the passengers aboard drowned. Passengers on boats that did get through were interned in special camps. Some "illegal" immigrants, coming overland through Iraq and Syria, made it to Palestine. After 1943, when news of the Holocaust leaked out of Europe, the British relaxed the restrictions somewhat, permitting Jews who were able to escape from Europe to enter Palestine. In all, between 1940 and 1945 some 61,000 persons entered Palestine.

When Germany's armies surrendered in 1945, the settling dust revealed the full extent of the devastation that the Nazis had inflicted on the populations of Europe, and especially on Europe's Jews. Of 70,000 Jews in Greece, 16,000 survived. Only 35,000 of 140,000 Jews in the Netherlands remained. Out of 650,000 Jews in Romania, 200,000 were left. In Germany and Austria 40,000 of 330,000 Jews remained. In the Soviet Union the Nazis killed 900,000 Jews of the Ukraine, 245,000 Jews in Byelorussia, and another 107,000 in Russia. But the cruelest blow was inflicted in

Poland where the greatest number of Jews had lived—3.3 million before the war. After, only 300,000 were left. Fully ninety percent of Poland's Jewish population—3 million men, women, and children—were murdered by the Nazis.

In the face of numbers like these—6 million of nearly 9 million slaughtered—words utterly fail to convey the full horror of what happened. Entire families, villages, and towns were lost forever. The cream of European Jewry was wiped out. Those who survived Hitler's death camps were left permanently scarred by the horror of the Holocaust. The Jews of Europe, in the description of one observer, were a people "racked and impoverished, decimated and rent."

For the 650,000 of Palestine, one lesson was paramount—the need for Jews to control their own affairs, their own destiny. The importance of the Holocaust as a factor in Israeli affairs cannot be exaggerated. The totality of the Israeli experience cannot be understood simply by understanding the effect of the Holocaust. But it is not possible to understand Israel and the modern Jew without also understanding the effect of the Holocaust.

The conventional wisdom holds that Israel would not have been established without the Holocaust. On the other hand, after this cataclysm the heart of the Zionist movement, the millions of Jews of eastern Europe who would have been willing immigrants to a Jewish state, were no longer alive. Many of those who came to Palestine and later to Israel were Jews who simply had no other place to go. Thousands of Jews who tried returning to their homes from the concentration camps found nothing left of their former communities. Or they were once again the victims of pogroms. For hundreds of thousands of Jews in postwar Europe, Israel was the only alternative to life in refugee camps—living off international charity. Immediately following World War II the British barred Jewish immigration to Palestine. The only Jews who came in were "illegal" immigrants, those who walked out of the displaced-persons camps where they had been living, made their way across Europe with the assistance of Zionist organizations, and boarded the leaky boats chartered to carry them to Palestine. Thousands more were intercepted by the British and sent to crowded camps in Cyprus or back to Europe to the same camps they had left.

R.H.S. Crossman, a member of an independent commission investigating the condition of refugee camps after the war, wrote this description after visiting one such camp:

These 98,000 people, most of them Polish Jews, had been deported to a foreign country [Germany] whose language most of them could not speak. They had been rescued by our armies from the gas chambers. If the war had gone on a few weeks or even a few days longer, none of them would have been alive. Nearly all of them were isolated survivors of families which had been wiped out. A large number, when the war ended, had walked hundreds of miles back to their home towns to find themselves the sole survivors of the Jewish community, living ghosts returned from the grave to reclaim property which had long since been shared out. So they had trudged back to the camps.

Even if there had not been a single foreign Zionist or a trace of Zionist propaganda in the camps, these people would have opted for Palestine. Nine months had passed since VE Day, and their British and American liberators had made no move to accept them in their own countries. For nine months, huddled together, these Jews had had nothing to do but to discuss the future. They knew that they were not wanted by the western democracies, and they had heard Mr. [British prime minister Clement] Attlee's plan that they should help to rebuild their countries. This sounded to them pure hypocrisy. They were not Poles anymore but, as Hitler had taught them, members of the Jewish nation, despised and rejected by "civilized Europe." They knew that far away in Palestine there was a national home willing and eager to receive them and to give a chance of rebuilding their lives, not as aliens in a foreign state but as Hebrews in their own country.

23

Despite her energetic efforts to keep Jewish refugees from Europe out of Palestine after World War II, Britain found the tide of worldwide public opinion against her. At the same time, within Palestine a vicious three-sided guerrilla war was under way —Arabs against Jews, Arabs against the British, Jews against the British. Differences emerged among various groups within the Jewish community of Palestine (the Yishuv) over the proper strategy. Groups like the right-wing Irgun Z'vai Le'umi (the National Military Organization, better known as Etzel or abroad simply as the Irgun) had already begun attacking the British before World War II was over. The British responded by capturing Irgun members. Some were hanged. The Irgun responded by hanging two captured British sergeants. Even more extreme in its approach was the Lech'i, or Stern Gang, an offshoot of the Irgun, which resorted to terrorism and assassination in order to drive the British out of Palestine and establish a Jewish state.

The main, and more moderate, military force of the Yishuv was the Haganah, meaning simply the defense. As its name implied, the Haganah was a reactive force, initially striking at Arabs only when provoked. It was designed to protect Jewish settlements from attack. But the Haganah still was an illegal, underground organization. Jews caught with weapons or suspected of belonging to the Haganah were imprisoned for long terms.

Between the external pressure of adverse world opinion and the internal pressure of an escalating civil war, the British government proved unable to maintain the Mandate over Palestine that had been granted to it by the League of Nations after World War I and continued by the United Nations after World War II.

Jewish leaders outside Palestine and the leaders of the Yishuv were pressing the United Nations to allow Jewish refugees into Palestine. They were able to present an impressive case based on the accomplishments of almost thirty years of Jewish pioneering under the British Mandate. Moreover, the Jewish case was buttressed by expert testimony detailing how modern technology could be harnessed to enable Palestine to support an enlarged population.

The Arabs of Palestine were hardly silent on the point. They had a legitimate case to make based on their presence on the land for centuries preceding the Jewish revival and return to Palestine. Arab spokesmen argued eloquently before United Nations bodies considering the problem that the Arabs of Palestine inevitably would be displaced by massive Jewish immigration.

It may be that had Britain taken a more conciliatory position toward Jewish immigration to Palestine after World War II, the historical outcome might have been entirely different. The war had produced any number of conundrums, not the least of which was where to put the hundreds of thousands of Jewish refugees rendered not only homeless but stateless. Britain's persistent refusal to allow more than token numbers of Jews into Palestine along with the relentless publicity given to the thousands of Jewish refugees in miserable camps or on board creaking freighters and, finally, the mounting viciousness of the terrorist campaign being conducted against the British in Palestine—all took their toll. At the height of the post-World War II period of the Mandate, Britain had eighty thousand army troops and sixteen thousand police in Palestine devoted to keeping order. British dependents were evacuated, and only essential British civil servants remained, living in security areas surrounded by fences and barbed wire. The effort was costing the financially strapped British government more than thirty million British pounds a year.

When British efforts to find a way to mediate the differences between the Arabs and the Jews of Palestine failed, Britain announced in February 1947 that she was referring the matter to the United Nations for decision. Britain had effectively washed her hands of responsibility for the fate of Palestine.

After months of study the United Nations voted on November 29, 1947, to partition Palestine, carving the country into Jewish and Arab sections. Jerusalem and Bethlehem were to be in a special, international zone.

The UN partition plan—though awkward and perhaps ungainly on a map—might have proved workable had goodwill existed between the Arabs and Jews of Palestine. But goodwill was practically—but not totally—nonexistent. The Jewish community, through its quasi-government in Palestine, the Jewish Agency, accepted the partition plan. The Arabs in Palestine, who had no counterpart organization to the Jewish Agency, spoke through action. A full-scale guerrilla war was started by the Arabs in and around Palestine even before the British pulled out. The Arabs made it clear that no Jewish state would be tolerated in Palestine.

The British, for their part, made only feeble efforts to keep the peace, often intervening when Jewish forces gained the upper hand, standing by when the Arabs were in control. Britain made virtually no effort to prepare for an orderly transition from Mandate to self-government, simply withdrawing and leaving it to the Jews and Arabs to fight it out between themselves for control.

Israel's War of Independence in fact began November 29, almost six months before the actual Declaration of Independence on May 14, 1948. It continued, with periodic cease-fires, until early 1949 when Jordan, Syria, Egypt and Lebanon were forced by their military position to agree to an armistice, while rejecting a full-scale peace treaty with Israel.* Although badly-outnumbered and outgunned, the nascent Israel Defense Forces had been able through skillful strategy and high motivation to repulse the Arab attacks. The final borders of the state, as outlined in the armistice agreements, gave Israel considerably more territory than the original UN partition plan had called for. But the borders still left Israel at a decided strategic disadvantage. The incipient nation shared a long border with Egypt on the Sinai desert where the Gaza Strip penetrated 20 miles along the coastal plain into Israel, putting Egyptian artillery within range of Tel Aviv and Israel's principal population concentration. In the northeast, Syria occupied the Golan Heights, looking down on the Jewish agricultural settlements of the Upper Galilee. Jordan occupied the high ground above a long, irregular border on the West bank of the Jordan, as well as the Old City of Jerusalem, leaving Israel with

---

* Iraq and the Palestinian Arab forces that also fought Israel have never agreed to an armistice and a state of war technically still exists between Iraq, the Palestinians, and Israel.

a narrow, vulnerable corridor into the Jewish section of Jerusalem in the western part of the city.

In the course of the war, more than 500,000 Arabs fled their homes, creating a refugee problem that continues to plague Israel. Roughly one percent of the entire Jewish population was killed in the War of Independence—more than six thousand soldiers and civilians. Arab casualties were not disclosed. Israel's economy was devastated by the conflict.

And yet, in spite of the enormous problems, the Jewish State of Israel survived and prospered. In its first three years Israel brought 687,000 immigrants to her shores, a figure equal to the whole Jewish population of Palestine. With contributions from world Jewry and massive infusions of foreign aid, the country was able to telescope the time period usually required for underdeveloped nations to industrialize.

The country's security position, however, was far from stable. Border settlements were periodically subjected to attacks by Arab *fedayeen*. Although armistice agreements were signed in 1949 with the countries bordering Israel, none of them was willing to conclude a peace treaty. In 1956, alarmed by a massive arms agreement between Egypt and Czechoslovakia, Israel—supported by England and France—cooperated in a lightning war against Egypt. In 1967, when Egypt knowingly committed an act of war by closing the Strait of Tiran to Israeli shipping—cutting off the vital Israeli Red Sea port of Eilat—Israel went to war with Egypt. Jordan, and Syria joined Egypt. The war left Israel with vastly expanded borders—in possession of the entire Sinai Peninsula and the Gaza Strip, the West Bank of the Jordan, the Golan Heights in the northeast and East Jerusalem, including the Old City with its places holy to Jews, Muslims, and Christians. For the first time in two thousand years Jerusalem was again under Jewish sovereignty.

The 1967 war occurred as Israel was suffering from a severe economic recession that had left the country in a state of psychological depression as well. The failure of Western democracies to come to Israel's aid and Arab rhetoric about pushing Israel "into the sea" raised the specter for Israelis of a new Holocaust.

The lightning victory of the Six Day War brought a dramatic

turnabout in Israel's situation—economically, militarily, politically, and psychologically. In a matter of months the country moved from depression to unprecedented prosperity. The addition of a million Arabs to the Israeli economy provided a major new market as well as a source of relatively cheap labor. Israel believed it had destroyed the armies of Egypt, Syria, and Jordan, putting them out of commission for several years at least, while strengthening her own security situation by occupying the Sinai Peninsula, the Golan Heights, and the West Bank. The additional territory shortened the borders that Israel had to defend, provided a buffer between Israel proper and her enemies, and left Israel occupying the high ground. Israel had demonstrated to skeptics that she was capable of defending herself, that the state would survive and that it was a force to be reckoned with in the Middle East. Psychologically, the Six Day War led Israelis to believe that the country had ended an era of isolation from its neighbors and that they would be forced to sue for peace on terms favorable to Israel. In the months immediately after the war, Israel was prepared to return the territory it had captured in return for what was called a "real peace." When that hope proved illusive, many Israelis assumed that they could hold the captured territories indefinitely—perhaps forever. To the ultrareligious nationalists of Israel the war seemed the fulfillment of God's promise to Abraham, Isaac, and Jacob to give the Land of Israel to the Jewish people. Certainly life, in a material way, had never been better. New buildings seemed to sprout like grass after a summer rain. Cars, refrigerators, washing machines, and the other creature comforts of a modern industrial society became commonplace items in more prosperous Israeli homes. And the number of prosperous Israelis increased.

In the midst of the general rejoicing at Israel's new comfort and security, troubled Israeli voices were raised questioning the new directions events were taking. The irony of one of history's most oppressed peoples suddenly cast into the role of imperial power ruling over a subject people was not lost on them. The growing dependency on Arabs to do the manual labor that Jews formerly did for themselves, the increasing consumption and materialism, and Israel's failure to reduce its dependence on external aid were additional sources of concern. Occasionally alarm was expressed that Israel was overextending itself. But for a people who had already done the seemingly impossible, the normal limitations that restricted other peoples seemed beside the point. The 1967 war produced a wave of euphoria and filled Israelis with enormous self-confidence that allowed them to disregard warning signs and questioning voices. Doubts were pushed aside until the Yom Kippur War of 1973 suddenly presented Israel with an entirely new situation—or perhaps the same old situation.

The war began on October 6 with simultaneous attacks by Egyptian forces crossing the Suez Canal and Syrian forces in the Golan Heights. Although Israeli intelligence had monitored the build-up of both the Egyptian and Syrian forces, their intentions were utterly misread by those responsible for analyzing the meaning of the information collected. Israeli troops suffered horrendous losses of men and equipment in the opening days of the war. Israel itself was hard pressed to turn the tide of battle, succeeding at first—after prodigious effort—to halt the attack and then to go over to the counterattack. The actual fighting lasted eighteen days and ended with the Egyptian Third Army surrounded and cut off, Israeli tanks on the road to Cairo, the Syrian forces decimated, and Israeli artillery within range of Damascus. Israel had suffered more than twenty-five hundred soldiers dead and more than three thousand wounded. A substantial part of the Israeli army—including reservists—remained under arms for another six months while the armistice negotiations dragged on.

The 1973 war destroyed the illusion with which Israelis had comforted themselves that the additional territory occupied after 1967 would protect them and their families from the ravages of war for another ten years at least. The 1973 war was savage, and it caught Israel seriously unprepared, materially as well as psychologically. The greatest weapon in the hands of the attacking Egyptians and Syrians was Israeli overconfidence.

The 1973 war, in retrospect, can be seen as a major turning

point in Israel's development. The war shattered the trust of the Israeli public in the ruling Labor Alignment's policies and led to the election of the right-wing government of Menachem Begin. Ironically, Begin, an implacable hard-liner in opposition, proved to be more moderate in power and was able to negotiate the peace treaty with Egypt that had been sought since 1948.

The signing of a peace treaty with Egypt in 1979 altered Israel's security equation and partially relieved the total isolation in which Israel had lived for thirty-one years, but the treaty failed to resolve a growing inner turmoil. Departures from Labor Zionist ideology had left Israeli politics more pragmatic and less fractious, but also without the sense of mission that had sustained Jews in Palestine and Israel in the dark days of the past. The old slogans and rallying cries seemed shopworn and naïve, anachronisms from another era whose relevance lay chiefly as a bench mark with which to measure the changes that had occurred in Israel.

Needless to say, the world of the 1980s is a far different place from the world of the late 1940s, 1950s, or even the 1960s. The world has changed. Israel has changed. Politically, economically, ideologically, militarily, and socially Israel has been transformed.

In the first thirty years of her existence Israel transformed herself from an underdeveloped country into an industrial and then a consumer society without becoming financially self-sufficient in the process. As a result, her dependence on external aid and her foreign debt have grown enormously in the past decade. The elaborate—and unique—labor union-industrial conglomerate structure (Histadrut) that served to organize the country's Jewish work force and to develop an industrial base has become a vehicle for shielding incompetent and unwilling workers from the harsher realities of Israel's need to produce more so that the country can stand on her own financial feet. The unpleasant truth is that Israel has become a country living on the dole, dependent on foreign aid not to assist her development but to underwrite maintenance of a comfortable standard of living higher than she could afford on her own.

The total population in 1948 was less than nine hundred thousand. In 1981 Israel's population was approaching four million. The composition of the population had also altered. Where before, the Jewish community had been dominated by immigrants from eastern and central Europe, more than half of Israel's Jewish population now traces its roots back to Arab and Islamic countries. This shift is more than statistical. It signifies a profound change in the attitude of the population toward the problems confronting Israel—economically, politically, and even diplomatically.

The hundreds of thousands of Jews who came in the 1950s and 1960s believed that they would be received and treated as equals. The immigrants from Islamic countries especially found the adjustment difficult. Often denigrated by native Israelis and Jews from Europe as "primitives," thousands of these Oriental Jews were shunted off to remote "development" towns or crowded into the slums of Haifa, Tel Aviv, and Jerusalem where their resentment toward the dominant European establishment of the country slowly festered. Because of the particular way Israel developed, this Oriental lower class turned not to the left, as is usually the case, but to the right, supporting the hard-line, ultranationalist positions of Begin's Herut party. The growth of the Oriental Jewish population and its increasing disaffection with the Labor establishment helped pave the way for the political shock of 1977.

In politics, the ruling Labor elite that governed the country for the first twenty-nine years of its existence found itself out of power in 1977 in an upheaval of profound proportions for the country. This ruling elite had become smug, arrogant, and corrupt. The right-center coalition that replaced the Labor Alignment, however, was characterized by inexperience in government, a rigid commitment to ideological principles of dubious relevance to Israel's situation, and an inability to fashion a program that relieved some of the more troublesome problems of Israeli society. The growth of Israel's Oriental Jewish population in the years of Labor control led, paradoxically, to the development of a right-wing working class hostile to the nominally socialist Labor elite. When Labor proved unable to satisfy the Oriental population's desire for better conditions, it turned to the Likud party, a coalition comprising the Herut and Liberal parties led by Menachem Begin.

By almost any measure, Israel's already serious economic problems grew worse in the years after 1977 during Begin's term as prime minister. A commanding figure in opposition, Begin proved a weak leader in power, unable to bring the various factions in his coalition to heel in order to put together a coherent program.

The Labor Alignment, strengthened by the failure of the Likud to improve Israel's domestic crises, still suffered from internal dissension that bordered on internecine warfare. Divided internally and unable to command an enthusiastic response from a public that remembered all too well its transgressions, Labor was vastly diminished from the days when the party and government were virtually synonymous.

Israel's proportional representation system of government dispersed power rather than concentrating it, leaving various constituencies in a position to block effective government action. This system, combined with the universal loss of confidence in the country's political leadership, constituted a crisis of authority for Israeli society.

The 1967 war had been unavoidable from Israel's perspective. Israel's lightning victory electrified the Western world, but her experience since has proved Nietzsche's observation that "there are victories that are harder to bear that defeats." Israel's transformation from tiny underdog to tiny empire, from democracy to dominator, left her divided internally and exposed externally. Paradoxically, unification of the ancient Land of Israel led to the shattering of the political consensus that had precluded exhausting controversy over security issues. Disposition of the territories occupied in 1967 became a major—and divisive—issue in Israel.

On the one side stood a significant number of Israelis who felt that retention of all or some of the territories was necessary to protect Israel and her population. Another significant portion of the Israeli public went beyond the security issue by asserting that Israel also had a historic and religious right to at least the land on the West Bank of the Jordan, the biblical lands of Judea and Samaria.

On the other side stood an equally significant number of Israelis who were concerned about the continued effect of the occupation on Israeli society itself in spite of the dangers involved in relinquishing control. "For all the shame and pain we feel over the harm done to us by our neighbors because of anachronistic perverse policies," Israeli historian Jacob Talmon wrote in 1980,

> our fear should be greater over what these acts will do to us, to the Jewish people and to our dream of social and moral justice and renaissance. For this dream was one of the vital and beautiful aspects of Zionism, setting it apart from other national liberation movements. The desire to dominate . . . leads to perpetual fear and mistrust of the subjugated people and creates terrible temptations that are stronger than any subjectively good intentions.

Zionism, which began as a movement of national rather than religious rejuvenation, was received with hostility by the Jewish religious establishment of the Old Yishuv in Israel and in eastern Europe. The conflict between secular and religious forces, which predates the State of Israel, persists. This conflict has been further complicated by the more recent growth of a religious-nationalist movement in Israel dedicated to establishing Israeli sovereignty over the territories captured in the Six Day War. This movement not only limits the maneuverability of Israel in its conduct of foreign policy but constitutes a threat to domestic security and the establishment of the rule of law within Israeli society. The movement's basic strength comes not from the number of followers it has but from the vulnerability of Israel's political system to splinter groups and from the basic ambivalence of Israelis themselves, unable to make firm choices among the conflicting requirements of security, democracy, and maintenance of Israel as a Jewish state.

Militarily, Israel is still the strongest power in the region. Israel has maintained a qualitative edge that offset the numerical superiority the Arabs enjoyed. That edge, however, has been maintained at enormous financial cost. The increasing expense of new weapons systems, the need to keep pace with arms purchases made by the Arabs, and Israel's growing economic problems threatened to undermine its security. Israel's financial condition— minimal growth, rampant inflation, increasing debt—has forced the government to make a Hobson's choice between the economy and security.

From the outset we are confronted with a problem of standards and expectations, of conflicting ideals and goals, of moral contradictions and dilemmas. The State of Israel is not, after all, two hundred years old, nor is Israeli society. But neither is Israel simply a dreamed-up country whose population was thrown together by lines drawn on a map to suit the convenience of a retiring colonial power. Regardless of where they were scattered for more than a thousand years, the Jewish people retained deep and lasting ties that held it together.

On the other hand, Israel has grown in less than forty years like some kind of pampered, force-fed prodigy that could not be left to develop normally. It is as though her arms are a bit too long for the stubby torso, the legs too short and a little too muscular. One never quite knows in Israel whether to expect more—or less. Technologically and scientifically, Israel is a modern, Western country. Her political institutions are Western in form, but half of the country's population owes its origins to the traditional cultures of Islamic societies and has had experience of only a generation or less with free speech, a free press, universal suffrage, and the spirit of toleration, moderation, and restraint without which democracy cannot function.

Israel's founding ideology was essentially agrarian. The Zionist ideal was of small, rural settlements and simple, ascetic living. Zionism was essentially democratic in spirit—socially and politically. Socialism was easily compatible with Zionism, and while many of the early settlers were socialists, many were not. Industrialization required a different ordering of priorities—encouragement of precision and individual excellence, differentiation according to ability and merit.

The commitment to socialist ideology was not necessarily shared by the immigrants who came in the late 1940s, 1950s, and 1960s, but the state's own commitment to Jewish immigration made the government, rather than the individual immigrant, responsible for his or her well-being. Thus, the stage was set for resentment on a massive scale as better-equipped immigrants and native-born Israelis were able to capitalize on opportunities while less well equipped immigrants—"disadvantaged" in the modern phrase—languished.

Zionists wanted to create a "normal" society for Jews, but remembering their Jewish heritage, they also aspired to something more, something better—a country adhering to a higher moral standard than that which prevailed among other nations.

The Jewish desire and need to return to the ancient homeland conflicted with the Arab right of prior occupation. The hostile reception by the Arabs presented the Jewish settlers with a dilemma, forcing a choice between moral aspirations and security. The humiliation of ghetto life—with the hated memories of the puny, defenseless Jew of the past—and the more recent horror of the Holocaust did not condition the Jewish settlers to withdraw in the face of a threatening force. From their perspective, they had no choice.

The Jewish past engraved a preoccupation with security on the Israeli mind. Security was a prime *raison d'être* for the state. From the Israeli point of view it was well enough for outsiders—Western intellectuals and diplomats—to preach a doctrine of self-restraint in the face of terrorist attacks.

Jean-Paul Sartre posed the question in these terms:

> Must Israel, as the Israelis themselves say, remain a state apart, or consider itself a state like all the others? That is to say: there are the Jews; they have been persecuted, they have something among them . . . this is, a kind of heritage of permanent persecution and which is their great value. If it

is thus, then the State of Israel must be an example, we have to demand more from this state than from others. Or you can say that Israel is like any other state, it is no longer a matter of Jews in Israel, but of Israel, and then we have to consider it as it is, and we must admit it has the same faults as the other states.

Remorse in Israel over the circumstances under which Jews had returned and the hardship their return has caused for Palestinian Arabs has not reached the point where Israelis are willing to accept "permanent persecution," in the form of terrorist attacks, as a logical extension of the Jewish heritage of providing a moral example. Daily, Israelis are reminded that their presence in the Middle East is unwelcome, that their lives collectively and individually are in danger. Did providing a moral example mean that Israelis had to wait for terrorists to strike before defending themselves? Or could Israelis seek to destroy the terrorists before they struck first? Israel is small enough so that Israelis can, without stretching their imaginations, put themselves into the crux of the issue. An Israeli army officer whose family lives near the border with Lebanon, where terrorists frequently try to cross into Israel, summed up his own view succinctly:

"What concerns me is not the threat to Israel. The [Palestine Liberation Organization] is never going to destroy Israel. What concerns me is the threat to my family, and to me my family is everything in my life."

Neither Herzl nor the Zionists who followed him saw that creation of a Jewish state would mean fierce, unrelenting hostility from the Arabs. Faced with an apparent choice between survival and serving as an "example," Israel has chosen survival. Should the original ideals and aspirations be the yardstick of judging Israel, or should Israel be excused by reason of hardship and imminent danger? How can we put Israel into its context as a Western-style society attempting to create a reality—not in Europe or next to the United States—but in the midst of a vast Arab sea where Israel's existence is still not accepted and where the prevailing view of life proceeds from an entirely different set of standards and assumptions from those of Western societies?

We find ourselves spectators at a kind of moral and intellectual tennis match, watching the ball being knocked back and forth with blinding speed. Israel, of course, is not operating in a vacuum. It is not as though Israel is the sole obstacle to ending the Israeli-Arab conflict, unless the expectation is that Israel should, in pursuit of peace, simply accede to all Arab demands and effectively cease to exist. In selecting standards with which to measure Israel it also would be well to keep in mind the nature of the countries surrounding Israel. Israel has attempted—with notable lapses—to construct a parliamentary democracy where individual rights are protected by due process of law. One does not see in Israel bodies hanging in public squares or public beheadings conducted as one can see from time to time elsewhere in the Middle East. The death penalty has been used in Israel only once, for the execution of Nazi mass murderer Adolf Eichmann, who received an open trial according to established principles of law.

Israeli officials do not boast publicly of the blood Israel's soldiers have spilled in the manner of the Syrian minister of defense who recounted before the national assembly the exploits of a war hero who had killed twenty-eight Israelis: "He butchered three of them with an ax and decapitated them. In other words, instead of using a gun to kill them he took a hatchet to chop their heads off. He struggled face-to-face with one of them, and throwing down his ax managed to break his neck and devour his flesh in front of his comrades. This is a special case. Need I single it out to award him the Medal of the Republic? I will grant this medal to any soldier who succeeds in killing twenty-eight Jews, and I will cover him with appreciation and honor for his bravery."

From the Israeli perspective, were it not for the presence of Jews in Israel, the world would pay scant notice to the problems of what would then be Palestine unless, of course, those problems had some practical bearing on the supply of oil to the rest of the world. In the face of what they see as a patent double standard— the United Nations routinely condemns Israel for taking action against Palestinian terrorists in Lebanon but says nothing about attacks on civilians inside Israel—Israelis have become cynical about moral judgments pronounced by anyone outside the conflict. "In India, in Africa, in Europe, millions of human beings have been put to flight, transported, enslaved, stampeded over the borders, left to starve, but only the case of the Palestinians is held permanently open," Saul Bellow has written.

> Where Israel is concerned, the world swells with moral consciousness. Moral judgment, a wraith in Europe, becomes a full-blooded giant when Israel and the Palestinians are mentioned. . . . What Switzerland is to winter holidays and the Dalmatian coast to summer tourists, Israel and the Palestinians are to the West's need for justice—a sort of moral resort area.

Perhaps. But does the cynicism and moral decrepitude infecting Western democracies cancel Israel's own moral aspirations and release her from the discipline of self-denial and self-restraint that characterized her early history? Despite the difficulties of geography and moral relativism the fact of the matter is that Israel holds herself out to be a civilized country—whatever the nature of her adversaries—and she deserves to be measured accordingly. Israel invites measurement as a civilized, democratic, modern industrial country, as well as being independent and self-sufficient, and it is from that perspective that Israel ought to be considered. "Each of us," Ben-Gurion said in the early days of the state, "is entitled to cling to the conviction that merely to be like all other peoples is not enough. We may pridefully aspire to bring true the words of the Prophet: 'I, the Lord . . . give thee for a covenant of the people to the Gentiles.' "

The conflicts and contradictions between Zionism's desired future and the hard realities of the present are reflected in serious conflicts and contradictions in Israeli society. These problems were bad enough, but they paled beside a problem of more profound and ultimately more pernicious consequences.

Zionism emerged in the late nineteenth century as a movement with a clear mission—the establishment of a national home for Jews, a state where they could preserve their national identity. In a difficult, often depressing present Zionism had looked toward a golden future. The importance of the future as a source of sustenance for the Zionist movement cannot be underestimated here. "One of the most potent attractions of a mass movement," Eric Hoffer writes in *The True Believer,*

> is its offering of a substitute for individual hope. This attraction is particularly effective in a society imbued with the idea of progress. For in the conception of progress, "tomorrow" looms large, and the frustration resulting from having nothing to look forward to is the more poignant. . . . In a modern society people can live without hope only when kept dazed and out of breath by incessant hustling.

In the period before the state was created, the more idealistic among its potential citizens and leaders entertained ideas about creating a model society that would carve a new path of progress and enlightenment in human development, guided by principles of social justice and equality. Dominated by hard-working socialists whose hands were calloused from years of physical labor themselves—building roads, working the land, constructing a foundation for future development—Jewish society celebrated work as a value in and of itself. They foresaw a time when technology and their own effort could provide a comfortable living standard for everyone. As socialists and democrats, they envisioned a society free of inequalities, with all of its citizens enjoying equal rights and privileges, based on the biblical injunction: "Zion shall be founded in justice and her people in righteousness."

Like the United States, Israel has a pioneering past that remains a real part of the national ethos. The passage of time, the onset of new problems, has softened the remembered harshness of Israel's pioneering past. Sitting in the midst of a relatively modern industrial state, Israelis reflect nostalgia for a mythical past, of simpler days with simpler issues rather than the complexities of modern times. Those early pioneers carried a vision of Eden in their minds. Israelis today rarely delude themselves in thinking that they are involved in the construction of a utopia.

That lost purpose and direction is sorely missed. It sustained Jewish pioneers through hardships, gave them strength to withstand deprivations and uncertainties. The failure of Israel's leaders to articulate any sort of vision, the slow realization that Israel may in fact be just another country, the transformation from an agrarian to an industrial society, the shift from group to individual values—all these changes have created a real crisis for many Israelis who had gathered strength from the idea that they were part of a great historic, even spiritual, adventure.

Sophisticated middle-aged Israelis can now recall with a mixture of embarrassment and nostalgia the pioneering songs of their youth, when the country was young and full of hope. Those songs seem affectingly innocent, extolling the virtues of the irrigation sprinklers that brought water to the parched land, exalting in the act of building ("I will dress my country in a gown of concrete and ribbons of steel"). The landscape is dotted with towns and villages whose names rejoice in the land itself—Splendor of the Carmel, Glory of the Sharon—or express the expectations of the settlers— Gates of Hope.

Not only were the Zionists inspired in their quest, but also the struggle for Jewish independence . . . the struggle for Jewish independence had the stuff of romance and legend about it, appealing to Westerners, who, Albert Hourani observed,

> were attracted by the gallant little people with a great and tormented past, by the pioneers taming the wilderness, the planners using science to increase production, the collective farmers turning away from the guilt and complexity of personal life, the terrorist making his gesture in the face of authority—all the images of a new world . . . hopeful, violent, and earnest.

Gradually, though, the romance wore thin. The West's infatuation with Israel was overshadowed by other interests and considerations. The "heroic days" could not last forever. David Ben-Gurion, the ruthless visionary who emerged as Israel's first—and still greatest—leader imparted a sense of destiny to Israel's small population. Israel sought out friendships with other emerging nations—especially in black Africa. Despite her own meager resources Israel gave technological aid and advice to these other developing nations, all seemingly partners in an exciting voyage to a brave new world of independence and progress. It is one sign of Israel's changed situation that virtually all of those black African nations severed their relations with Israel after the 1973 war. Israel's closest associate in Africa now, less by choice than by force of circumstance, is the repressive regime in South Africa.

The 1973 war obviously was a major event in Israel's short history. The war shattered not only the ruling Labor Alignment's grasp of power and the population's absolute confidence in the Israeli army, but most seriously, Israelis' belief in their own destiny. By some perverse irony it happened that despite the long-sought blessing of a peace treaty with its largest and most important neighbor that followed in the wake of the 1973 war, Israel in its fourth decade was in a state of crisis. Israel, to be sure, had had crises before and weathered them. The difference this time was that Israel's crisis was one of spirit and self-confidence, purpose and direction.

The malaise afflicting the country was summed up by a kibbutz member in 1981, asked his reaction to a movie showing the determined struggle of concentration camp survivors—some aged and infirm—who literally clawed their way over frozen mountain passes in Europe to make their way to Palestine in the late 1940s, carrying their only possessions on their backs. "What I saw," the kibbutznik said, "was people who had nothing, but they had hope. What I see now is people who have everything, but no hope."

The despondency he described was real and it echoed through scores of conversations in private and public forums throughout Israel. "Once," another Israeli said, "we had a saying that even the impossible is possible here. Now we say that even the possible is impossible."

For a secure and prosperous country, for a country whose population is not simultaneously threatened with extinction and lured by comfort available elsewhere, the lost sense of purpose might be lamentable but not particularly worrisome. In Israel's case the sense of mission was everything—the indeterminate factor that made all the sacrifice and hardship bearable and worthwhile.

When the seeds of this fall from grace were planted cannot be determined with absolute certainty. Certainly many of Israel's problems have their roots in times that predate the creation of the state. Yet it seems clear, in retrospect, that the catalyst for this mood of self-doubt and shattered trust was, paradoxically enough, Israel's greatest success—her smashing victory in the Six Day War. The 1967 war facilitated development of an Arab underclass, which performs the low-paying, unskilled jobs that Jews would rather not perform. The inability to conclude a peace treaty with Jordan has forced the Israeli democracy to employ the repressive tactics of an occupying power. Disposition of the territories occupied since 1967 has become the dominant—and potentially the most divisive—issue in Israeli politics. The perception outside the country of Israel as the most serious obstacle to Palestinian self-determination has isolated Israel internationally to an unprecedented degree.

But the 1967 war also touched off something in Israel psychologically—a mood of self-indulgence, an inflated sense of proportion that corrupted the spirit of the country. Geographically, psychologically, and economically, Israel had existed within narrow limits prior to 1967, living a relatively ascetic life, characterized by self-discipline and self-restraint.

"Until 1967," the Israeli intellectual Yehoshafat Harkabi wrote,

> Israel insisted on keeping to the realistic, middle way, taking pride in its capabilities but never losing sight of its limitations. That is why it accepted partition, and when there was no way out, even retreat. Its leaders were fully aware of the dangers of rising above reality and losing touch with it.
>
> After the 1967 war, however, what had previously appeared to be unrealized was suddenly within grasp, for the outcome

of the war exceeded all expectations. The question arose: Why remain satisfied with little if it is possible to achieve gigantic national objectives? The objectives therefore became inflated; the Israeli self-image swelled: and the old frontiers that were once bearable became indefensible. The spiritual climate changed and this affected the quality of life generally. After all, if the state is a power to be reckoned with, then its citizens, who made it great, are great, too, and so deserve large salaries and a high standard of living.

In the years following the 1967 war Israel contracted the same case of hedonism that had already invaded the democracies of Europe and North America. "The difference between then and now," said an Israeli woman who had been active in the days before the establishment of the state, "is that people then thought in terms of 'us,' and now they think in terms of 'me.' "

The difference, in part, was accounted for in the transformation from a voluntary society whose members freely accepted obligations to a state where citizenship carried compulsory responsibilities backed by law and enforceable by coercion when necessary. The most difficult task for any revolutionary movement is to institutionalize the ideological fervor that sustains its disciples. In this, Zionism was no exception. The Jewish state—the professed goal of Zionism—had been created. The land had been settled. The 1967 war had made Israel secure. The results of the old virtues of hard work and abstemious living had paid off in unprecedented prosperity.

In a certain sense the life of Israel paralleled that of her greatest ruler, King David, three thousand years before—first the rise from humble poet and shepherd to great warrior, conqueror of Jerusalem and ruler of an empire, and then the succumbing to the temptations of the flesh. No more poignant symbol of Israel's transformation can be presented than the odyssey of Yitzhak Rabin, commander of the victorious Israeli forces in the Six Day War and later the first Israeli-born prime minister. Less than three weeks after the conclusion of the Six Day War, Rabin accepted—as

43

an honor bestowed on the entire Israel Defense Forces—an honorary doctorate from the Hebrew University in Jerusalem. In an acceptance speech that electrified the nation, Rabin credited Israel's victory to the "power of moral and spiritual values." Ten years later Rabin was forced to resign as prime minister in disgrace after lying publicly concerning an illegal foreign bank account maintained by his wife.

In her fourth decade, struggling with problems of her own making and those she was powerless to affect, Israel was also a nation and a people in desperate search of her own identity and character —for better or for worse.

2 / THE CHARACTER OF ISRAEL

Our doubts are traitors that make us lose the good we oft might win by daring to attempt.

Measure for Measure

A nation's vices are the excess of its virtues.

Anonymous

"I can see easily enough," Mark Twain wrote during his nineteenth-century visit to Palestine,

> that if I wish to profit by this tour and come to a correct understanding of the matters of interest connected with it, I must studiously and faithfully unlearn a great many things I have somehow absorbed concerning Palestine . . . I must try to reduce my ideas to a more reasonable shape. One gets large impressions in boyhood, sometimes, which he has to fight against all his life.

Each person forms for himself the images that sum up a place, an experience, or a people. Occasionally the image we form bears no relationship to the reality or, as in Twain's case, we find that our images are out of all proportion. The Sea of Galilee, as Twain discovered, is in fact a rather modest inland lake. The Jordan River might be considered nothing more than a humble stream or creek to anyone who has seen the Nile, Amazon, or Mississippi.

Israel has never lacked for symbols to reflect the reality of its experience: the bronzed kibbutznik of either sex, standing amidst blooming crops; the young soldier keeping vigilant guard in a lonely outpost; the dark-skinned Yemenite Jew praying at the Western Wall. Or more recently: the religious zealot occupying a barren hilltop; an Israeli soldier in riot gear confronting an Arab demonstrator; a maimed Arab official smiling defiantly from his hospital bed. Each of these presents an aspect of life in Israel. None captures, or even approaches, the totality.

Similarly, other symbols that may have expressed some vital truth about Israel at one time or another either have been exaggerated to the point where they distort the truth or they no longer reflect reality. Golda Meir's ascension to the prime ministership in 1969 encouraged the false impression that Israel is a country where the sexes are truly equal.

Plato was one of the earliest writers to assay the distinction between appearance and reality. In an age where hundreds of millions are spent to present the proper "image," the distinction is especially relevant. The symbols we select to understand the underlying reality have to be selected carefully. We must remember that bare symbols may fail to convey essential nuances and that societies are not composed of progeny cloned from a single source. Israel is a complicated society for all of its smallness. Baffling contradictions are embedded in the life of the country.

As a point of departure it would be worthwhile to consider some basic characteristics that have shaped the Israeli response to the challenges and crises the country has experienced. *Characteristics*—it may be too soon yet to speak of an Israeli *character*—form the crucible in which the response is shaped.

Mark Twain would have branded a fool anyone who had predicted one hundred years ago that the land that has become Israel could support a modern, industrial economy with lush fields and abundant produce. The land Twain saw then was a wasteland, stone and sandy soil, stripped of foliage, desolate and damned.

And yet the heart of the Israeli experience has been to refuse on an individual and collective level to take no for an answer, to deny

what appear to others to be insurmountable obstacles and insuper-
able limitations. At times the entire country seems to be participating in an enormous act of levitation, defying natural laws in a
mass demonstration of mind over matter.

"If you will it," Theodor Herzl admonished the early Zionists,
"it is no dream." Optimism, determination, a belief in the ability
of men to determine events—these were the traits that shaped
Israel in the years that preceded the establishment of the state in
1948 and in the years that followed. Barely three years after the
stench had cleared from Hitler's crematoria, the new Jewish state
was established, fulfilling a two-thousand-year-old dream.

In its early years the myth of Israel appealed to Western liberal-
ism, and perhaps helped ease the sense of guilt felt by those who
had done little or nothing to aid Jews in their time of distress.
Israel was the Jewish phoenix sprung from the ashes of the Holocaust. Israel's struggle to survive was a latter-day version of David
fighting Goliath. Jewish ingenuity and Jewish muscle employed
modern technology to "make the desert bloom."

The emphasis on the positive in Israel, the upbeat, "can-do"
attitude carries over into various aspects of Israeli life. The Israeli
army as well as the country's agriculture and industry is based
largely on self-teaching—learning through trial and error. An Israeli executive said that when he advertises to fill a vacancy, he
customarily includes a line suggesting that a minimum of experience is required from applicants. Nevertheless, he said, a large
number of applicants invariably show up who have no experience
at all. "If I ask them why they came when they had no experience,
they tell me, 'Show me what needs to be done, and I'll pick it
up.' "

Israelis pride themselves on their ability to improvise and to
fashion solutions to both mundane and desperate problems as they
occur. Since almost every adult male has at least two jobs to begin
with—the one he performs in civilian life and his job in the army
(which often bears no relation to his civilian work)—it is not
beyond the realm of expectation that a prospective employee will
be able to "pick it up." An American television journalist said
that when his network switched from film to videotape, it took the

Israeli camera crews a matter of hours of working with the new equipment to master it. The comparable time for retraining in the United States, including formal instruction that the Israelis did not receive, was several months.

Optimism is a quality that Israelis esteem. Optimists, from the Israeli point of view, are good because they act and don't worry about the future. Pessimists are deprecated because they sow doubt and uncertainty, preventing action. Israel is a society that values action. Intellectuals are appreciated, especially if their thinking leads to concrete results, but intellectuals who are skeptical or cynical are frequently written off as pessimists. During a meeting to discuss the future of Jerusalem, one of the speakers—a man in his mid-forties—told the audience bluntly that he was pessimistic about the future of the city. When he finished, another speaker on the panel—a white-haired, leathery-skinned, calloused kibbutznik in his eighties but still strong and alert—rose and chided the younger man. "How can you be so young and be pessimistic?" the octogenarian asked. "If we had had your attitude, nothing would have been accomplished here."

The concept of *ein breira*—no choice—is fundamental to understanding Israel. Israelis live in a world where they are constantly being reminded of limitations and constraints—narrow borders, a small population, hostile neighbors, lack of natural resources—so that they have had to learn, in order to survive, to exploit each situation to its maximum tolerance and to continuously test apparent limits to see if they can be extended. Israelis learned long ago that necessity is the mother of invention and further that what looks impossible when merely desirable becomes feasible when there is no choice. From the beginning, the odds have been against Israel and it is only a dogged determination and a repeated willingness to attempt the seemingly impossible that has kept Israel alive through more than three decades.

Israelis, faced with situations involving no choice beyond sink or swim, do or die, learned to do and to swim, and in the process they developed what often seems a cold and unsentimental view of the world. Questions that can trigger exhaustive debate and moral agonizing in the comfortable quarters of the Western world very often are tersely answered by Israelis, who find themselves in tighter circumstances. Israelis generally accept moral restraints on what is permissible in combat, but they have little patience or tolerance for fellow Israelis who attempt to evade combat for reasons of conscientious objection—a position generally regarded as a moral luxury that cannot be afforded in Israel. "We are very few," an Israeli army officer said. "We can't afford to be too moralistic. If you refuse to fight, I have to fight twice as hard. Why should I have to do your dirty work for you? This is a sort of Sparta here. You have to fight to survive."

In Israel there is a continuous sense of being up against it, with life making its demands clearly and unmistakably. Whatever the ideals and aspirations of the early Zionists and pioneers, whatever utopian visions that motivated them, Israel now is a fact—a home for 3.2 million Jews. "Israel," an Israeli said with visible emotion, "is *not* an experiment. We are trying to build our life and not experiments. It's not trial and error. It's not we are trying this and if it doesn't work, we'll try something else. This is it."

This hard view of the world also helps explains the prevailing macho syndrome of Israel. Despite all the hardships shared by male and female pioneers alike in the early years of the Zionist enterprise in Palestine, Israel is very much a male-dominated society. One of the basic stereotypes, as psychologist Amia Lieblich notes in her book, *Tin Soldiers on Jerusalem Beach,* is the "famous Israeli type who can function under all hazards and hardships. You don't think too much, but you act swiftly and effectively." One encounters this Israeli time and again, the Israeli equivalent of John Wayne, Humphrey Bogart, or Gary Cooper— the strong silent type. In no small measure the pose is consciously constructed. Emotions are repressed or hidden as are expressions of concern or alarm. Grace under pressure is the order of the day. To be—or to appear to be—nervous or emotional is a sign of weakness.

The result is a dead-pan, flat reaction to the world, a certain lack of humor, spontaneity, and *joie de vivre,* as though to admit to emotion is to provide a weapon that can be used against one. The classic example is the interview conducted by Jewish author Elie Wiesel with Colonel Mordechai Gur, commander of the paratroop forces that captured the Old City of Jerusalem in the 1967 war and one of the heroes of that conflict. As one of the first Israelis to break through to the Western Wall and the Temple Mount, the single most revered site in Judaism—restoring it to Jewish control and sovereignty for the first time in almost two thousand years—Gur might have been expected to have a great deal to say about his feelings at the moment of victory.

> WIESEL: Were you excited?
> GUR: What do you think?
> WIESEL: Did you cry?
> GUR: No, I did not cry.
> WIESEL: Why not?
> GUR: I don't know. I don't like tears.
> WIESEL: Did you feel any?
> GUR: Of course. Like all the others. But I didn't cry.
> WIESEL: What *did* you feel?
> GUR: I don't think I can put it into words.
> WIESEL: Try.
> GUR: No, I don't think people should discuss their feelings.
> WIESEL: What should people discuss?
> GUR: Who says you've got to discuss anything?

At this point, Wiesel, a Jewish survivor of the Nazi concentration camps exploded, asserting that Gur, a sabra (native-born Israeli) had a "duty" to talk about his experience. "Maybe you're right," Gur agreed, recanting. Pressed by Wiesel to reveal his thoughts, Gur added: "I won't tell you. All I'll say is that what I felt was something very deep."

Expressions of emotion, however normal they might seem to non-Israelis, are deprecated. Indeed, one of the issues that separate European Jews in Israel from Oriental Jews is the higher degree of emotionalism shown by Oriental Jews, who are much less restrained and more demonstrative in expressing themselves, while European Jews often tend to be, like Gur, laconic, if not downright phlegmatic. When Israeli president Yitzhak Navon, a Jew of Oriental origin, was told by physicians that his wife was suffering from cancer, he reportedly broke down and wept in front of them. An Israeli newspaper reported the incident, along with the reaction of the nurses who witnessed the scene and who were embarrassed by this public, unmanly—in their view—show of emotion by Israel's president.

Emotion, of course, is not suppressed altogether. Grief for the thousands killed in Israel's five wars (counting the 1969–70 war of attrition with Egypt) is institutionalized in a Memorial Day, celebrated in the spring. The nation's cemeteries are literally filled with mourners, and the entire country stops all activity at a fixed time to honor the war dead. Every military ceremony similarly includes a moment of silence. Memorial Day has deliberately been placed immediately before Israel's raucous Independence Day celebration as a reminder to Israelis of the price that has been paid to preserve the state. And as soon as Memorial Day ends, Independence Day festivities begin. Life goes on.

The stress on the positive in Israel makes a virtue of necessity. Confronted by hostile neighbors who refuse to recognize her existence, Israel lives in a constant state of alert against an attack that could obliterate the country. Israel's economic problems are enormous. Israeli life is permeated with a melancholy sense that it is a game without end, a sort of perpetual elimination contest in which all the teams—save Israel—will live after defeat to play another day. In Israel there is always this impending sense of doom, a sense of a community with one foot planted in oblivion and the other in glory. It is perhaps significant that the favorite pastime of Israelis at the beach is a game played with ruthless abandon regardless of surrounding sunbathers. It is called matcote, a cross between Ping-Pong and paddleball. What makes the game distinctly Israeli, an Israeli pointed out, is that it is a game without rules, without a winner, and without an end.

It may seem contradictory on the face of it to say Israelis are both optimistic and fatalistic, but optimism for Israelis is an operating principle rather than a set of expectations. Optimism is a discipline reflecting a determination to think positively even though one may suspect in his heart of hearts that the ending may be bad. "We do what we can," Israelis seem to be saying. "The rest is a matter of Providence or fate."

Israelis are fond of quoting their first prime minister, David Ben-Gurion, to the effect that "anyone who doesn't believe in miracles isn't a realist." This emphasis on the positive can become pathological. In extreme moments, some Israelis seem to suggest that the only limitations that exist are in the mind rather than in a material reality. One of life's larger philosophical problems is knowing the limits of reality, the fine line that separates the possible from the desirable. The conflict dates almost from the beginning of Zionism between those who—while positive—were more prudent versus those who believed in lightning strokes to accomplish the collective will.

"If there is any other way of building a house save brick by brick, I do not know it," Chaim Weizmann, then president of the World Zionist Organization, told the Zionist congress in 1931. "If there is another way of building up a country save dunam by dunam, man by man, and farmstead by farmstead, again I do not know it."

Israelis find themselves in a difficult situation. To do things in the conventional way, to take it slow and to be sure of every step before taking it, is a luxury that the nation cannot always afford. Individual Israelis demonstrate a clear existentialist, live-for-the-moment attitude. This attitude is not so much an expression of confidence as it is just the opposite, a profound lack of confidence —not so much in their own talents or capabilities—but in the whole course of events that are largely outside of their control. Because Israel is a small country, Israelis are acutely aware of their inability to affect very much of the world beyond their immediate surroundings. Every little external tremor sets off vibrations that reverberate in Israel. After four wars in less than thirty years,

52

Israelis have become grimly fatalistic about the present. One Israeli argued quite persuasively that living beyond his means—a national institution in Israel—made perfect sense. "Why shouldn't I borrow money and overextend myself to take a trip abroad?" he asked. "If I wait until I save the money, I might be dead. Better to go now and enjoy it. I can worry about paying for it later."

On the other hand, a lack of restraint, which is to say action that goes too far, can be disastrous. In events large and small, from the way the country conducts its affairs with the world at large to the way Israeli drivers hurtle down the country's streets and highways, the clear impression is of a death-defying high-wire act performed to a perpetual rolling of drums. Occasionally the performer slips. Israel has one of the highest automobile accident rates in the world; interestingly only twenty-five percent of the country's households own cars. The high accident rate doubtless reflects incompetent driving, but it also reflects a cavalier disregard for the limitations imposed by human abilities and physical circumstance. Since the State of Israel was established, it has gradually accumulated a debt that now exceeds its gross national product. Unlike the United States, where much of the debt is owed by the government to American citizens, the Israeli debt is owed to governments and persons outside of Israel. Servicing this debt—paying the annual interest and principal payments—has become a major problem of the Israeli economy. All of the economic aid that Israel receives annually from the United States now does nothing more than to repay the United States money due on the loans Israel has taken from the United States.

To ask the average Israeli about these problems is to receive in response an elaborate shrug and noncommittal facial expression. *"Yeheye beseder,"* the Israeli replies. "It will be all right." Or, *"Yeheye tov,"* he might say. "It will be good." These two expressions, used interchangeably, are an expression of a mixture of confidence and blind faith in the future. Said in a dark moment, the expression is an affirmation of faith, of confidence, or of belief in divine help or in plain dumb luck. *"Yeheye beseder,"* can also be a statement of defiance in the face of peril, a refusal to be cowed by an apparently desperate situation, a kind of "Damn the torpedoes, full speed ahead!" attitude.

Still the problem of limits remains. Not every situation can be overcome by a sheer act of will. The danger is that success can lead to an overemphasis of the positive attitude, ultimately leading to a misperception of one's own abilities or of basic facts. Israel's lightning victory in the Six Day War in 1967 had this effect on the Israeli leadership and public, with disastrous consequences. "The ugly truth is that we became slightly arrogant, slightly fat, and—most damaging of all—slightly careless," Jerusalem mayor Teddy Kollek wrote in his memoirs. "The tragedy is that it cost us a few thousand of our young men's lives [in the Yom Kippur War]—our most precious commodity—to come to grips with the distortions in our self-image, and I'm not sure that many people in Israel have really woken up yet."

Israel is very small, about the size of New Jersey with a population roughly equal to Maryland's. The country's smallness is not only a condition of geographic and demographic fact but also a circumstance with profound implications for the economic, strategic, political, and social climate of the country. Smallness means no room for error, no margin of safety. Israel has no Siberia for its soldiers and population to retreat into against the advancing armies of her would-be conquerors. "I can travel from one end of Israel to the other in about the same time that I used to travel from one end of the United States to the other," Israel's former ambassador to the United States Simcha Dinitz joked once. "The difference is that in the United States I flew in a jet. In Israel I'm driving in my own car."

Israel's small size means that relations of all kinds are much more intimate. Maintaining anonymity and privacy requires a positive effort. The likelihood of two Israelis who have never seen each other finding friends in common within a matter of minutes after meeting is very high.

In January 1968 the Israeli submarine *Dakar* was expected back in Israel after a training mission. News reports had announced that the Israeli navy had lost contact with the submarine five days earlier. Nevertheless, the morning the submarine was expected, a rumor started in Haifa and quickly spread through the country that the submarine had been sighted. The rumor, as it turned out, was baseless. The *Dakar* never returned to port and has never been positively located. All hands aboard were lost. In the wake of the incident, however, an Israeli research institution decided to do a survey about the dynamics of a rumor's spreading. Based on the rather small sample of about 180 persons, the survey found— among other things—that roughly twenty percent of the persons interviewed for the study either knew someone on the submarine's small crew or knew someone with friends or relatives aboard the boat.

Despite the difference in background, education, and culture in the Jewish population, the country's small size makes it virtually impossible for one person to be oblivious to another's problems. Even the most remote sections of the country are no more than a three-hour drive or bus ride from Jerusalem or Tel Aviv, making it difficult, if not impossible, to "tuck away" problems out of sight. When a nine-year-old boy who lived in a wealthy Tel Aviv suburb was kidnapped, the sense that the entire country was hanging on every news report was palpable. Aboard the public buses, which have radios and play the hourly newscasts, conversation stopped so that the passengers could hear the latest news about the case. When the boy's body finally was found, the incident was a national trauma for Israelis. Although an aberration, the incident was taken as a personal blow by Israelis, who reacted as though an intruder had violated the sanctity of their own families as well.

This sense of living in a very small world is pervasive. Although obviously not every Israeli knows every other Israeli, the feeling of being in a very small goldfish bowl is inescapable. When an American woman mentioned to two Israeli women that she was going to visit an Israeli friend in Tel Aviv and asked if they knew her, one of the women said yes, she had served in the army with the American's friend. The other Israeli woman said, no, she did not know her. "I know her sister," the other woman said. "I studied with her in the university."

An Israeli journalist who writes about economic affairs for a daily paper spent an evening regaling friends with stories from his youth about one of Israel's industrial leaders. "We were together in the youth movement," the journalist said. "We grew up together. I know all about him."

"Knowing all about" someone means that it is very difficult for that someone to surround himself with any kind of mystique or pretension. It is not impossible, of course, but when intimate details about one's past are common knowledge—as intimate details about one's present are as well—one has a harder time passing oneself off for very long as something that one is not.

Smallness in this sense is antidote to illusions, which is another way of saying *ein breira*. It is difficult to harbor the hope that somewhere in the country is a person or group that can suddenly emerge to turn the country in a new direction. The chances are negligible for a new personality to emerge suddenly onto the scene and rise immediately to the top. When an American journalist asked two very shrewd Israeli political experts if they foresaw any chance of a new, unknown figure "coming out of nowhere" to capture the Israeli public's imagination, both men immediately said no. "There is no 'nowhere' in Israel for someone to come out of," one of them answered.

Israelis consequently confront the world with few illusions about what they can expect from others. Whether in the country's larger cities or the smaller towns, they live close enough to each other to penetrate the facade with which we all try to surround ourselves. They either know enough, or hear enough, about the personal lives of the country's major figures to know that they, in fact, are not much different from themselves. Although David Ben-Gurion managed to screen his own romantic affairs from public view, he was the exception rather than the rule. When Moshe Dayan's first wife, Ruth, went to Ben-Gurion in tears to complain to him about her own husband's affairs, Ben-Gurion reportedly told her: "You have to get used to it. Great men's private lives and public lives are often conducted on parallel planes that never meet." This stark realism (not to mention male chauvinism) reflects a certain brazen quality that Israel's smallness encourages.

Dayan, among Israeli public figures, was notorious for his reputed extramarital affairs, for his famous and legally questionable collection of antiquities, and for his flouting of conventional morality. Prevented by proximity from harboring illusions about their leaders, Israelis appear to manage to deal with their performance in office as a matter separate and apart from their personal character or exploits. To do otherwise might leave the State of Israel without any eligible candidates for public office.

Israel's smallness also means that maintaining a separation between supervisor and employees in the workplace is more difficult than in larger, more anonymous societies.

"Look," one Israeli executive explained, "I have to constantly be aware that some friend or relative of my secretary may be in a position to do something for me. So if I'm too tough on her, it may wind up making my own life more difficult. Or, it's entirely possible that one of my subordinates here may be my superior in the army and I may need a favor from him sometime. So relations here are much more complicated than in a bigger country."

This smallness has some obvious benefits. It is much more difficult to develop a feeling of alienation and estrangement from the rest of society in Israel. The psychological pressures resulting from this enforced intimacy are not insignificant. But smallness also brings with it a greater sense of community, a feeling of being able to identify for oneself his or her place in the order of things and to comprehend his or her own worth in the common effort. Smallness also means that the sense of knowing one's neighbor—in principle if not in fact—is greater. As a result, the sense of identification of one person with another is greater than in a larger society. Children in Israel are treated like a national resource. Strangers will stop to help a small child cross the street or to scold the careless child attempting to cross without due care, much as one might scold one's own child. Getting into a crowded bus on a rainy winter's night can seem like entering a warm kitchen, with the same sense of familial closeness.

Sometimes, things can get *too* close in Israel. The whole concept of space in Israel is entirely different. Standing in line at the bank, it is virtually impossible to conduct one's business in private, since the next person in line invariably is looking over one's shoulder to see what is happening. The sense that one has no secrets—whether strictly true or not—leaves one with a feeling of walking naked in the world. People who value their privacy must work much harder to maintain it in Israel than is the case in larger societies.

Even though Israel is surrounded by other countries, the hostile relations with all but Egypt means that Israelis cannot travel outside the country with ease. Obviously, Israelis who can afford it can get on a plane or a ship and fly to Europe. But the number who can afford a vacation abroad on an annual basis is a distinct minority. "Getting away" inside Israel is next to impossible. As Israel returned the Sinai Peninsula to Egypt as part of their peace agreement, the space available in which Israelis could roam free shrank considerably. Unlike the United States, Israel is a place where one cannot travel very long without encountering a border.

A small, closed society can give one a sense of intimacy and shared purpose, it is true, but the other side of the coin is that such intimacy can be stifling, even suffocating. As Israeli psychologist Amia Lieblich has written,

> A person growing up in a particular neighborhood is likely to have the same children as peers for a long time to come: from kindergarten, through elementary and high schools, even to the army. Emigrants are regarded as traitors and the fallen in wars are mourned collectively. The accepted norms are very strong and any deviation meets with suspicion and at times even sharp criticism.

Israel's compactness means that the experience of the place is also somehow more intense. The impression is not entirely one of perception. Roughly sixty percent of the population lives on a narrow strip of land between Tel Aviv and Haifa. Israel has more vehicles per mile of paved road than any other country in the world. These conditions do not make for peace and tranquillity. "In order to keep our sanity," one Israeli said, only half joking, "my wife and I have determined that we have to live one year out of every four outside the country. Otherwise, we'd crack up from the intensity of the life here. It's just too much."

The idea of borders, of being confined to a small, well-defined place is not new to Jews. The desert fortress of Masada, where more than nine hundred Jewish zealots committed mass suicide in A.D. 73 rather than surrender when Roman soldiers laid siege to them after the Jews escaped from embattled Jerusalem, is a prominent symbol of the modern Israeli state. In eastern Europe and the Islamic world Jews often were confined to ghettos. In Russia, by decree of the government, Jews were limited to the Pale of Settlement and excluded from living in Russia proper. Hitler confined Jews to concentration camps, where the Nazis methodically worked at exterminating them.

Even in Israel, the homeland and safe refuge for Jews, the feeling of security is mixed up with the feeling of being finally, once and for all, trapped. The land evokes a sense of both safety and love as well as the more ominous overtones of fear.

"Many were the stories I was told of Jerusalem under siege," writes Amos Oz, one of Israel's most prominent authors.

> Jewish children always died in these stories. They died heroically, or were slaughtered, but the stories always ended with the town burning and the children dying. Sennacherib, Titus, the Crusaders. Riots, terrorists. Military rule. The High Commissioner, searches, curfew. Abdullah, the desert king. The guns of the Arab Legion. The convoy to Mount Scopus. The convoy to the Etzion bloc. An incited rabble. Inflamed mobs. Blood-thirsty ruffians. Brutal armed irregulars. All forever aimed at me. I always belonged to the minority, to the besieged, to those whose fate was sealed, who lived a life hovering on the brink of disaster.

Jews, of course, are a majority in Israel. But it is never very far from the mind of any Israeli that their country is a tiny, narrow island surrounded on every side but one—the sea side—by a vast expanse of Arab countries. The sense of being under siege, the

Masada complex of popular psychology, is never very far beneath the surface. Physically and psychologically, the existence of a siege is real and felt in Israel. The eagerness with which Israelis rushed to make contact with Egyptians after the peace treaty between the two countries was signed—an eagerness that prompted some Israelis to express embarrassment at the ardor with which their countrymen were lavishing affection on the Egyptians—reflects a deep craving for acceptance by Israelis, isolated and rejected in the Middle East for more than thirty years.

The recurring votes of censure and condemnation from the United Nations—seemingly regardless of Israel's actions or those of her adversaries—both depress Israelis and inspire a mood of defiance in them. If the world already has rejected them, the argument from some Israelis goes, why bother worrying about what the world reaction will be to a particular action? As Israel's friends in Europe put a greater distance between themselves and Israel, the Israeli sense of isolation grows and with it a feeling that perhaps Israel can get along without the rest of the world. It is an illusion that only an isolated country, cut off from daily intercourse with other nations, could harbor.

One might think that, given Israel's smallness and intimacy, people would treat each other with courtesy and consideration. The fact of the matter is that Israelis are not, on a casual, daily level, very nice to each other. The kind of formal politeness and consideration that characterizes life in the United States or England is not something one can take for granted in Israel. This situation is not new. "In our country," David Ben-Gurion wrote in 1954,

> even personal manners are deficient. Many of our inhabitants, including Israeli youth, have not learned how to respect their fellow citizens and treat them with politeness, tolerance and sympathy. Elementary decency is lacking among us, that decency which makes public life pleasant and creates a climate of comradeship and mutual affection.

No one would ever contend that Israel is dull. The entire country throbs with raw, restless energy and seems to move in rhythm to a subconscious beat that everyone is tuned in to. This kinetic energy can be exhausting as well as invigorating, wasted as well as purposeful, chaotic as well as organized. Israelis seem always to be in a hurry. At traffic lights they are honking and flashing their lights the moment the light turns from red to red-yellow before turning green, prodding the lead car to get moving. To see them crowding on to buses raises visions of refugees fleeing before the advance of a rapacious army. The puzzle is that once they have arrived at their destination, the sense of urgency evaporates and a tranquil, even torpid calmness overcomes them.

For the native Israeli who has never been outside the country this state of affairs may seem perfectly normal. For the outsider it is a dash of cold water in the face. The disorderly nature of Israeli life, the lack of tidiness and symmetry, and the apparent lack of order ought not to be exaggerated. A quick trip to Cairo, only a forty-five-minute flight from Tel Aviv, provides an immediate, stark contrast that suddenly presents Israel as a model of efficiency and discipline in comparison. Cairo can be a nightmare of hours-long traffic jams, telephones that simply do not work, and petty corruption unfathomable to a Western visitor.

But Egyptians are unfailingly courteous and charming, polite and gracious. Israelis are ever eager to get down to business, to get right to the heart of things. The little extra graces that give the Middle East its charm and style are seen by Israelis as useless decorations, impediments that only waste time.

The difference between the direct, even blunt approach of Israelis and the more rococo style of the Arabs is full of significance for Israeli-Arab relations. "The Arab," Israel's first president, Chaim Weizmann, wrote with scarcely concealed frustration,

> is a very subtle debator and controversialist—much more so than the average educated European—and until one has acquired the technique one is at a great disadvantage. In particular, the Arab has an immense talent for expressing

views diametrically opposed to yours with such exquisite and roundabout politeness that you believe him to be in complete agreement with you, and ready to join hands with you at once. Conversations and negotiations with Arabs are not unlike chasing a mirage in the desert: full of promise and good to look at, but likely to lead you to death by thirst.

A direct question is dangerous: it provokes in the Arab a skillful withdrawal and a complete change of subject. The problem must be approached by winding lanes, and it takes an interminable time to reach the kernel of the subject.

Israelis, by contrast, want to talk *tachliss*—the equivalent of getting down to brass tacks. "What do you want?" is not an uncommon greeting delivered by the more imperious Israeli clerk or bureaucrat. An attempt to explain a general situation may be cut short by the listener with an impatient *"Nu?"* ("So?") or *"Oz ma?"* ("So what?"). "Get to the point!" they seem to be saying to each other. Everything up front, without pretense, matters are stripped down to bare essentials.

It might be deduced from what has always been described that Israel—despite the conventional wisdom shaped by official versions of Israeli life—is a country where women take a position distinctly behind men. The characteristics Israelis respect—toughness, straightforwardness, self-control—are also traits they associate with masculinity. The enduring popular image of Israel is entirely different. Israel is widely considered to be a country where sex discrimination is largely unknown, where women are free to pursue careers on a competitive basis with men in circumstances of basic equality. Officially, legally, and ideologically women in Israel *are* the equal of men. Considering the subordinate position of women in Israel's neighboring countries, Israel is a progressive society. Women have the right to vote in Israel. They have a literacy rate roughly equal to men. They serve in the armed forces and in the Knesset (parliament).

When Golda Meir became Israel's fourth prime minister in

1969, her ascendance seemed to symbolize the role of women in the Jewish state. On closer inspection, however, it becomes clear that Meir's rise to power in 1969 was little more than symbolic. Meir, in fact, had risen *despite* her sex, had overcome her femininity rather than asserting it, by establishing that she could be as tough and unyielding as any man could be in a tight situation.

Despite the official version, the popular image, and the illusion inspired by Meir's tenure as prime minister, the role of women in Israel is subordinate to that of men. At present in Israeli politics not a single woman plays a major role in any of the major parties or in any policy-making forum. Women are vastly underrepresented in the Knesset itself. Only 11 of 120 members of the ninth Knesset and eight members of the tenth Knesset were women. Despite legal prohibitions on discrimination in employment, women in Israel frequently receive lower wages for performing the same work as men.

Despite the symbolic emancipation that Israeli women have experienced, the reality of the situation is that in terms of sexual equality Israeli women probably lag behind American women. The guarantee of equal treatment promised by Israeli law is effectively restrained by social, cultural, and religious considerations that relegate Israeli women to inferior—albeit protected—status in Israel.

Israeli law forbids discrimination in wages. Women working in the same job classification as men must receive equal wage treatment. But Israeli law does not prevent employers from giving women lower classifications and consequently lower wages than given to men even when much the same work is being performed. Women in Israel, according to a report prepared by a prime minister's commission appointed to study women's problems, receive wages that are only 60 to 80 percent of what men earn. Attempts to get the Histadrut, the labor union representing a majority of the work force, to file lawsuits against employers violating the spirit of the law are discouraged by the hierarchy of the Histadrut, a male-dominated institution.

A visit to the average factory or office in Israel will find men in managerial positions, doing heavy work and filling supervisory and executive jobs, while women perform blue-collar jobs or work as secretaries and clerks. Women, according to the report of the prime minister's commission, are concentrated in the lowest and middle levels of their professions. At the five highest levels of government service, women constituted only 17 percent of the employees, and in the highest levels women were only 4 percent. In all, 40 percent of government workers were women, but in the Begin government no women served as ministers, as directors-general of ministries, and only one woman served as a deputy director-general. Out of nine judges on the Supreme Court in Israel, two are women, but only 8 percent of all judges in Israel are female.

The percentage of Israeli women who work outside the home, although slowly increasing, is significantly lower than in the United States. About 35 percent of the female population of working age is employed outside the home in Israel, compared to 50 percent in the United States. Although the percentage of working Israeli women is increasing, the *rate* of increase appears to be slowing down. In 1955 only about 25 percent of Israeli women worked. By 1966 the figure was 30 percent. And fifteen years later 35 percent of Israeli women worked outside the home. For a country facing a labor shortage this failure to fully utilize a potential labor resource may, at first blush, be puzzling, but it has to do with deeply entrenched social, cultural, and religious attitudes that are widespread in Israeli society.

One need only sit in a café in Tel Aviv or ride the bus in Jerusalem to pick up the almost palpable vibrations of the macho syndrome in Israel. Women who observe conventions and accept their inferior status are honored with certain benefits and placed on a pedestal. Mothers with newborn children receive three months' leave with pay. Mothers with young children are permitted to leave work an hour earlier than other employees. Women in the Israeli army are barred from participating in combat. The status women enjoy in Israel is one of *protection* rather than equality, and the protection they receive reflects a view of women as the weaker sex, as persons whose primary role in life is that of wife, mother, and homemaker rather than career woman.

Perhaps nowhere else is the contrast between the promise of a new society and the discrimination of old practices more glaring than in the kibbutz—that symbol of Israeli progress and enlightenment. One might expect—if the kibbutz took equality seriously— to find men and women working side by side in the nurseries, in the laundry, in the kitchen, in the classrooms. In fact, it is rare to find a man in any of these places (save perhaps doing heavy lifting in the laundry or washing dishes in the kitchen). For the most part these positions are the bastion of women. Men do not work in the children's houses. Elementary school teachers in kibbutzim are almost never men (nor do men teach elementary school outside of the kibbutz very often, either).

When I remarked once to a kibbutznik on the dearth of men in children's houses or in other places "traditionally" associated with women, he explained to me that the reason why women dominate in child rearing, in the kitchen, the laundry, and other domestic places was because "it's generally agreed that women are more suited to this kind of work than men are. Men don't do this kind of work well."

A woman friend, who had herself left her kibbutz after finding the atmosphere too constricting, recounted the experience of a relative who had also left the same kibbutz to join another because she did not want to work in the kitchen or the nursery—the only jobs open to her. The kibbutz she joined put her to work in the cow barn, a much coveted job on a kibbutz. After some months, during which she enjoyed working in the cow barn, the kibbutz developed a problem and the young woman was told that she would have to give up her job in the cow barn and go to work where she was needed—in the nursery.

The traditional role of a woman as a wife and mother is venerated in Judaism and is reflected in the biblical proverb that is an ode to the perfect wife: "A woman of valor who can find? Her price is far above rubies. The heart of her husband trusteth in her;

and he shall have no lack of gain. She doeth him good and not evil all the days of her life. She seeketh wool and flax, and worketh willingly with her hands."

In a country where Jewish population growth is critical to the nation's survival, the role of the woman as mother and homemaker is paramount. The state pays subsidies to large families in order to encourage propagation. (Ironically, Israeli Arabs who also receive the family allowance, are substantial beneficiaries of this policy since the birth rate is higher for Arabs than Jews.) In traditional families the decision about whether or not to have another child may not be the woman's alone. It may not be for her and her husband to decide. An Israeli from Iran with seven children of his own spoke about his brother who had three children, the youngest of whom was thirteen. His sister-in-law was pregnant again, the man said, and wanted to have an abortion, "but we"—meaning the extended family—"don't want her to."

"It's God's will," his wife added.

Until 1979 Israel's abortion law amounted to abortion on demand, with the state or the various medical plans paying the cost of the procedure. But then the ultrareligious Agudat Yisrael party in the Knesset demanded, as the price of its continued support of the Begin government, that the law be changed to remove the "social" clause, permitting abortions without requiring medical or psychological justification. The practical effect of the change was to deny poorer women abortions, since more affluent women could still—as they did in the days before the law was liberalized—see a physician privately to get an illegal abortion. Since poorer women are also those who tend to have the largest families, the tightening of the restrictions on abortions strikes where it hurts the most—in the poorest families which have the most pressing problems and consequently present Israeli society with its most urgent domestic concerns.

Women are also protected in their army service. Women in general are barred from combat. But Israeli law also exempts from army service women who object to serving on religious grounds. Prior to 1978 a woman who invoked religious reasons in order to avoid service had to submit herself to examination by a three-member board. Giving way to religious demands, the Begin government amended the law in 1978 to permit the exemption of women on their uncorroborated assertion that they were prevented from serving for religious reasons.

Only about 52 percent of Israeli women of army age served in 1979, an estimated drop of 3 percent from the previous year. Something over one fourth of women liable for military service in 1978 were exempted, an increase of 7 percent over 1976 (before the law was relaxed), and claims have been made that in 1979 another 14 percent were exempted.

Women serve in the army for two years (as opposed to three for men) and then—if not married or without children—they are eligible for reserve duty until they are twenty-five. Increasing exemptions for women aggravates the burden on men (who serve three years in the army, are eligible for reserve duty until age fifty-five regardless of family status and who must serve forty-five to sixty days a year in the reserves).

Within the army women may be subjected to sexual pressures from male superiors, although sex is officially discouraged on army bases and women can file formal charges against men who assault them. The commander of the Israeli navy was dismissed in 1979 following his acquittal on assault charges by a court-martial. The commander was dismissed after the court ruled that it believed the charges filed by the plaintiff, a female noncommissioned officer, but could not convict the defendant for technical reasons.

Another alleged assault was brought to public attention by a female member of the Knesset who charged that the case involving the navy commander was only one of dozens of instances of sexual abuse in the armed forces. She charged that a religiously observant army colonel who was married and the father of five had abused his eighteen-year-old secretary. His defense, according to the Knesset member, was that his secretary's presence in the army was proof that from a religious person's perspective the woman was already "loose," so where was the harm?

Israeli attitudes toward virginity and rape display an absolutist frame of mind. In traditional families maintenance of virginity is an essential for any unmarried woman. In extreme instances the woman in a traditional marriage must establish not only to her husband but to the community that she was a virgin at the time of the marriage. My wife attended the marriage in the early 1960s of an Israeli couple of Kurdish origin where the wedding guests were invited into the conjugal bedroom after the marriage was consummated to examine the bedsheets as proof of the bride's virginity.

Women in rape cases must have corroboration of their charges in order to have an alleged rapist convicted. Once a woman has sacrificed her virginity, Israeli men have a difficult time understanding why she resists any man's overtures. "If I say I'm not interested," an Israeli woman said, "they tell me that I must be a lesbian. They can't imagine that you just might not fancy them. They think that there's something wrong with you."

The veneration of women in Israel is clearly not without exception, in principle or practice. If Judaism extols the virtues of the "woman of valor," the treatment of women in religious dogma also reveals a barely concealed attitude of contempt, an expression of the idea that women are a necessary evil. "A man should be careful not to pass between two women, two dogs, or two swine," the code of Jewish law admonishes. "Nor should two men permit a woman, a dog, or a swine to pass between them."

In Orthodox synagogues women are compelled to sit out of sight of the men, who are seated closer to the Torah, (the first five books of Moses) for fear that the presence of women might distract men from purer thoughts. Women, in fact, are not even obligated to attend services. It is not unusual to pass a synagogue and to find women standing in the street, peering in at the service through a window because the tiny women's section is already filled to capacity.

Obviously, the attitudes of the ultra-Orthodox do not govern the behavior of Israeli society completely, but the attitudes of Israeli men cannot but be influenced by the deeply ingrained restrictions and proscriptions of Jewish law regarding women. A distinction has to be drawn, however, between the prevailing attitudes toward women and sex in families of Oriental and European background. Although ultra-Orthodox Jews among Europeans tend to be more rigid and puritanical in their sexual attitudes than Oriental Jews, Oriental Jews in general tend to be more traditional in their attitudes than nonobservant European Israelis.

Oriental Jewish families still have stronger ties to a way of life in which the man of the house was an all-powerful patriarch. In some Arab countries from which they emigrated to Israel (Yemen, for example), Jewish men were accustomed to having more than one wife. But it isn't necessary to take an example that extreme to understand that Oriental Jews—who are roughly half of Israel's population—still harbor attitudes toward women that make it difficult for them to understand why a woman should be treated on anything like equal footing with men, inside or outside the home. Although Israeli-born women have roughly the same literacy rates as Israeli men, the rate of illiteracy among Israeli women born in Oriental countries is higher than among Israeli women born in European countries. Deficient education continues to plague Israeli women of Oriental origins into the second generation as well. About eighty percent of girls who are not drafted into the army because of deficient education are from families of Oriental origin.

Despite the veneration of women suggested by the biblical proverb, wife beating is a relatively serious problem in Israel. Between 50,000 and 60,000 cases of wife beating occur annually in Israel (out of 860,000 Jewish households in Israel), suggesting that many Israeli men see it as their prerogative to use physical force against their wives.

Given this backdrop, it is hardly surprising that Israel presents a relatively unsympathetic atmosphere for the working mother. Roughly half of all women with children under thirteen in Israel work, but their employment is carried out in circumstances hardly conducive to work, much less a career. The school day in Israel runs from 8:00 in the morning until 2:00 P.M. at the latest for elementary school children. Working mothers can put their children into a day-care center—if they can find an opening—or they can hire someone to care for their children, but both choices will discourage all but the highest-paid women from working.

In the earliest days of Jewish pioneering the position of women was somewhat different. Then women were on a level roughly equal to men (although in her autobiography Golda Meir describes in colorful detail her toils in the kitchen of the kibbutz where she worked on first coming to Israel). Israel has no shortage of heroic women from that early period.

What changed the role and status of women—if we can speculate on causes for a moment—was, first, the nature of the settlers coming to settle in Palestine and, second, the needs of the Jewish community.

The transformation of the Jewish defense forces from a band of partisans into a regular, disciplined army with the establishment of the state meant that fundamental decisions had to be made about the character of the society that was to be built. The kind of society that approves sending women into combat in less than life-and-death situations is a fundamentally different society than one that actively opposes women fighting.

In its early years Israel desperately needed population growth, and it served the purposes of the new state to see women not as warriors or as the equal of men but as reproduction machines. The traditional role of women as wives and mothers coincided with the needs of the Jewish state. Jewish women, according to Ben-Gurion, had "a sacred duty" to have as many children as possible: "Any Jewish woman who, as far as it depends on her, does not bring into the world at least four healthy children is shirking her duty to the nation, like a soldier who evades military service," he wrote.

From a feminist point of view the position is outrageous. But Ben-Gurion's statement sheds light on part of the reality in Israel. The demands and considerations of Israeli life are different from the rest of the Western world. The womb may not, as one Israeli humorist put it in satirizing Ben-Gurion's position, "belong to the motherland," but Israeli women have to consider themselves and their problems as women in the context of the country's basic situation. As one of Israel's leading feminists has pointed out—in explaining the work of the prime minister's commission on the status of women—Israel has not reached the point where women's problems can be singled out for treatment without considering the broader picture.

Israel's continuing security problems not only prevent it from developing as a "normal society" but prevent development of the issue of women's rights. Politics has not been a fruitful area for correcting the situation. Judging by the limited success of candidates who have championed women's rights in Israel, the climate of public opinion is not receptive to a full-scale attack on practices that put women in an inferior position. Feminist candidates have not been able to win more than two or three seats at most in the Knesset.

Women's rights, like the issues of individual and minority rights in Israel, have been subordinated in this case to the prevailing concern of the collective for the general well-being rather than to focusing on any of its parts.

From the outset of the Zionist movement until the proclamation of Israel's independence on May 14, 1948, the emphasis has been consistent: the purpose of the Zionist movement was the redemption of the Jewish *people.* The movement, and later the state the movement succeeded in creating, focused on the group rather than the individual. One reads Israel's Declaration of Independence in vain for any mention of the individual. In the new state the emphasis was to be on the common rather than the individual interest. In Israel, one learns very early in life, the group is what counts.

In their first days in school Israeli children are introduced to the children who will form the basis of their circle until they are teen-agers, perhaps even beyond. Activities are done in concert. One of the highest compliments one Israeli can pay another is to describe him or her as a "real *chevraman,*" a term that means a person is not only a devoted member of the group but puts its interests above his own.

Practical as well as psychological reasons explain this emphasis on the group. The earliest Jewish pioneers arriving in Palestine, and those who came after, found fairly quickly that succeeding by themselves was a challenge beyond their abilities. Unskilled, not used to manual labor, at the mercy of hostile bands of Arabs, and weakened by malaria and other diseases, they found that pooling their resources was a necessity. Those who succeeded by going it alone did so only with the help of Arab labor, a practice that was anathema to Zionists dedicated to the principle of *Jewish* labor.

There were psychological reasons for this emphasis on the group as well. The goal of Zionism was self-realization through the restoration of the Jewish people. In emphasizing the primacy of the group effort, encouraging the individual Jew to find an identity in the group, Zionism was a classic mass movement. "A mass movement, particularly in its active, revivalist phase, appeals not to those intent on bolstering and advancing a cherished self, but to those who crave to be rid of an unwanted self," Eric Hoffer has written.

> A mass movement attracts and holds a following not because it can satisfy the desire for self-advancement, but because it can satisfy the passion for self-renunciation. . . . Their innermost craving is for a new life—a rebirth—or, failing this, a chance to acquire new elements of pride, confidence, hope, a sense of purpose and worth by an identification with a holy cause.

Although Israel's mythology includes any number of examples of individual acts of heroism, Israeli heroes are celebrated for what they have done for the group, for the society, for the nation. The rugged individual who builds dams, roads, or great empires, who invents a miraculous new device, who amasses a great fortune for himself—a Thomas Edison, Andrew Carnegie, Henry Ford, or Cornelius Vanderbilt—has no counterpart in Israeli folklore. Individuals stand out from the group but only when their contribution to the group is exceptional. Israel's liberal parties, with their classic emphasis on the primacy of the individual, have received relatively insignificant support from Israeli voters who have shown a preference for the ideologies of parties—both left and right—that emphasize the collective. One of the surest ways to discredit a politician or a movement in Israel is to establish that their motives in undertaking a particular action were less than selfless, that they profited personally from a particular venture.

Because of Israel's tenuous security situation the demands made on the individual for the collective welfare are considerable. In addition to mandatory military service for both sexes, taxes are confiscatory. Israelis cannot afford to forget, ultimately, that their survival and well-being rests on the cohesiveness of the group. Israeli leaders are constantly warning against internal divisions that will weaken Israel in the face of its enemies. Criticism of Israel abroad by Israelis is taboo since it weakens the country directly and suggests a less than united front.

The ultimate betrayal in the eyes of Israelis is to leave the country permanently. The Hebrew word for emigration, *yerida,* comes from the verb meaning "to go down." The Israeli emigrant, or *yored,* is treated as an apostate. Rare is the sabra living abroad who will admit that his departure from Israel is permanent. If one confesses to having no intention of going back to Israel, the statement is usually accompanied by an elaborate, passionate explanation of the horrors and ills of Israeli society. Leaving Israel is something that no sabra can do casually.

Considering the demands on an Israeli's financial resources, time and ultimately even on life itself, it is clear that Israel is not the kind of society where one can remain aloof from what is happening around him. Obviously this situation creates internal tension, since it is not possible for any movement to sustain a high pitch of ideological commitment indefinitely. Zionism has succeeded in creating the "new Jew," and he and she are now living in Israel under difficult, but not unbearable conditions. They show every sign that they would like to be relieved of some of the collective burden they are carrying in order to pursue their own individual interests.

The concept of individual rights is in its infancy in Israel. The country has not yet put behind it the vocabulary and thinking of the days that saw its citizens and new immigrants as soldiers in a cause. Because Israel lacks a constitution or any document resembling the American Bill of Rights, individual rights remain undefined. Unlike America, created to secure the rights of the individual in the context of a long struggle with the British Crown, Israel was established to safeguard the people, the group. Up against the group in Israel the individual has little chance. The concept of democracy in Israel is taken to mean majority rule. Protection of individual rights and interests is achieved not by the self-restraint of the majority but by the minority finding ways in the political process to block the majority from infringing on what the minority sees as its rights. One well-publicized case involved a resident of a new apartment building who found that the garbage cans for the building's other seventy-nine residents were located outside his bedroom window. When he complained, government authorities responded by producing a petition signed by the building's other residents protesting any change in the arrangement because it would entail additional expense to them. The aggrieved resident, the government authorities said, would have to live with the problem since the government could not thwart the will of a clear majority whatever the inconvenience to him.

The subordination of individual rights to the will of the majority is seen most clearly in the approach to minority rights in Israel, especially among Israeli Arabs, who may find their right to hold public gatherings canceled by state fiat, whose land is seized, and whose cars are searched—all in the name of security.

Standing on his own in Israel, without the benefit of an institution or a powerful friend, the individual runs the definite risk of being lost in the shuffle of organized competing interests and institutions. Nowhere is the relative unimportance of the individual more apparent than in an encounter with the Israeli bureaucracy. The Israeli system, which owes its posture and techniques not to the British Mandate but to the arbitrary mentality of czarist and Bolshevik Russia, presents itself to the Israeli citizen not as a guardian and servant but as a warder. "The mentality of this country is that the time of the person doesn't count," a member of the Israeli Knesset said. "The whole system is designed as though the state was created so that the clerk has his desk and he sits here and you stand there in a queue. And if the line isn't long enough, the clerk isn't important."

An Israeli woman related how she received a notice from the tax authorities informing her that she was "ordered to report" by a fixed date or a police file would be opened against her. "You have been warned," the notice concluded. Panic-stricken, the woman asked her lawyer to find out what law she was being accused of breaking. The lawyer found that the woman was being called in to answer questions on a questionnaire that she was supposed to have submitted to the tax authorities but had, in fact, never received from them.

The stories about the indifference and callousness of the Israeli bureaucracy in the face of the individual are legion. One Israeli received a notice from the municipal government of Jerusalem that was supposed to have had a tax bill attached to it, but the bill was missing. He gave an account of his experience: "I went to city hall to ask about the bill. I was given a form to complete and told to take it to another office. I returned the following day to the second office. The official there told me how much I owed. I took out my wallet to pay. 'You can't pay here,' the official told me. 'You have to go to the treasurer's office,' which was three blocks away.

"At the treasurer's office, where only one window was open, I waited in line for an hour. When I reached the window, I was told by the clerk that I needed a separate, *payment* form, which she could not give me. I had to go to another office. The clerk who gave me the payment form told me that after I paid, I would have to return to get an approval stamp before I could take the bill back to the original office. I went back to the treasurer's office and found a second, shorter line open. After a twenty-minute wait, I reached the payment window and started to pay with cash. 'I can't take cash, only checks,' the woman behind the window told me, although no sign warned that cash wouldn't be accepted. 'If you want to pay in cash, you have to go to the other window.' At that point, I blew up, startling the various clerks who couldn't understand what could have angered me."

A self-employed Israeli photographer told me how he attempted for more than a week to have his telephone repaired. His telephone was his lifeline to his clients and therefore an essential part of his business. His repeated efforts to have his phone fixed were received by the government clerks responsible for telephone repairs with impatient irritation and curt assurances that the phone would be fixed as soon as possible.

Making a delivery to a client, the photographer was not surprised to learn that the client had been trying—without success—to contact him. "Where have you been?" the client asked.

"My phone's not working," the photographer said.

"Why didn't you tell us?" the client said. "Come with me." The client took the photographer to an elderly man who worked as a guard in the client's office. "Tell him your problem," the client told the photographer. The photographer, not understanding how the grizzled old guard could help him with his telephone, nonetheless explained the problem.

The guard nodded knowingly and asked the photographer's phone number and address. "Your phone will be fixed this afternoon," the guard said. "Don't worry about it."

"He used to work for the phone company before he retired," the client explained. "Whenever we need our phones fixed, we ask him to take care of it. He calls up his cronies and they do what he asks."

What had been incomprehensible to the photographer immediately became crystal clear—he had discovered a source of *proteksia*, also known in Israel as vitamin P, the Israeli equivalent of "clout," "pull," or being "wired-in." In the absence of well-defined individual rights *proteksia* is a system, like political machines, that helps the individual navigate the rocks and shoals of the Israeli bureaucracy, but also, perversely, makes one more dependent on connections to avoid being another faceless citizen standing in an endless line. *Proteksia* corresponds to the Arab institution of *baksheesh*, a form of tip or bribe firmly entrenched in countries like Egypt but largely unknown in Israel, at least at lower levels.

Proteksia is only one of the ways that Israelis escape or avoid the frustrations of dealing with the state, the coercive authority of

Israeli society. Another way Israelis adjust to the burdens and obligations of citizenship is by avoiding them altogether. "I don't know anybody here who doesn't cheat," an Israeli said. "You have to just to survive." Israelis need look no farther than their own leaders whose bending of the rules for personal gain and profit are well known and widely reported in the Israeli press.

Indeed, the system in Israel encourages evasion, cheating, and winking at the law. The tone occasionally is set by the government itself. In 1979 a series of mail strikes delayed the delivery of tax bills to Israeli citizens. Although it was widely recognized that the government would have to extend the deadline for payment of the bills, the government waited until a day after the bills were due to advertise in newspapers that the payment deadline was being extended. Since the annual inflation rate was more than 100 percent, even a month's delay in paying the tax would mean a significant saving for the taxpayer.

"A proper government," an Israeli lawyer commented, "would have advertised before the deadline. The way they actually did it, whoever paid, paid. Whoever didn't pay, got an extension. I'm sure the government official who dreamed this up got a pat on the back for playing part of the population a sucker."

Israelis are far from being marionettes. If anything, Israel suffers from a reaction to the heavy-handed attempts to regulate the lives of its citizens. Rules exist, frequently honored more in the breach than in the observance. The natural rebelliousness and resistance to authority that human beings demonstrate in the presence of overbearing authority is well represented in Israel. The safety valve of Israeli society in the face of constant demands on the individual for sacrifice is a kind of anomic, antisocial behavior, a general flouting of laws and elementary courtesy. The discipline simply becomes too much. Israelis let off steam by disregarding whatever seems to them to be unessential for the general safety and survival. No movie is shown in an Israeli theater without being preceded by a notice that smoking is prohibited. The appearance of the notice on the screen is taken as a sign for the moviegoers to light up. The floors of the theater are littered with forbidden sunflower seed husks. City sidewalks become impassable from the presence of illegally parked automobiles. Individualism in this setting becomes resistance to an ever-present, overwhelming, overbearing authority constantly demanding money, time, or—in the most extreme instance—one's life or one's children—for the good of the community. This is not the sort of atmosphere in which a strong sense of individual rights develops. Whatever individual rights or rewards one obtains in Israel, it is quickly learned, one gets by being aggressive, wily, manipulative, or through *proteksia*. Little comes simply by way of right without a fight.

Two millennia of living under the rule of foreign governments and the more recent experience of the British Mandate in Palestine have left Jews with a distrust of and hostility toward government. During centuries under regimes that often treated them as foreigners, Jews developed a sense of government as an obstacle and threat to be circumvented whenever possible. The government, after all, was not their government in most cases, since they were not integrated into the society in any meaningful way. Jews were often merely tolerated and sometimes not even that. With the rebirth of Jewish nationalism and the move toward Palestine, Jews came under the rule of yet two other foreign governments—first the Turks and then the British. Loyalty to either was clearly not the highest priority of the Jewish pioneers coming to Palestine. Their chief obligation was to the Jewish community —to the Yishuv—and to furthering the ends of Zionism.

One Israeli, whose experience was far from unique, served in the Mandatory British police. He was also a member of the Haganah—the secret, illegal Jewish defense force—and, as such, he was a Jewish spy. In his own mind, resisting British authority— undermining it when necessary—presented him with no conflict. Today he is an exemplary citizen of Israel.

But the transition from insurrection to statehood is not always made so easily. Once resistance to authority is sanctioned, especially when a higher purpose is being served—whether the higher purpose is the establishment of a Jewish state or resettlement of the land in fulfillment of a perceived right or a biblical promise—

the habit dies hard. So long as some group's ideological agenda remains unfulfilled, the potential for serious conflict is present.

"Creating facts" in defiance of the law is an honored tradition in Israel. In 1946 eleven settlements were established, literally overnight, by Jewish pioneers in contravention of British edict, to establish a Jewish presence in the Negev on land that the Jewish National Fund had purchased for that purpose. The Jewish settlers put up a prefabricated stockade with a watchtower and shelter in the span of a single day, taking advantage of a provision in a still-applicable Ottoman law that barred destruction of a dwelling—even if illegal—once the roof and walls were built.

Gush Emunim, the ultranationalist religious group founded to press for mass Israeli settlement of the West Bank, appealed to this tradition of "creating facts"—first implicitly and later explicitly— when they established their presence on the West Bank over the Israeli government's opposition to their settling.

When Gush Emunim settlers on a particular West Bank settlement decided, without government authority or permission, to expand their settlement's perimeter, Israeli soldiers were sent to enforce a government decision that the settlers had to withdraw. The military commander informed the settlers that they would have to move.

"Listen," a spokesman for the settlers told the army commander, "we want to explain why we're doing this. Let's sit down and develop a discussion."

"I haven't come to understand you," the commander reportedly said. "I have no time. I have a technical problem. You have to leave this area."

"But you have to understand us," the spokesman said.

"Look," the commander told him, "drop by my house whenever you want. We'll talk all night. Right now I've given you an order. As a citizen of the State of Israel you're required to obey it. That's all."

The issue is seldom drawn so starkly. Gush Emunim presents rather a special case in Israel, since supporters of the movement sincerely see themselves as continuing in the best traditions of Zionism, "creating facts" in defiance of world opinion and more timid souls among their countrymen. Of course, the conflict between religious zealots and secular authority goes back hundreds and perhaps even thousands of years. (The Bible taught to every Israeli child in school presents the conflict between the ancient kings of Israel and the prophets.)

Besides this conflict with religious zealots appealing for justification to a higher authority, Israel must also contend with political parties that predate the state, a labor union and industrial conglomerate (the Histadrut) that predates the state (and often is described as a state within the state), a strong grouping of self-governing socialist farm communities that predate the state, and a variety of private organizations funded by people and groups outside of Israel who don't necessarily coordinate their activities with the Israeli government or any other central planning authority. In each instance the state has to compete with institutions that predate it and have their own—sometimes conflicting—view of what ought to be.

What is true for institutions also is true for individuals. Israelis, according to Hebrew University Professor S. N. Eisenstadt, demonstrate "an unwillingness to accept authority, which derives from the supposition that no group or individual is more qualified than any other to impose authority."

Of all these forces the most serious threat to orderly government comes from groups like Gush Emunim pursuing a vision of their own. Some Israeli experts who have studied Gush Emunim find it has a deep-seated commitment to its own ends that takes it out of the consensus and places it on the extremist fringe in Israel, prepared to take desperate action in pursuit of its own vision of the future.

But the conflict between order and chaos in Israel is seldom presented in such terms. In exceptional as well as commonplace situations an order from someone in authority is an invitation for an Israeli citizen to debate rather than an occasion for prompt compliance. Some Israelis (and outsiders) find this characteristic appealing, and it's certainly true that this resistance to authority offers a profound obstacle to the establishment of an authoritarian government in Israel. In its homier manifestations this trait may be amusing, charming, and even at times endearing. But it also creates disorder and leads the citizen who does obey the law to question on occasion whether he or she isn't something of a sucker for having done so.

The tradition of "creating facts" was also confronted in a different form in late 1980 in the celebrated case of Gad Greiver, a rather prosperous Israeli who had built an expensive home for himself, illegally, on land earmarked for agricultural purposes. Greiver, one of thousands of Israelis (Jews and Arabs alike) who had built homes illegally on state-owned land, fought a five-year battle with the Israeli government to keep his home. Despite government orders, backed by the Israeli Supreme Court, Greiver managed to keep the authorities at bay, while trying to enlist public and influential support to save his house from destruction. One argument made in his favor by many Israelis was that even though his house had been built illegally, it should not be destroyed because it would be a shame, in a country trying to encourage Jews to come settle and build, to tear down a Jewish house. The contrary argument, which ultimately prevailed, was that the law could not be circumvented—whatever the reason.

This is a struggle that goes on all the time in Israel. On Israel's Memorial Day, a somber occasion when those killed in the country's several wars are honored, an Israeli who had been one of the heroes of the 1967 war offered to take me to the national cemetery in Jerusalem, on Mount Herzl. We arrived very near to the time that the ceremony started, and my companion drove past the point on the crowded road where policewomen were directing cars into a dusty parking lot. About one hundred yards up the road he pulled his car up on the curb and parked. As we started walking away from the car, a policeman approached.

"You can't park here," he told us. "You have to park back in the field behind you."

"How was I supposed to know that?" my companion asked. "Nobody told me."

"Even so," the policeman said, trying to argue and direct the line of cars at the same time, "that's where you're supposed to park. You can't leave your car there."

"Well," my companion asked, digging in, "what do you want me to do now? I can't back up, and if I go to look for a spot, I'll miss the ceremony."

Exasperated and thwarted, the policeman turned his back and continued directing the traffic. "Let's go," my companion said, "before he changes his mind."

The house where we lived the first year we were in Jerusalem was on a narrow street that had been recently changed from two-way to one-way because of numerous accidents. When cars approached and saw the No Entry sign barring their way, the drivers often hesitated and then decided to enter the street anyway, since their alternative was a three-block detour to reach their destination, which was actually only a block away. My neighbors, my wife, and I took it upon ourselves to stop cars entering the street illegally, and the drivers invariably were bewildered as to why we were bothering. Nor could they understand that they were doing anything improper. It made no sense to them to drive three blocks out of their way to reach a point they could see was reachable directly—law or no law.

Resistance to authority and orderly procedure is a current that runs deep in Israeli society. In its most extreme instances, resistance to authority leads to what one Israeli expert on the subject has characterized as *illegalism*, a view that treats the law and regular procedures as something to be observed only when there is no choice. The law, illegalism suggests, applies to others, not to oneself. Considering the history of Israel's establishment, the sacrifices the state has asked of its citizens in the past, and the constant demands it continues to make, it is no accident that among the most popular Israeli folk heroes are three men—Moshe Dayan, Ezer Weizman, and Ariel Sharon—with well-established reputations as mavericks, individualists with an unconventional approach to dealing with problems, men who succeeded within the system but who show an impatience with formal procedure and more than a faint hint of the proscribed tendency to rugged individualism.

If it is true, as General Yitzhak Rabin said weeks after the 1967 war, that Israelis are a people who "rise above themselves in times of crisis," it is also true that in times of quiet the country not infrequently seems to compensate by glaring lapses in manners, courtesy, and general regard of one person for another. Debates in the Knesset are marked with interruptions and heckling that go far beyond the give-and-take of the British House of Commons. The formal, mannered politeness of the United States Senate where no one is ever addressed by name and interruptions are preceded by a request for the "gentleman to yield for a question," would appear ludicrous in the free-for-all atmosphere of the Knesset. The lack of order in the Knesset is echoed in the rowdiness that pervades Israeli cinemas, in the unruliness of school classrooms, in the hooliganism that follows soccer games.

"Israeli society," wrote one Israeli analyzing the failure of the country's education system to turn out self-disciplined, well-mannered children,

> is aggressive, authoritarian, competitive, sexist, impatient and discourteous. And these are the qualities that can be found in the institutions of Israeli society. The Knesset is one example, and the schools are another. Israeli parents are unreliable in business, cheat the income tax and drive on the roads in disregard of other users and personal consequences. In public life, it is the man with the loudest voice and the biggest belly who gets what he wants. But the children of these parents and this society are expected to sit in rows in classrooms, quietly, well-mannered, considerate of others, careful of school property, to be stuffed with education like Strasbourg geese are stuffed with grain.

It is perhaps no accident that Hebrew lacks a word of its own for "gentleman." The word used is borrowed bodily from the English, suggesting that the entire concept is one foreign to Israeli society and that an Israeli who wishes to be a gentleman will have to look outside his country for a model to emulate.

Israel is not on the edge of anarchy by any means, despite what visitors may think or Israelis may say in a moment of customary excess. Crime, though a growing problem, does not even begin to approach the levels found in the United States or other Western countries. Urban Israelis take elaborate precautions to make their houses secure from the growing number of burglaries. Israeli police, who have their hands full maintaining security against terrorists, concede that they are overwhelmed with more serious problems and do little more than record break-in complaints so that the victims can collect on their insurance policies. Nevertheless, Israel's streets are relatively safe to walk at night. When the power went out all over the country in the late afternoon of an autumn day, life went on much as normal. Horrendous traffic jams did not occur. Police and soldiers were not needed to prevent looting. No rapacious mobs roamed the streets. What might have been a crisis elsewhere—New York springs to mind—was no more than an inconvenience in Israel.

Considering the lack of courtesy and civility in Israeli society, the hammer-and-tongs way that Israeli politicians go after each other, the prominent place that war and lesser skirmishes have played in Israel's history, and the seeming ubiquity of rifles and small automatic weapons, Israel is a relatively nonviolent society. It has far fewer than one hundred murders a year, and many of those involve violence in the Arab population where the tradition of the blood feud and the obligation of one man to uphold the honor of his family against some perceived slight is still well-established. Israelis concerned about the quality of life in their country worry aloud about "verbal violence," but physical violence is far less prevalent than in the United States where the surface is more civilized but the undercurrents are more volcanic. Violence as a means of settling conflicts within the Jewish community, within the group, is not unknown, but it is a long way from being an honored tradition.

On the other hand, courtesy and regard for others is lacking enough in daily life that Israelis themselves are aware of it. Israelis have begun talking about a new type of Israeli—not a starry-eyed idealist or a sun-bronzed farmer working the fields from dawn to dusk, but a new model—the Ugly Israeli. In his or her mildest form this new type of Israeli is exemplified by the woman who was interviewed one night on Israeli television. The woman was approached by a television reporter as she was leaving a picnic site she had occupied with her family. The family was packing, but was leaving its trash behind. Why, the television reporter asked her, didn't she throw away the trash? "I pay my taxes," she replied. "Let the government clean it up."

Efforts to change this situation, to introduce an element of courtesy, orderliness, and regard not only for the law but for other people doesn't always encounter a warm reception in Israel. An American woman who had been living in Israel for almost twenty years recounted how she was watching a group of small children while she was standing outside the relatively luxurious apartment building where she lived in Jerusalem. The children were grouped around an ice cream truck, waiting their turn, when a much larger teen-ager elbowed several of the smaller children aside and placed his order.

When she complained to the teen-ager, he told her, "It isn't for me, it's for those two guys over there," pointing at two adults playing tennis on the nearby court of a private club. She turned her attention back to the line only to find, a moment later, that the boy was back. When she complained again, he said: "They told me to do it. They're in a hurry." She stepped out of the line and walked over to speak to the two men. "Look," she said, "why are you encouraging him to break into line? How's he ever going to learn to do things properly if you encourage him to be rude?"

"Go on!" one of the men told her. "This is Israel. You're from the United States, aren't you? Don't try to impose your American ways on us. That's the way we do it here."

Any number of social commentators have remarked that manners and civility inevitably suffer in a democracy. Critics of democracy, especially reactionary critics, have faulted it for being a great leveler of society, reducing everyone to the lowest common denominator of the least cultured, least educated elements in a society. Israel is far from being a classless society, but the divisions

—at least among the Jewish population—do not present insurmountable obstacles to upward movement as one's education and income improve. An air of informality pervades Israel. People invariably introduce themselves to strangers using only first names. Employees are accustomed to calling their employers by their first names. Elementary school students also call their teachers by their first names.

Israelis have little patience for formality or protocol, for complicated ritual and procedure. Israeli politicians, mingling among their fellow Israelis, rarely wear a coat and tie. (Israeli politicians rarely wear ties in any case, since most Israeli men are usually not so formal.) Because the country is so small, because much of the experience has been shared, it would not do for one Israeli to present himself in public as somehow different or better than his fellow citizens. The most prominent exception to this principle is Abba Eban, former Israeli foreign minister, and former ambassador to the United States and to the United Nations. Something of a political matinee idol in the United States, where his fluent English (he was raised in England) and his brilliant oratory make him a popular lecturer, Eban is especially popular among Jewish groups. He is also fluent in Arabic and several other languages. His Hebrew is equally polished and ornate—so much so that he is a source of amusement for less polished Israelis, who speak in a simpler, coarser vein. As a public figure in Israel, Eban occupies a position similar to that held by the late Adlai Stevenson in the United States. Stevenson was often faulted, as a politician, for talking over the heads of the people and for appearing slightly too patrician. Israelis may stand in awe of Eban's rhetorical ability, but he fails to touch their souls in a way that ignites them. Precisely those qualities that make Eban so popular in the United States—his polished smoothness and worldliness—are a deficit in Israel, where the expectation is that the leadership should have the same kind of blunt straightforwardness that the rest of the population possesses in such large measure.

The complaint about Eban in Israel is not so much that he presents himself as somehow superior to his fellow Israelis as that he places too much emphasis on talking and gentility and not enough on action. At the other extreme is a politician like Ariel Sharon, with a reputation for bombast and seemingly impulsive action that emerges from a deep wellspring of raw, restless energy. Sharon is single-minded, and aggressive to the point of boorishness, in the estimation of some of his colleagues, but he is also a popular figure, especially among Oriental Jews.

In certain areas Israelis revere excellence, brilliance, and profundity. Scholars and scientists occupy roughly the same status in Israeli society that saintly rabbis inhabit among the strictly Orthodox. Yet, anyone who wants to be involved in contemporary affairs, although aspiring to be a member of the elite, cannot appear to be elitist. The nearest thing Israel has ever had to an elitist educational institution was a handful of agricultural schools whose graduates emerged with muscles and dirt under their fingernails. No one deprecates education in Israel—it is generally understood that the country's survival depends upon maintaining a high technological level—but education and learning flaunted arouse suspicion and hostility. The vaguest suggestion of personal superiority can damn one's chances of success regardless of the brilliance of the argument or performance. One of the more insulting remarks one Israeli can make about another (although not libelous, according to an Israeli court ruling) is to call someone a *yekke*. Although the term originally was used to describe Jews coming from Germany, it is now used to denote anyone who pays too much attention to detail, to finer points, or is overexacting (or exacting at all in some cases) in some matter or dealing.

Social democracy in Israel is not entirely or even predominantly negative. Israelis display an openness and frankness that encourages one person to speak one's mind and offer one's opinion freely to another without feeling that one is being presumptuous in doing so. Israelis respect experts, but they also respect their own experience and knowledge and have few inhibitions about putting in their own two cents' worth when they disagree with what an expert may be saying.

My wife and I traveled to the north with a fairly high government official whom I had asked to explain the government's settlement policy in the Galilee. The official took us in a car with a driver, who happened to double as a tour guide when taking tourists around the country and who considered himself, we discovered later, an amateur historian. As we drove along, the conversation ranged over a variety of topics. The government official offered his explanation of a particular situation. When he had finished, the driver, who had not spoken at all up to that point, interjected: "The situation is actually more complicated than he's explained it. This has to do with history, which is my field." He then launched into his own explanation of the situation. The government official listened carefully and commented seriously on what the driver had said, accepting his analysis as that of an equal—socially and intellectually—rather than as coming from someone performing a menial job who should be seen and not heard.

The sort of separation that exists in other Western democracies between important dignitaries and ordinary citizens is rare in Israel. One evening I went with some friends to a small Jerusalem restaurant. The maître d' motioned us to a table off to one side. As we walked to it, we noticed suddenly that we were being seated about twenty feet from the table where the president of Israel, his wife, and another couple were sitting, rather inconspicuously. They were not, as one might expect, surrounded by security guards. In fact, we didn't even see a security guard anywhere around (although they certainly were nearby). Anyone who wished to was able to approach the president's table and apparently could do so without being stopped. Several persons did approach him and spoke with him. The waiters did not fawn over the president and his party. One was left with the clear impression that he was just another customer and was getting that kind of treatment—no more and no less.

The president's wife often walks by herself in Jerusalem's shopping district. She buys groceries herself in a supermarket near her home and has her hair done in a rather modest salon. None of this simplicity was affected or strained in an effort to be one of the people. The president of Israel *is* one of the people and remains so by refusing to be insulated from his fellow citizens. A former president of Israel, returning from a trip abroad, waited for two and a half hours with his fellow passengers for his luggage before he could pass through customs and go home. He neither asked for nor received special treatment.

Considering the distance between politicians and their constituency in the United States and the abuse of privilege in the last decade or so, this kind of public humility has more than a little appeal. But Israelis pay a price for having their leaders live so close to them. Yaron Ezrahi, an Israeli political scientist, argues persuasively that democracy is a great destroyer of political leadership, not only in Israel but through the Western world. Democracy erodes the aura and mystique with which leadership surrounds itself, destroying the charisma so necessary for effective leadership. If, after all, the leader is no wiser and no different essentially from the rest of the population, then his arguments lose much of their persuasiveness. If his opinions have no special insight, why should they be valued above others?

Ben-Gurion, though a more controversial figure during his tenure than is generally recognized in the United States, chose to live a simple, unpretentious life close to the population. But he needed none of the trappings of power because he was widely perceived to be possessed of a vision that gave his public pronouncements an almost prophetic weight. His successors have been less successful, to the point where the authority of leadership in general has declined in Israel. Part of this decline may be explained by a Russian proverb: "Under great oaks, only mushrooms grow." Meaning that after the founding generation of leaders it is inevitable that men and women of greatly diminished stature would follow. Part of this decline may also be ascribed to growing problems, diminished competence among the leadership, arrogance, and the corruption that comes from holding power too long. But much of this decline can also be accounted for by the discovery on the part of Israelis that their leaders are, in fact, only human and that they have feet of clay and are prone to error. Israel could not continue indefinitely with a heroic struggle. Inevitably, order had to be established. With order comes routine and with routine comes the organization and its apparatchiks.

The fall from grace may not have been so hard had the country's leadership been more responsive and closer to the population on a *political* as well as a *social* level. And it is small consolation for Israelis to know that they are suffering the same crisis of leadership that plagues other Western democracies. As with everything else, because the general situation in Israel is more tenuous, the problem is more serious. The decline of ideology, the waning of national spirit, the breakdown of the consensus in the country, all make it that much more difficult for Israel's political leadership to find support to deal with the severe problems facing the country.

Manners, courtesy, and civility are another victim of social democracy in Israel. This situation is not necessarily inevitable for a democracy. Norway is also a social and political democracy and yet Norwegians are exceptionally polite. But Israelis have yet to reach such a state of social grace. The debate in Israel goes on continuously as to whether or not public manners are getting better or worse. One of the casualties of social democracy is decent, cheerful service in restaurants, hotels, or other establishments where clients are waited on. Tourists fall outside the Israeli social order and may not be affected by the Israeli habit of demonstrating equality by showing contempt for the customer. (On the other hand, the tourist may suffer equally or even worse, depending upon the psyche of the individual employee.) Occasionally, an Israeli worker will decide to humor a countryman. Otherwise, the Israeli customer can generally expect indifferent, cheerless—occasionally surly—service, as though one is being done a reluctant favor that constitutes a thoughtless imposition on the employee, who has far more important things to do. When the customer becomes known as a regular, of course, the situation changes, but that suggests that the customer and the employee have established a relationship in which the employee can make it clear that he or she is a social equal. Once that principle is established, service may still be deficient—form, as I have said, is not a strong point in Israel—but the general atmosphere will improve markedly.

Israel is also still close to its origins, which were primarily egalitarian and socialist. The aristocracy of the country is not marked by wealth but by accomplishment in a sleeves-up, muscular tradition of tilling the land, of working long hours to found this or that labor institution, or of smuggling "illegal" Jewish immigrants past British authorities. This is not the stuff of grand manners and drawing rooms. Where a family may have had a maid, she likely was seen as part of the family and saw herself in the same way. Israel was and still is too small for the most part for anyone to withdraw from the rest of the population without actually leaving the country. (For one thing, everyone—or at least every eligible male—has his annual reserve duty to do, a quick reminder to every Israeli that no one is so special that he can rise above that onerous duty.)

But even beyond the nature of Israel's own history is the history of the Jewish people. Almost by its very nature the Jewish people do not easily lend themselves to pretentiousness. Aside from a few—very few—"noble" families like the Rothschilds or the Montefiores, the average Jew can, within one or two generations, trace his or her family back to some hovel or ghetto where an ancestor eked out a miserable living and depended for well-being and security on the help and support of fellow Jews. Everyone understood that as Jews their fate was tied together, so that few could consider themselves so important as to be able to rise above the community.

The rich literature and folklore of the eastern European ghetto, which played such a critical role in shaping the culture and institutions of Israel, is replete with images of the *little* Jew up against the world, fate, God, or whatever. Such Jews survived by their cunning and developed a sense of humor about themselves and their life that deflated pretentiousness. In that sense social democracy is a Jewish—or at least an eastern European Jewish—quality that the earliest immigrants brought with them when they came to resettle the land. Political democracy springs from social democracy and it is not surprising, as a result, to find that Israel has many of the same democratic traditions and institutions found in any other democracy—with some notable differences and wrinkles that are distinctly Israeli.

* * *

After living in Israel for a year, we were visited by some friends from the United States. I was left momentarily speechless during a conversation I had when one of our friends suddenly asked, "What are people like here?" The question was so bold in its straightforwardness, so innocent in its simplicity that I was overwhelmed by it. It was a question I felt unable to answer, and in a way it confronted me with the presumptuousness of what I was attempting to do myself. What, after all, is Israel like? No matter what statement one makes about the country, it is possible to find the exception that challenges it. If matters are distilled to essence, they may be oversimplified. If we try to look at things in all their complexity, the situation may seem hopelessly muddled.

Still, Israel is different from Egypt or Italy or the United States, and not just in obvious ways. The heart of the matter, it seems to me, is the admonition that an Israeli gave me soon after our arrival. "You must remember," she said, "we are a desert country. Things here need constant attention. Nothing takes care of itself. If we're careless for a moment, it could all slip away."

At the bottom of the characteristics we have been looking at— obsessive optimism, geographically reinforced intimacy, emphasis on the group—is the scarcely concealed anxiety that what is ultimately at stake here is not some vague question of quality of life or larger purpose, but survival itself.

Every little tremor from the outside is seized upon, dissected, and analyzed in terms of the same recurring question: "What does it mean for us, for Israel?" Ancient history and modern experience both teach Israelis that they can trust nobody completely except themselves, that nothing can be taken for granted.

It is characteristically Israeli to see the world and themselves in terms of absolutes. Things are either one way or entirely the opposite. "Either," Israeli author Amos Oz observed, "we are the greatest, the most—or the hell with us." Israelis, former Defense Minister Ezer Weizman said once, see the world divided into two groups—pro-Israelis and anti-Semites. Not to have a positive, optimistic outlook is to be pessimistic—defeatist—to wallow in self-doubt while the entire enterprise so painfully and carefully constructed over the years slides back into the oblivion of almost two millennia of exile in the Diaspora, or—worse—extinction.

Thus, Israeli soldiers are taken to Masada, symbol of the fanatic last stand of Jewish zealots in A.D. 73. The zealots committed suicide rather than surrender to the Roman soldiers who had besieged them after destroying the Second Temple in Jerusalem. Today's Israeli soldiers are brought to Masada to swear, under the flickering light of torches in a ceremony designed to conjure up mystical connections with the past, that "Masada will not fall again!" Other countries may worry about war or invasion. Israelis worry about extinction. In Israel the lesson drawn from history and experience is that none of the *other*, the outside can ever be relied upon, that the only reliable help in the end is self-supplied. In Israel the enemy is always at the gates, even when he puts on a moderate face. "Once the Jewish people did not believe the book *Mein Kampf*," former Israeli Prime Minister Yitzhak Rabin has warned ominously. "I don't advise them not to believe the Palestinian Covenant."

Much of the Israeli approach involves skating along a thin edge, pushing situations to their limits. It is not a pattern of behavior designed to win Israelis friends among more prudent secure peoples whose own experience has taught them different lessons.

The question, of course, is how much one's approach determines the response. In their worst moments, when their aspirations and desires get the best of them, Israelis turn their backs on the outside world, treating it as though it were not a factor and that it will not respond. Self-involvement can lead ultimately to a form of autism, which is nothing more than an absorption in fantasy at the expense of external reality.

The question of survival so dwarfs everything else that it hardly seems possible that Israelis would have energy left to consider other issues. During the 1948 War of Independence, Jerusalem resident Harry Levin observed in his diary, members of a kibbutz fretted over how the fighting was disrupting their lives: " 'A workers' settlement,' one member wrote in the kibbutz journal," the diarist recounted, quoting from the journal, "finds it hard to reconcile itself to a situation in which we must curtail our productive work and give more and more attention to war." . . . Another settler, who signs himself *Tarbutnik* (slang for "one concerned with culture"), pleads for the maintenance of cultural activities in spite of the demands of defence. I find a bit exasperating this worship of culture in every kind of circumstance; like the people who feel dirty if forced to miss a day's bath.

Israelis have, of course, concerned themselves with more than survival alone. The maintenance of Israel as a civilized country depends upon its upholding certain standards in the midst of the challenges confronting it.

In their best moments Israelis project an appreciation of the philosophically absurd position they are in. They show a fatalistic sense that they must look at their own condition without sentimentality or illusions, calculate what is needed to survive while remaining true to their own self-imposed sense of decency and human dignity, and after that proceed. But the essence of this approach is an ability to accept the situation with a cold-blooded discipline that eschews fruitless complaints about perverse luck or fate, and concentrates instead on finding the inner strength to measure up, to be equal to the need of the moment. In their best moments Israelis can be self-effacing, self-disciplined, and self-sacrificing.

Obviously Israelis are not always at their best. More than occasionally uncommon generosity and selfishness are at war within the same soul. "The land of Israel is Gulliver," artist Siona Shimshi said, "and we are a generation of giants, yet Lilliputians in everyday life." Shimshi's characterization catches the contradictions of Israeli life—the tension between great accomplishments and egregious pettiness, between majesty and meanness, between great purpose and the mundane demands of everyday life, between the hopes Israelis harbor and the grim reality to which they have had to accustom themselves. The whole setting and circumstance of Israel—the denial of limitations, the cultivation of art and music in the midst of constant readiness for war, the determined effort to "make the desert bloom," the massive contradictions one confronts everywhere—are evidence of a kind of Sisyphian struggle going on. Constantly under siege and threatened with extinction, every day in the life of an Israeli is an act of affirmation, like Melville's Queequeg in *Moby-Dick*, "holding up that imbecile candle in the heart of that almighty forlornness . . . the sign and symbol of a man without faith, hopelessly holding up hope in the midst of despair."

3 / THE ECONOMY

Labor is a lofty human ideal, an ideal of the future. . . . Our condition in the past, our situation in the present can teach us that we must take the lead in this—we must all work.

A. D. Gordon

The respectability of work has gone into exile.

Shimon Peres

In the Jewish state that the early Zionists constructed in their minds, the concept of work was enshrined in an exalted place. Work was part of the program of "self-realization" for the Jews returning to the homeland. Where the Jew of the Old World had become separated from the soil and had lost the skill of his hands, the new Jew would be strong and self-sufficient—a farmer and laborer—building the Jewish homeland with his own sweat and muscle.

As visions go, it was harmless enough. As a motto, "The conquest of labor" set a positive and constructive tone for the Jewish national movement, promising to channel energies into peaceful endeavors. The early settlers sang a simple Hebrew song—"We came to rebuild the land, and to be rebuilt by it."

As a goal it was ambitious but far from utopian, despite the doubts of some contemporary observers who underestimated the energy and will of the people driving the dream forward. If they could return, the early settlers in Palestine might marvel at what has been accomplished in scarcely a century. The land has been

cleared; swamps have been drained; cities, towns, and villages have
been built. Modern technology has enabled Israelis to make the
desert bloom. But rebuilding the land was only half of the dream.
The other half was to *be rebuilt* by it. Here the outcome is less
certain. The original vision of a hard-working, self-sufficient people paying its own way in the world has been less successful.

Where Israelis once venerated work, they now joke about it,
mocking themselves in the process. Israelis are fond of telling the
story of a symposium held to discuss increasing industrial efficiency
in their country. One of the speakers at the meeting suggested that
rather than having a Sunday-through-Friday work week, Israelis
should emulate the United States and work five days a week. "Too
ambitious," the president of the Israeli manufacturers disagreed.
"Why not start with one day?" he asked.

Without a doubt the economic development of Israel is one of
the miracles of the post-World War II era. Israel has transformed
itself from a country that had to import more than 50 percent of
its food to a country that now grows 90 percent of what it eats and
pays for the rest with its own agricultural exports. No other country, dictatorship or democracy, can claim to have simultaneously
quintupled its population, equipped a modern army virtually
from scratch, built a modern industrial plant capable of making
sophisticated goods that compete successfully on the world market,
and increased its exports by 3,600 percent in thirty years.

Impressive accomplishments, but at the same time Israel suffers
from chronic high inflation and has never had a year in which it
sold more on the world market than it bought. The country's
foreign debt—the money it owes to other countries—has grown
dramatically, but its productive capability has not kept pace. Israelis live at a standard that they cannot, in fact, support without
outside help.

In headier moments Israelis like to describe their country as
"the Switzerland of the Middle East." It's true enough that Israelis, when they have a mind to, display technological proficiency,
a dexterity and ingenuity that rival any other modern industrial
country. But Israel is *not* Switzerland—at least not yet. During the
1973 Yom Kippur War, Israeli army units captured, intact, an

entire Egyptian antitank unit near the Suez Canal. Since the Israelis were desperate for ammunition, they quickly set out to master the operation of the Soviet antitank missiles they had captured. Among the captured equipment was an electronic device used to train the troops in the operation of the missile. After a few days of intensive use, however, the device burned out. Army technicians opened it and were dismayed to find that it used vacuum tubes, long since made obsolete by transistors. The technicians announced that the device was irreparable.

The officer in charge, however, was determined to have the device back in operation since the need was urgent. He sent it to one of Israel's biggest electronic firms, which returned it thirty-six hours later, fully operational. The firm's technicians had torn out the guts of the device, redesigned it, and installed transistors where the vacuum tubes had been used. All in all, it was a real feat of technical know-how and persistence.

"How long," the officer in charge asked an official of the electronics firm, "would it have taken you to do what you did if this had not been an emergency?"

"Six months," the official replied.

The Israeli economy, like the rest of Israel, is not one thing but many, and often contradictory at that. Despite its pretensions and accomplishments Israel is still located in the Middle East—subject to the arcane, byzantine ways of the area, with Israel adding a few unique contributions of its own.

Agriculture, which was once one of the principal employers in Israel, now accounts for only about 6 percent of the work force and only slightly more of the gross national product. Industry accounts for 24 percent of the work force and 23 percent of the GNP. As an employer, industry is overshadowed by public and community services, government agencies, social service organizations and the like which employ 28 percent of the work force and account for 21 percent of the GNP. Tourism employs about 12 percent of Israeli workers and accounts for 10 percent of the GNP. Construction, business and finance, transportation, storage and communication together employ about 21 percent of the work force and account for 31 percent of the GNP.

In agriculture, citrus is one of the big cash crops, along with cotton and fresh flowers, which are flown to European markets. Israeli industry has begun marketing innovative electronic devices throughout the world, along with high-fashion clothing, polished diamonds, and sophisticated weaponry ranging from light arms to jet fighters. Precisely how much munitions Israel is selling abroad is difficult to say, but the most informed estimate is that roughly $1 billion and perhaps as much as $1.5 billion of Israeli exports are accounted for by armaments and related equipment.

The economy of Israel, like the state itself, is largely the product of planned effort rather than the result of individual initiative. The Israeli economy is not centrally planned and controlled like the Soviet Union's, but neither is it a creature of market forces like that of the United States. Even before the State of Israel was established, groups and organizations were working to build an industrial base that would provide work for Jews coming to Palestine to establish a Jewish homeland. This goal of providing work for Jews to further the aspirations for a homeland and ultimately a Jewish state is central to the Israeli economy. Israel is still benefiting—and suffering—because of this central purpose.

A more unlikely place than Israel for development and a more unlikely people than the Jews to develop it would have been hard to imagine one hundred fifty years ago. "The idea of making farmers of the Jews is vain," Herman Melville wrote when he visited Palestine in the 1850s.

In the first place, Judea is a desert with few exceptions. In the second place, the Jews hate farming. All who cultivate the soil in Palestine are Arabs. The Jews dare not live outside the walled towns or villages for fear of the malicious persecution of the Arabs and Turks. Besides the number of Jews in Palestine is small. And how are the hosts of them scattered in other lands to be brought here? Only by a miracle.

Melville put his finger on two problems. First, the land itself was barren, stripped of foliage by the Turks, so that the winter rains eroded the soil with their runoff. In summer the land was hard, caked. Without water, it wasn't possible to grow anything, and it did not as a rule rain in Palestine from April until November. Second, the Jews of Palestine—indeed the Jews of the world—had been divorced from the soil for hundreds of years. All over the Middle East, North Africa, Europe, and even North America, wherever Jews *were* found, they were *not* found working the land. Jews had been forcibly kept from the soil for so long that they had lost the skill. They had become merchants, moneylenders, small artisans, and tradesmen—doing the only jobs that they were legally permitted to do, not the jobs that they necessarily wanted to do.

In any case, the Jews that Melville saw were pious Jews who had come to Palestine not for economic betterment—Palestine hardly offered that—but to achieve the epitome of their religious experience—studying the holy scripture (Torah) and commentaries in the Land of Israel. These religious Jews, some of whom came from Europe and others from Oriental countries, lived largely off of the charity of Jews from other countries, who considered it a *mitzvah* ("good deed") to give money to support Jewish scholars or simply Jews in need.

The confinement of Jews to ghettos throughout much of the world and the restrictions on the kind of work they could do had left its cultural mark. Manual work was disparaged by Jews.

But even as Melville was writing in the mid-1850s of the unlikely prospects for Jewish reclamation of their ancient homeland, economic and social currents were moving to dislodge the Jews of eastern Europe from the ghettos where they had been segregated—and also sheltered—from the world outside. The economy of Europe was changing rapidly, and economic functions—like banking and moneylending—that had been barred to Christians and therefore filled by Jews, were opening to Christians. The functions that Jews had historically performed now could by done by non-Jews, and therefore, the social utility of Jews declined. Jews, rather than performing a service, created an obstruction. Anti-Semitism, if held in check at all, had been restrained because Jews had served a practical need of the community; as the need diminished, anti-Semitism grew.

Gradually, the idea took hold that the path of redemption for

Jews, the way that would enable them to take their place among other nations and other peoples in the world was to become once again a whole people. Jewish organizations sprouted in eastern Europe, France, and Palestine dedicated to the principle of work and to a reunification with the soil.

If a single individual served as a prophet for this movement, it was A. D. Gordon, who preached the "religion of labor" for Jews. "We were defeated through lack of labor," he wrote. "Work will heal us. In the center of all of our hopes we must place work; our entire structure must be founded on labor." After two thousand years of being divorced from the land and from manual labor, Gordon wrote, Jews could not again be a living, "natural, working people" unless all their energy was directed toward labor—"labor by which a people becomes rooted in its soil and in its culture."

Gordon—or at least Gordon's philosophy—made a lasting impression on Israel and Israelis, even among those who today have never heard of him. Work—labor as a value to be prized in and of itself—still is part of the national credo, part of the mythology that Israeli politicians invoke when they exhort their countrymen with patriotic calls. Nor is it entirely empty rhetoric. It is possible to find in Israel places—especially kibbutzim—where ideology emphasizes work as a value by itself, rather than as a means to an end. When I asked a kibbutznik once how kibbutz members dealt with another member who was a shirker, he gave me an indulgent smile, suggesting that the problem rarely comes up.

Gordon's philosophy also shaped the thinking of the early settlers who called themselves *halutzim* ("pioneers") quite consciously setting out to redeem the land by working it and to redeem themselves in the process. That the work had to be done by Jews was a cardinal principle. A Jewish society could not be built with Arab labor. This insistence on Jews doing the work created tension and conflict with the Arabs. The principle of Jews performing the work was seen by the Jewish pioneers as a part of the process of national redemption, rather than a position hostile to Arabs. It was not enough that the land in Israel should be productive, but the Jewish people also should be.

Between 1882 and 1903 approximately twenty-five thousand

Jews came to Palestine, mostly from eastern Europe. Most of these new immigrants were members of an organization calling itself Bilu, an acronym from the Hebrew biblical passage, "O House of Jacob, let us go up." In Palestine they settled largely in the cities and villages, but a fraction returned to the land, founding small settlements or working in an agricultural school founded by the Paris Alliance Israélite. These were the settlers of the First Aliyah, or first immigration. The vast majority of the twenty-five thousand who came between 1882 and 1903 left Palestine. Finding life too hard, they went back to Europe or on to America. Those who stayed found their socialist principles gradually transformed into capitalist convictions. When the immigrants of the Second Aliyah began arriving in 1905, they found a class of Jewish employers firmly implanted, engaging Arab workers to farm their land.

The Jewish landowners were more interested in making money than in providing employment for fellow Jews. The settlers of the Second Aliyah, overwhelmingly from eastern Europe, were coming from the ferment that ultimately produced the Bolshevik Revolution. These settlers were committed to Zionism—a return to the Jewish homeland—and to socialism. It was understood that both programs would take time to realize.

The life remained hard. "For a year," one young settler later wrote, "I sweated in the Judean colonies, but for me there was more malaria and hunger than work." This particular young settler was David Ben-Gurion. He came from Poland in 1906 with the wide-eyed idealism and fiery dedication that was typical of the pioneers of the Second Aliyah.

All three—work, hunger and malaria—were new and full of interest. Was it not for this that I had come to the land? The fever would grip me every fortnight with mathematical precision, harass me for five or six days, and then disappear. Hunger too, was a regular visitor. It would come to lodge with me for weeks at a time, sometimes for months on end. During the days I could dismiss it in all sorts of ways, or at least I could stop thinking of it. But in the nights—the long racked vigils—the pangs would grow fiercer, wringing the heart, darkening the mind, sucking the very marrow from my bones, demanding and torturing—and departing only with the dawn. Shattered and broken, I would drop off to sleep at last.

In this fashion, days of work alternated with days of fever and hunger, and then the recurring night. But the enthusiasm and the joy faded not at all. Who worried about malaria in those days? The few who did not suffer from it were a little shame-faced before the rest of us who did; imagine coming to the Land of Israel without savoring its fever!

Some of the pioneers of the Second Aliyah—a fraction as it turned out—stayed on in Palestine. Most left, perhaps as many as 80 to 90 percent. Propelled by ideology and pragmatism, the young pioneers who remained began establishing collective settlements—kibbutzim and moshavim—to farm the land, reasserting a Jewish presence in Palestine on land purchased by the Jewish National Fund from contributions made by Jews all over the world.

In 1923 the British Mandate in Palestine was formally established, although the British had actually been in control since the end of 1917. England had already given its formal support through the Balfour Declaration in 1917 to the principle of a Jewish homeland in Palestine. Even before the formal establishment of the Mandate concern was growing within Jewish labor circles in Palestine about conditions for Jewish workers there. Motivated by this concern, some four thousand Jewish workers banded together to establish the General Federation of Jewish Labor in Palestine, commonly known then and today as the Histadrut. Ben-Gurion was chosen as the Histadrut's first secretary-general.

As originally conceived, the Histadrut was a labor union. As Jewish immigrants continued to show up in Palestine, the focus of concern shifted somewhat for the Histadrut. New workers were coming in faster than the economy could employ them. Wage rates would become depressed if work were not provided. To avert that situation the Histadrut formed a Workers' Corporation (Hevrat Ovdim), using workers' dues to fund businesses that employed workers, who in turn became members of the Histadrut and who were paid—by the Histadrut.

The Histadrut quickly expanded its functions to meet other needs of the emerging Jewish community (Yishuv). Health services were provided through the Histadrut's health plan—Kupat Holim. Within a matter of years the Histadrut established a bank (Bank HaPoalim), a construction company (Solel Boneh), a central purchasing and marketing company (Hamashbir), an agricultural marketing organization (Tnuva), an insurance company (Hassneh), and a daily newspaper (*Davar*).

By the eve of World War II the Histadrut was indistinguishable from the Jewish community. The Histadrut's existence gave the leadership of the Jewish community, which was dominated by the same Labor hierarchy that controlled the Histadrut, an ability to coordinate and control activities in the community toward the ultimate goal of establishing a Jewish state. In 1942, with World War II in full swing, three fourths of the Jewish workers in Palestine were represented by the Histadrut, which was also the largest industrial producer in the country.

The Histadrut now is a mighty force in Israel. No less than twenty-five percent of the goods and services Israel produces and sells—chemicals, drugs, computers, shoes, tires, steel, electrical appliances, skyscrapers—are built or manufactured by a Histadrut concern. Only the Israeli government employs more workers. At the same time, the Histadrut is the labor union for seventy-five percent of Israel's work force.

The dual role of the Histadrut—as employer and union—presents both opportunities and problems for the organization and for Israel. The existence of a well-organized, disciplined, and controlled labor force was doubtless invaluable to the establishment of the Jewish state. The ability of the Labor-dominated government to call on the Histadrut for aid and assistance in Israel's early years was also critical.

On the other hand, the dominant position of the Histadrut and Histadrut-owned business and industry in the Israeli economy contributes to some of the serious problems that Israel faces today.

In the early years of Israel's existence the country's leadership believed it was essential that the flood of immigrants have work to do instead of spending their time on the dole while living in the transit camps (ma'abarot) that the government put up to house them temporarily. Factories were established, operating with government subsidies, to provide work for these new immigrants. Within a few years a series of "development towns" was constructed—especially in sparsely populated areas of the north and south. The Histadrut played a critical role in building factories in many of these towns to provide work for the new immigrants who were settled there.

To keep its separate functions from being confused the Histadrut is divided into four major departments: trade union, Hevrat Ovdim, health and welfare, and education and culture. The four departments are separately run and maintained, reporting to the Histadrut's governing convention through the executive structure. With this organizational structure, the workers may be said to own the Histadrut's factories without directly controlling them. Some Histadrut factories are well-run and highly profitable. Others are less so. Where a Histadrut factory is unprofitable, the factory manager can expect to be removed after two consecutive years of running at a loss a plant expected to make a profit.

Worker-ownership does not ensure that a Histadrut's plant will be free of strikes or tension. Histadrut factories are struck, although the incentive to find a quick resolution of disagreements is greater in such plants than in privately owned (as opposed to worker-owned), and efforts are made to avoid strikes wherever possible.

The executives of the Histadrut factories meet union leadership to make broad policy and to negotiate contracts for the workers under union control. Below the boardroom level where these major policy decisions are made for the industry as a whole the interplay between labor and management is similar to what one would find in other Western industrial, capitalist countries. Workers within a Histadrut-owned plant are represented by a workers' committee in the same way that workers in a privately owned plant are. The workers' committee presents grievances to management on behalf of employees and negotiates local conditions with the plant management. Negotiations on specific working conditions other than wages and hours (which are negotiated for the industry as a whole) are conducted annually. If an issue cannot be resolved within the plant between the management and the workers' committee, it is referred to the central Histadrut organization for arbitration.

Histadrut factories commonly feature some type of profit sharing for employees, in addition to bonuses and other incentives paid to individual workers.

The influence of the workers' committee in Histadrut plants varies, as it does in privately owned plants, according to the personalities involved, the competence of the management, and the aggressiveness of the workers. In some, the workers play a major role in choosing the managers, an arrangement that does not always produce the kind of management that runs a plant in the most efficient manner.

Nor is everyone within the Histadrut enthusiastic about a system that puts so much power into the hands of a work force whose motivation to work is often a problem. When I asked the manager of one Histadrut factory whether the workers' committee in his factory played any role in choosing the factory's management, he bristled. "No" he replied angrily, "this plant is run properly."

Unique as the Histadrut is as a meld of labor and management, union and ownership, the atmosphere and working conditions of a Histadrut-owned factory or business are not noticeably different from the atmosphere in a private plant. Nor are the problems markedly different.

Because of the way Israel's economy developed before the establishment of the state, labor unions are considerably stronger in Israel than in other countries that are at a similar stage of development. The usual pattern in the West was for industry to develop first and for the work force to organize itself later. The reversal of this pattern in Israel has special implications for Israel's economic situation.

Prior to 1948 labor-management relations were dominated by the Histadrut, which had two major considerations—establishment of a Jewish state and realization of socialist ideology. Histadrut businesses and even privately owned plants were often started less to make a profit than to provide jobs for Jewish workers and to develop the Jewish homeland—in other words, to further the Zionist program of reclaiming the land and restoring life and culture to the Jewish people. Employer-employee relations in Israel were more democratic from the outset than they were in other countries, because the motive for being in business was different. The profit motive was often secondary, a means rather than an end. In many prestate Histadrut enterprises workers were paid on the basis of their individual need rather than the work they performed. It was not unusual to find a manager with a small family making less than a janitor with more children. The janitor's needs were greater; therefore his salary was also greater.

After the founding of the state, the Israeli economy was in dire straits. A flood of new immigrants forced the government to impose severe economic controls and high taxes on the population. Factory owners and managers were inclined to make nonmonetary concessions to workers simply because there was little money to be paid out. Additionally, as an Israeli economist pointed out, socialist ideology was very strong in Israel in its early years. Owners felt a little embarrassed at being bosses, so they involved the workers in the process of managing the factories.

Israeli plant managers today running factories where workers wrote the work rules, face problems similar to that of an American company that has made work condition concessions rather than paying monetary benefits. Once workers are given authority over the conditions of their employment, they are understandably reluctant to give it up.

Most factories, including those that are privately owned, have some degree of worker participation in decisions ordinarily reserved for management. In 80 percent of Israeli plants, according to a study done by Israeli economist Abraham Friedman, the union is involved—through the workers' committee—in the process of disciplining workers. In 25 percent of Israeli plants the union alone disciplines employees. In 35 percent of Israeli plants discipline of workers is a union-management concern only when the employer is involved in the problem. Otherwise, the union alone disciplines the worker. And in 36 percent of the cases discipline is always jointly administered.

In 37 percent of Israeli plants, Friedman found, the shop steward *always* intervenes when a worker is moved from one job to another even if the transfer is only for two hours. In 66 percent of Israeli plants promotion is a *joint* responsibility of workers and management. In two thirds of these plants promotions are made from a list prepared by the workers' committee, giving it effective control over the whole process. "Which means," Friedman says, "that management is less efficient and less effective, which means promotion is based on seniority and not on merit, which means you have many managers who don't know how to manage."

A highly visible example of management paralysis is Israel's national airline, El Al. Once a nominally profitable venture, by the late 1970s El Al had become a major burden on the Israeli government, which had to make up a $25-million deficit in 1978 and a $100-million shortfall in 1979. Although much of El Al's problems resulted from forces out of the company's control—a substantial increase in fuel costs, deregulation of air fares in the United States leading to increased competition from American air carriers—El Al was unable to respond to the problem in an imaginative or creative way.

El Al's employees were represented by eighteen different unions, each of which was in a position to ground the airline when it saw fit to do so. (In 1978 El Al employees struck for twenty-one days.) "You cannot give orders in this place," one El Al official complained publicly. "You can only make requests. The request will be submitted to the relevant workers' committee for their consideration. Everything becomes rigid."

Over a period of time El Al had entered into contracts with its flight crews whereby much of their salaries were paid in American rather than Israeli currency. They were paid a higher rate during flights to compensate for not providing meals (even though enough food was supplied to feed the passengers that the crew was able to eat at El Al's expense after all), and the company paid the crew members' income taxes.

When the airline attempted to increase its income by introducing a new class of passengers who would bring their own food on board—flying for less but reducing the number of cabin crew needed—the cabin staff vetoed the proposal and it was dropped. Although El Al had a perfect safety record, its flights were so frequently late that passengers joked that El Al was not a name but initials standing for "every landing always late." Service aboard El Al flights was generally cheerless at best and surly at worst—if available at all. A survey of major international airlines in 1979 placed El Al at the bottom of those studied. Israelis, encouraged to fly El Al for reasons of security and national pride, began taking competitive lines if they had to be certain of arriving on time.

El Al's situation began to improve only when the company's management, prodded by firm warnings from the government, made it clear to the airline's employees that the company would be closed and all of its employees dismissed if the unions did not allow management to make necessary changes. The new crisis atmosphere did not, however, prevent various parts of El Al's work force from periodically disrupting the line's operation and threatening its continued functioning.

The right manager *can* make a difference. The manager of a factory—owned by the Histadrut as it happened—said that one of his assistants made an unexpected visit to the factory one evening to find an employee sleeping. The employee, as it turned out, was the chairman of the factory workers' committee. The manager decided to punish the offender, who retaliated by calling a strike in protest. The manager then decided to make an issue of the whole affair, closing the factory and informing the Histadrut that it would not reopen until the employee was fired. After two days the worker was fired and the factory reopened.

But the system doesn't always work that way. Another executive recounted the story of a man hired as a watchman in a Histadrut hospital. Before the watchman had worked six months—at which point he would have had tenure and could not have been fired—he discovered that some employees were stealing. He reported the situation to his superiors. The workers' committee at the Histadrut hospital where the incident occurred responded by bringing pressure, successfully, to have the watchman fired.

In long-established factories, especially those set up to provide work for new immigrants, a variety of incentives are employed to make sure that the worker shows up for work, is on time, and actually does something while on the job. As a result, Israeli workers receive a variety of bonuses and benefits on top of a basic salary. "The normal attitude in Israel," one executive said, "is 'I get paid my salary just for coming to work. If you want me to do something, you have to give me something more.' "

The general practice in factories is to pay a basic hourly wage and then to give a bonus based on productivity, a separate bonus if the employee shows up for work every day, and still another bonus for being punctual.

The payment of bonuses for not missing work is a reflection of workers' attitudes coupled with an anomaly in the Israeli tax system. At one time in Israel it was possible to miss a day's work every few weeks, collect sick benefits from the National Insurance Institute (similar to the Social Security Administration in the United States), and come out ahead, since compensation paid for missing work was nontaxable.

The bonus system is designed basically to get the Israeli worker to produce. "We give salaries that we know are impossible to live on," a textile factory manager in a development town told me. "So then we have to offer bonuses. The system encourages that." The standards set for production are ordinarily well below what a worker is able to produce. In one factory I visited, ninety percent of the workers were performing above the norm and therefore were getting production bonuses. I asked the factory manager why he didn't raise the norm, since almost everyone was performing above it. "You have to give something to the people," he answered. "If you don't give them something, they have no incentive." Roughly half of the workers in this plant, a prefabricated concrete factory near Ashqelon, were earning half their pay in bonuses, and a few of them were managing to make more than the factory manager as a result of the bonus system.

An alternative to paying bonuses—which is a reward for workers —is to dismiss the unwilling or incompetent worker. Israeli workers, however, are rarely fired. "We have a saying," an Israeli told me. "Hiring a worker is like driving a nail without a head into the wall. Once you put it in, it's almost impossible to get it out."

The extreme degree of union organization in Israel gives the worker a protected status that makes his or her welfare and well-being as important, if not more so, than the health of the business enterprise. Union organization is not limited to factories and blue-collar jobs. Teachers at all levels—including the universities—are union members, along with office workers, government employees, doctors, nurses, and scores of other jobholders. Virtually the only workers not unionized in Israel are policemen and soldiers (policemen have attempted unsuccessfully to organize).

Part of the reason for the protected status of the Israeli worker is the socialist aversion to exploiting the laborer. The Histadrut was in a position well before the state was established to dictate the terms of labor employment for new businesses.

After the state was established in 1948 a flood of immigrants poured into the country who had to be given work. Immigrants to Israel were not coming because the country offered opportunities but because they had no place else to go. Resource-poor, almost entirely dependent on imported raw materials with which to make the products she exported, Israel had to *create* opportunities for employment. This process was exactly the reverse of what happened in the United States in the nineteenth and twentieth centuries, when immigrants streamed to America to fill waiting jobs. In Israel the emphasis was on Jewish immigration for its own sake.

111

The purpose of Israel's establishment was to reconstitute the Jewish homeland and rebuild the Jewish people.

Jobs and opportunities had to be created to make immigration to Israel possible. Jobs and industries were created with an eye on immigration rather than on profitability or efficiency. The determination was made early in the state's existence that it was demeaning, demoralizing, and generally undesirable to have large numbers of immigrants sitting idle in immigration camps, especially when security demanded quick settlement of the sparsely populated parts of the country. Immigrants were sent to new towns—"development towns"—where factories were built and jobs were created for them. The government provided large subsidies to companies to get them started in order to produce work. A coffee plant intended to package coffee for export marketed its product abroad for one cent less than the cost of the raw materials that went into it—not to mention the cost of labor, transportation, and overhead. Yet the company showed a "profit"—for a time— because the enormous subsidies paid to it by the government made it profitable to sell finished coffee for a price that was, in effect, less than what the company paid for the beans.

Jobs created at public expense are not necessarily worthless. There is a certain value to having people work, if for no other reason than to preserve their own self-esteem, no small consideration in a country trying to revive a dormant people. Beyond that motive, though, is the value that some make-work can fulfill. Public-works projects, for example, often provide sorely needed improvements. The vast network of flood-control projects and public building financed by the federal government in the United States during the Depression of the 1930s is an example of "make-work" that benefited the public despite the criticism of the projects at the time. Similarly, in Israel jobs created for new immigrants for the sake of providing employment were the target of derision from other Israelis.

"Basically," an Israeli said, "these jobs were given to new immigrants, for example, planting new trees on the mountains. Everyone just laughed. You know, they said, 'These people are just scratching the land.' But if you move around Jerusalem now, you see forests. They didn't drop from the sky. Suddenly you find out that these jobs, which were really hated then, which were created for the sake of creating jobs, suddenly are fruitful, really something for the benefit of the whole country."

In the more than thirty years since the state was established, Israel's economic situation has changed dramatically. Israel has a number of substantial industries whose growth is hampered by a shortage of labor. The Israeli government continues to be the major employer, with hundreds of thousands of employees. This high percentage of the labor force in government jobs deprives Israeli industry of the workers required to expand exports and earn badly needed foreign exchange.

The Israeli government's policy in creating work had another effect. It also created an expectation that the state would provide work, would take the initiative in providing for the general welfare. Israel, one high official said, "is a typical case of a state that tried to provide from womb to tomb. We've raised a generation that no longer knows of the old frugal ways. We have two sayings that sum up the whole problem—'Lo ichpat li,' and 'Magia li,' 'It doesn't matter to me' and 'I've got it coming.' Israel doesn't have the incentive of the United States because jobs are more secure here than they are there and we don't have the compulsion to make people work the way they do in a totalitarian country."

The basic problem of the Israeli economy is finding ways to produce more and to increase efficiency. Anything that reduces the amount of time that workers are actually at their jobs reduces Israel's labor productivity. Israel's basic security situation is one major cause of diminished labor productivity. Another is unauthorized strikes.

The cost of security for Israel is enormous. As a percentage of the government's budget from 1970 to 1980, defense spending fluctuated between 29 and 49 percent, and averaged about 36 percent. From 1970 to 1980 Israel spent roughly one quarter of its gross national product on defense—five times the comparable figure for the United States. The cost of security goes beyond what the government pays for weapons, construction, and salaries of the men and women who serve in Israeli armed forces. To understand the real cost of security for Israel other expenses have to be considered—the necessity of building a wall or fence around every school in the country; the stationing of civilian guards at every school entrance during hours when children are present, as well as at movies, concerts, department stores, supermarkets, government offices, and other public gathering places; and the requirement that all eligible men between the ages of twenty-one and fifty-five who are not serving their obligatory three-years military service must spend thirty to sixty days annually in the military reserves.

The costs of reserve duty are both direct—salaries paid to reservists, housing, and food—and indirect. It may be that the indirect costs are even more substantial than the direct ones since requiring productive men, who are the bulk of the labor force, to serve between one twelfth and one sixth of the year in the military deprives Israel of enormous productive capacity. The cost can be estimated by the calculation that although the nominal Israeli work week is 48 hours, Israeli workers actually work only an average of 35.8 hours a week (compared to 44 in England, 43.5 in Spain, 44.7 in Switzerland, 41.2 in France, 35.7 in Sweden, and 35.6 in the United States). A principal reason for the discrepancy between the number of nominal hours worked and actual average is the amount of time Israeli men have to spend in the army reserves every year.

The statistics fail, however, to describe the added costs of dislocations and inconveniences that result from having such a large reserve requirement. At one factory I visited, all of the engineers from the engineering department had been called into the army at the same time, leaving the section empty. The factory manager was expecting a visit of some officials from Pirelli, the Italian tire firm, as well as some Dutch industrialists. The visitors represented a potentially important source of business for the factory and the manager needed the engineers present to meet them, but, he said, there was nothing he could do. "I don't know how to get them released from the army even for one day," he said. "It's a big problem for us." In general, he calculated, he had ten percent more workers than he actually needed working at his factory, just so that he could keep the plant operating while employees were in the reserves.

At another factory three of the five crane operators had been called into the army at the same time. The factory manager had hired two temporary crane operators as replacements, but he had to pay three times the normal wages for them and, he said, they were "much less" efficient than the men whom they were replacing. This manager estimated that he lost eight percent of his factory's productivity—calculated in time—because of employees fulfilling their reserve obligations. If he calculated the costs in lost profits, he said, it would be much higher.

Since this particular manager was a reserve officer in the tank corps, a decorated officer at that, his open questioning of the wisdom of the army's reserve politics took on extra weight. Why, he wondered out loud, couldn't the army hire people to serve as guards, since that was the duty performed by many reservists? "They don't save anything by doing this," he asserted. The answer seems to be a matter more of social policy than economics. Not requiring all able-bodied men to serve at least some time, and roughly equal time at that, would be socially disruptive and divisive.

For entirely different reasons strikes are also a substantial cause of diminished productivity in Israel. Though perhaps not a way of life in Israel, strikes are certainly a well-entrenched local custom. In 1978 more than one million workdays—equivalent to the annual work of more than thirty-seven hundred workers—were lost because of strikes. This figure amounts to roughly double the average for workdays lost because of strikes in the United States on an adjusted basis.

During the fall of 1979 a strike and subsequent lockout closed Israel's largest bank—Bank Leumi—which handles the personal accounts of about fifty percent of all Israelis. Doctors refused to treat patients, restaurants turned away patrons, gas stations refused to sell gasoline—all because the potential patients or customers lacked cash and wanted to pay instead with checks drawn on their Bank Leumi accounts.

During my first year in Israel I kept a list of strikes. A partial accounting (the list in its entirety is too long to present here) includes strikes by: elementary and high school teachers, university professors, court clerks, bus drivers, gas company deliverymen (cooking gas must be delivered since underground pipes do not exist), produce suppliers, egg farmers, physicians, bakers, state prosecutors (who submitted their resignations en masse but later recanted), the Red Magen David (the Israeli Red Cross, which traditionally serves as the emergency night-treatment center for subscribers to Israel's largest medical plan), Tel Aviv's garbage collectors (who struck several times), and Israel's airport employees (Israel was closed to the world for twenty-four hours). In addition, Israel's *judges* threatened to strike.

Although many of these strikes were approved according to regulations adopted by the Histadrut, most strikes in Israel are not authorized in advance by the central union body.

With seventy-five percent of the country's work force enrolled in the Histadrut's membership, the central union should be a powerful organization with firm control over the work force. The reality is not so simple. In the first place, it is possible to belong to the Histadrut and still work in an office or factory that has not been organized by the union, or in a work place where a majority of the workers are not Histadrut members. Membership in the Histadrut is independent of employment in a union shop, and many members of the Histadrut join it only to be eligible for its medical care plan.

Over the years there has been a separation between the Histadrut's top leadership and the rank and file. The central leadership of the union has always been closely identified—some would say synonymous—with the leadership of Israel's principal labor political party, Mapai, and with its successor, the Labor Alignment. The Mapai leadership, which was also the Histadrut leadership, used the Histadrut as an instrument of national policy —directing development into areas where it was needed, placing

factories where employment opportunities were lacking, and restricting wages when the country's economy demanded it. As a
result, a gap opened between the rank and file, which had one set
of interests, and the union leadership, which had a somewhat different set of priorities.

The nature of the work force changed as well. In the years
before the state the work force was strongly imbued with socialism
and a commitment to Zionism. Members of the work force came to
Israel for religious reasons or because they could no longer live in
the Arab countries where they had abided. Israel was their only
alternative.

The top leadership of the Histadrut is chosen in an indirect
process somewhat similar to the national elections for the Knesset.
All Histadrut members vote for delegates to the Histadrut convention. Convention delegates run on party lists, and each party is
entitled to a number of convention seats proportionate to the
number of votes cast for its list. The convention appoints the members of the union's executive council, which appoints the members
of the executive committee, which in turn appoints the forty-
three members of the trade union department. The function
of the trade union department of the Histadrut is to negotiate
national and industry-wide collective agreements according to the
wage policies of the Histadrut, to approve strikes and settle disputes through mediation and arbitration, and to formulate policy
concerning specific and general problems.

The trade union department, however, operates at a level far
above the individual Israeli worker. Of much more importance to
the individual worker is the leadership of the workers' committee in his or her own plant or office. Unlike the leadership of
the central union, the workers' committee chairman and members
are selected by the workers directly. A factory may have more than
one workers' committee—one or more for blue-collar employees
and another for white-collar employees.

The workers' committee has the right and power to negotiate
wages and working conditions that go beyond the minimums negotiated on an industry-wide basis by the trade union department.

The power of the workers' committee varies from one work place to another, depending upon the quality of leadership and the pattern of concessions that the local management has made over the years.

Because the leadership of the workers' committee has real power and because it is elected directly by the workers in the plant or office where it operates, the employees take a more active interest in who their leaders are. And the leaders, directly responsible to the members, tend to be more responsive to the rank and file at the work site and less responsive to the central union leadership. Since, in most instances, workers are compensated for work time lost during an unauthorized strike, the pressure to call a strike to protest a particular grievance can be strong—regardless of what the central union leadership may want.

Israeli economist Friedman, who has studied unauthorized strikes in Israel, attributes their frequency to the Histadrut's "structural dualism," that is, to the incompatible interests of the central leadership—which has long term goals in mind—and leaders of local workers' committees—who are interested in the short-run economic well-being of members at the shop level. "This discrepancy between the goals of the two organizations results in a large number of unauthorized strikes, most of which are conducted by workers' committees," according to Friedman.

The "discrepancy" Friedman describes reflects the weakening of ideology among rank-and-file union members, a process that has been going on since the state was established and mass immigration began. With the anti-Histadrut Likud coalition controlling the government, the conflict between Histadrut rank-and-file membership and the top leadership was muted—even though the number of strike days more than doubled. But there is every reason to expect that the return of the Labor Alignment to power would not reverse this separation, unless the top leadership opts for paying more attention to the demands of its membership and less to the longer-term outlook of the government.

With one brief exception in the mid-1960s, the official policy of the Israeli government has insured that virtually everyone seeking a job has had work. From 1967 until late in 1979 the Israeli economy was basically running at a level of full employment. Israel has been able, since the state was established, to maintain a well-trained and reasonably well-equipped army, to provide better than adequate medical care for its population, to improve the amount and quality of food and ensure that everyone has enough to eat, to provide decent housing for most of the population (though overcrowding and substandard housing are still a major problem), and to increase production and consumption of consumer items—all simultaneously. How was all of this possible?

Unlike other Middle Eastern countries and other developing nations, what has been done in Israel has been done largely by Israelis. The technological expertise to do much of what has been done either already existed in the country or it was learned and then applied. Israel's principal institutions of higher learning—the Hebrew University in Jerusalem, the Weizmann Institute of Science, and Technion (Israel Institute of Technology)—all preceded the establishment of Israel by many years, laying the intellectual, scientific, and technical foundation for the future. Additionally, Israel was given immeasurable assistance by the immigration of highly skilled professionals both before and after the state's establishment. Literacy was not a serious problem in the prestate era, when the Histadrut as well as religious and political groups all operated schools.

The Israeli economy today produces sophisticated electronic equipment, precision medical devices, tools for heavy industry, jet aircraft, tanks, and a whole range of other products that must meet exacting standards. Israel's military industry developed as a response to necessity. After the Six Day War in 1967 France—which had been a principal supplier of weapons to Israel—refused to continue supplying either new weapons or spare parts. As a result, Israel decided to make her own weapons, to the extent that she could, because of the uncertainty of finding another supplier. This effort, however, is a tremendous strain for Israel, even if some of what is produced eventually can be exported.

"One of the things I argue is that we have a huge shortage in technicians and skilled employees," an Israeli economist said.

"The basic problem is that it's a built-in deficiency, a built-in shortage. Think about a country with a million and a quarter wage earners that can produce its own tanks, planes, and missiles, as well as boats. We demand more from ourselves, more than a country like this can give. It gives a lot to the Jew who comes to Israel and says: 'Wow! Israelis are really building planes.' But most of this economic activity puts a burden on the labor market, because you can't take an unskilled employee and make him a skilled employee in two weeks.

"The point is that we demand from ourselves more than in a very logical analysis we could have demanded if we take the example of other countries. But if you would argue about this with any of our politicians, they would say: 'You know this was said about Israel from the time the first Jewish settlements were established in Palestine. And we survived. That's the only way in which we expand.' "

There's much to be said for this point of view. Without a doubt, great challenges produce greater effort. Israel, however, did not pull itself up entirely by its own bootstraps. Israel has been the recipient of an extraordinary amount of foreign aid—in the form of loans, outright grants, subsidies in the purchase of equipment, and military assistance. Even before the establishment of the state, Israel was able to call on the resources of world Jewry. From 1950 through 1975 Jews all over the world gave or loaned Israel $9.5 billion. Since the loans were generally made through the purchase of Israel bonds, which carried a relatively low interest, the loans were extended at favorable rates to Israel. Additionally, Israel and Israelis received about $3.9 billion in reparations and restitution from Germany to settle claims growing out of the Holocaust. The United States gave or loaned Israel more than $14 billion in the period from 1949 through 1979. Israel received roughly $3.2 billion in aid from other sources. The total aid Israel has received in the form of outright gifts or loans since 1949 is in excess of $30 billion. This aid has been extended to a country with a population that has never exceeded four million persons.

A closer examination of the aid pattern shows that assistance from the United States, the largest single source of aid for Israel, has increased enormously in the last ten years. From 1949 through 1970 the United States extended about $1.2 billion in aid to Israel. Between 1970 and 1980 Israel received $12.8 billion in aid from the United States, and $5.4 billion of that aid was extended between 1977 and 1980. In 1981, Israel received $785 million in economic aid as an outright grant and $1.4 billion in military aid—$900 million in loans and a grant of $500 million.

Israel's foreign debt—the money Israel owes to other countries and to persons living outside of Israel—has steadily grown since 1948. Since Israel has never had a year in which its exports totaled more than its imports, it has relied on grants and loans to make up the difference. Israel's foreign debt was $2 billion in 1969, $12 billion in 1978, and will be approaching $30 billion sometime in the mid-1980s or sooner.

Israel's debt can be seen in two different ways. On the one hand, debt is a sign that a person, a company, or a country has trouble living within its means. Or, an Israeli economist suggested, "you could say that the money was available and so we decided to seize the opportunity and use it for development." Businesses borrow money all the time to expand their production capability. Countries do the same thing. Israel has used gifts and loans to increase her capacity to grow food, to produce industrial goods, and to support her security forces. All of those accomplishments are attributable, in part, to the availability of foreign capital, which gave Israel the ability first to survive and later to expand. The problem for Israel, however, is that the economic aid it now receives is being used not for economic growth but instead for the purchase and consumption of consumer goods, which add little or nothing to Israel's productive capacity and her ability to be self-sufficient and economically independent. This outside assistance also has caused the Israeli economy to develop in ways that may not be in the long-term interests of Israel.

Before the founding of the state, in the period of the British Mandate, Jews in Palestine received substantial help from the international Jewish community. Land purchases, redevelopment projects, and other services were made possible by the contributions of world Jewry. After 1948 that aid increased substantially as the new state struggled to survive and to cope with a rapidly increasing population. From the northernmost point of Israel in Metulla to the southern tip of the country in Eilat, the country is filled with schools, community centers, hospitals, parks, playgrounds, swimming pools, museums, and a variety of other public buildings that are a monument to the generosity of Jews living in the Diaspora. Besides these tangible examples a wealth of social, scientific, educational, and cultural programs are funded with money from Diaspora Jews.

Israel's financial problems in the early years were also eased considerably by an agreement reached with West Germany in 1953 that provided for the payment of hundreds of millions of dollars in aid to Israel. This aid was enormously important in developing Israeli industry as well as in providing the army with badly needed equipment. Besides the aid to the State of Israel, Germany agreed to pay reparations to Israelis who had suffered at the hands of the Nazis.

An immediate effect of the reparations payments to individuals was the creation, virtually overnight, of a relatively prosperous class of Israelis—Israelis of European origin—who were able to move from crowded living quarters into more comfortable surroundings, to buy automobiles, to take expensive trips outside of the country, and to buy other comforts that poorer Israelis could not afford.

This veritable flood of foreign money that poured in was viewed with alarm by some Israelis, who saw it as a corrupting influence— "easy money" they called it, or "free money"—"money that nobody made."

"If people can earn money in this country without doing a day's job because people outside Israel want to be helpful, and someone can live at a certain level without working, then it's difficult to change people's habits," one Israeli businessman said. "If the United States sent us an additional two billion dollars in foreign aid every year, then my plant wouldn't work anymore because my employees would get some kind of make-work, government job."

Zionism in Palestine was a reaction, among other things, to the practice of *chaluka,* the distribution of money from Jews living abroad to poor Jews in the Holy Land who would not or could not work. For early Zionists this tradition was a shame and a disgrace, a sign of the abnormality of Jewish existence. Israel shows signs on a national scale of becoming similarly dependent on foreign aid and money from abroad. "It wouldn't be unreasonable to argue as a proposition that we would have been better off if foreign aid had stopped twenty years ago," one prominent Israeli economist said.

Breaking down the income and expenditures of Israel on a national scale is a complicated affair since a considerable portion of what Israel spends comes from outside the country and is not spent in Israel at all. American military aid, for example, is spent almost entirely in the United States, although Israel appears to have been successful in convincing the United States to allow Israel to use American military aid to purchase equipment from itself.

When trading internationally over the past decade, Israel's deficit has ranged each year between a low of about $1 billion and a high of $4 billion, with the amount usually in the vicinity of $2.5 billion. The bulk of this annual deficit has been made up with American foreign aid, although world Jewry contributes about $500 million to Israel and restitutions from the German government to individual Israelis bring in another $250–$300 million. Israel continues to be able to borrow at reasonable rates from commercial banking institutions.

By 1979, Israel's gross national product was between $17 billion and $18 billion. Government expenditures were roughly one-third of the GNP. Over the ten-year period from 1970 through 1979, Israel consumed considerably more than it produced.

Domestically, the Israeli government has resorted to the simple expedient of printing money to make up the difference between its income from taxes and its expenditures. Internationally, where Israel also habitually spends more than it earns, it has become increasingly reliant, as we have seen, on American foreign aid to bridge the gap.

Much of the foreign assistance Israel has received was used to great advantage. Israel has four major universities—Tel Aviv, Ben-Gurion, Haifa, and Hebrew universities—as well as the Israel Institute of Technology (Technion), and the Weizmann Institute of Science. Israel has a greater number of professors per capita than any other country in the world (excluding the Vatican). Israel's ability to conduct high-quality scientific research and to train first-rate engineers has been of incalculable help to the country's rapid growth. Israel also has been able to maintain a cultural base far greater than it could have afforded on its own. Foreign donations substantially paid for the construction of the Israel Museum in Jerusalem and Tel Aviv Museum. Israel has five orchestras, including one—the Israel Philharmonic—of world-class quality. A country of Israel's size with no financial resources beyond her own could not afford to support, much less to have developed, institutions such as these.

Some Israelis—a minority to be sure, but an influential minority —argue that aid from Jews of the Diaspora and from other countries is positively harmful to Israel, that it merely prolongs the day when Israel can stand on its own. "What we don't need," one Israeli said, "is money to build another institution that will drain our work force even more. We simply don't have the people to man these places." Just as serious as the drain on the work force, from this viewpoint, is the psychology of *schnorring* ("begging") that foreign contributions create, a throwback to the old days when religious Jewish men spent their time in yeshivas studying, sending fund raisers to beg money from Jews who did work to support these penurious students. Israel has an elaborate apparatus geared to the needs and desires of visiting Jewish contributors—especially from the United States—to see to it that groups of visitors are "shown" the country and impressed with Israel's financial need.

Large Israeli institutions, like the Hebrew University, Tel Aviv University, and the Technion, have boards of directors with at least fifty percent American membership in order to comply with American law, enabling contributions to the institutions—via an intermediary organization—to be tax-deductible in the United States.

One example of the dislocating effect of foreign money in the Israeli economy is the existence of no less than four medical schools, and pressure from religious Jews both within Israel and abroad is being exerted for a fifth. These schools are substantially funded by foreign contributions to their parent universities. Israel, however, already has a *surplus* of physicians. Israel has a higher number of physicians per capita than any other country in the world with the unlikely exception of Albania. Israel cannot employ more than a fraction of its medical school graduates. The rest must look outside the country for work. The combination of weak health-planning controls and the relatively easy availability of funds supporting the medical schools adds up to a significant waste of human resources for Israel, which pays the price, not in money spent for educating the medical graduates—that comes from abroad—but in the loss of their labor.

One of the most serious negative consequences of this enormous foreign aid is that Israel has a severe problem in getting Israelis to work in factories. The dependence on foreign aid, according to Israeli economist Nadav Halevi, "has been a major reason for the peculiar distribution of the labor force: fully one-half of Israel's employed are in public and private services, finance and trade. Clearly, this distribution is not consistent with future requirements."

Israel suffers from a severe labor shortage in industry, where workers are needed to manufacture the goods needed to increase exports in order to reduce the country's foreign debt and break its dependence on foreign aid. The Bank of Israel's 1978 report, analyzing problems facing Israel, complained that

[in] recent years there has been a marked structural change in employment, with the public services sector absorbing most of the additional manpower. Since the government's ability to siphon off more money through taxes is limited . . .

and since a diminished dependence on external sources of finance [foreign aid] has become a prime national target, there is no escaping the need to reduce the share of public services in total resource use. In other words, the freezing, and perhaps even absolute decrease, of public sector employment is necessary for relieving pressure in the labor market and making more resources available to the business sector.

The largest single employer in Israel is government, which has increased its employment proportionately in the ten years from 1970 to 1980. In other words, not only are more Israelis working for governmental bodies than ever before, but a greater share of the work force—roughly three out of every ten workers—is employed by government. The percentage of workers in industry— actually making products for export—has grown numerically in the same period, but has *declined* proportionally.

Compared with seven leading industrial countries (the United States, Germany, Japan, Canada, the United Kingdom, Italy, and Sweden), Israel has the lowest percentage of workers employed in industrial jobs except Canada. Only Canada and the United States have a higher percentage of workers employed in service jobs than Israel. In the absence of the enormous foreign aid of all types that Israel has received, it would not have been possible for it to support such a high proportion of its work force in government and service, rather than industrial jobs.

Low unemployment—or overemployment as some Israeli economists and businessmen characterize the situation—has a direct effect on the attitude of the work force. Between 1967 and 1979 more job openings existed than workers available to fill them. Workers could be reasonably sure under those circumstances that they could leave one job and always find another. "This creates one hell of a problem in terms of productivity and efficiency, in work ethic and in discipline since an employee can say, 'Fire me and give me my severance pay,' knowing full well that he can go get a job elsewhere," an Israeli business expert told me.

The combined elements of powerful unions protecting the

worker and a labor shortage yielded low standards of productivity. A certain factory in Israel manufactured equipment requiring the drilling of very small holes. Workers who were just learning the job could turn out sixteen pieces an hour. After two months' time, having learned the job, the workers turned out six pieces an hour. When someone familiar with the factory was asked why productivity went down instead of up after the workers had learned the job, the answer was straightforward: "Six an hour is the going rate."

In an industrial setting the combination of strong unions combined with a work force emerging from nonindustrial cultures results in workers with minimal interest in actually working. "You have to consider," an Israeli industrial expert explained, "that many of these people are coming out of countries where the attitude toward work was entirely different. In some Islamic countries the worker would work until he had made enough that day to support his family for the next twenty-four hours. He didn't see any reason to work more than that. So imposing industrial discipline on someone like that isn't easy. If you compare us with the United States, which has a head start of a hundred and seventy years, we're bound to come off second best."

It would be easier to make allowances for Israel's status as a still-developing country were it not for the impressive accomplishments of which Israelis are justly proud. These accomplishments make it more difficult to accept Israeli protestations that the country is still underdeveloped—not just physically but temperamentally. An American psychologist who has been living in Israel for more than fifteen years said that he continually finds Israelis in his profession doing substandard work. "When I criticize the situation, they tell me, 'You can't possibly apply American standards to the way we do things here. We're still an underdeveloped country.' But I don't accept that. I think it's just a crutch they use to excuse themselves for not doing better."

Israelis who chafe under what is commonly described as the "declining work ethic" often complain about the "Levantinization" of Israel. Workers in service industries frequently give the impression that they are doing the customer a favor by taking care of him rather than conducting business. One woman recalled how she tried to order cooking gas by telephone (a standard procedure) without receiving any answer. She concluded that the phone was not working. The following day, her husband stopped in to place the order in person. Three women were sitting next to each other behind a counter. The middle woman was on the phone, taking orders for gas.

"My wife called all day yesterday," the man told one of the other women behind the counter. "There was no answer. Apparently the phone wasn't working."

"It was working," the woman said. She gestured to the woman on the phone, taking orders. "She wasn't here yesterday. She was sick."

An American approached an official of the Histadrut with a proposal to help the Histadrut's medical plan obtain surplus U.S. government equipment at a substantial savings—a fraction of the cost—under a provision of American law making such equipment available to certain institutions. The Histadrut clearly qualified. The American, who spoke Hebrew fluently but preferred conducting business in English, explained the procedures to the Israeli Histadrut official during a meeting attended by another American and an Israeli. As the American explained the procedures that would have to be followed, the Histadrut official remarked to his colleague—in Hebrew, not knowing the American understood—"This will be a lot of work. I'd have to do all this! I don't want to do all this work. It's too much."

The opportunity was not pursued.

A small number of Vietnamese refugees who found sanctuary in Israel in the late 1970s quickly established a reputation for being hard workers, a quality that one would normally think would make them a welcome addition to a country. *Ma'ariv*, Israel's afternoon newspaper, reported that a group of Vietnamese refugees working in the central part of the country had been warned by Israeli workers "not to make too much of an effort" and that, in one plant, "there was great tension around the Vietnamese workers' productivity." The situation was finally eased, according to the report, after some Vietnamese workers left the plant and those that remained "slowed down their pace and have grown accustomed to Israeli norms."

Another result of overemployment is that people who are underqualified will be used for jobs where qualified people cannot be found. "It's hard enough to find a secretary who knows Hebrew well enough to do the job, much less English," an Israeli said. "The government is constantly lowering its standards in order to fill jobs. And there's no incentive to perform well since promotions are independent of performance."

A university professor described an encounter with the bureaucracy of his school. He was called by an administrator asking him to complete some forms required so that merit wage increases could be paid to his staff.

What, the professor asked, if his staff didn't deserve merit increases? "I was told," he recalled, "that the increases were a matter of common practice, but that they couldn't be paid until I submitted the forms. But, in fact, it wasn't up to me at all, even though these people worked for me. The supposed merit increases were regarded by everyone as something they had coming—regardless of merit."

An Israeli who was putting together a business venture using American and Israeli money said that during a meeting with the Israeli participants, one of the Israelis suggested that the Americans should pick up certain expenses that were actually the financial responsibility of the Israelis.

"I asked them why the Americans should pay," the Israeli wondered, "and they said, 'Well, they're Americans, aren't they? They have lots of money.' "

At a later point in the meeting, this same Israeli said, the Israelis threatened to pull out altogether if the Americans insisted on receiving what would normally be considered a fair rate of return on their money. The Israeli participants said that they would simply close the Americans out and turn to the Israeli government for the capital needed to finance the project. "The Israeli government is dying to attract private capital into Israel and here is a perfect example of how government investment money—which is really money given by Jews abroad—is discouraging private investment," the Israeli said. "And it doesn't even stop there because these American businessmen I was dealing with are also big contributors to Israel. So, in effect, they're competing with themselves. Their charitable contributions are loaned out by the government on such attractive terms that Israeli businessmen aren't interested in doing business on a normal basis."

"The problem of fifty percent of Israeli industry," another Israeli businessman added, "is that it thinks it can *survive* by making products for the local market, and it doesn't have enough initiative to go out and see what's going on and develop new products."

Until the mid-1970s Israeli businesses operated behind protective trade barriers that made it profitable for them to manufacture products for the home market rather than for export. As part of the reciprocal trade agreement with Europe's Common Market countries, Israel is gradually lowering its import taxes on Common Market goods. What this change means in practice is that European goods that were artificially priced out of the range of Israeli consumers by Israeli import taxes are now becoming relatively cheaper. And Israeli businesses that enjoyed the protection of trade barriers and subsidies are finding themselves in competition with European businesses. Theoretically, the agreement with the Common Market offers a tremendous opportunity for Israel to expand production, increase exports, and become more self-sufficient, but only if it can come to terms with deeply ingrained habits and work practices that put it at a disadvantage.

The manager of a dental products factory, who has succeeded in transforming a near-bankrupt company into a profitable venture, told how he had to begin by reshaping the attitudes of his employees. "It's difficult to get someone to come in here and work at a very precise Swiss standard when the moment he leaves the factory, everything changes. The way people drive, the way they throw their cigarettes anywhere, the whole general carelessness of

Israelis—just getting people to talk in a low voice—everything is a problem."

Only about half of the employees who apply for work in the factory, which makes precision dental and medical equipment, are able to meet the manager's exacting standards. When he took over the existing factory, with its employees, one of the manager's first moves was to fire the head of the workers' committee. The move precipitated an immediate crisis with the Histadrut. "I told them that I would close the company rather than give in," the manager said. "I made the issue the continuation of jobs for thirty employees. And finally, the chairman of the workers' committee resigned, collected his benefits, and left." Other employees also left over time as they found the new regime too demanding. But the factory prospered as the manager, and the engineers in the factory, found ways to improve products made elsewhere and to market those products abroad.

"I believe that the real meaning of leadership is that an employee believes that if he follows my order, he will have something from it," this manager said. "Basically, the people here believe that if they follow me, their conditions will be better. I consult the workers, but *I* am the manager of the company. If somebody wants to manage behind me or above me, that is the end of the story."

The difference in whether an Israeli business—like any business anywhere—is profitable or not appears to be the quality and skill of the people directing the company and the spirit that they are able to inspire among the work force.

One of Israel's largest—and most successful—businesses is the government-owned Israel Aircraft Industry, which has grown from an aircraft maintenance company with one hangar and a few hundred employees in 1953 to a conglomerate making or offering more than four hundred products or services with twenty-two thousand employees.

In contrast to the eighteen unions at El Al, the Israel Aircraft Industry has only one union to which most employees (including the company's president) belong. The Israel Aircraft Industry was established initially to service Israeli military aircraft, but it has expanded its operation into the manufacture of jet fighters, executive jets, and a lightweight cargo-and-passenger propeller aircraft, as well as missiles, radar, boats, and a variety of electronic equipment. More than half of the company's revenues—in excess of six hundred million dollars by 1980—come from exports.

From the time IAI was established the company's management refused to allow the workers to have a formal role in choosing managers and discussing promotion of workers, although the workers are "consulted" through the shop steward. The final decision remains firmly in the hands of management. Workers are arranged into production teams, which are paid bonuses according to whether they meet or exceed schedules set for them by management. "If Joe doesn't perform" a company official explained, "Moe will come along and tell him, 'Come on. Let's go.' When one person slacks off, it costs the others money." The company also has an extensive program of cash bonuses and other rewards to encourage employees to make suggestions to improve the product or increase efficiency. "The essential point here is that we're a team. We're in this together. Everyone who works here is a partner in this venture. That's what we're trying to get across to our employees." Signs hung all over the factory encourage the workers to make suggestions, admonish them to exercise care (Are You Ready to Fly on the Part You Are Making?) and to take pride in their work.

The approach apparently works. The Israel Aircraft Industry has never had a strike. It appears to be profitable, and it receives no government subsidies. (Questions of subsidies and profits are extremely complicated since long-term investments and pricing policies have to be taken into account. Israel's aircraft industry was not started to make money so much as to ensure adequate maintenance of Israel's aircraft and later an adequate supply of the aircraft themselves. As a result, the success of Israel's aircraft industry has to be measured by more than the financial balance sheet. Even if the aircraft industry were not profitable, Israel's security considerations provide a strong incentive for maintaining it.)

The Israel Aircraft Industry represents a concerted effort to free Israel—as much as possible—from dependence on foreign suppliers for weaponry. But the company has spawned a number of subsidiary, privately owned high-technology companies that are looking for foreign as well as domestic markets.

It is a paradox that Israel is attempting to become more self-sufficient militarily at the same time that it is becoming more dependent economically on foreign assistance. Despite the example of the Israel Aircraft Industry and other relatively efficient Israeli companies, Israel's economy appears to have become addicted to foreign aid. Although not in danger of imminent collapse, despite rampant inflation, a number of signs indicate that foreign aid has become a necessary factor for Israel—not to increase its ability to produce more, but simply to subsidize its standard of living.

The transformation of Israeli society has not gone unnoticed or unremarked in Israel itself. Amnon Rubenstein, a Knesset member and former dean of Tel Aviv University's law school points out that a survey of Jewish Palestine in 1945 found that only 24 percent of the population had been involved in productive professions (industry, agriculture, construction, transportation) before coming to Palestine, but that after coming 69 percent were engaged in such enterprises. By 1975, Rubenstein writes in his book *To Be a Free People,* the number of workers involved in such productive labor had dropped 23 percent, a change Rubenstein describes as movement "from a productive society to a dependent one."

Rubenstein cites the change in economic role as an example of a curious passivity that has overcome Israelis, in place of the "self-confidence and belief in their cause" that gave them the ability "to do the impossible." Where they once asked themselves individually what they could do for the common purpose, Rubenstein argues, today the buck is passed to an anonymous, detached "them."

Rubenstein is not alone in seeing a psychology of dependence

133

growing. The entire economic aid package of roughly $700 million in 1980 from the United States did no more than to pay back the United States the principal and interest due on American loans to Israel. In the absence of domestic energy supplies, Israel has had to buy oil on the more expensive spot-market because of difficulties in finding foreign suppliers willing to make long-term contracts with Israel. Without increasing energy consumption appreciably, Israel's energy bill went from about $775 million in 1978 to more than $2.1 billion in 1980 and will increase more as the decade proceeds. Although exports increased, the amount was not sufficient to make up this deficit. In the absence of greatly increased foreign aid—which seems unlikely—Israel will have to expand her exports, which suggests that her labor force has to produce more, which probably means that more people will have to go work in factories and those already working in them will have to work more efficiently.

At the same time, though, Israel may have to accept a lowered standard of living. Israel managed to increase its production considerably during the 1970s, but at the same time—for a variety of reasons—it consumed more of what it produced. In 1972 Israel consumed 83 percent of what it produced. By 1978 the figure had grown to 93 percent, which means that in the intervening six years what Israel had left to sell to the rest of the world *declined* as a proportion of what it made and consumed itself.

The fact is, as any visitor discovers rather quickly, that compared to neighboring countries and those in Eastern Europe, Israel is awash in affluence. Store windows and private homes are full of expensive consumer items—small and large appliances, Japanese watches, color televisions, and other symbols of the good life. More than a quarter of all Israeli households have a private automobile (compared to 4 percent in 1962); 90 percent own televisions (compared to 50 percent in 1970); 70 percent of the households have washing machines (compared to 16 percent in 1960); 97 percent had refrigerators (compared to 47 percent in 1960). One out of seven Israelis has been able to vacation abroad in recent years.

Considering staggering taxes, inflation, and relatively low salaries (by American and European standards), how Israelis manage to live as well as they do is a puzzle to outsiders—as well as to Israelis themselves.

A good Israeli salary—not necessarily the top salary—but an amount that an Israeli in a management position might aspire to is about $1,000 a month. Only twenty thousand Israelis reported incomes of more than $10,000 in 1979 (although, as we shall see, Israeli tax reporting is something less than a clear indicator of what people actually earn).

Like the United States, Israel has a system of graduated income tax, so that the percentage of tax one pays increases as income increases. Israelis who earn $5,600 per annum or less before taxes must pay 25 percent of their income to the government. In other words, a wage earner making $5,000 a year has to pay $1,250 in taxes, leaving $3,750 in money to spend. From that point the taxes increase sharply, so that someone making little more than $12,000 a year has to pay half of everything over that amount in taxes and those earning more than $16,000 a year pay taxes of 60 percent on everything they make over that amount.

In addition to the income taxes, Israel has a value-added tax (or VAT, which is equivalent to a sales tax) of 12 percent on most purchases and services other than food items. On top of these taxes, Israelis (including apartment dwellers), pay a property tax, license fees for their cars, import taxes of one hundred percent or more on import items, a fuel tax, and a monthly payment to the National Insurance Institute for unemployment, disability, and retirement compensation. From time to time the government has also required Israeli wage earners to buy defense bonds. As a result of these and still other taxes, no one in Israel talks about gross salaries because the figure is meaningless. What counts, as wage earners all over the world know, is what they have left to spend after the government gets through taking its share of a worker's earnings.

A skilled worker in a typical factory, with three children, earning top wages, makes about $7,400 per annum before taxes. With deductions for taxes, health insurance, and other required payments, the worker has about $4,750 a year left—about $400 a month. Top pay in the same factory, which happened to be for the chief engineer and not the plant manager, is about $17,460 before taxes and other deductions. The chief engineer's net annual salary, after taxes, is $7,560—$630 a month.

Executives also get fringe benefits, not the least of which is a company-owned car to use for business (and often for pleasure), with the business paying for the gasoline. Many businesses also pay the cost of an employee's home telephone. Army officers and police officials with access to cars customarily use them for personal business or pleasure during off hours.

In addition to the relatively low net wages Israelis earn is the high cost of basic commodities—food, clothing, and shelter. A family of four with two small children, eating meat or chicken only two or three times a week, will pay $250 to $300 a month for groceries. Beef and chicken are more expensive in Israel than in the United States. Milk, eggs, cheese, and butter cost roughly what one would pay for them in the United States, meaning that Israelis—who earn less—pay proportionately more. Only bread, one of the few remaining items to receive a government subsidy, remains relatively inexpensive, and it is a staple of the Israeli diet.

Comparatively few Israelis rent housing. About seventy percent own their dwellings and an additional seven percent live in houses or apartments under a quasi-purchase agreement called key money, which requires them to purchase the right to live in the apartment from the previous tenant at a mutually agreed-upon price and then to pay a monthly amount for rent. The remaining families rent their apartments from private landlords or from the government. The cost of purchasing a new apartment—houses are usually for only the relatively wealthy—begins at around $10,000. That figure is misleading since it applies to only a relatively few apartments available in development areas where the government offers subsidies, loans, and other inducements to encourage young couples to move there. The basic starting price for an apartment (not in Jerusalem where prices are considerably higher) is about

$30,000. Since mortgages in Israel are ordinarily available for only a small percentage of the purchase price of an apartment and often not at all, the bulk or all of the purchase price has to be paid in cash.

Where does a young couple with an annual income of $5,000 or less find $30,000 or more to purchase an apartment? They turn to their parents for help in the form of a loan or an outright gift of money. Many parents take what little money they have saved and buy apartments, which they then rent, against the day that their children will need a place of their own to live, in much the same way that Americans start saving early for their children's college education. Or the couple may rent an apartment instead of buying, even though ownership of an apartment is generally acknowledged to be the best hedge against inflation that an Israeli can have, and renting costs them more in the long run. Or the couple may continue to live with one set of parents, sleeping several to a room. Israel has a severe shortage of housing, the more so when one considers that a substantial part of the housing was built in a hurry and much of that is in need of renovation now.

I am not speaking here about how Israelis in the higher income brackets live. Their housing situation, although somewhat easier, is still difficult. A "luxury" apartment by Israeli standards—which means a kitchen large enough to eat in, a living room, bathroom (perhaps two), and three bedrooms costs at least $100,000 and usually much more. Although luxurious by Israeli standards, such a building would be considered far from plush in the United States (where housing costs are also admittedly high). The difference between the United States and Israel is that although housing may cost the same in the two countries, income in the United States is significantly higher. Israelis wind up paying a far higher proportion of their income for housing under financial conditions far more burdensome than those Americans face.

The cost of furnishing an apartment or house is also extremely high. A standard refrigerator costs more than $1,000, a washing machine more than $800. Almost no one owns a dishwasher. Furniture is also expensive, since the wood to make it must be imported, along with fabric, nails, and whatever else goes into its manufacture.

Machines and appliances in general cost roughly twice as much in Israel as in the United States—though the high cost hardly seems a deterrent to ownership. Roughly one fourth of the households in Israel own a car, though the cost of a very small ordinary, nonluxurious model begins at $10,000 and costs more than $20,000 for heavier, fancier models. Gasoline costs two and a half to three times what it costs in the United States. Spare parts, like the cars themselves, cost roughly twice as much as in the United States. Little wonder then that Israelis treat their cars like a member of the family—sometimes even better—covering them in the summer with a custom-made cloth to shield them from the sun, nursing them along for years.

How then do Israelis manage to get by? One answer, offered by almost any Israeli one cares to ask, is that they don't. An Israeli, who was self-employed, described to me during a conversation a sort of financial musical chairs he played with his monthly income. He owed the grocer, the bank, the butcher, the fruit and vegetable man, and so on. He distributed his check around in such a way that he rarely fully repaid anyone, but instead made a mark on his debt so that each of his debtors saw that he was at least getting *something*.

Most Israelis never see their monthly salaries directly. (Israelis are generally paid once a month.) The money goes directly from the employer to the employee's bank account, which facilitates the use of one device that has become very popular in Israel—the automatic personal checking account overdraft. Many Israelis live with a perpetual negative balance in their checking accounts, so that their monthly paycheck does nothing more than to pay back a portion of their debt, enabling them to borrow more from the bank—at interest rates exceeding the inflation rate—and live another month.

Poorer Israelis do without. They rarely eat meat. They do not own cars. They live in small, overcrowded apartments. They take simple vacations if they take any at all. They ride buses, which are subsidized by the government and are relatively inexpensive. (An intracity ride costs about twenty cents.) Families of lower-class and lower-middle-class Israelis tend to be larger than families of middle-class and upper-middle-class Israelis. Women in poorer Israeli families are less likely to hold jobs outside their homes than women in more affluent families. Roughly thirty-five percent of all married Israeli women work, and the percentage increases as the amount of education a woman has increases.

Another obvious source of extra income comes from working overtime or moonlighting. Israelis ordinarily do not hold more than one job as a matter of course. Less than ten percent of all Israeli males moonlight, and the number of women is even smaller. But moonlighting is not at all unusual among Israeli professionals and administrative workers whose time is more flexible and who come into contact with more opportunities for moonlighting than do industrial workers.

A typical moonlighter in Israel, not unlike the United States, would be a college professor who earns one salary as a teacher and then earns another as a consultant to private industry or to government institutions. Almost all physicians work as employees for one of the various prepaid health plans or hospitals in Israel. They supplement their income by seeing patients in off-hours, generally in a clinic set up in their home or in some other private facility where they can offer better service than available in health plan clinics to patients willing to pay out of their own pocket. (The average patient in a health plan sees his or her doctor for less than five minutes during a visit.)

Industrial workers, of course, work overtime in order to increase their income. Some of them do work additional jobs, but an industrial worker's schedule is generally less flexible than a professional's. A garage mechanic, for example, may perform minor repairs on cars at his home—at a cheaper price than for work done in a garage. A carpenter employed in a furniture factory may also make cabinets on the side.

All this sounds as though Israel is a nation feverishly at work, but that impression is somewhat off the mark. The mailman for one Jerusalem neighborhood told a resident, who had asked why deliveries seemed so infrequent, that deliveries *were* infrequent. "He told me he delivers only twice a week—Mondays and Thursdays—because he has another job," the resident said.

Why should the post office tolerate that kind of service? "They have a hard time getting mailmen," the resident said.

The contempt Israelis show each other in the form of poor service is nothing compared to the contempt that they show for the tax collector, which suggests yet another way that Israelis manage to pass through narrow financial straits. An Israeli friend recommended to me that when my car needed repairs, I should take it to a mechanic he used who not only was extremely reliable but also was cheaper than his competitors. This mechanic worked out of his home. When the time came to pay him, I started writing him a check and he frowned. "Something wrong?" I asked.

"Cash would be better," he said.

"I don't have enough," I told him.

"Okay," he said, "so pay me what you can in cash and give me a check for the rest."

I did that and he gave me a receipt—but only for the amount I had paid by check, and the receipt noted that the money was for parts, not labor. The rest of the money I paid the mechanic undoubtedly had become what Israelis call black money.

Daily, Israeli newspapers carry reports of government tax authorities swooping down on a business of one sort or another to seize property or cash because the hapless victim was cheating on his taxes—a national institution in Israel. In one instance a wedding was disrupted when the tax authority officials arrested the bandleader, the caterer, and the manager of the hall where the wedding was performed—all for nonpayment of taxes.

Felafel stand owners are another favorite target of Israeli tax authorities. Felafel, ground chick-peas rolled into a ball, fried, and served inside hollow, flat bread with salad, is a national dish in Israel, like hot dogs or hamburgers in the United States. A felafel costs about seventy-five cents. Felafel stand owners generally keep their money carelessly stashed in a drawer rather than a cash register and are reluctant to record their sales. They deal in volume, and it would be too cumbersome for them to write a receipt each time they sell what is essentially a fast-food item. The Israeli government is pressing felafel stand owners to install cash registers, which would provide a record of sales and thus give the tax authorities a record to check.

To outward appearances the felafel stand hardly seems the kind of place worth bothering with. The operator is usually a middle-aged man with at least a day's growth of beard, or his equally unkempt, tired-looking, and harassed wife or another member of the family. Since it's only a stand and not a restaurant, overhead is kept to a bare minimum—no tables, chairs, or ambiance at all, just felafel.

This modest facade apparently hides a gold mine. Driving from Tel Aviv one hot summer afternoon, my wife stopped at a military hitchhiking station to pick up a soldier. An older man, described as "grimy and grubby-looking" by my wife, got into the car. As they rode toward Jerusalem, the soldier—who was coming home after completing his army reserve duty—complained to my wife about how he was constantly being harassed by government tax agents. He owned a felafel stand near Mahane Yehuda—Jerusulem's open market—a prime location for felafel. Since it was not out of her way, my wife dropped the man at the building where he lived, which turned out to be one of Jerusalem's most luxurious. His felafel stand, we learned later, provided a comfortable living not only for him but employed three of his brothers as well.

Estimates of how much income in Israel is not reported vary widely, since no one can be sure precisely how much business is conducted away from the prying eyes and outstretched hand of the tax authorities. Conservative estimates begin at around 8 percent of the country's gross national product—a considerable sum—and go up to a staggering 25 percent. When an Israeli sees another Israeli with a fancy car, a watch, a color television, or some other tangible artifact of conspicuous consumption, the knowing comment is, "Black money."

Friends who purchased a rug costing more than six hundred dollars in Jerusalem found that the merchant refused to accept a check as payment. His motive became clear when, after they had worked out a satisfactory payment scheme—with the merchant getting paid in cash—he resisted giving them a receipt as well. He simply wanted no record of the transaction.

Black money transactions are often not even conducted in an atmosphere befitting violations of the law, since both parties to the transaction stand to gain immediately from doing business under the table. It is not uncommon, when a plumber or some other repair person presents his bill, that payment is requested in cash without a receipt being offered. An Israeli woman told about one such experience when she requested a receipt. "Oh," the worker replied, "if you want a receipt, I'll have to charge more." Giving a receipt meant collecting not only twelve percent more for the Value Added Tax, but also enough additional to cover the income tax the worker would have to pay for the money received plus various other taxes. The price of his services was kept lower by keeping the entire transaction off the books.

Traditionally, being caught not paying taxes has not been the occasion for a jail sentence or a stiff fine, but rather the first step in negotiations between the tax delinquent and the state. One grocer boasted that he had paid no taxes whatever for the first thirty years of Israel's existence as a state. When the tax authorities caught up with him, the grocer negotiated with them and paid a considerable sum—but still a fraction of what he owed.

More recently, though, the government has started getting tough with tax dodgers. Judges *have* been giving stiff fines and even jail sentences to tax offenders. But the enforcement still appears to be a hit-or-miss, uneven affair. The Israeli government also has tried to enlist private citizens in the attempt to enforce tax payments by urging them to request receipts, which they can use to qualify for a kind of lottery. The lottery is advertised on television with encouragements to obtain receipts for all financial transactions.

A more drastic measure taken by the Israeli government was to change currencies, substituting the shekel for the Israeli lira and clamping down on the amount of foreign currency Israelis are permitted to hold. As part of this effort some government officials wanted to break into safety deposit boxes of persons suspected of holding large amounts of black money in cash. This step was resisted, however, when several government ministers protested that it would be an unprecedented and unwarranted invasion of privacy. Knowledgeable and more cynical Israelis doubted from the outset the effectiveness of changing the currency, since most of larger holdings of black money were generally considered to have been taken out of the country far in advance of the government's crackdown.

Various explanations have been given for this Israeli penchant for evading taxes. Economists have found in general that when tax rates go above a certain level, tax evasion also increases. Since Israelis are—nominally, at any rate—the most heavily taxed people in the world, it should not be surprising that tax evasion is rife in Israel. Another explanation given is that Jews—who historically lived as aliens and outcasts in other peoples' countries—have not developed the habits of good citizenship attendant upon people with a state of their own. Whatever the explanation, it is paradoxical that the same Israelis who are so conscientious and quick to volunteer in times of war and crisis should be so cavalier about supporting their own institutions financially as well.

Black money no doubt accounts for a major portion of the consumption that goes on in Israel, all the more so since the country suffers from chronic inflation that discourages saving. Although inflation became severe in Israel at the end of the 1970s and early in the 1980s—reaching three digits—it has been a recurring problem for Israelis.

An Israeli went to his bank in the spring of 1980 to cash what amounted to a five-year certificate of deposit. The deposit did not carry a fixed rate of interest but rather was "linked" so that it would not lose its value whatever the inflation rate. In other words, the bank promised to hold constant the value of the money he deposited by linking the interest to the rate of inflation. Since small savers are the first to be hurt when inflation gets out of hand, it was a deal too good for him to pass up. Just to sweeten it slightly, the bank offered an interest rate of ten percent on the initial deposit, not on the full amount at the end. In 1975 he had deposited 4,000 Israeli pounds. When he returned in 1980 to withdraw his money, his initial deposit was worth 45,000 Israeli pounds—almost the entire increase accounted for by inflation. The bank told him to return in a month to collect his money, after he gave them notice of his intention to withdraw his deposit. When he returned to collect the money after a month, he realized that the ten percent bonus promised him by the bank had been consumed by one month's worth of inflation. He left the bank with 41,000 pounds more than he had deposited, but in fact not a cent—or an Israel agora which is even less—wealthier in real terms than he had been before. This experience does illustrate, however, how Israelis managed to cope with inflation. If this small saver was not ahead, because of inflation, he was not behind, either. His money had more or less kept its value, which is more than most savers in the United States or Europe could say.

Inflation in Israel isn't necessarily any different from inflation anywhere else in the world. There just seems to be more of it. It is a chronic problem—more severe in recent years—but a problem in general. To say that Israel has triple-digit inflation—more or less—does not give an accurate picture of the situation, since Israelis find a variety of ways to manage. To say that they live happily with it would be stretching the point. Almost no one enjoys a situation where the price of basic goods and services—milk, eggs, bread, meat, heating oil, bus fare, gasoline, electricity—doubles or triples in a year's time.

Small businessmen, obviously, are able to raise their prices on items that are not subject to price control. The increases may lag behind the rate of inflation (or they may be ahead of the inflation rate and contribute to it), but at least a businessman is able to protect himself to some extent—or even profit from inflation, if he is shrewd.

Workers covered by contracts negotiated between the Histadrut and representatives of all employers are periodically given increases based on the cost-of-living index kept by the government through a survey—or "market basket"—of representative goods and services. Wages are raised on a quarterly basis, according to the increase in the cost-of-living index, and the process—known as indexing—is widely used in countries with high inflation rates. A variation of indexing—"escalator clauses" or "cost-of-living increases"—is employed in the United States on a less extensive scale.

The problem with indexing, escalator clauses, and cost-of-living clauses in general is that the payment of the increase in wages follows the increase in prices, and the longer it takes to raise the wages to make up for increased prices, the more the worker loses. As a result, labor unions generally press for as short a period as possible between increases. In Israel the increases are generally paid once every three months, which reduces the impact of inflation somewhat.

Workers are not alone in having contractual hedges against inflation. Building contractors customarily put a clause in their contracts "linking" payments to the inflation. Banks also link interest rates to the inflation rate.

Time becomes even more valuable when inflation rates climb. Every day's delay in paying costs someone—or increases someone else's profit. If prices are increasing at the rate of ten percent a month, one month's delay in paying a bill can mean substantial savings for a business. It is not unheard of or even unusual for Israeli businesses to stall for six or nine months to make payment for goods or services they have received.

To hedge against that kind of delay in payment of bills, some Israeli businesses and even private citizens protect themselves by demanding payment in foreign currency—usually American dollars—which are thought to be more stable than Israeli currency. The use of foreign currency to cover the cost of internal transactions indicates the lack of confidence that Israelis have in their own currency, a trend that makes the situation even worse for the local currency, since the rush to convert Israeli currency into dollars, deutsche marks, Swiss francs, English pounds, gold, or almost

145

anything else further diminishes the value of Israeli currency. After a three-year hiatus during which the Israeli government lifted controls on the amount of foreign currency Israelis were allowed to hold, the controls were reimposed in early 1980, leaving many Israelis—who were holding contracts calling for payment in American dollars—in the lurch, since they were no longer permitted to hold more than a minimal amount in foreign currency.

The problem of inflation is not entirely of Israel's making. Israel is particularly vulnerable to developments outside of the country. Almost everything made in Israel is fashioned from raw materials that are imported. Israel is a country extremely poor in natural resources. Attempts to find desperately needed oil reserves have so far proved unsuccessful. Hence Israel has remained vulnerable not only to price increases in oil and other imported raw materials, but also to politically motivated boycotts.

Israel's citrus industry is a prime example of the country's economic vulnerability. Roughly 43 percent of Israel's agricultural exports (15 percent of the total) are citrus fruits. In the flat, coastal plain surrounding Tel Aviv—in communities like Petah Tikva and Hod HaSharon—one passes mile after mile of orange and grapefruit trees heavy with gold and yellow fruit. Oranges and grapefruits are precisely the kind of big-ticket luxury export item Israel needs to support her relatively high living standard.

From the point of view of Israel's economic development, citrus farming offers two principal advantages: first, a citrus grove requires less labor than other crops; and second, citrus groves provide a higher rate of return per square foot than other crops. But Israel is not the only country that finds citrus an attractive cash crop. More than half of Israel's citrus products go to the eight countries of the European Common Market, who have been conducting negotiations with Spain and Greece over entry into the free-trade area. Spain's entry especially has the potential for seriously cutting into Israel's citrus market.

Israel might also drastically reduce her prices, but that would mean a reduction in Israel's living standard. When the subject of the economy comes up in Israel, veteran Israelis who recall the days of austerity with a kind of perverse nostalgia invariably assert that Israelis are living too well. "We cry, we cry," goes a popular Israeli song, "but we're living well."

Do Israelis live above their means? As a nation, Israel has borrowed heavily. It now has the highest external debt per capita— more than $5,000—of any country in the world. It continues to be heavily dependent on foreign aid. On an individual level, Israelis are also chronically overextended financially.

How Israelis manage their personal finances is something of a mystery to outsiders and only slightly less so to Israelis. According to one story Israelis tell, when Prime Minister Levi Eshkol visited the United States and was talking to President Lyndon B. Johnson, he expressed some interest in how Americans spend their money.

"Well," President Johnson is said to have replied, "they spend about a quarter of what they make on housing, another quarter on food, another forty percent on clothing and transportation."

"That's ninety percent," Eshkol replied. "What about the other ten percent?"

"We're a democracy," Johnson said, "so we don't ask. But tell me about your country. How do people spend money there?"

"About thirty percent goes for housing," Eshkol supposedly replied, "another forty percent for food, twenty percent for clothing, ten percent for transportation, and ten percent for entertainment."

"But that's one hundred ten percent of their income," Johnson said. "Where does the extra ten percent come from?"

"We are also a democracy," Eshkol replied. "So we don't ask."

Although figures show a high degree of personal savings, middle-class and upper-middle-class Israelis do not, for the most part, save money.

With inflation a chronic problem, saving money doesn't always seem to make sense—at least on a visceral level. If one can afford to buy *things*, which are always going up in price, the pressure becomes very strong to buy now before whatever it is becomes more expensive. This is a traditional inflationary mentality and Israelis are susceptible to it like everyone else, especially perhaps with black money needing to be disposed of. As a result, Israelis often are overextending themselves to buy a car, an apartment, a vacation, a refrigerator, or whatever. It will never get any cheaper and will probably become more unattainable if they don't seize it now. Because of agreements reached with the Common Market countries, the Israeli government's ability to discourage imports of consumer items has decreased.

Something else is at work here, however, and it goes well beyond inflation and gets to the heart of the Israeli experience in a very real sense. "Somewhere in your analysis," an Israeli admonished, "you have to account for the impact of five wars in thirty years and the effect that's had on the collective psychology here." The uncertainty of the future is always a consideration in Israel and cannot be discounted as a factor in guiding behavior. Living for the moment can easily become a national habit.

Israel's financial situation would be eased immeasurably if the country's future became more certain, which is to say if it were able to reach a firm peace agreement with its neighbors. Then the enormous share of time, energy, and resources devoted to security could be shifted somewhat and Israelis could shoulder more of their load themselves, without—or with less—outside help.

Short of that kind of an agreement Israel's continued well-being depends on its ability to retain a well-educated, technically proficient professional class that has the expertise to keep Israeli technology up-to-date with developments in other industrial countries. One of the more serious consequences of weakened ideology as a motivating factor in Israel is that economic well-being has become more important for deciding whether to stay in Israel or whether to emigrate. Israel may be paying more than it can afford to provide its citizens with a level of services and standard of living that will keep them content.

Israeli economists and others who worry about Israel's economic performance do believe that Israel can be put on a sound financial footing. In 1975 and 1976 the gap between exports and imports was decreased to a point where it became possible to foresee the day when the gap *could* be eliminated altogether. Once before, prior to the Six Day War in 1967, the gap was similarly narrowed without relying on increased foreign aid. But these two periods have been the exception rather than the rule. The situation for Israel, while not yet desperate, is becoming extremely serious.

"We must realize that our future is at stake," Arnon Gafny, the governor of Israel's central bank, the Bank of Israel, told a group of Israeli businessmen in late 1980. Israelis have become accustomed to these warnings, but there are reasons now for believing that the situation for Israel has undergone a sea change, but not for the better. Israel's development in her first twenty-five years occurred during a period of unprecedented world prosperity and relatively cheap energy. Those conditions have obviously changed, and Israel is discovering that it will have to make some fundamental changes as well.

Enforced austerity has potentially disastrous consequences for Israel. The period of greatest emigration from Israel was not after any of her wars but in the period from 1951 through 1955 when economic hardships were the most severe. A reduction in the Israeli living standard may result in an increase in the emigration rate. Well-educated, innovative, capable professionals are in demand all over the world, and Israel already is experiencing a "brain drain" as her own scientists, engineers, and other professionals leave for greener pastures.

Economically, Israel appears to be in a box—not entirely of its own making perhaps—but a tight corner nevertheless. So long as Israel is surrounded by hostile countries, she will have to continue spending an inordinate amount of money to support an outsize defense establishment.

Like every other country in the world that has to import energy, Israel will find its energy costs going up throughout the next decade. Meanwhile, interest payments for past loans are increasing.

To offset these growing financial drains, Israel can look for more foreign aid—which will be increasingly difficult to obtain. If aid were provided, however, Israel would face a different problem. They would have to sacrifice that much more of the freedom of action Israelis assert they must have in order to chart the independent course they believe is necessary for their survival and well-being.

The incongruity of straining to become militarily independent while becoming more financially dependent has not been overlooked by concerned Israelis. During the 1977 Knesset election campaign, Yigael Yadin—running at the head of the centrist Democratic Movement for Change ticket—warned, "There is no greater danger to our spiritual future and our independence . . . than the aid we get from our brothers and friends." Another DMC Knesset candidate, Meir Amit, who had served as the head of the Histadrut's conglomerate arm, Koor Industries, was explicit. "Two thirds of our national deficit is covered by the Americans," Amit said. "We are becoming increasingly dependent on the United States . . . exposing ourselves to strong political pressures which will be accompanied by painful economic sanctions."

To avoid increased foreign aid, Israel could attempt to solve its own economic problems through increasing productivity, reducing services, and perhaps even reducing its living standard. It may be too much to expect a spontaneous rebirth of the sacrificing spirit of the early pioneers that would be necessary to bring Israel out of its current economic morass. One prominent Israeli economist said that if American foreign aid were reduced by about twenty-five percent, Israel would be forced to make hard—but necessary—decisions. A prominent Israeli businessman advocated changing the way American foreign aid is given to Israel to channel it directly to businessmen—in much the same way that Marshall Plan aid was channeled to European businessmen after World War II.

Israel's history since 1948 shows that the country is capable of overcoming seemingly insurmountable obstacles through innovation, the ability to improvize, and acts of will. Ingenuity is an enormous asset for nations as well as people, and its loss, through increased dependence on outsiders, can be critical.

However serious their economic situation is, Israelis have not lost their characteristic ability to see it and themselves in bittersweet terms. According to one story Israelis tell, the archangel

Gabriel returned to heaven after being sent to earth on an intelligence mission by God himself.

"What did you see down there?" God asked Gabriel.

"In Africa," Gabriel said, "the situation is very bad. People are starving and there doesn't seem to be much that can be done."

God nodded impassively and gestured for Gabriel to go on. "In Europe, although people are living well," Gabriel said, "they're unhappy because they have to pay higher prices and they see that all their money is going to countries that sell them oil."

"What else?" God asked, still showing no sign of emotion.

"In Israel," Gabriel said, "the situation is puzzling. Inflation there is more than two hundred percent, taxes are very high, and yet everyone is living well, eating well, going on vacations. People seem to be very happy despite all the problems."

At this point God put his hands to his head and a look of dismay came over his face. "What's wrong?" Gabriel asked, concerned at the change of expression.

"It's clear," God answered. "They're counting on me to pull them through again."

4 / THE SECOND ISRAEL

We must ask ourselves a question that no other people asks: Are we really a people? As I see it, we are not yet a people. . . . This historic process, which is only just beginning, is a very prolonged one.

David Ben-Gurion

The feeling that there is discrimination, as well as the apparent evidence that there are two societies, separate and unequal, has reached a psychological boiling point.

Nessim Gaon

Like the United States, Israel is a country that brings together people who have emigrated from many other countries—more than one hundred in all. In the two thousand years since the destruction of the Second Temple, Jews had scattered literally all over the globe. The "ingathering of the exiles," the Herculean effort by the newly born Jewish state, was one of the efforts made in Israel's early days to fulfill the promise of the Zionist dream. In Israel today fair-skinned Jews from the Netherlands stand beside dark-skinned Jews from India and the Falasha from Ethiopia. Israel has Jews from Germany, Poland, and Russia, of course, but also Jews from Iran, Kurdistan, Afghanistan, Yemen, Turkey, Argentina, Chile, and the Philippines.

On the streets and cafés, in a hundred little towns and villages all across the country this tremendous diversity of populations gives Israel a richness and variety that one would not normally expect in a country with fewer than four million inhabitants. The news on Israeli radio is carried not only in Hebrew and Arabic but also in English, French, Spanish, Yiddish, Ladino (a kind of Yiddish for Spanish-speaking Jews), German, and Russian.

Again, as in the United States, the ideal image is of Israel as a melting pot, one country with equality for all citizens. Yet even when the question of the Arabs is put aside, in reality Israel is a divided country—economically, culturally and ethnically. Significantly enough for the future stability of Israel, the divisions are parallel so that regardless of what factor we consider—wealth, education, ethnic background—the line cleaves Israeli society into the same two basic groups. The fact is that despite a common heritage that goes back more than three thousand years and a more recent history approaching four decades as a sovereign nation, Israel is not yet one society, but two.

There is one Israel that is Western, relatively prosperous, well-educated, and substantially in control of the country's institutions. The other Israel, the second Israel as it is often called, is Oriental, relatively poor, unskilled, and although a numerical majority, under-represented in the inner power sanctums.

The tensions between the "two Israels," between the dominant Western Israeli society and the subordinate Oriental or "second" Israel, are always present, if not on the surface then directly below it. In 1980 when Minister of Religious Affairs Aharon Abuhatzeira was accused of bribery and corruption, the investigation was seen by Israel's Oriental, or Sephardic, community as an example of the persecution of Oriental Jews for Abuhatzeira was the scion of a proud, old Oriental family from Morocco.

The two principal ethnic groups are the Ashkenazim and the Sephardim. Strictly speaking, Sephardic Jews are those who can trace their origins back to Spain or Portugal. The word *Sephardi* comes from the Hebrew word for Spain, *Sepharadh*. In Israel, Jews from the Islamic countries of North Africa as well as the Middle East and Turkey are referred to either as Sephardim or as Oriental. Similarly, Jews from eastern and central Europe are Ashkenazim, although as used in Israel the word means Jews of European background generally.

Prime Minister Menachem Begin, an Ashkenazic Jew, but one with a considerable following in the Oriental community, made a public appeal to Oriental Jews not to allow the investigation to become an ethnic issue. Israel's President Yitzhak Navon, the country's first president of Oriental extraction, made a similar appeal. Nonetheless, these appeals did not stop many Oriental Jews from seeing the whole affair as a way of somehow embarrassing them and deflating their growing power and influence in public affairs.

The tendency of Israelis to speak in terms of "us" and "them" when discussing the Ashkenazic-Sephardic situation in Israel is a clear indication that a schism exists. Although some observers think the problem will disappear with time as the two populations are assimilated, a significant number of Israelis, feel that the problem of "two Israels" represents a serious and continuing threat to the stability of the state. This feeling became especially sharp during the 1981 election campaign when the ethnic division manifested itself in overt ways.

Oriental Jews are still the lowest paid workers in Israel. Although incomes in general have risen in Israel, the overall, relative position of Oriental Jews has not changed significantly in the last decade. In 1971, about 73 percent of all Oriental families were in the bottom half of Israeli families according to income. In 1978, the figure was 72 percent.*

---

* As usual with statistics, the picture changes somewhat, depending upon what set of numbers one chooses to use. The overall conclusion—that Oriental Jews remained rooted at the bottom of Israel's wage-earners, remains. In 1968, the average income of an Oriental Jewish wage-earner was 78 percent of the national average, 78 percent of what Israelis whose fathers were born in Israel earned, 71 percent of Israelis of European-American origin and 127 percent of Israeli Arabs' income.

By 1978, average Oriental income was 72 percent against the total average: 70 percent of what Israelis of Israeli origin earned, 68 percent of European-American, and 94 percent of Israeli Arabs. The problem of isolating two years for comparison ought to be noted, but even when that deficiency is taken into account, what remains clear is that Oriental Jews in Israel have not made much progress toward eliminating the income gap separating them from the rest of Israeli society. In fact, in terms of improving their income position against Israeli society in general, Israeli Arabs appear to have made more progress than Oriental Jews.

The more crowded the living conditions, the greater the likelihood that the family living in the housing unit is Oriental—more than 14 percent of families with a father born in Oriental countries lived in what the Israeli government classified as "crowded" conditions, compared to 5 percent of families with Israeli-born fathers and 2.5 percent of families with European-American born fathers.

In education the situation is much the same. Among the Israeli-born a child with a father born in Israel is twice as likely to attend a university as a child with an Oriental father, and a child with a European-American born father was three times more likely to attend a university.

These facts seem to point to a classic case of a disfranchised, "poverty" class that becomes more marginal and problematic with each passing generation. Although the situation of the "second" Israel has parallels with the situation of black Americans in the United States, a comparison demonstrates that there are more fundamental differences than similarities in the two cases:

> Oriental Jews did not come to Israel as slaves. They came willingly, even eagerly, as free men and women.
>
> Israel has no history of discrimination institutionalized in law and formal practice.
>
> Oriental and Ashkenazic Jews share an ancient culture and religion. In Israel, they face a common threat.
>
> Oriental Jews are not necessarily physically distinguishable from Ashkenazic Jews in any way. Some Oriental Jews have darker skin than Ashkenazic Jews, but not necessarily.
>
> Oriental Jews are a majority of the Jewish population in Israel, not a minority. They have full access to democratic institutions and the likely prospect, in time, of becoming the dominant political force in the country.

Nevertheless, although Oriental Jews constitute 55 to 60 percent of the Jewish population in Israel, they are a minority in the places that count—in the Knesset, the Histadrut, the universities, the educational institutions. Not surprisingly, a study in

1977 to determine who constituted Israel's elites—the persons perceived by others as holding power and influence—found that Jews of central and eastern European background dominated the major institutions of power in Israel. The total Oriental representation in Israel's elites was only 10 percent. Of 428 persons who served in Israel's first nine Knessets, only 10 percent were Oriental Jews. In the ninth Knesset, elected in 1977, roughly 17 percent of the members were of Oriental origin.

In one sense, much of the anguish expressed in Israel about the condition of society, the erosion of values and the old idealism, and the decline of the work ethic reflect a thinly veiled resentment toward the growing numbers and cultural influence of Oriental Jews. Their presence was denied for years, even after they approached a majority of the population. Amos Elon, in *The Israelis: Founders and Sons*, his superb study of Israel at the end of the 1960s, summed up what he saw as the shaping force of Israeli society:

> In the day to day life of Israel, in the flavor of its politics, its traditions of social radicalism, the manners of its people, their passionate argumentativeness, their belief in ideology, their incorrigible addiction to theoretical formulation, their worship of labor and the soil and the virtues of simple peasant life, even in their attitude to the industrial West— a mixture of envy and disgust, provincial admiration and self-righteous superiority—in all these, echoes of Eastern Europe reverberate like an old tune through the cacophony of ultra-modern electronic music.

Elon described the original settlers of Israel, not the Israel of today. Elon was describing a rapidly vanishing world, its fate perhaps sealed once and for all by the victory of the Likud government of Menachem Begin in 1977. With that election the Oriental population of Israel served notice on the Eastern European power structure that it wanted a seat at the table. It is not a prospect that meets with universal approval among the Ashkenazic population where warnings are sounded of the "Levantization" of Israel, of growing "primitive" antisocial behavior—code words that refer to the growing influence of Oriental Jews.

The problems Israel had in integrating the hundreds of thousands of European Jews into the population after independence in 1948 were substantially mitigated by the cultural similarities between the new immigrants and those Jews already settled in Israel. These new immigrants also had at least passing familiarity with political Zionism and with socialism.

From 1919 through 1948—the years of the British mandate—Jewish immigration to Palestine had been dominated by European Jews. Only about ten percent of the Jewish immigrants were Jews from countries other than Europe. Even in those early days, coming as they were from relatively backward societies, poor, unskilled Jews from Asia and North Africa occupied an inferior social, economic, and political position in the Yishuv, or Jewish community. The motivation of these Oriental Jews in coming to Israel had less to do with Zionism—a movement that had barely touched their former homelands—than it did with religious reasons—the realization of the traditional Jewish dream to return to the Holy Land. The father of a woman I met in Israel was arrested and imprisoned in his native Yemen on a charge based on false evidence. Conviction would have meant certain death for him. In the depth of his despair this religious Jew committed himself to the most solemn promise he could think of—that, if freed, he would make his way to Palestine, back to the ancient Land of Israel. With the intervention of the leadership of the Yemenite Jewish community, he was freed and then he kept his promise.

Other Oriental Jews came for less dramatic reasons, often religious but also in the expectation that they might improve their lives materially. But even if their lives did improve economically, they found themselves cut adrift from the culture and traditions with which they had grown up. Huddling together in the slums of Jerusalem and Tel Aviv, they managed to preserve some of their traditions, but they also found themselves—with few exceptions—

157

at the bottom of the social ladder in the Yishuv. With its different customs, culture, language (Arabic instead of Yiddish) and even religious rituals, the Oriental Jewish community fashioned certain institutions of its own.

Before Jewish immigrants began arriving in large numbers in Palestine in the 1880s, a substantial community of Sephardic Jews already was settled there, especially in Palestine. These Sephardic Jews, many of whom could trace their roots in Palestine back for several generations, were relatively more prosperous and more worldly than the ultrareligious Ashkenazic Jews who depended upon charity from Europe and America for their survival. This Sephardic community constituted something of a Jewish aristocracy in Palestine at the beginning of the twentieth century, when the Labor Zionists began coming from eastern Europe. With the arrival of large numbers of Zionist pioneers, the character of the "Old" Yishuv was substantially transformed and the influence of the established Sephardim was substantially diminished in the Yishuv. The Yishuv had two separate spiritual leaders, a chief Sephardic rabbi and a chief Ashkenazic rabbi, reflecting the differences in religious traditions and observances within the two communities. In some instances Oriental Jews broke completely with the past and were able to integrate successfully into the dominant Western culture and growing new Jewish community.

After 1948, however, the situation changed dramatically. Zionism demanded the "ingathering of the exiles." Jews were driven out of Islamic countries by regimes hostile to their presence and began emigrating to Israel in large numbers. More than 45,000 Jews came from Yemen. In 1950, following enactment of a special law by the Iraqi parliament permitting Jews to leave provided they took less than twenty dollars with them, 120,000 Iraqi Jews emigrated to Israel. The largest group of Oriental Jews began arriving in the mid-1950s when nationalist sentiment in Morocco made the position of the country's Jewish population less secure. By 1972 more than 250,000 Jews had come to Israel from Morocco. As a result, besides native-born Israelis (sabras), Moroccan Jews now constitute the single largest ethnic group in Israel.

In the first five years of Israel's history as a state, about 350,000 Oriental Jews immigrated. By the mid-1960s, when the period of mass immigration to Israel had ended, about 700,000 Oriental Jews had come to Israel, compared to roughly 580,000 from Europe, the United States, and South Africa.

Absorbing such a large number of immigrants—representing approximately one third of Israel's population in the mid-1960s—would have been difficult under the best of circumstances. But the Oriental Jewish immigrants were not arriving under the best of circumstances. The literacy rates for both men and women were significantly lower than for the European immigrants, almost all of whom could read and write. Only one fourth as many of the Oriental Jews coming to Israel had professional skills in comparison to European Jews. Twice as many Oriental Jews were classified as unskilled laborers. In short, Oriental Jews were entering a society that could survive and thrive only by concentrating on modern Western methods. And yet they lacked the very talents they needed to prosper in this strange new world. To make matters worse, the wealthier, better-educated elements of the Oriental Jewish communities—especially those from North Africa—chose the good life of Paris over the hardships of the pioneer in Israel. The Moroccan Jewish community, the largest of the Oriental Jewish groups that emigrated to Israel, came to Israel short of skills and shorn of leadership to guide them through a difficult period.

As they arrived, these newcomers were packed off by the government to "development towns" in relatively remote regions of the country—especially in the Negev—where they were cut off from the main currents of Israeli life. Or they were squeezed into slums in Jerusalem and Tel Aviv, sweltering in summer and suffering in the damp, chilly winters. In other instances they were formed into groups and settled in cooperative farming communities, moshavim, where they became farmers under the tutelage of the Jewish Agency and the government.

Many prospered in their new country. And many did not. By the mid-1960s it was becoming clear that the dream of a single, united Jewish people living in Israel was not being realized. Two

Israels were emerging—one highly literate, educated, relatively affluent, and not coincidentally, Western; and the other relatively poor, unskilled, uneducated, and not coincidentally, Oriental in origin.

The problem simmered, undiscovered by the outside world until the early 1970s when a group calling itself the Black Panthers (with an eye definitely turned in the direction of Western journalists) came on the scene. In fact, however, Israelis had known that a "problem" existed at least since 1959, when riots had broken out in the Wadi Salib section of Haifa, a shabby, over-crowded slum inhabited mainly by Oriental Jews. At the time of the riots a clear separation was already evident. The bottom 10 percent of Israeli households, overwhelmingly Oriental and predominantly Moroccan, were receiving 1.6 percent of the nation's income, while the top 10 percent of Israeli households, almost entirely Ashkenazim, received about 24 percent. Of one hundred thousand students registering to begin high school in 1958 (tuition had to be paid and attendance was not compulsory), only four thousand were Orientals. Poorly educated, Oriental dropouts were suited for unskilled, low-paying employment, while the better-paying more prestigious work went to the better-educated, better-prepared Ashkenazim.

The rift had been forming from the onset of the mass immigration to Israel, perhaps even before. Although the official ideology spoke of a "melting pot," the reality, in fact, was a mold, a form into which the new immigrants were expected to fit as part of the program to build the state. "The immigrants," Ben-Gurion declared,

> must be taught our language and a knowledge of the Land and of the pains of immigration. They must conceive what the first settlers did with their bare hands, how they fought with the desert, with an inept government in the Turkish days and obstructions under the Mandate; and what they nevertheless did. Being privileged to enter Israel, they must be told that they, too, must toil, if perhaps less than their forerunners.

Precious little was said about concern for the immigrants' past, their customs, or culture.

Presiding over the "ingathering of the exiles" were Jews who had been living in Israel since the 1920s and 1930s, and they were in large measure Jews from eastern Europe—the Jews who became known to the Orientals derisively as the *vusvusim*. Significantly enough, the term grew out of the Yiddish language—the mother tongue for Eastern European Jews—and the term symbolized the cultural and communication gap separating the two groups. When immigrants arrived, they were met at the boat or plane and taken to transit camps for processing. In the course of the procedure the new immigrants were often interviewed by Russian or Polish Jews, and if the answer was not understood, the Ashkenazic Jew—reverting to Yiddish—might ask: *"Vus? Vus?"* ("What? What?"). And inevitably, the people who repeatedly asked *"Vus?"* became the *vusvusim*.

The language difference has diminished somewhat as Israelis of all backgrounds increasingly rely on Hebrew, but the subject of Yiddish and the domination of the Yiddish speakers in Israel remained a sore point for years. ("Golda," the Black Panthers chanted bitterly in the early 1970s when picketing Prime Minister Golda Meir, "teach us Yiddish!")

The heart of the problem was a kind of cultural imperialism practiced by the dominant Ashkenazic culture over the incoming Oriental culture. "We must melt down this fantastically diversified assemblage and cast it afresh in the die of a renewed nationhood," Ben-Gurion said in 1951.

> We must break down the barriers of geography and culture, of society and speech, which keep the different sections apart, and endow them with a single language, a single culture, a single citizenship, a single loyalty, with new legislation and new laws. We must give them a new spirit, a culture and literature, science and art.

Implicit was the idea that the immigrants had no "culture," no literature, no art of their own, that they were somehow backward and primitive. When officials of the Jewish Agency went to Morocco to encourage Moroccan Jews to come to Israel, they also discouraged the immigrants from bringing their traditional clothing and jewelry with them on the grounds that it would be out of style and useless in Israel. To this day children from lower-class Oriental homes are referred to often as coming from a "culturally deprived" background.

"This is what happened in the schools," an Israeli said. "For many years everyone felt that we needed to try to make everyone Western and that the major culture should be the culture of Eastern European Jews—German Jews, Russian Jews, Jews from America—that these were the things one should be striving for."

An Israeli whose parents came from Kurdistan and who grew up in a predominantly Kurdish neighborhood of Jerusalem, recalls that his teachers, who were for the most part Ashkenazim, communicated a sense that he was somehow inferior. "The teacher," he said, "gave us a feeling that our values were not good, like their values. For example, in music, before I went to school, I really liked Oriental music. But the teacher said to me that this music was 'primitive.' It made me feel that my music wasn't any good. On the radio all I heard was Western music. So I said, 'My teacher is okay. She's right.' All around me was something else. I felt maybe my family didn't know that they were primitive."

Not only the music played on the radio in the early years was almost exclusively Western music, but the literature taught in the schools was Western. "When I was a girl in school in Tel Aviv," a woman whose parents came from Yemen recounts, "they taught us about Bialik. Okay. So it's good to know something about a Russian Jewish poet. But why didn't they teach us anything about my people, too?"

"I think," one Israeli observed, "that from the very beginning the idea has been that everyone says we have to create a Jewish society, but actually we're always trying to create a Western society."

The rage expressed in the Wadi Salib riots in 1959 and in the Black Panther demonstrations of the late 1960s and early 1970s had its roots in the familiar problems of perceived discrimination and the conflict between rising expectations and stark limits of reality.

"I think," an Israeli social worker observed, "one of the major problems was that North African Jews thought they were going to be accepted as equals, and then they realized that as a group they weren't being accepted because they have a different culture, different traditions, different personal habits, different languages, et cetera. What has happened here—especially for those North African Jews who came—they were leaving countries where they were discriminated against, where they didn't feel at home, and they thought they were coming to a country where their personal situation, where their economic situation and their status, would change in an essential way. They thought they would see themselves as better. They would be totally integrated and accepted because this is a Jewish country. They told themselves: 'We're not arriving as foreigners. We're arriving as Jews who are being asked to return,' the 'return of the exiles.' When many North African Jews arrived, they found they weren't seen as equals and they weren't accepted as equals and that even though it is a Jewish state, perhaps they don't have some of the problems they had in their countries before, here they have other problems. We're all Jews and we're all equal, but perhaps some are more equal than others."

One of the earliest victims of the Oriental immigration—especially among North Africans where the cultural gap and the leadership problem were the most severe—was the integrity of the family unit. Oriental Jewish families reinforce the religious tenets that give primacy to the father as head of the family. But in the new world Oriental Jews had entered, with its new values and new priorities, a conflict emerged between the family and the state. Ben-Gurion, characteristically adverting to the Bible for precedent, referred to the "desert generation," the generation that emerged from slavery in Egypt but then had to wander forty years in the desert in order to produce a generation of children who had no memories of a slave past and who could live as free, fierce, and proud men.

"All these families were traditional," an Oriental Jew who

managed to escape the trap said, reminiscing. "They came from big families. The father was everything in the family, and his children respected and obeyed him. Maybe that continued for the first years in Israel. But during the years the authority of the father was broken in the family. The children felt if their father wasn't a doctor, a lawyer, some kind of professional, he was nothing. And if he said to them, 'Do this,' or 'Do that,' they would laugh at him. In schools what the teachers taught was mostly Ashkenazim, nothing about Oriental values and culture. When we came home, we felt as children that maybe something was wrong with our families and with our fathers. This is the most important thing that happened because it's still going on. So what happened, in several cases, is that the boys felt that they couldn't get anything of value from their families. They didn't succeed in reaching their goal in the society of Ashkenazim—they didn't go to high school, or become lawyers, or doctors, or professionals themselves. They thought they could do that. They felt the gap—they weren't this and they weren't that. They lived in two worlds. They wanted to be like the Ashkenazim because they felt that this was a good thing to be."

In the cities the Oriental immigrants lived in the worst neighborhoods with the worst schools and reputedly the worst teachers. In the development towns, on the remote fringes of the country, the teachers were often well-meaning but underqualified or simply unqualified. If the development towns were near a large city— Haifa, Tel Aviv, or Jerusalem—perhaps teachers were brought to their towns during the day. "They were all Israeli-born or European-born," an Israeli observed. "They'd leave [their homes in the city] every morning and come by bus, or a government car would bring them. They'd teach until one and then they'd go back . . . and that was the end of their day. What happened was that many of the traditions and much of the culture remained because the people were living together, but the establishment kept telling them, 'Look, you're going to have to be different.' But people didn't know how to become integrated. The schools were separate. Even in the cities the schools were separate. Many felt that the only real melting pot was the army because this was where they all get together."

Ultimately, perhaps inevitably, as the old traditions were broken down and before new roots could be formed, the signs of social decay began to appear—most notably crime. Crime began developing as a serious problem in the mid-1950s when not only the number of crimes increased—a consequence that could be expected with a growing population—but the amount of crime per capita also increased, indicating that a significant change was occurring. The number of reported crimes of all types increased from about 22,000 in 1950 to 213,000 in 1978. Thefts increased from about 9,000 in 1950 to 99,000 in 1978. Other types of crime— rape, assault, and a particularly vicious form of robbery where the homes of old persons were broken into and the victims were beaten as well as robbed—also increased.

An analysis of government statistics revealed that a disproportionate number of crimes were committed by the Oriental population, and more specifically, by Jews from Morocco or the children of Moroccan Jews. The crime rate among Moroccan-born Jews was the highest for any group—50 percent higher than for Israel-born Jews, almost 100 percent higher than for Jews from Asian countries (Turkey, Iraq, Yemen, India) and almost 400 percent higher than for European and American-born Jews. Although only about 15 percent of the population, Moroccan Jews accounted for 42 percent of Israel's prostitutes, according to a survey.

In an atmosphere of increasing alienation, crime offered the promise of quick and easy wealth, or at least a way for an uneducated, unskilled population to make its way in the world. An Israeli social worker who worked closely with street gangs said that the young, budding criminals with whom he worked saw crime as their only means of social advancement. "They feel that the only way for them to get ahead is through crime," he said. "And they don't feel as though they're doing anything wrong. They say to me, 'The only people we do things to are the Ashkenazim.' So they don't think they're doing anything wrong."

Israel now has a flourishing, largely Oriental underworld—drug dealers, pimps, hustlers, extortionists, loan sharks, car thieves, hit men, and petty criminals of all types. Juvenile delinquency is a serious and growing problem.

For years the problem of a Jewish underclass had a vicious-circle quality to it. Coming from families that were poor, unskilled, and uneducated, Oriental children left school early. Lacking skills, they were unable to get decent jobs. Some of them turned to crime, were caught by the police, and convicted. Once convicted, they were considered undesirable for the army. Or even if they had not become involved in criminal activity, their performance on screening tests often was so poor as to prevent their being accepted for otherwise mandatory army service. Once the army rejected them, however, they were doomed to a life on the bottom because few employers would take on a young man who had failed to serve in the army.

More recently, however, because the government has realized the Gordian knot it creates when it bars "undesirables" from the army, and because of the army's increased need for manpower, these former "undesirables" have been accepted for service, eliminating one major obstacle to their integration into the mainstream of Israeli society.

The problem of Oriental Jews in Israeli society is not only one of poverty, however. In many instances Oriental Jews have succeeded financially only to find that "integration" into Israeli life is not simply a matter of a higher living standard. "A lot of them have money," an Israeli whose parents were European in origin said, groping for the right word to express herself. "It's a matter of—culture."

European Jews find much of the unrestrained and occasionally unabashedly sensuous behavior of Oriental Jews embarrassing and "primitive." It isn't hard to understand why people of European background would find Oriental Jews "primitive" if the observation stops at surface impressions. In contrast to the Western preference for emotional control, Oriental Jews tend to give full expression to themselves. No celebration goes by without the women attending ululating in a manner often heard in Arab countries. Disconcerting when heard the first time, the sound is an expression of happiness—used to greet an honored guest as well as for events like weddings, bar mitzvahs, and similar celebrations. Similarly with anger, it is not unusual for Oriental Jews to vent their emotions publicly without paying attention to who is watching.

What is described as "primitive" behavior by European Jews can also be characterized as earthy and natural, simple and unaffected. The annual celebration of L'ag B'omer in Israel brings thousands of Jews to the northern town of Meron, near the city of Safad. The holiday, commemorating the time when Israel was under Roman rule and Jews had to study the Torah clandestinely, is a popular one among Oriental Jews, who come by the thousands to Meron to camp for several days. Moroccan Jews especially turn out, setting up elaborately decorated tents filled with comfortable furniture, often transported from their living rooms and bedrooms at home. The decorations may include painted walls on the tent, couches, rugs, and electric lights powered by portable generators brought by the campers.

During my own L'ag B'omer visit to Meron, the celebration went on well into the night. In one tent a woman was singing songs in Arabic to a packed crowd of fifty or sixty persons, accompanied by a band playing behind her on a makeshift stage. Along the way, as my wife, son, and I stopped to talk to the campers, we were invited into the tents to enjoy cake, cookies, and other sweets. Several times we passed carcasses of recently slaughtered sheep and goats hanging outside. Live sheep and goats were tied up near the tents. The animals had been brought by the campers to be slaughtered and eaten on the spot, since part of the Oriental celebration esteems eating meat that has been slaughtered in Meron.

In contrast to the Oriental observance of L'ag B'omer was the more demure behavior of very religious Hasidic Jews who had also made the pilgrimage to Meron. The main gathering was at the tomb of Rabbi Shimeon bar Yohai, a second-century biblical scholar and Jewish leader who opposed the Roman occupation of Israel. His body is buried in Meron along with that of his son.

On the roof of Rabbi bar Yohai's tomb fires were burning in oil drums in the traditional manner. Hasidic Jews—members of ultra-religious sects from Eastern Europe, some of whom still dress in the manner of eighteenth-century Polish noblemen—were dancing in a circle (men only). For the Hasidim, L'ag B'omer was every bit as much of an event as it was for the Moroccan Jews who had assembled from all over Israel. But the Hasidic observance concentrated on the religious aspects of the event and lacked the Roman orgy quality of the observance by the assembled Oriental Jews.

Israelis of European background had spoken about the L'ag B'omer celebration with scarcely veiled distaste, describing it as a sort of pagan rite. The event itself fell far short of that kind of wild scene, but the fact is that the annual L'ag B'omer observance in Meron is something of an embarrassment and nuisance to the Israeli government, which has to detail thousands of policemen and soldiers to the area to protect the campers and to preserve order.

A considerable gap exists between the L'ag B'omer celebration and a society that produces state-of-the-art electronic equipment competitive in international markets and modern jet aircraft flown by some of the finest pilots in the world. The difference is between a traditional society based on informal, personal relationships and a highly complex, impersonal society relying on bureaucracy and disciplined procedures to establish and meet its goals. Israel can scarcely survive as a country if it does not adapt itself to Western standards, but it does not seem to occur to Israelis of European background that they might have something to learn from Oriental Jews. As more than one Israeli intellectual (usually Sephardic) has remarked, an Oriental Jew is said to be "integrated" when his behavior emulates the customs and manners of Ashkenazic Jews rather than the other way around.

In politics, too, Jews of Oriental origin find it difficult to become integrated. The mayor of Beersheba, Eliahu Nawi, who was born in Iraq, quit the Labor Alignment ticket during the 1981 Knesset election because he failed to be given a position on the Labor list that would guarantee him a seat. Nawi later recounted

for reporters the following conversation between himself and
Labor Alignment Chairman Shimon Peres:

PERES: You don't know what pressures I've had to withstand.
NAWI: Withstanding pressures is a characteristic required of a
leader and I don't see you doing that.
PERES: There are too many Iraqis at the top [of the list].
NAWI: I've been in Israel more than fifty-six years. Do you think
there is ever a chance I'll be [recognized as] an Israeli?
PERES: This is not what I think but that is what people say.

Much about the Oriental outlook and approach to life ought to
be appealing to Israelis of European origin. The Jewish emphasis
on the family is especially strong among Oriental Jews. No less
religious on the average than their European counterparts, perhaps more so, Oriental Jews manage to observe the imperatives of
Jewish law without imposing themselves on others as more religious European Jews—particularly Hasidim—often do. If anything, Oriental Jews demonstrate an almost existential attitude in
their religious observance, seeming to say: "This is our way. We
understand that yours may be different." The incidents reported in
Israel of religious zealots trying to impose their views and practices
on the rest of the community invariably involve European Jews.
That kind of narrow self-righteousness is not the style of Oriental
Jews, who tend to be reserved, moderate, and tolerant in their
religious observance, tempering a strict approach with common
sense.

According to one story popular in Israel an American woman
boarded an Israeli bus and sat down next to a Hasid, who immediately jumped up and took another seat rather than sit next to a
woman. The woman, offended and upset, turned to another pas-
senger and said, "Did I do something wrong?" The other pas-
senger assured her that she had done nothing wrong, it was simply
that the Hasid, because of his religious convictions, would not sit
next to a woman. A few moments later a Sephardic rabbi boarded
the bus and despite several seats being empty, he chose the one

next to the American woman. Bewildered, the woman could not resist asking the rabbi to explain his actions. "I don't understand," she said. "That other rabbi has a beard like you. You both have a cane. You're very much alike. Yet he moved when I sat down here and you deliberately chose this seat. Why?"

"It's simple," the Sephardic rabbi replied. "He is a Hasid. I am a *hacham* [wise man]."

The conflict and tension between the two cultures is often on a rather mundane level and contains an element of humor. An Israeli, who is of Ashkenazic origin but who is often mistaken for a Sephardic Jew because of his olive-colored skin, recalled how he had been waiting for a bus in Tel Aviv once to take him to Jerusalem. Two older women, clearly of Oriental extraction were sitting on the sidewalk, also waiting. They asked him to tell them when the bus arrived since they were unable to read Hebrew and would not be able to identify the bus they were waiting for.

"I told them no problem, not to worry since I was waiting for the same bus. I stood where the line would form and when the bus came, I told the women to get on. Another person waiting in line, an older man who wore a black coat and who was clearly a religious Ashkenazi said the women should go to the end of the line. I told him that they had been waiting since before he came, although not in the line. No matter, he said, they should go to the end of the line. I let them get on in front of me in spite of him. So then he complained to the driver, really made a fuss and said the driver should take me to the police. The driver shrugged his shoulders. One of the old women pulled me aside, and obviously assuming that I was also Sephardic, said to me, looking at the Ashkenazi, 'They're always like that.' "

Homely incidents like these serve as reminders of a continuing perception on both sides of "us" and "them." As long as poverty is identifiable as a particularly Oriental malady, the problem will probably remain. Conflict in Israeli society is aggravated by the commitment of the Israeli government to the principle of facilitating Jewish immigration from other countries. Since the Soviet Union is the only remaining potential source of large-scale immigration, this policy means that the Israeli government, directly and through the Jewish Agency, is offering benefits to Russian Jews that are denied to native Israelis. This disparity is a special source of tension and anger for Oriental Jews living in crowded apartments who cannot understand why immigrants who have not served in the Israeli army, and who have not fought in any wars to protect Israel, should receive benefits and assistance denied to persons already in Israel.

Since the early 1970s the Israeli government has begun several programs consciously aimed at improving the condition of Oriental Jews. In the country's larger cities an effort has been made to integrate high school populations as far as is practically possible. Government statistics indicate that, on paper at least, the educational gap between children of European-American and Oriental origins is being eliminated. In 1967 Oriental children were about one half of the country's population in the 14–17 age group, but only 36 percent of the school population for the same group. In 1979 Oriental children were 58 percent of the 14–17 age group population and 52 percent of the student population for the same age group. The gap between the percentage of Oriental fourteen-to-seventeen population and Oriental school attendance had been narrowed from 14 percent to 6 percent.

Disparities still exist, however. Oriental children in 1979 constituted a disproportionately large part—64 percent—of the students attending agricultural and vocational schools, while only 39 percent of the students in academic high schools were of Oriental origin (as opposed to 25 percent in 1967). In Israel's universities more than 72 percent of the students were of Western origin in 1978, as opposed to 18 percent of Oriental background. In 1965, 12 percent of university students had Oriental origins.

Optimists in Israel note that with time and patience ethnic differences in Israel will be largely erased by intermarriage. More than 20 percent of marriages in Israel annually are "mixed," and the number is increasing by about .5 percent a year.

The impression left by looking at these statistics is that the situation of Oriental Jews in Israel is slowly improving. But it

171

would be a mistake to assume that what the statistics reflect is necessarily what the population feels. Government attempts to erase educational and economic differences between Ashkenazic and Oriental Jews have resulted in a predictable backlash among some Ashkenazic Jews who resent what they see as unjustifiably preferential treatment. The "us" and "them" perception of each side toward the other, the grievances and recriminations expressed, the sense of mutual disdain lying just below the surface— all of these unquantifiable factors indicate that Israel is far from a fully integrated society.

This appearance is borne out by election results. Although Israel has so far avoided developing overtly ethnic parties, a pronounced split is developing in the electorate. Both the Labor Alignment and the right-wing Herut party campaign for the Oriental vote (as does the National Religious party). Oriental voters, who voted primarily for the Labor Alignment and its predecessors in the 1950s and 1960s, have been gradually moving to the right, toward Herut. In 1969 the Labor Alignment received 55 percent of the Oriental vote; in 1973, 38 percent; and in 1977, 32 percent. At the same time, the Herut-dominated Likud party and its predecessor, Gahal, received 26 percent of the Oriental vote in 1969, 39 percent in 1973 and 46 percent in 1977, clearly eclipsing the Labor Alignment as the party of choice for Oriental voters. The phenomenon of a right-wing proletariat, not entirely exceptional, is still unusual. It was largely because of the growth of the Oriental community and its shift away from the Labor party that Menachem Begin was elected prime minister in 1977. In power, the Likud party (of which Herut is the dominant faction) did not significantly improve the most serious material problems of Oriental Jews. In fact, since inflation generally hurts poorer members of society the most, Oriental Jews economically may have been worse off after four years of Likud government.

Despite these economic difficulties Oriental Jews appear to be staying with the Likud, a shift that reflects the more hawkish, conservative, chauvinistic sentiments of the Oriental community in Israel. These attitudes are also reflected in the rightward drift of the Labor Alignment. Older Israelis of European background appear bewildered by the change that has come over the country, by the gap that has grown between Jews of Oriental and European background, and by their own diminishing power within Israeli society. Still the dominant force by virtue of their control of major institutions, Ashkenazic Jews are becoming acutely aware that their pre-eminence is being challenged. The growing influence of Oriental Jews in Israeli society means that they not only have greater visibility and power in politics, but also that attitudes and public policy may change. Oriental Jews are more isolationist and less sympathetic to the rights of Israeli Arabs than Ashkenazic Jews, who are steeped in the more conciliatory ideology of Labor Zionism.

The rise of Oriental Jews in Israel has coincided with, indeed has contributed to, the decline of Labor Zionism as the dominant power in Israel, a change of profound significance for Israel.

5 / POLITICS

At the ebb of its political fortunes in 1974, with the country still suffering from the trauma and near disaster of the 1973 war, Israel's ruling Labor Alignment turned to Yitzhak Rabin to head a coalition government and restore public confidence in the Israeli government and the party.

On the face of it the choice was a masterstroke. Rabin, fifty-two when he became prime minister of Israel, was the youngest person ever to serve as head of government. Shy and somewhat withdrawn, Rabin was the first native-born Israeli to be prime minister. His Labor Zionist credentials were impeccable. Although he had spent almost his entire adult life in the Israeli army, he had been educated at the Kadouri Agricultural School in the Plain of Esdraelon (Jezreel Valley)—the Choate and Exeter of the prestate Jewish community (the Yishuv). Rabin had served with distinction in the Palmach, the shock troops of the Yishuv, then rose through the ranks of the Israel Defense Forces, eventually planning and commanding the incredibly swift, brilliantly executed victory in 1967. The year following the war Rabin moved to Washington as Israel's ambassador, consolidating the closer ties between Israel and the United States that had been developing through the 1960s and acquiring for Israel badly needed sophisticated weapons systems. In 1973 Rabin returned home, not many months before Egypt and Syria attacked Israel.

Having been absent from Israel much of the time since 1967, Rabin was one of the few public figures whose image was not tarnished by the 1973 war. With a party and government largely controlled by septuagenarian immigrants from Eastern and Central Europe, Israel was ruled by men and women who had less and less in common with the new generation of sabras born and reared in Palestine or Israel. With Rabin's ascension, it seemed possible that the Labor aristocracy could maintain its grip on power to some extent, bowing to the inevitable passage of time but without undergoing a radical transformation.

The Labor Alignment's gamble on Rabin did not pay off. The party was already badly split. The intelligentsia and middle-class, which had grown up and prospered under Labor rule, had become dissatisfied with the party's inability or unwillingness to deal with chronic domestic problems, with Labor's inflexible and unimaginative policies regarding the Arabs, and with growing incidents of corruption. Either because his political talents were unequal to the task or because the task was too great for even the most skilled politician, or perhaps because of both, Rabin failed to revive the ruling Labor aristocracy's declining fortunes. In the 1977 elections, for the ninth Knesset (Israeli parliament), the Labor Alignment was turned out of office by the right-wing Likud coalition party and its leader Menachem Begin. For the first time Israel had a non-Labor government. The country had embarked on a new era in its political history.

Although the point was not immediately grasped at the time, the 1977 election may well have signaled the beginning of an entirely new direction for Israeli politics. The most immediate interpretation of the 1977 upheaval was that the Israeli electorate was expressing its disapproval if not disgust with the Labor Alignment which, in one form or another, had formed the government since independence.

But deeper forces than simple disapproval were at work, forces that became clearer with the 1981 election when Begin and the Likud not only won another mandate to form the government, but increased their representation in the Knesset from 43 to 48 seats. The Likud was able to win in 1981 despite economic policies that had driven inflation to an annual rate of 135 percent and increased the dependence of Israel on American foreign aid and a foreign policy that had made Israel more isolated in the world community than at any other time in her history. Despite the ineptitude of the Likud in power, the Israeli electorate refused to restore the Labor Alignment to govern. New forces were asserting themselves—forces that found more in common with the tone and style of the Likud than with Labor.

At the same time, the bold attempt at political reform championed by the newly formed Democratic Movement for Change in 1977 had died by 1979. The reformers found that they not only had failed in their main objectives—changing the electoral system, curbing the power of labor unions, reducing Israeli dependence on American aid to name just a few—but, by opening the door to the Likud's entry to power, had discouraged any further efforts at reform for years to come. Reform-minded Israeli voters who had defected from Labor in 1977 in the hopes that they could encourage "their" party to alter its course, flocked back to it in 1981 for fear that their failure to support Labor—however unenthusiastic they were with the prospect—would open the way for Begin and the Likud to govern for another four years.

Indeed, a principal feature of the 1981 election campaign was the distaste with which many Israelis viewed both major parties. Labor was seen as having failed to use the four years out of power constructively to put its house in order. Begin and the Likud, after four years of hyper-inflation and several painful but unsuccessful attempts to bring the problem under control, were an equally undesirable alternative. The Hobson's choice facing Israeli voters was summed up in a joke told across the country prior to the election:

Two Israelis, Moshe and Amos, met on the street in Tel Aviv. Moshe announced to Amos that he was leaving the country, probably never to return.

Knowing that Moshe was an ardent patriot, Amos could not believe the news. "What is it?" Amos asked, deeply concerned. "You have a good job, a nice apartment, you love it here. What's making you leave?"

"I have two reasons," Moshe answered. "First of all, I just can't stand the government anymore. They're driving me crazy. I can't take Begin. I can't take the rest of them. I've got to get out."

"Okay, okay," Amos said, understanding and placating. "I know what you mean. I can't stand this government, either. But be patient. The Labor party will be back in power in another year or so."

"That's the second reason," Moshe said.

In fact, Israel's political problems go beyond the stagnation and corruption of the Labor Alignment on the one hand and the inadequacy of the Likud on the other. The current crisis of Israeli politics and government reflects changes in the composition of the population, the shattering of the consensus that had united Israelis until the 1967 war and a political system that frustrates efforts to put aside differences in an effort to fashion broad solutions to complicated problems.

Profound changes have overtaken Israeli politics since the state's establishment. Grasping at symbols and mouthing rhetoric from a vanished past, Israel in the 1980s was a country vastly different from what it was in 1948, or even 1968. The crisis of Israeli government and politics has to be understood first against the backdrop of the Israeli system of government and, second, in terms of the issues dividing Israeli society.

Some of Israel's problems are rooted in a system, never intended to be anything but temporary, that has endured for more than thirty years. Israel is a parliamentary democracy. The 120 members of the Israeli Knesset are elected every four years (or earlier if the Knesset calls for early elections). As with other parliamentary systems, if the government falls in a vote of confidence, a new government must be formed that has the confidence of the Knesset. The prime minister is customarily a member of the party with the largest representation in the Knesset. The other government ministers come from the prime minister's party and from some of the other parties composing the government coalition. Although it is theoretically possible for one party to win an absolute majority of seats in the Knesset, making coalition government unnecessary, in practice no party has ever done so. As a result, the dominant party has always been forced to seek the support of lesser parties in order to constitute a majority. This need represents one of the great weaknesses of the Israeli political system and accounts for much of the trouble that Israeli governments have experienced from time to time over the past several years.

Unlike the United States, the Israeli president is elected by the Knesset and is given largely ceremonial duties. The president serves as the formal chief of state, but the head of government is the prime minister. The president is not necessarily an inconsequential figure, though. Although basically apolitical, the men chosen to be Israel's presidents have been well-respected figures—academics as well as politicians and statesmen—whose pronouncements on current issues are usually couched in broad terms. Israel's judges, appointed for life, or until they decide to retire or reach age seventy—whichever comes first—are nominated by a special commission. The judges nominated by the commission are appointed by the president, who has no authority to reject the commission's recommendations. For the most part, Israeli judges do not have authority to strike down laws passed by the Knesset—although the Israeli Supreme Court has, on one occasion, done so, and the Knesset accepted the decision. On the other hand, the courts can and do issue orders restricting and barring actions taken by the government if the actions are contrary to law.

Because of fundamental differences over basic questions, Israel lacks a constitution. It is generally agreed in Israel that any attempt to write one would split the country and cause serious conflict within the Jewish community. Rather than drafting a constitution, the Knesset has passed a series of "basic laws," that can be changed at any time by a simple majority of the full Knesset.

Although theoretically supreme, the Knesset in fact is directed by the cabinet, whose ministers usually also sit as Knesset members. The Knesset's agenda is largely determined by the government, which also decides—through the prime minister—when to invoke party discipline, requiring members of the governing coalition to support the government. Once party discipline is invoked, if the government fails to win a majority vote, it must resign. Like the British model, only the Knesset can dissolve itself and call for new elections. The Knesset can also—by majority vote—extend its life, as it did in 1973 during the Yom Kippur War.

Knesset members are not elected from geographical districts as members of the British Parliament or American Congress are, but rather under Israel's proportional representation system they are elected from party lists according to the number of votes cast for the party. Thus, the higher a candidate stands on the party's list, the more chance he or she has of serving in the Knesset. The selection of candidates, though nominally democratic, is open to the same sort of manipulation by a small coterie of powerful individuals found in any political system—whether democracy or authoritarian state. Other countries employing proportional representation generally combine it with other systems. Israel is unique in using the system in its pure and undiluted form.

The great strength of Israel's political system is also its great weakness. The system assures that any minority of one percent or more of Israeli voters who feel strongly about a particular issue can be represented in the Knesset. In other words, roughly seventeen thousand voters can elect a member of the Knesset. Voters who care passionately about a single issue—even if they are thinly dispersed around Israel—may be able to muster enough votes of like-minded people to elect one or more members to the Knesset. Once elected, such a member or members will be part of a group of 120 and obviously will have difficulty accomplishing much of a controversial nature, yet they will have one vote and when circumstances work in their favor can bargain with that vote to great advantage.

One immediate effect, then, of Israel's political system is a proliferation of small single-issue or minority-interest splinter parties. As a result, no major party has ever been able to win a

LAWRENCE MEYER

majority of seats and must, therefore, negotiate with smaller parties to win majority support and form a government. Parties themselves may represent an uneasy alloy of factions, which further complicates negotiations. In the ninth Knesset, for example, twenty-four factions were represented (including fourteen in the government).

Israel's system presents political parties with an entirely different set of problems from those faced by parties in countries with single-member districts. Political candidates from single-member districts run in a winner-take-all contest that encourages them to take a position appealing to the broadest possible base. Focusing on a single issue may win a candidate the devoted following of a minority of voters, but not the election.

In a single-member district election the candidate must address a broad range of issues, fashioning a comprehensive program based on compromises and moderate rather than hard-line positions. The voter must buy a "package" even though he may not support all of its parts. On the other hand, the Israeli system allows for the proliferation of special interest candidates and parties. If neither of the two major parties offers a mix that is appealing, the voter can turn to the National Religious party or to the even more rigidly Orthodox religious parties that offer candidates, to a left-wing party that emphasizes reconciliation with the Arabs, to a right-wing party that supports getting tough with the Arabs, or to a moderate party emphasizing consumer rights or civil liberties or the needs of working mothers. Arab voters also can choose among special lists of Arab candidates offered for them by the major parties or the list of the Arab Communist party. The only time a vote is utterly wasted is if the voter's choice of parties fails to win the requisite minimum number of votes to qualify for one seat. Once elected, small-party members can bargain with the winning party, which is looking for enough votes in the Knesset to form a majority. In the right circumstances small minorities can have enormous influence. The National Religious party—never able to win more than fifteen percent of the vote in any election—has participated in every government, securing major concessions on behalf of religious interests, concessions that a majority of the population is either indifferent to or, in many cases, opposes.

This political system has its roots in the prestate Zionist movement, when Herzl and his successors were trying to win support for the Zionist program among the far-flung Jewish communities of the world. A system of proportional representation guaranteed minority participation, allowing minuscule groups to have their say. Better, the Zionist leaders decided, to have a large movement with turmoil within than to have a small movement of like-minded persons. Prior to the creation of the state four basic groups composed the Zionist movement: the Labor Zionists, comprising a range of left-wing movements from democratic socialists to Marxist-Leninists and Stalinists; General Zionists, who focused on the general issue of creating a state with less interest about its economic form; religious Zionists, who were concerned with the spiritual foundation of a Jewish state; and anti–Labor Zionist Revisionists who were antisocialist and also militant in their demands for a Jewish state comprising all of Mandatory Palestine (both sides of the Jordan River). These four basic groups by no means exhaust the points of view that existed in the Zionist movement, but they represent the largest groupings.

Since the State of Israel was born under duress, in time of war and without an orderly transition from colonial rule, Israel's first government had to be installed without first holding lengthy deliberations and negotiations to establish a form for it. The quasi-governmental institutions of the Zionist movement and the Yishuv were simply transformed overnight into the government of the State of Israel. Proportional representation was one of the institutions "temporarily" adopted by the new state.

Once instituted in Israel, though, the system of proportional representation was virtually impossible to alter without one political party or another winning a majority of seats and voting to change the system. The attraction of the system for minor parties is the influence it gives them with the major parties when they are forming a government, and afterward when they are actually governing. The slimmer the majority—especially when the par-

181

ticipating parties have little in common other than a desire to share power—the greater the leverage the small party has over the large party forming the government. Rather than encouraging compromise, the system leads to fragmentation.

From the outset Israel's first prime minister, David Ben-Gurion, attempted to alter the system, which he saw as responsible for Israel's recurring government crises. Although nominally more democratic because it allowed a "fuller, more accurate, and more faithful reflection of public opinion," proportional representation, according to Ben-Gurion, was in fact a less democratic system than single-member districts because elected representatives were responsible not to a constituency but to their parties. The party chose them to stand for election, determined their position on the list (the higher the placement, the better the chance of election), and decreed what they should vote for and what they should vote against.

After Israel's first election, Ben-Gurion noted,

> the small factions, without whom no majority government could be formed, were interested in preserving the proportional election system. Thus there came into being a large number of small parties whose programs held no interest for the majority of the nation, which was denied its basic democratic right of a real choice of the government. Its composition was decided after the election by the parties alone.

The voter, Ben-Gurion noted, had no direct connection with the representatives for whom he or she voted, and the representatives had no voice in drawing up the list of candidates. The interests of the party, as dictated by an inner circle of party leaders, became supreme. In the elections for the second Knesset, 800,000 voters chose among 17 party lists, of which 15 won one or more seats in the Knesset. In the third Knesset, 10 factions were represented (12 after Mapam—a left-wing party—split). In the ninth Knesset, 13 parties won representation. In the tenth, 31 parties offered lists and 10 won representation.

Rather than uniting the country, Ben-Gurion and other critics argue, the electoral system Israel uses results in a multiplication of parties that aggravate divisions.

From a practical point of view, this system also poses profound problems. Unlike Great Britain, Canada, or the United States, where the electoral system works to limit the number of parties, the opposition in Israel is a collection of disparate forces—left and right, Zionist and anti-Zionist, socialist and capitalist—that have little in common beyond their opposing the government. Most important, the opposition in Israel is not prepared to govern because its elements have so little in common they are not able to offer a practical, programatic alternative to the government. Thus, the opposition in Israel cannot be responsible in the sense of offering an alternative to the government. The opposition can say only "no," and, Ben-Gurion observed, "It educates its public to national irresponsibility."

Israel's system also hampers the governing coalition which must act, and must maintain a majority to do so. Ben-Gurion wrote:

> Yet in a situation of party fragmentation, when no one party has a majority, even a relatively large party, without which no government can be formed, requires the cooperation of smaller factions, which affords opportunity for subtle moral extortion by these groups. They appeal to a small minority only, not in the name of the needs of the nation as a whole but in the name of marginal interests with only minority appeal. Yet they are able to impose upon the majority policies it might have rejected outright had it been truly free to do so. Owing to the nature of coalition governments, it has no choice. Without these small factions, there can be no majority, while the opposition is incapable of forming a government. The door is thus open to improper extortion, and a proportional election system provides practically no means of correcting this grave fault.

In addition to the problems proportional representation presents, there are other structural quirks of the Israeli system that make governing more difficult.

Until 1981, the prime minister could not dismiss a minister who refused to resign. The only way the minister could be removed was to dismiss the entire government and re-form it without him or her. The law was changed in 1981 to give the prime minister authority to remove individuals, but as a practical matter it still is difficult to remove a minister when he belongs to a party other than the prime minister's.

Furthermore, the prime minister, though nominally the head of government, cannot control the action of another minister or the ministry that he directs. Each ministry is a semi-independent branch of the government, often working at cross-purposes to other branches—especially since the ministers represent different parties with different priorities.

The prime minister even lacks control of the government budget, unless he chooses to be finance minister himself. Otherwise, the prime minister must find a finance minister willing to coordinate the national budget with the government's program as determined by the cabinet.

Since particular parties may control certain ministries for years on end, those ministries may become instruments of the party controlling them rather than instruments of the state. The National Religious party, for example, has controlled the Ministry of Interior for years, using the ministry to distribute government funds to selected religious institutions in a way that strengthens the religious party's political base. No effective mechanism exists to hold the ministry accountable for the way it disburses the funds.

Every government, attempting to enact and implement long-term programs, has to make political compromises with groups whose immediate interests are affected. Israel's system of government makes long-term planning even more difficult by denying the government a stable majority that gives it a margin of time and breathing room in order to pursue its policies.

This system never worked well in Israel, but it functioned adequately so long as a consensus existed on the most important issues confronting Israeli society. When deep disagreements arose—occasionally threatening to aggravate divisions within the country—short-run accommodations rather than solutions were found, since the system enabled minorities to block long-range answers. With the present absence of a consensus on vital issues, with the country divided on a number of questions, with leadership weak and uncertain on what direction to take, Israel's system encourages inaction and stagnation, drift rather than initiative, while the problems grow, becoming more serious, more difficult to master.

The Labor Alignment's status is greatly diminished today from what it was in the prestate era and in the first two decades of Israel's history. Although the name and even the composition of the Labor coalition changed in the period between 1948 and 1977, the central core remained the same. The coalition was dominated by the same moderate socialists who were preeminent in the Yishuv. Because political parties in Israel preceded the state, and because of the quasi–self-governing nature of the Jewish community before the state's creation, the Mapai party was involved in a number of enterprises. The leadership of Mapai was, for all intents and purposes, also the leadership of the Histadrut. This centralization of leadership gave the new state a tremendous leg up in its early years, since the energy and resources of labor could be put to use serving the purposes of the new government, avoiding draining, counterproductive struggles among unions, industry, and government. Although disagreements might emerge within the organization, policy could be made under one roof and coordinated to maximum effect. Once the government decided to locate a development town, the Histadrut could be called upon to set up a factory there to provide jobs, while the Histadrut's medical service, Kupat Holim, would open a health clinic. These moves, in turn, strengthened the Histadrut and the governing Labor coalition.

Prior to 1969, when a merger of parties was achieved within the Labor bloc, the principal Labor party was Mapai, an acronym meaning "the Land of Israel Workers' Party." The history of Mapai gives an idea of the peregrinations of political groupings in Israel. Mapai was formed in the prestate era of 1930 by the merger of two groups—Achdut Ha'Avoda (the Union of Labor) and

185

HaPoel HaZair (the Young Worker). These original foundations were not firm. In 1944 the Union of Labor broke away from Mapai to become an independent party, and then in 1948 joined with the left-wing HaShomer HaZair (the Young Watchman) to form the Mapam Party (United Workers), a Marxist-party. In 1954 the Union of Labor group split off from Mapam, formed a separate party for a time, and eventually rejoined Mapai to form the Ma'Arach (Labor Alignment). By 1969 Mapam also had softened its Marxist line and had rejoined Mapai in the Labor Alignment.

The issues causing these various shifts and schisms may seem trivial or quaint now, but they were real enough at the time. Some of them had to do with how best to approach Israel's Arab neighbors, others with how Israeli socialism should confront Stalin's communism. Time has softened the divisions among Labor's left-wing factions, especially as the Israeli electorate has grown more conservative, but scars remain from earlier battles, complicating relations within the Labor Alignment.

Although never able to win an absolute majority of seats in the Knesset, Mapai or the Labor Alignment, which succeeded it in 1965, was the major party in each of the coalitions forming the government from 1949 until 1977. That preeminence helps explain how Mapai's leaders were able to confuse the party with the government and the government with the state. In the prestate period Mapai was associated with the kibbutz movement, with pioneering efforts to resettle the land, with industrialization, with formation of a defense force, with provision of health and medical services, and of course, with the formation of the country's largest labor union. Mapai did not, in the prestate period, bear the ultimate responsibility of governing. That responsibility rested with the British.

When Israel became a state, Mapai was clearly the core of the establishment in Israel, a status that gave the party great strength but also lay at the heart of Mapai's future problems. A classic kind of power elite existed in Israel, a relatively well-defined circle whose members were able to move from one institution to another

—from army to industry, from Histadrut to government—under the guidance and protection of Mapai.

Although Israel is not and was not a one-party state, and Mapai never had a monopoly of power, its dominance was so complete that the party and government were virtually synonymous. Other political parties saw their role as moderating Mapai's direction rather than replacing it. An illustration of Mapai's preeminent position was given in a 1956 report of a Mapai party official:

> I once came to a regional council and spoke on a particular subject. A member got up and asked: Why is there no doctor here? I said to him: I come from Mapai headquarters and not from *Kupat Holim* [the Histadrut Sick Fund] headquarters. He answered me: "Everything here is Mapai . . ." For this member and many like him there is only one address. He sees the party at the head of the government, at the head of the Histadrut, at the head of the municipal authorities, at the head of the local government authorities, at the head of *Kupat Holim*, at the head of *Solel Boneh* [Israel's largest construction company], at the head of the labor exchanges and before him there is drawn the image of a party that can do everything, and therefore he directs all his demands to it, and rightly so.

Mapai's dominance was enhanced after 1948 by the dismantling of many institutions set up to perform government functions in the prestate era. Private militias affiliated with political movements—the left-wing Palmach and the right-wing Irgun Z'vai Le'umi paramilitary forces—were disbanded. Separate educational institutions maintained by various political parties, were merged into a state system. (Significantly, though, religious schools were permitted to continue, under state supervision if not always under state control.)

The Histadrut was not dissolved, nor was its medical service, the largest supplier of health care in the country. The country's kibbutzim and moshavim (collective and cooperative farms), also closely affiliated with Mapai, were not disbanded. The political and social consensus of Israel in its early years was decidedly left of center. Until 1969 left-wing parties held no fewer than fifty-nine seats in the Knesset, with the balance of power tipped in Mapai's favor by the dominant labor-oriented HaPoel HaMizrachi faction of the National Religious party. Mapai was able to maintain the support it enjoyed among Israelis who had come to Palestine prior to the establishment of the state and to use its dominant position to offer assistance and guidance to new immigrants who understandably had difficulty distinguishing between Mapai—whose tentacles reached everywhere—and the state. The shrewd immigrant learned early that allegiance to Mapai had its benefits, especially in the form of *proteksia.* One story popular in Israel's early years described how a new immigrant, briefed to announce his loyalty to Mapai early and often, made his way through the entry procedures immediately upon arriving in Israel. When he stopped at the customs counter, the clerk looked up and asked the immigrant, "Have you anything to declare?"

"Yes," the immigrant blurted out. "I'm a member of Mapai."

Although democratic in formal procedure, Mapai's internal style in those early years is better characterized as Bolshevik. Decisions were made by a tight inner circle of party leaders and passed down through the hierarchy. The party leadership developed a paternalistic attitude toward the citizens of the country. The party was seen as being, through the government, the source of benefits for the people rather than as an instrument for governing. At the top of this structure stood one of the party's founders and its most illustrious leader—David Ben-Gurion.

Although some Israelis today still bristle at the mention of his name, Ben-Gurion was one of those rare leaders who was able to meld ideology and pragmatism, a vision of the future with the demands of the present. With his high-pitched voice and Polish-accented Hebrew, his diminutive stature and shock of unruly white hair, Ben-Gurion was an unlikely figure for a charismatic leader. But he possessed an iron will, a keen intellect, and a gift of oratory that enabled him to dramatize situations and rally support to his position. In the early days of the state, when confronted by opposition within his own party, Ben-Gurion was able to carry the day on several occasions by threatening to resign, a move that would have left Mapai without its most readily identifiable popular symbol.

Even with Ben-Gurion at the head of the Mapai ticket, the party was never able to win 50 percent of the vote. Mapai's best showing with Ben-Gurion at the top of the list was 40 percent in 1959. Consequently, Mapai always had to enter into coalitions with other parties. Its principal and perennial coalition partner was the National Religious party, itself the product of a merger of two religious factions—Mizrachi and HaPoel Mizrachi.

Until 1967 the National Religious party (NRP) focused its concern almost solely on domestic issues, primarily on matters directly involved with religious affairs—observance of Sabbath, supervision of dietary laws, and prevention of any change in the law defining "who is a Jew"—as well as welfare services. In return for being given its way in these areas—within limits—the NRP lent its support and its votes to Mapai and its successors, providing it on several occasions with the margin of majority. The alliance was not always an easy one, since elements within Mapai were antireligious and elements within the NRP were antilabor. The relationship endured until 1976 when a nominally religious issue —the ceremonial reception by the government of new fighter planes in Israel on the eve of the Sabbath—broke up the relationship. The real reason for the split was far deeper and more serious, revolving around the changing politics of the NRP and the territories captured in 1967.

The 1967 war injected a new issue into Israeli politics—the disposition of territories captured in the war. The most tangible result of the war had been the occupation by Israel of the Sinai desert, the Gaza Strip (a thin salient extending from the Northern Sinai into Israel on the coastal plain), and the Golan Heights bordering Syria and the West Bank of the Jordan; and the unification of Jersualem. In the initial period after the Six Day War in

1967, it might have been possible for Israel to negotiate with some or all of the combatants in the war—Egypt, Syria, and Jordan—for the quick return of some or all of the territory Israel had captured. Israel did not seek the initiative in negotiating with the Arabs. Israel's position was characterized by the statement made soon after the war by then Minister of Defense Moshe Dayan. "We're waiting for a phone call," Dayan said.

The phone never rang. Negotiations did not take place in that early postwar period, prior to the hardening of positions. Sentiments began to develop in Israel against returning the territories. Within a month of the war's finish the Knesset enacted legislation facilitating the annexation of Arab Jerusalem, so that Jerusalem—divided since 1948—was entirely under Israeli sovereignty. Steps were quickly taken to "create facts," in the time-honored Zionist tradition, so that Jerusalem could not again be redivided. Concerning Jerusalem, opinion was virtually unanimous that Israeli sovereignty over it should not be relinquished.

The reasons for opposing return of the territories ranged from expressions of concern for security and the need for maintaining defensible borders against future attacks, to unvarnished imperial urges, overlaid with arguments about historical boundaries of ancient Israel, and a religious view of the war as the modern fulfillment of God's promise to the Jewish people to grant them dominion over the biblical Land of Israel. ("To your descendants I give this land from the River of Egypt to the Great River, the River Euphrates" [Genesis 15:18].)

The religious view focused on the West Bank territories—the biblical lands of Judea and Samaria—which contained several sites of religious importance for Jews, including the burial place of the Jewish (and Arab) patriarch Abraham, of his son Isaac, and of Isaac's son Jacob; the resting place for the Ark of the Covenant near Shiloh; Rachel's Tomb in Bethlehem; as well as a number of other dwelling places and shrines. Since God, according to this view, had promised this land to the Jewish people, it was only natural that Jews should be allowed to settle it, and sentiment began to develop within Orthodox religious circles in Israel to permit Jews to return to Judea and Samaria and to establish permanent settlements there. This sentiment ultimately crystallized around the Gush Emunim (Bloc of the Faithful) movement, a group with a fervent sense of its mission and purpose in establishing settlements in the territories.

The Labor Alignment, with a more pragmatic attitude, tended to see the captured territories as a strategic asset, although some sentiment existed within the party for a more imperial view. For the most part, settlements sanctioned by the Labor government after 1967—in the initial period in any case—were in the Jordan valley, along the new border with Jordan, on the Golan Heights, and later in the northern Sinai, just south of Gaza. The reasons for these settlements had less to do with sentiment, imperialist urges, or religious nostalgia than with constructing a line of defense around Israel in the absence of peace agreements with Egypt, Jordan, and Syria.

Although the issue had created conflict within Mapai, the party's basic position had historically been to accept a division of Mandatory Palestine between Jews and Arabs. As early as the 1930s Ben-Gurion had been willing to settle for much less than all of Palestine (for less, in fact, than what Israel ultimately got after the War of Independence in 1948–49). Under Ben-Gurion's prodding, Mapai, although it assumed a Jewish right to all of the Land of Israel (as defined in the Bible and promised in the Balfour Declaration), was willing to make a pragmatic compromise for a State of Israel covering something less than the ancient land. Other groups in Israel—most significantly Zionist Revisionists—never gave up the hope that one day the borders of the State and Land of Israel would be the same.

Prior to 1967 this hope was submerged, since no one advocated fighting to gain control of Judea and Samaria (the only areas of interest from a religious point of view since neither the Sinai nor the Golan Heights were part of the biblical Land of Israel). After 1967 religious-nationalist sentiment began growing for permanent retention of Judea and Samaria. The Labor government, still relatively strong, resisted attempts to establish religious settlements on the West Bank, although a few settlements were grudgingly allowed. A younger, more militant group of politicians within the NRP started pressing for settlements on the West Bank, challenging the older, more moderate leadership of the party which had traditionally allied itself with Labor.

The 1967 war had released other currents within Israel that were weakening Labor's grasp. As the party of the establishment, Labor was, despite its socialist ideology, the party of the middle class, of professionals and academics, of Israelis who had been able to prosper with the growth and increasing affluence of Israel. Predominantly of European and American origin, nonreligious, socialist, and Zionist in outlook, Labor's constituency moved further and further from its proletarian origins with each generation. Far from being the party of the working class, Labor had become the party of management, of the bureaucracy, of thousands of persons who held government-supported jobs.

In the early years of the state, Labor's constituency was the bulk of Israel's population. In the early 1950s, though, a different kind of immigrant began arriving in Israel, not from Europe or America at all, but from Islamic countries—from Morocco, Tunisia, Algeria, Iraq, Syria, Yemen, and Turkey. These immigrants spoke Arabic rather than Yiddish. They tended to be religious. Their motivation for coming to Israel had less to do with Zionism—a movement about which they knew next to nothing—than with escaping religious persecution and economic deprivation, combined with a religious attachment to Israel. These immigrants had no feeling at all for the social and political currents of eastern Europe that had produced Israeli socialism. The bulk of them came without skills. Many were illiterate, emerging from societies that were still preindustrial.

These immigrants of "Oriental" background never found a comfortable home within Mapai or its successors. Wherever they turned, they found instruments of the ruling Labor aristocracy. Unskilled and unprepared for life in an industrial society, they constituted the core of the new proletariat in Israel. Jobs were provided, directly or indirectly, by the government. Welfare programs designed to ease the hardship and mollify them created the classic resentment found among welfare clientele. These Oriental Jews became the new underclass of Israeli society, shunted off by the government in the early years to "development towns" relatively remote from the population centers of the country, cut off from their birthplaces, traditions, and familiar culture.

Whatever economic problems hit Israeli society hit this group the hardest—housing shortages, unemployment, rising prices. Neither under Ben-Gurion nor under subsequent leadership did Mapai or its Labor successors adequately confront the challenge posed to its continued political domination by the enormous influx of nonsocialist, preindustrial, religious Jews who emerged from a non-Zionist background into Israel. For one generation, perhaps out of an urge to assimilate into their new country and because the Mapai was the source of its benefits—housing, jobs, subsidies—these Oriental Jews supported Mapai, but not necessarily with enthusiasm. The ideal of a socialist society had little meaning and no particular attraction for them. If they turned to farming, it was within the confines of the cooperative moshav rather than the collectivist kibbutz.

As they became more prosperous, but still less prosperous than the dominant European class, their dependence on Labor declined and their resentment—or their children's resentment—increased. The Ashkenazim had higher incomes. Ashkenazi children received a better education. The Ashkenazim profited from German reparation payments. It was Ashkenazic music that was played on the radio. Ashkenazim composed the leadership of the Labor party and its primary instrument, the Histadrut. The Oriental population constituted the underclass. Oriental Jews earned less and were the bulk of the population in the country's slums and remote development towns. Oriental Jews also suffered the most when a government-orchestrated recession struck in 1966.

Ultimately, the Labor aristocracy became the focal point for the resentment and pent-up frustration of the Oriental population. The Labor party in Israel was not, despite its assertions, an instrument of antiestablishment reform. Labor *was* the establishment in Israel and those disaffected with the establishment had to look outside of Labor for change.

Besides the economic difficulties Oriental Jews faced, they shared a memory of wrongs and indignities perpetrated against them in many of the Islamic countries from which they emigrated. They shared a hostile attitude toward Israel's Arab adversaries that found its expression in the supernationalistic program of Menachem Begin's Herut (Freedom) party. With each passing year the percentage of Oriental Jews in the population grew. By 1977 Oriental Jews were more than fifty percent of the population. This growth in Israel's Oriental population translated itself into increased support for Herut.

The Herut party traced its origins back to the Zionist Revisionists, the militant Zionist movement whose philosophy had been laid out by Vladimir (Ze'ev) Jabotinsky, a Russian Jewish journalist. The Revisionists had split off from the mainstream World Zionist Organization in the early 1930s when the WZO, under moderate leadership, had declined to assert openly that a Jewish state was the goal of Zionism. That difference was only one of many between the hard-line, uncompromising Revisionists and the moderate elements within the Zionist movement.

Herut, consistent with its Revisionist origins, believed strongly in a Jewish state occupying *all* of Mandatory Palestine, including that part of Palestine that is now part of Jordan. Herut also favored private enterprise rather than socialism, looking for support among the thousands of small merchants and tradesmen who came to Palestine from Poland in the 1920s and 1930s.

The spiritual essence of Revisionism was a belief in strength. Jabotinsky had been a tireless advocate in World War I of the formation of a Jewish legion to fight alongside the British. Within Palestine the Revisionists came over time to be identified with the Irgun Z'vai Le'umi (National Military Organization), or more simply, the Irgun, which had split off from the Yishuv's main defense force, the Haganah.

Where the Haganah focused on self-defense, the Irgun did not hesitate to attack Arabs in retaliation for attacks on Jews, or to attack the British for obstructing immigration of Jews from Europe to Palestine. On more than one occasion the differing convictions of the Irgun and the Haganah resulted in violence. During the War of Independence the conflict between the Irgun and the Haganah almost came to full-scale civil war between contending Jewish forces.

Jabotinsky, described by contemporaries as a spellbinding orator and a charismatic leader, was a brilliant translator, a poet, and a writer of some renown. He was also a romantic, given to grand gestures, florid manners, and blue-sky ideas. Chaim Weizmann, Jabotinsky's contemporary, described the Revisionist leader as having a "dual streak." Warm-hearted and generous, ready to help a friend in distress, "all of these qualitites were, however, overlaid with a certain touch of the rather theatrically chivalresque, a certain queer and irrelevant knightliness." Jabotinsky, according to Weizmann, lacked realism. "He was immensely optimistic, seeing too much and expecting too much." For his part, Jabotinsky, whose position came to be characterized as "maximalist," looked on Weizmann and others of more moderate persuasion as being "minimalist" Zionists.

The Revisionist movement depended upon the charisma of Jabotinsky to hold it together. Herut also has largely depended upon the personality of one man, Menachem Begin.

Begin, a soldier in the Free Polish forces, left the Polish army after arriving in Palestine during World War II. A lawyer by training, Begin was courtly in manner, bombastic in his oratory. He looked up to Jabotinsky, who had been his mentor in prewar Poland, and he, too, possessed many of the same romantic qualities that had characterized Jabotinsky. After Jabotinsky's death in 1940 the Revisionist movement was essentially leaderless. Begin's arrival in Palestine provided the Irgun, which had fallen into disarray, with a leader able to command the allegiance of the disaffected forces of the Irgun.

Begin's underground background as commander of the Irgun, his antisocialist politics, and his savage attacks on Ben-Gurion and other government officials as leader of the Opposition after the creation of the state effectively froze him and the Herut party he founded out of any government role for most of Israel's history prior to 1977. Ben-Gurion's firm rule had been that any party was a fit candidate for coalition partnership with Mapai "except for Herut and the Communists." Save for an interlude from June 1967 until 1970 when Begin (as minister without portfolio) and a few other Herut Knesset members had been invited to participate in a government of national unity during the crisis of the Six Day War and its aftermath, Begin and Herut had been in a state of permanent opposition to the government. This opposition, though short of violent, was not the tame variety of Her Majesty's Loyal Opposition in England or of Republican opposition to years of Democratic dominance in the American Congress.

Herut members, Arthur Koestler wrote in 1949,

> have inherited the Revisionists' maximalist program, their contempt for the official Zionist leadership, their sense of grievance and hatred of the parties of the left; but nothing of Jabotinsky's liberalism, Western orientation, European spirit. Their ideology was primitive chauvinism, their language a stream of emotional bombast accompanied by biblical thunderings.

With Begin as Herut leader and spokesman and Ben-Gurion as head of the government, the nature of the opposition took on a personal quality. In a very real sense the conflict between Begin and Ben-Gurion, between Herut and Mapai began in the state's first months and was not resolved for years after Israel's independence.

The most dramatic incident of many occurred during the midst of Israel's War of Independence in June 1948, when a small cargo ship loaded with Jewish refugees, weapons, and ammunition paid for by Irgun supporters was fired upon and sunk (after the refugees had debarked) by Israeli army forces acting under orders from Ben-Gurion. The sinking of the ship, the *Altalena,* followed negotiations between the government and the Irgun about control of the *Altalena*'s cargo. The government insisted that it was to have control of the cargo, since all military forces were by then under government command. The Irgun wanted to reserve a substantial part of the ammunition for its use, a position that Ben-Gurion and others saw threatening the sovereignty of the nascent state. When agreement could not be reached, the ship was ordered to be sunk. Both sides suffered fatalities and injuries, but civil war was averted by Begin's order to his followers not to retaliate. Nevertheless, the incident deepened the rift between the ruling Mapai and Begin and his followers. Echoes from the sinking of the *Altalena* still reverberate in Israeli politics.

For better or worse, the isolation of Begin and his party was virtually complete after the formation of the state. The major institutions of the new state—the Histadrut, the army, the Knesset—all were dominated in one way or another by Mapai.

At times Herut's opposition under Begin's direction took on a desperate quality. When Ben-Gurion proposed an agreement with Germany in the early 1950s calling for reparation payments by Germany to Israel and to individual Jews, Begin—though a member of the Knesset—incited a violent march and riot outside the Knesset building by opponents of the agreement. "There are some things worse than death," Begin declared in a speech to an assembled crowd. "This is one of them." Referring to the sinking of the *Altalena,* Begin said: "When you fired at us with a cannon, I gave an order, 'No!' Today, I shall give the order, 'Yes!' This will be a battle of life and death." In the ensuing melee, ninety-two policemen and thirty-six civilians were injured. The Knesset chamber was littered with glass and stones. (The Knesset was then located in the heart of downtown Jerusalem.) Order was not restored until Ben-Gurion called the army in to disperse the crowds. The following day Ben-Gurion told the Israeli public in a radio address that the state possessed "sufficient forces and means to protect Israel's sovereignty and freedom and to prevent thugs and political assassins from taking control and [to foil] prolonged acts of terror within the state."

While Begin referred to Ben-Gurion, from the dais of the Knesset, as "a fascist and a hooligan," Ben-Gurion could not bring himself to speak Begin's name, referring to him in his diary as "the leader" and on the Knesset floor as "the man sitting to the left of Yohanan Bader [Begin's deputy]."

Effectively frozen out of power for the first twenty-nine years of the state, Herut experienced much the same alienation from the dominant institutions of Israel that the dispirited Oriental population felt. While the Labor party was primarily a movement of Jews from Eastern Europe, Herut began attracting support from Israel's Oriental population. Begin's strident criticism of Labor's failure to improve the social and economic conditions of the so-called second Israel, his firmly nationalistic and unforgiving attitude toward the Arabs, his greater sympathy for religious observance, all won him a wide following among Oriental Jews.

As the Labor position after the 1967 war hardened concerning peace with the Arabs, Begin's position seemed comparatively less inflexible than it had previously. In 1969 Leonard Fein in his highly respected book on Israeli politics, *Israel: Politics and People*, dismissed Begin's call for permanent retention of the West Bank in a footnote: "True to his party's tradition, Menachem Begin presented a plan calling for permanent annexation of the West Bank and disfranchisement of its citizens. The plan was doomed, for most of Israel's leadership recognized it as a prescription for permanent instability." Time and circumstance proved otherwise, and Begin's proposal survived to form the heart of his plan—as prime minister—for autonomy for Arab citizens of the West Bank.

In 1965 Begin and Herut finally achieved the respectability and recognition they had so diligently sought. The Liberal party, a bourgeois, middle-class party of moderate to right-wing views, which traced its origins back to the mainstream General Zionist movement, merged with Herut to form first Gahal and then the Likud party. From the head of a large minor party Begin had emerged as the spokesman and leader of the Opposition by the mid-1960s. And from that point the fortunes of his party continued to rise.

By 1977 the Labor Alignment—in one form or another—had been in power for twenty-nine uninterrupted years. The period had seen remarkable accomplishments in Israel. The country's population had more than trebled. The population had become comfortable, even prosperous. But internal divisions, subordinated to the external security threat prior to 1967, had surfaced. No longer the party of revolution and change, Labor had become the party of the status quo; whereas Begin's Likud party—despite its right-wing nationalist orientation—had become the party of Israel's largely Oriental working class. The observation of French political scientist Maurice Duverger applies to the Labor Alignment of 1977: "When a left-wing party becomes dominant, its appetite for revolution is dulled. . . . Domination takes the zest from political life, simultaneously bringing stability. The dominant party wears itself out in office, it loses its vigor, its arteries harden."

By the late 1960s and early 1970s, the population of Israel was getting younger, while the leadership of the Labor Alignment was getting older. Ben-Gurion had split with Mapai in 1965 to form a rival faction. One of the issues that drove him out of the party was his demand that the older leadership give way to younger men and women, an idea that received a cold reception from the aging functionaries who were in control of Mapai and who had long chafed under Ben-Gurion's leadership. The immediate cause of Ben-Gurion's departure was the Lavon affair, a controversy dating back to the mid-1950s when Israeli secret agents in Egypt attempted to rupture relations between Egypt and the United States by blowing up an American installation in Cairo. The effort ended in disaster, with Israel's agents picked up by Egyptian authorities. The Israeli public learned of it only years later when information about the "security mishap" began surfacing in Israel, focusing on Pinchas Lavon, the minister of defense at the time of the original incident. The Lavon affair ultimately snowballed into a national furor, splitting Mapai and leading to Ben-Gurion's resignation as prime minister in 1963 and his departure from the party in 1965 after the Mapai leadership refused his demand for a full-scale investigation of the original incident to determine, among other things, "who gave the order."

Ben-Gurion's relations with the rest of the party leadership had become fractious by the time of his resignation. When he bothered to consult with his fellow cabinet ministers before making major policy decisions, Ben-Gurion often resorted to threats of resignation if he failed to get his way. Increasingly, his view of Israel's needs differed from theirs, and the bruises from past battles still smarted. When Ben-Gurion resigned as prime minister in 1963, the party chose Levi Eshkol—Ben-Gurion's personal favorite—as his successor.

The ascendancy of Eshkol, a shrewd if uninspiring politician, did not represent a continuation of Ben-Gurion's control and influence but rather what one student of Labor politics, Peter Medding, has called the triumph of organization over charisma and "institutional power over prophetic morality."

When Ben-Gurion left Mapai in the early 1960s, it was still unthinkable that the ruling aristocracy could be dislodged, even by its most popular symbol. The Labor aristocracy had had forty years to institutionalize its power—in much the same way that political machines in democracies everywhere become entrenched —by distributing patronage, finding jobs for supporters, doing favors, short-cutting bureaucratic procedures for supporters, and so on. Whatever Ben-Gurion's popularity, he could not hope to overcome self-interest in one stroke. The loss of Ben-Gurion and his supporters was compensated for by a rapprochement with Achdut Ha'Avoda, a kibbutz-based faction that split away from Mapai in 1944.

Ben-Gurion's imperious style of directing government affairs was replaced by a more collegial system, in which Eshkol was the first among equals, the choice of the apparatchiks of the Labor aristocracy who were in control of the party and the government. When Eshkol died in 1969, the crisis of succession was resolved with the choice of Golda Meir, whose selection was intended to be temporary, until someone acceptable to all factions of the party could be found.

Tough and courageous, Golda Meir came to the job of prime minister at the age of seventy-one. She was inflexible in her attitude and actions toward the Arabs and paternalistic in her view of the constituency to which she was ultimately responsible. Israel's position regarding negotiations with the Arabs hardened during Meir's premiership. It was also during her tenure as prime minister that the Israeli government, spurred on by Defense Minister Moshe Dayan and others in the cabinet, began constructing security settlements in the Jordan valley, the Golan Heights, and south of the Gaza Strip.

The government's strategic assumption after the 1967 war was that another war would not occur for at least ten years if Israel retained the territories captured in 1967. As doubts began to be raised about the validity of the assumption, criticism within the Labor Alignment was suppressed by attacking the critics in tones suggesting that they were disloyal. Between 1967 and 1973 whatever initiatives were launched, whatever "feelers" were sent out or received, no progress was made toward peace between Israel and its Arab adversaries.

These were years of unprecedented prosperity, although little progress was made toward eliminating the gap between Israel's poorest Jews—for the most part of Oriental background—and its wealthiest Jews—for the most part of European background. A vague feeling was growing among the educated and among the more idealistic segment of the Israeli population that something was going wrong with the Zionist dream. Israel was becoming an occupying power, even if the Arabs of the West Bank were prospering under Israeli rule. The old virtues of hard work and simple living were giving way to conspicuous consumption and growing dependence on Arab labor. And with much of the land already settled, no outlet existed for further pioneering.

Labor had come to be an organization with a vested interest in the status quo. Israeli politics were stable to the point of stagnation. Organization had long since replaced ideology, and the machine worked to keep itself in power rather than to pursue any bold or imaginative programs. Since disagreements over policy did exist, decisions were often deferred to avoid debates that could fracture the organization and loosen its grasp on power. This situation was tailor-made for drift, for decision by inertia, and for demagogic tactics designed to win support for one or another contender for power inside the organization.

After 1967, as no progress was made toward peace, criticism of the government's hawkish position began to be voiced by intellectuals and others concerned with the lack of movement. The critics were publicly rebuked with not so thinly veiled suggestions that they were undermining Israel's security. The party invoked the security situation to stifle criticism and public debate and to avoid discussion of controversial issues. This policy may have maintained a surface impression of consensus, but underneath the surface unrest and discontent were growing.

The Labor Alignment's machinery was increasingly dominated by party officials and functionaries, so that by 1971 more than eighty-five percent of the members of the party's dominant committee were insiders. Without an outlet for expressing its restiveness a large segment of the party's traditional constituency was becoming discontented. In the absence of a catalytic event, however, the curious passivity that infects Israelis when they are dissatisfied prevented any kind of meaningful protest.

With the approach of elections for the eighth Knesset in the autumn of 1973, the Labor Alignment based its platform on the twin planks of peace and prosperity. "There is peace on the banks of the [Suez] Canal, in the Sinai desert, the Gaza Strip, the West Bank, Judea, Samaria, and on the Golan," Labor boasted in its political placards. "The lines are safe. The bridges are open. Jerusalem is united. New settlements have been established and our political situation is stable. This is the result of a balanced, bold and far-sighted policy."

Labor's balanced, bold, and far-sighted policy was disrupted on October 6, 1973, when Egyptian commandos and tanks crossed the Suez Canal, while Syrian tanks, moving under a murderous artillery barrage, attacked Israeli forward positions in the Golan Heights. The Yom Kippur War had begun. When it was over, the political career of Golda Meir was effectively over, too, though she would remain in office for several more months. The Labor Alignment's platform of peace and prosperity, of self-confident assurances about Israel's continued security, had been rendered meaningless.

The elections were postponed two months. When they were held in December, Labor did not alter its slate from its original composition and managed to win 51 seats (as opposed to 56 in the previous elections in 1969), while the Likud (Herut and the Liberal parties combined) increased their representation in the Knesset from 26 to 39 seats. The elections had been held too soon after the war to allow new parties to be formed in opposition to the government's policy. Israeli political pundits read the 50 percent increase in the Likud's vote as a protest and speculated that Likud had reached the peak of its popularity.

Golda Meir experienced severe difficulties in forming a new government with her party's weakened mandate. Relations with the NRP were becoming increasingly strained, and she faced the possible departure of Defense Minister Moshe Dayan and Transport and Communications Minister Shimon Peres because of criticisms of Dayan within the party. At one point Meir proposed a minority government that would have had the approval of only 58 of the Knesset's 120 members. Ultimately, though, with Dayan and Peres agreeing to participate, Meir presented a government that was approved by the Knesset 62–46.

The situation was extremely fragile, however. Immediately after the war, criticism of Meir's diplomatic and security policies had been voiced within the Labor party. The government's stand-pat position that retention of the territories would protect Israel from attack for ten years had been ridiculed by the war. The arrogant and heavy-handed suppression of any criticism within the party or outside before the war only served to intensify feelings after it. Soldiers released from their units came, still in uniform, to protest the mismanagement that had left Israel so ill prepared for the 1973 war.

A special commission, headed by the president of the Israeli Supreme Court, Dr. Shimon Agranat, was appointed. An interim report, submitted to the government and made public in early

April 1974, called for the resignation of the army's chief of staff, David Elazar, and several other high-ranking officers. The report stopped short of holding Dayan or Meir responsible, however, for Israel's performance in the war.

When the report failed to include Dayan in its recommendations for dismissal, public demonstrations and meetings were organized calling on him to resign. Dayan supporters argued that if he resigned, Meir and her other advisers should also resign. Public pressure and debate mirrored the conflict within the Labor Alignment, giving public opinion leverage it normally lacks in Israeli politics—save at election time. Faced with the prospect of a Knesset debate over security policy in which she would be unable to win a vote of confidence, Meir resigned, automatically dissolving her government. It had lasted only a month, the shortest-lived cabinet in Israel's history.

The Labor Alignment was deeply divided over security policy, between those who wished to maintain the rigid prewar policy of integrating the territories into Israel and those who wanted to seek some accommodation with the Arabs in light of the war. More than that, however, Israel's performance in the war had underlined a growing feeling in Israel that political and moral corruption had infected the government as well as the society. The party had reached the point where major policy decisions were made by a handful of leaders at the top and passed down for rubber-stamp ratification by the appropriate bodies below.

When Meir announced her resignation and the powerful finance minister, Pinchas Sapir, declined to take her place as prime minister, the way was opened for an unprecedented vote between Rabin and Peres, the first time the party's leadership had been opened to a real contest. Rabin was selected by a vote of 298 to 254 of the party's central committee.

The contest between Rabin and Peres marked not only the passage of power to a younger generation of Israelis, but the end of Mapai's supremacy within the Labor Alignment. Neither Peres, who had deserted Mapai with Ben-Gurion, nor Rabin, who had been a member of the left-wing Palmach (shock troops) during the War of Independence, was a creature of the Mapai apparatus.

In the subsequent Rabin cabinet, Peres served as defense minister. As erstwhile rivals for the top position, Rabin and Peres were constantly at odds, privately and publicly, deepening divisions within the party. A politician more skillful and restrained than Rabin might have been able to cope with the situation, but Rabin, a moody, introverted, and complex man, was unable to heal the rifts within the party or to prevent Labor's traditional coalition partner, the NRP, from drifting farther away. More significantly, Rabin was unable to revive the party from the stagnation that had overcome it. Too long in power without any meaningful opposition, Labor had grown arrogant, assuming it ruled by right, protective of its vested interests and unable to respond in a creative or effective way to the growing problems of a changing population.

The firm consensus that had prevented any meaningful discussion of peace with the Arabs started pulling apart with the Six Day War. On the left it became possible for Jewish Israelis for the first time to engage in public debate and criticism of a rigid government policy that had reached a dead end with the 1973 war. In the absence of any change in Israeli policy, it was argued, Israel could only look forward to a succession of wars that would slowly bleed the country white.

On the right, with its traditional platform calling for retention of all territory from the historic Land of Israel, the Likud was finding support from new quarters. The militantly nationalist elements within the NRP, opposed to any territorial settlement, were pulling the NRP away from the Labor Alignment. Labor was fighting a losing battle against establishing new settlements in the occupied territories in addition to the "security" settlements already established in the Jordan valley, the Golan Heights, and the northern Sinai. Pressure was coming from these ultra-religious, supernationalist groups to allow them to settle near populated areas on the West Bank, not for strategic reasons, but to establish a Jewish presence in "all of Israel." These religious activists, employing the familiar rhetoric and displaying some of the outward spirit of early Jewish pioneers, were making a Zionist appeal that many Israelis found hard to resist. Although Rabin did resist the settlers, they received support from Peres, who did not avoid policies that brought him into open conflict with the head of the government in which he served.

The NRP, faced with a growing militant movement of young voters within its own ranks, no longer could be a silent partner in the Labor coalition, passively giving its proxy to the government in matters of foreign policy and security. The more Rabin resisted the demands of the settlers and the weaker the Labor government's position seemed, the more the NRP looked for a way out.

The split finally occurred when the ultrareligious Agudat Yisrael party offered a motion of no confidence in the Knesset after a ceremony held to welcome the arrival of the first F-15 fighter planes came close to infringing on the start of Sabbath observance. When two NRP ministers abstained in the vote—a breach of the coalition agreement—Rabin seized on the occasion to dissolve the government and call for new Knesset elections in May 1977—six months early.

The public mood was hardly favorable to the Labor Alignment. Rabin had not been able during his period in office to overcome the trauma that the Israeli public had experienced from the 1973 war. Israelis still felt betrayed by a government that had assured them, up to the eve of the war, that war would not come for years. When it came, the army was less than prepared and only a desperate effort by Israel—ultimately successful but at a dear cost of blood and treasure—saved the country. Even with the military success that was achieved in the war, many Israelis emerged from the experience disillusioned, distrustful, and convinced that something real in strategic terms had been lost by Israel, which had counted on its ability to deliver a swift and mortal wound to deter any Arab initiative to start a war. More than the strategic setback, however, the 1973 war also removed a bond of trust between Israel's citizens and its leadership. The war seemed to sum up much of what was wrong in Israel.

Labor had run out of program. Discontent was rising among the lower economic classes, which were not improving their relative position even as a new class of millionaires was growing, getting fat—according to conventional wisdom—on defense contracts and other government programs. Better-educated Israelis, the moderate left-wing elite of the society, found the Labor Alignment's approach stale. They also found that they had no effective voice in deciding Labor's policies, a reflection of a system that relies on party organization and discipline to maintain it. Labor had no adequate mechanism for keeping in touch with the wishes of its constituency.

The smell of corruption was in the air. In the months preceding the 1977 election two prominent members of the Labor Alignment were publicly accused of criminal wrongdoing. Asher Yadlin, director of the Histadrut's Kupat Holim health services and Rabin's nominee for governor of the Bank of Israel, the country's central bank, was convicted of accepting bribes and making a false income tax declaration. During his trial Yadlin claimed that the money had been turned over to the Labor party, and he implicated other prominent party members in illegal fund-raising activities.

A month and a half before Yadlin's conviction, Minister of Housing Avraham Ofer committed suicide, protesting his innocence, after charges were published accusing him of corruption as well.

The coup de grace came when a newspaper article revealed that Rabin's wife, Leah, maintained an illegal foreign-currency account in a Washington bank. Rather than admitting the charge at the outset, Rabin dissembled, offering a series of explanations of the account—undermining public confidence in his integrity as well. Ultimately, Rabin was forced to take a leave of absence as prime minister since legally he could not resign as head of a caretaker government, and he stepped down as his party's candidate for prime minister in the approaching elections.

These scandals made Labor rhetoric about socialism and equality appear a sham. In fact, Labor had long since done little more than pay lip service to socialism, relying on welfare programs, subsidies, and a complicated system of compensatory allowances for workers instead of making any concerted effort to realize equality between the more affluent voters who were its constituency and the less affluent who increasingly were not.

In the May 1977 election for the ninth Knesset, the Likud party, led by Menachem Begin, picked up 4 seats, increasing its strength to 43. Had Labor been able to limit its losses to those 4 seats, it would still have had 47 seats in the Knesset and would have had the right to try to form the government. Labor, however, lost not 4 seats but 19, leaving it with only 32. It had suffered massive defections, especially among the remaining Oriental voters in its constituency. Labor also lost votes to the centrist Democratic Movement for Change, a kind of good-government, reform party that included Labor party defectors, moderate liberals, and political neophytes like Professor Yigael Yadin, the army's second chief of staff and a renowned archaeologist. As a new party the DMC won an unprecedented 15 seats. A profile of the typical DMC voter showed him (and her) to be better educated and more affluent than the average voter, of European origin, and a resident of a large city rather than a development town or an agricultural settlement. Despite the rather elitist nature of the DMC the party's platform promised to make closing the social gap a priority item, along with moving the Israeli economy away from dependence on foreign aid and toward self-sufficiency. The DMC also tried to appeal to Labor's disenchanted constituency by holding out the prospect of democratic party procedures that would make it responsive to voters.

The Likud also suffered losses to the DMC, but these defections were more than compensated by the votes Likud picked up from voters who had previously backed the Labor party. Once in power, though, the strange alliance that constituted Likud started showing strains. Likud had been formed by the merger of the middle-class, bourgeois Liberal party, and the staunchly right-wing, nationalist, largely proletarian Herut party. What the two groups shared was a desire for power. Beyond that, however, their interests were not always the same, especially on economic matters. The Liberal party, which remained a formal faction intact within the

Likud (as Herut did also) had traditionally advocated a free-enterprise economy, a nationalist point of view (although moderate compared to Herut), the right of Israel to all of historic Palestine, religious tolerance for the rights of nonobservant Jews, and a pro-Western policy position.

Though Begin had long been the strong man of Herut and was the unchallenged leader of Likud, in power he proved unable to enact any major portion of his party's program beyond consolidating Israeli control of the West Bank. The Begin government's major accomplishment—the conclusion of a peace treaty with Egypt—was approved by the Knesset only with substantial support from the Labor Alignment. The Likud had no reservoir of talent because it had never held power before and it lacked appropriate institutions for developing talent.

Economic matters were largely turned over to the Liberal party, which lifted stringent currency controls that Israelis had lived under for twenty-nine years. Within two years, with the Israeli economy flooded with relatively cheap money borrowed abroad (where interest rates were lower than in Israel), inflation had increased from roughly 30 percent a year to 100 percent. The government lifted subsidies on basic food items to try to curb inflation. The hardest-hit segment of the population were the lower classes—Herut's basic constituency. Food prices shot up. Milk became a luxury item for poorer families.

At the same time that the government was reducing subsidies, millions of dollars were being spent to build new settlements on the occupied West Bank. Under relentless pressure from the militants of Gush Emunim, their supporters in the Knesset, and from Agriculture Minister Ariel Sharon, the government pursued a policy designed to tie the hands of future governments in negotiations concerning disposition of the territories.

Inevitably, though, the government's determined policy of establishing settlements on the West Bank created overt conflict within the Begin coalition, which soon deteriorated from a cohesive whole into what it in fact was a collection of factions with different—often clashing—priorities and programs.

Begin's proposal for limited autonomy for West Bank Arab residents failed to win the support of the government's foreign minister, Moshe Dayan, who eventually resigned and became a vocal public critic of the government and its policies. Similarly, Defense Minister Ezer Weizman, at one time one of the most popular figures in Israeli politics, began publicly criticizing Begin, the government, and its policies while still a member of the cabinet. Weizman finally followed the logic of his convictions and also resigned. Begin's government moved from one crisis to another, unable to enact any legislation beyond what was necessary to hold his fragile coalition together. On two occasions the superreligious Agudat Yisrael party pressured Begin into making changes in laws governing medical practices (abortion and autopsies) as the price for its continued support of the coalition. This pressure was the sort of "subtle moral extortion" that Ben-Gurion had warned Israel's system of proportional representation invited. Gush Emunim, by virtue of its ascending position in the NRP and the NRP's crucial importance to the government's existence, also was able to exert influence over policy far beyond its numbers.

Begin's West Bank settlement policy, pursued partially out of conviction and partially for political reasons, strained relations within the government and with Israel's principal ally, the United States. Liberal party members publicly complained at the government's open courting of Gush Emunim, a relationship that often seemed to have the tail wagging the dog. Herut members blamed the Liberals for the state of the economy. Other factions within the Likud made no secret of plans to withdraw and stand separately for election. When Begin tried at one point to assuage the Liberals, who complained they were underrepresented in the cabinet, he was blocked by the NRP and the DMC cabinet ministers, who resented any increase in Liberal party influence.

The Israeli public was treated to frequent public squabbles and abusive language from putative members of a government team. What in fact held them together was less a shared vision of Israel's needs and future than a desire to retain power, and the apprehension of many—which proved unfounded as it turned out—that years would pass before they would again have the opportunity to be in government. The government stood fast despite widespread defections that left it with only a bare majority in the Knesset. Public disaffection with the government grew but without effect on its ability to survive. In a system where the members of parliament are responsible to a constituency, a majority of parliament may decide to bring down the government in response to public pressure, individual members hoping to salvage a political future for themselves in the process. But in Israel members of the Knesset are responsible to the *party,* which places them on the ticket and determines, by position on the list, whether they have a realistic chance of election or not.

The problem was especially severe for Herut, which remained largely the creature of one man—Menachem Begin. Unlike the Labor Alignment, where organization had triumphed over charisma with Eshkol's succession of Ben-Gurion, Herut has little such organization. Herut is not a network of organizations in the sense that the Labor Alignment is. This difference gave Begin considerably more room for maneuver than a Labor leader might have, but it also called into question the future of Herut without its aging and ailing leader.

Begin's forte was rhetoric rather than organization, and he failed to institutionalize party leadership. On the contrary, Begin had discouraged the development of leadership by isolating and eventually driving out of the party anyone who opposed him. Ezer Weizman, a potential successor to Begin, had a kind of love-hate relationship with him. Despite his protests of allegiance Weizman often seemed to be measuring Begin's chair for his own future occupation. Begin viewed Weizman with suspicion, and the two finally parted company after Weizman's public criticisms of the government and his resignation as defense minister. Weizman ultimately was expelled from Herut in 1980 after he voted against the government (along with Dayan) on a vote of confidence.

The falling-out between Begin and Weizman left Herut without a single strong leader to succeed Begin who was able to appeal to a wide segment of the Israeli public. More than ever, Israel's system of government seemed ill-suited to the prevailing conditions. Personalities rather than ideologies were coming to dominate the political arena, and the fragmentation that proportional representation facilitated also opened the door to mischief.

The political crisis precipitated by the 1973 war is far from over in Israel. It has entered a quieter, less dramatic stage, but deep and significant problems—partly systemic and partly substantive—remain. A descending spiral of weak governments, unable to implement strong, necessary legislation could lead to further splintering of the consensus, making it that much more difficult for a strong, stable government to emerge.

Israel's central institutions are experiencing significant changes at a point when the economy, the society, and the country are under strong pressure internally and externally.

On the left the Labor Alignment, though still able to command a substantial portion of the vote, continues to suffer internal divisions growing out of battles over issues long since irrelevant.

Labor's constituency appears to be dwindling as well. It may be that Labor will have to choose between close adherence to its old socialist ideology, and its traditional constituency in the collective kibbutzim and cooperative moshavim on the one side, and the growing Oriental population, with its more conservative, nationalist views on the other.

The Oriental population is clearly taking hold of political institutions at the grass roots levels. The leadership of small towns and Histadrut workers' councils all over Israel is now predominantly Oriental. The top leadership of the Histadrut, a central institution of the Labor Alignment, continues to be dominated by European Jews, Labor's old guard, while the rank-and-file blue-collar membership is Oriental. The Histadrut has been gradually transformed from a labor *movement,* an organization with political purposes, to a trade union and conglomerate. Without a high level of ideological commitment to socialist principles among its membership, Histadrut membership becomes little more than a vehicle for increased wages and benefits for the worker. The distance between the Labor Alignment's leadership and the Histadrut's membership has grown.

Labor can no longer take its claim to power for granted as it did before 1977, a change with important, though still unclear, implications for the party's future. In the aftermath of Ben-Gurion's departure from the party, Labor was left with several power centers—the kibbutz movements, the Histadrut, the left-wing Mapam, and other factions—with different and sometimes conflicting programs. Holding this grouping together while reaching out to a portion of the public that has little or no interest in ideological disputes is a central problem for Labor's leadership.

Ben-Gurion had a personal following in the country. His successors were creatures of the organization, bound to work within it, rather than able to step outside it or appeal over the heads of the party functionaries to the Israeli public. Neither Eshkol nor Golda Meir had a mass following within the country that gave them an independent power base and the derived capacity to force acceptance by the party for programs that the organization opposed. In contrast, Ben-Gurion, holding out the needs of the state, was able to dissolve the elite Palmach units in order to depoliticize Israel's army. Later, despite internal party opposition, he was able to arrange German reparation payments because he had a personal following.

Far from having a personal constituency, in two salient events Eshkol and Meir were forced by the public to take actions against their wishes. Eshkol, on the eve of the Six Day War, was forced by a combination of external public and internal party pressure to relinquish control of the Defense Ministry to Moshe Dayan, despite the opposition of elements in Mapai to Dayan (who had left the party with Ben-Gurion in 1965). Meir, in 1974, was forced to resign as head of the party when it became clear that her leadership had been called into question by the public because of the 1973 war, even though Labor had retained control of the government after the war.

Rabin, a compromise candidate who had had only tenuous connections with politics before his formal entry in 1973, was really a creature of no faction. Rather than working to form his own broad-based support within the party, Rabin profited by being free of the taint associated with the 1973 debacle. He left the old divisions substantially as he had found them.

After Rabin's ignominious departure—following four years of acrimony with his original competitor for the party leadership, Shimon Peres—Peres took over control of the party. But Peres had been identified closely with Ben-Gurion and had left Mapai with Ben-Gurion, however reluctantly. Peres's identification with Ben-Gurion and those past battles was a stigma he continued to bear (along with suspicions about his integrity and trustworthiness).

Like Eshkol and Meir, Peres was not a Labor leader with widespread public support. Rabin had spent his entire period as prime minister fighting a series of skirmishes with Peres. When Peres succeeded Rabin, Peres had to worry continually about the dissident forces that grouped themselves around Rabin in opposition to Peres's leadership.

Leadership in the Labor party became steadily weaker after Ben-Gurion. While the inner circle that controlled Labor was able before 1973 to keep the peace and maintain its hold by mollifying a discontented but still relatively passive constituency, the 1973 war fractured the Labor leadership's hold, and the 1977 election found the party organization in disarray. The Likud victory broke the Labor party's monolithic hold on the institutions of power in Israel. Labor's status was changed irrevocably, and in comparison to its formidible position in the past, the party had lost the mystique of authority, no longer able to command the automatic support that had kept it in power for twenty-nine years of statehood.

The Labor Alignment continued to be torn by factional strife that centered not so much on issues but on personalities and control. The party organization made an attempt to open itself to influence from party members, especially from those who had deserted it in 1977. Even in returning to Labor's fold these former supporters did so less out of conviction than with a dispirited sense of resignation that they had no alternative, especially after the inept performance of the DMC, which fell apart less than two years after the 1977 election and had virtually no positive impact (judged by its party platform) on government policy.

The 1981 election established, among other things, that the

Likud's victory in 1977 had not been a fluke but rather signaled a profound change developing in the thrust of Israeli politics. Since the early 1950s, Begin and his Herut party (which merged with the Liberal party to form Gahal in 1965 and the Likud in 1973) had been capturing a steadily increasing portion of the vote.

Herut's improving fortunes were tied to the growth of the Oriental Jewish population in Israel and its increasing disaffection from the Labor Alignment. Although Israelis prided themselves on avoiding ethnic politics, the results of the 1981 election confirmed that an ethnic split was developing politically as well as socially. Neither party made overt ethnic appeals, but the political style and tone of the campaigns of Labor and the Likud were designed with ethnic targets in mind. The results of the 1981 election showed a majority of Oriental voters gravitating toward the Likud and a majority of European voters moving toward Labor.

Neither Likud nor Labor, however, was able to capture a majority of the total vote. In the 1981 election, the Likud won 48 seats to Labor's 47. Some of the small parties, especially on the left, were obliterated as Israelis concentrated on the two main parties, which together received 75 percent of the vote. In the ninth Knesset, thirteen parties were represented. In the tenth Knesset, elected in 1981, only ten parties won seats. The largest of these parties, besides Labor and Likud, was the National Religious party, which won six seats—half of what it had had in the ninth Knesset.

Ironically, despite the smaller representation of the NRP in the tenth Knesset (the more extreme religious party, Agudat Yisrael, won the same number of seats—four—in 1981 that it had received in 1977), its bargaining position with the Likud was stronger than ever. Since Labor refused to consider forming a government of national unity with the Likud, Begin had nowhere to turn to form a majority but to the religious parties, which exacted a heavy price for their support of the government—including increased exemptions for religious Israelis from military service and stricter enforcement of prohibitions of work on the Sabbath.

The political balance of power appeared to have shifted to the right with the 1981 election. Labor's electoral support, although roughly fifty percent more than it had received in 1977, was down considerably from the elections of the 1950s and 1960s when left-wing parties received a clear majority of the votes. Reflecting a consensus away from collectivism in Israel, the Labor Alignment in its 1981 campaign avoided mentioning socialism. In this paler incarnation, left-wing parties received only about forty percent of the vote. Indeed, it was possible to argue that center and left-of-center parties had not increased their representation at all in the Knesset between 1977 and 1981. Rather, Labor's increased vote in 1981 was at the expense primarily of left-wing and moderate parties, whose supporters were decidedly unenthusiastic about Labor's returning to power, but even more fearful of another four years of the Likud.

With the religious parties showing a clear preference toward aligning themselves with the Likud rather than Labor, Israeli political pundits were beginning to talk in terms of the Likud's remaining in power for a generation, as Labor had for Israel's first twenty-nine years. Since the Oriental Jewish population was growing faster than the European, Labor's problem was to find a way to correct the disaffection of Oriental voters to it or face the prospect of being a minority party indefinitely.

Regardless of whether the Likud remained in power or was replaced by Labor, it seemed likely that the political stalemate would produce a series of weak coalition governments, forced to trim policy to the lowest common denominator rather than taking any sort of creative initiative toward fundamental change. Considering the critical problems Israel faces, another ten years of government by indecision and drift would not improve her situation. The country needs tough policies to straighten out its economic problems, social programs designed to eliminate the gap between the country's two Jewish communities (or programs that at least would convince Oriental Jews that progress was being made) and a coherent policy that comes to grips with the conundrum of the territories occupied in 1967.

The situation seemed tailor-made for some kind of a grass roots citizens movement appealing to a shared sense of the public interest rather than to narrow, individual concerns. The Democratic Movement for Change was that kind of a movement and its failure —partially because of the inexperience of its leadership and partly because its platform aroused unrealistic expectations about what could be accomplished—discouraged subsequent attempts.

One reason why grass roots movements have difficulty in Israel has to do with a curious passivity among Israelis when it comes to politics. On one level Israelis are deeply involved in national affairs. An hour barely passes without an Israeli turning on a radio to hear the news bulletin. Conversation on buses becomes more subdued when the familiar tones of the "Voice of Israel" come over the air on the hour and the driver turns up the radio so everyone can hear. Attempting to get Israelis to show up for a social event before the nightly televised news is over (usually around nine thirty) is virtually impossible. At the Friday night social gatherings that are a national institution the government's policies and the country's problems are routinely dismantled by the panel of self-styled experts who gather to drink coffee and tea (seldom anything much stronger) and to eat cakes and sweets.

Although well-versed on what's happening in their country, the participation of the overwhelming majority of Israelis in public affairs is verbal. Politics is a universal avocation in Israel, but relatively few Israelis get involved beyond expressing an opinion (something that almost no Israeli is reluctant to do) or voting. Israel lacks a network of nonpartisan civic organizations that stand outside the political system but try to influence it. When the Israeli government appeared to be faltering in May 1967 in the face of bellicose statements from the surrounding Arab countries, popular pressure forced Prime Minister Levi Eshkol to relinquish to Moshe Dayan the post of defense minister, which Eshkol also held. After 1973 a groundswell movement also forced the government to inquire into the conduct of the Yom Kippur War. But in neither instance did these movements make an attempt to build any kind of permanent organization to institutionalize their efforts. Once the immediate purpose had been accomplished, the movements evaporated.

Part of the reason for the ephemeral nature of these efforts is the impervious nature of politics in government. Israeli politics, unlike American politics, is built around parties—however weak or shifting their form may be. Parties are the source of livelihood for thousands and thousands of Israelis, and it makes no difference whether the party is the Labor Alignment, the Likud, or the National Religious party (the three main groupings). Knesset members and party functionaries owe their political (and often their economic) life to the party. Political affairs in Israel are not organized for individual Knesset members to respond to what their constituents want. They have no constituents. Only their party has constituents. Should a member of Knesset resign his or her seat in protest, or for any other reason, the party replaces the member with the next person on the list. If a Knesset member becomes too outspoken in the criticism of the party's policies, the member runs the risk of being dropped to a lower place on the list in the next election, diminishing his or her chances of being elected, or being dropped from the list altogether.

Getting the party to change means taking on a relatively well-organized machine whose members depend on it for their livelihood. Anyone who wants to take on a political party has to contemplate an enormous undertaking (on an Israeli scale) of lining up money and supporters to challenge the status quo. Given the entrenched nature of the political parties, the undertaking seems too much for most Israelis, already hard-pressed to stay afloat financially and giving one month or more a year (male Israelis, at any rate) for army reserve duty.

Given this nature of political organization in Israel, inertia becomes somewhat more understandable. The lone candidate, even if elected, cannot accomplish much outside a party structure. As soon as a group becomes large enough to make a difference, unless the consensus within the group is very strong on all the important issues, the inherent tendency toward fragmentation of Israel's system threatens to pull the movement apart. One reason Israel's Peace Now movement, a broad-based citizens' pressure group, resisted becoming a political party was because its leaders feared it would be pulled apart by disagreements on issues other than peace.

The reasons for Israeli political passivity are not entirely structural, though. The explanation also has something to do with a certain decline in civic spirit in Israel—or with the failure to develop such a spirit in the first place. On a certain level, to be sure, it is not difficult to get Israelis to volunteer to take on small tasks. With minimal encouragement and almost no arm twisting, parents of school children agree to take on tasks to assist their children's teacher in doing things for the class. In emergencies the willingness of Israelis to pitch in is legendary. But on a daily basis, for the little things that improve the quality of life in a neighborhood, community, or country, Israelis still have not developed a sense of civic obligation that looks toward improving the quality of life for everyone. The lack of courtesy Israeli drivers show each other and pedestrians, the widespread tax evasion, and the littering of public parks and beaches, are minor and major examples of Israel's failure, until now, to forge a public civic spirit in the poststate era. The difference between the present and the prestate era, according to many Israelis, is the decline of voluntarism as a result of the state's creation.

"The establishment of the State of Israel was a trauma for the people living in Israel," one sabra explained. "One of the problems for an organization that has a super goal is what happens to the organization when it reaches the goal. You had the same problem with the March of Dimes and polio in the United States. You have an organization dedicated to the cause and suddenly you reach the cause. So what do you do with it? Dissolve the organization?

"Before the creation of the state, people in Palestine felt it was their duty to help in settling new immigrants. But after the state was created, the citizens moved to the opposite pole. They said, 'It's none of my damn business. They have a special agency. They have special people. Don't bother me. You have problems? Go to welfare. Don't bother me. I'm an ordinary citizen.'"

The transition from British colony to independent country was an abrupt one for Israel, with little time for the kind of spadework and psychological preparation that the British were known for in their other colonies prior to granting independence. Israel had no shortage of trained personnel nor was the population illiterate, unable to fend for itself. But the institutions of the country— the political parties, the Histadrut, the paramilitary organizations —had taken on a life of their own. Much of the life of the Jewish community had come to be centered on these institutions, which had to be broken down in order to integrate the citizenry into the state. When Ben-Gurion dissolved the Palmach, and later, party-run schools, he did so in order to consolidate the power of the state. But he also destroyed major vehicles for dispensing ideology.

As a movement Zionism had little to say about what form a Jewish state should take once achieved. Herzl, in his political novel *Altneuland* (*Old-New Land*), described a society in Palestine that was in reality a futuristic Vienna transplanted to the Middle East. As a realistic model for emulation Herzl's vision was largely irrelevant. Within the Jewish community of Palestine no common vision existed of the coming Jewish society, but rather a number of competing visions—socialist, capitalist, religious, supernationalist. The state, after its establishment, was something more than a neutral body for realizing Jewish national independence.

The state also became a political vehicle that offered the possibility of one group implementing its vision of the new society. Hence allegiance to the state from those who held a different vision could not be taken for granted. To a member of the Irgun, a follower of Begin and Jabotinsky, the State of Israel looked suspiciously like the Mapai party of David Ben-Gurion wrapped in a blue-and-white flag.

This is a process that still is not settled, although with the passage of more than thirty years these partisan ideological struggles have abated and the authority of the state has been more firmly established. But the decline of the voluntary spirit that characterized the prestate era cannot be taken as a progressive step toward creating a democratic society in which rights and responsibilities are shared.

What distinguishes American politics is that the parties and politicians competing for office share a basic centrist view of goals and the means to obtain those goals. Israel, at least in its early years and to some extent even today, was substantially different. Disagreements among various Zionist factions were sharp, especially in the prestate era, and they became more so as pressure on Jews in Europe intensified. The issues dividing one group from another were perceived—with justification—as having life-and-death importance, and the groups acted accordingly. The competing groups also had profoundly different views of what kind of society they believed should be created, and each group had an abiding sense of being right. As a result, violence was not an uncommon event. The murder of Chaim Arlosoroff, a moderate socialist, on a Tel Aviv beach in 1933 was generally blamed on the Revisionists, and the killing inflamed animosity between Labor Zionists and Revisionists in Palestine.

The style of political leadership in Israel is given to a level of intense personal animosity rarely experienced in democracies like the United States or Great Britain. The Zionist movement before the creation of the state set the tone. Herzl fought a series of battles within the movement, including an epic struggle with Chaim Weizmann and other younger Zionists. Weizmann, in his memoirs, managed to mention Ben-Gurion only four times—and only briefly at that—although the two men dealt extensively with each other during the prestate period. Their relationship became increasingly fractious, despite Ben-Gurion's protestations of affection for Weizmann. Ben-Gurion, as already mentioned, could not bring himself to speak Begin's name. Rabin, after serving as prime minister, viciously attacked fellow Labor Alignment member Shimon Peres, who had served as defense minister in Rabin's cabinet.

The debates in the Knesset, punctuated by persistent heckling, go far beyond the relatively restrained atmosphere of the English Parliament or the American Congress. When President Jimmy Carter visited Jerusalem in 1978 to negotiate the peace treaty between Egypt and Israel, television viewers saw Prime Minister Begin continually interrupted by heckling from Knesset members, one of whom was finally ejected from the chamber for her behavior.

When Ezer Weizman resigned from Begin's cabinet, he was not content to write a *pro forma* letter of resignation. Rather, Weizman publicly castigated Begin for having missed opportunities to make peace and to improve conditions in Israel. Begin responded with a remarkable diatribe, delivered in front of Israeli television cameras in a public meeting, accusing Weizman of hypocrisy, disloyalty, and duplicity.

These outbursts tend to give Israeli politics a certain savage quality, regardless of the smiles that often break out after the attack is over. The atmosphere of Israeli politics, while no longer violent, is still far from civil. The Begin government was especially noted for its discord. One of the national pastimes of Israel during the Begin government was turning on the Sunday night televised news to watch a reporter covering the weekly cabinet meeting give a verbatim report—reading from a leaked transcript—of the squabbles that occurred in the meeting. On one occasion Agriculture Minister Ariel Sharon threatened Deputy Prime Minister Yigael Yadin, "I'll strip you naked across the table." On several occasions reports were carried—never denied—of shouting matches, of personal insults being levied, of officials storming from the meeting. This atmosphere was not created by the Begin government, though it undoubtedly became worse than it had been previously.

Israel's smallness, the intimacy of the country, also contributes to this savageness in politics. Politics is another arena in which the smallness of Israeli society affects the nature of the system. It is entirely likely in Israel that members of the political leadership not only know each other but have known each other for years. Deputy Prime Minister Yadin once recalled how, when he had been army chief of staff, he had given Ezer Weizman a piece of philosophical advice about how to conduct himself in life. Thirty years later both men were members of the government and Yadin mused that the advice he had given then still held. To Yadin, Weizman was "Ezer," someone he had known well since both were youths. The likelihood of one member of the Israeli elite knowing another is high, and the potential for shielding one's secrets, for having a private life, for safeguarding one's weaknesses and innermost thoughts, one's vulnerabilities and peccadilloes from one's fellow Israelis is rather remote. Not only is a public official's marital infidelity public knowledge, but the identity of his mistress is as well. (All the more so in this instance, since marital fidelity in Israel occasionally seems to be as much honored in the breach as in the observance and since Israeli men are notoriously indiscreet about their exploits.)

As a result of this enforced intimacy Israelis often know more about their leadership than perhaps is good for the maintenance of any kind of image—if illusion is necessary for strong leadership. The intimate environment in which Israelis live has more in common with a small town than with a large nation. Considering Israel's isolation in the region where it finds itself, the country continues to be a ghetto of sorts, and it's not surprising that the atmosphere of the eastern European *shtetl* so well-known to Jews is re-created in spirit in Israel. Everyone's business is everyone else's affair. Secrets are hard to hold. Anonymity is almost impossible.

This intimacy breeds a kind of claustrophobia, which combines with an argumentative and querulous quality that is peculiarly Jewish. The result is not particularly appealing, and it creates a spectacle often embarrassing to some Israelis who worry about the lack of civility in Israeli behavior; but it is also a characteristic that seems unlikely to evaporate overnight. Many Israelis contend that, unappealing as the spectacle may appear to an outsider, it is all a rather harmless working off of steam, more bark than bite. "Israelis *say* terrible things to each other," one Israeli remarked, "but they don't *do* terrible things to each other."

The coarse nature of Israeli politics also reflects the style of men who cut their political teeth in a climate where ends were more important than means. Given the life-and-death nature of the issues at various points in Israel's history, it may have seemed genteel to a fault to be worrying about procedures and courtesy.

223

Those times are not so far removed that they have lost their impact on Israeli life, especially since they reinforced something of a preexisting natural tendency.

In the rather unsubtle atmosphere of Israeli politics grievances over past battles are not easily put aside. Some old Herut members cannot forget that Ben-Gurion ordered the sinking of the *Altalena*. Some old members of the Labor Alignment, who once stood in opposition to Ben-Gurion, cannot forget what he and his lieutenants did to them in the course of any number of political skirmishes. A veteran Herut member said that it took years before he was ever invited to appear on the government-owned radio because "Herut members were not allowed to speak on the radio."

The description of Israel as a democracy has to take into account a certain lack of tolerance and restraint in Israeli behavior, not to mention real problems of security that inhibit the free exercise of individual rights. Israel clearly has democratic *forms*—periodic elections by secret ballot in which opposing candidates seek to be chosen to run the government; limited government guided by rules accepted by the major participants in the system; the right of free speech, a free press, and the freedom of assembly; majority rule with respect for minority rights. These principles are formally established in Israel, but in each case major caveats have to be stated. The quality of Israeli democracy is impaired by the continuing threat to its security from the surrounding Arab countries, by the presence in Israel of a substantial, potentially hostile Arab minority, and by the continuing domination of Arabs in the territories who have no effective voice or control in the government that makes major decisions for them.

Except in matters that the army censor determines concern national security, newspapers and other media are free to publish and broadcast without restraint. The press in Israel is vigorous and often vociferous in its criticism of the government. Israel has three major independent Hebrew daily papers (and a fourth, if the English-language *Jerusalem Post* is included, although the *Post* is substantially owned, if not directly controlled, by the Histadrut, which in turn is closely tied to the Labor Alignment). Besides these independent papers several political parties publish their own papers, which operate with the same freedom and restraints imposed on the independent papers. Radio and television, although state-owned, often air controversial matters despite the opposition of the government.

Although it is true that newspapers can publish freely, the power of army censorship has been invoked from time to time to prevent disclosure of facts not clearly related, in the opinion of some, to Israel's security. In 1979, following the March 1978 invasion of southern Lebanon by the Israeli army in retaliation for the murder by terrorists of more than thirty-five persons, it was revealed that an Israeli army officer had been court-martialed, convicted, and sentenced to military prison for his actions in the "Litani operation," as it was called.

The officer in question, Lt. Daniel Pinto, was tried and convicted for the killing of two Palestinian civilians, suspected of being collaborators with the Palestine Liberation Organization. The bodies of the two civilians were found at the bottom of a well, their hands lashed behind their backs. They had been strangled. According to testimony at Pinto's court-martial, he had boasted to another officer that he had tortured and killed four Palestinians during the Litani operation.

Pinto's original sentence was commuted by the Israel Defense Forces' chief of staff, Lt. Gen. Rafael Eitan, to one quarter—less than two years—of the original sentence levied by the military court that convicted Pinto.

Although the facts of the incident gradually became known to Israeli journalists, the military censor barred them from publishing details of the incident. Since Eitan had reduced Pinto's sentence, arousing considerable controversy within Israel over the affair, many Israelis believed that the censor's action had less to do with security than it did with quieting a political issue that threatened the chief of staff.

On another occasion, a relatively high-ranking military officer said that a senior military official serving outside the country was under investigation for questionable practices in his official capacity. The Israeli press was aware of the charges, the officer said, but could not print them—although no security issue was involved—because the military censor was blocking publication. "It isn't security that's blocking it," the officer said. "It's political. The Defense Ministry doesn't want to be embarrassed by this."

The situation is somewhat different with the state-owned radio and television station. (It is also possible to receive transmissions from Jordan and Egypt television without much difficulty.) The Israel Broadcasting Authority is politically appointed. In the early years of the state, Israeli radio (there was no television until 1968) was little more than a mouthpiece for the government. Every broadcast began and ended with a report on something that Ben-Gurion had said or done. Over time, radio broadcasts and television news have become substantially more independent, but political considerations still have some influence, even if indirectly. After the Likud's victory in 1977 the composition of the governing authority was changed, a new director was appointed and the content of the news came under scrutiny for "leftist" tendencies. On several occasions friction turned into open conflict among the news staff, the director, and the broadcasting authority over items that had appeared or were planned for broadcast. During one televised newscast, transmission was interrupted for about four minutes. When the news continued, the announcer apologized for the interruption without explaining it. Later, it was reported in the newspapers that the director of the broadcast authority had intervened to prevent the airing of an interview with a West Bank Arab mayor. Since the interview could not be shown, the professional staff of Israeli television showed nothing for the length of time the report would have taken.

These incidents should not be exaggerated nor should it be inferred that the news in Israel is propaganda. Taking into account the independent as well as political-party newspapers, Israeli television and radio, and several weekly news-magazines, Israelis know a great deal about what happens in their own country, in the occupied territories, and abroad. Israeli radio and television are considerably freer than Jordanian television, which is a government propaganda organ and Israeli television is probably more independent of political controls than French television, which is also government-owned. After three years of trying to bring Israeli television to heel, the Likud government showed signs of throwing in the towel when a number of cabinet ministers proposed that a second, commercial station be licensed in order to allow a version of the news more favorable to the government (and the Likud) to be shown.

Nevertheless, Israel's security problems impose restraints on publishing and broadcasting in Israel beyond the formal restrictions. One Israeli journalist wrote a column following a spate of reports on various sensitive subjects complaining that government officials talked *too much* and that too much sensitive information was finding its way into print. This opinion reflected a certain Israeli sentiment that some things do not need to be known generally.

I was entertaining some Israelis in my home one evening, including an Israeli businessman and another Israeli who worked for the Ministry of Defense, but in what capacity precisely he had never told me. After a long evening of discussion the businessman turned to the government employee and asked (since the government employee looked rather young), "Do you work or do you go to school?"

"No, I work," the other Israeli answered.

"What kind of work?" the businessman asked.

"I work for the government."

"Oh," the businessman said, "what ministry?"

"Defense."

"With the army, or something else?" the businessman asked.

"No, using my background from the university in Arab history," the other Israeli answered.

At that point the businessman nodded his head knowingly and changed the subject, without a single additional question. Nothing in the other Israeli's tone or manner suggested that there should be no more questions. The businessman had simply run up against that wall where Israelis understand that they need to know nothing more and that their own interest would be better served by no further inquiry—certainly not in the presence of an outsider like myself.

As it turned out, the young Israeli—I later learned purely by chance—worked for the Shin Bet, the Israeli security agency. Although one might have guessed, from the reluctant way he answered questions, that his work involved security, a certain reflex prevented him from openly saying so. The official biography of Yitzhak Shamir, foreign minister for a time in the Begin government, described him simply as a former government official who served in Paris. Shamir worked for the Mossad, the Israeli civilian intelligence agency, a fact well-known in Israel. But discretion prevents Israelis from acknowledging officially what everyone knows privately.

Similarly, the general assumption in Israel is that Israel has a nuclear weapons capability and possesses several nuclear devices. But when France sold weapons-grade nuclear material to Iraq, increasing the prospect that Iraq would have a nuclear capability of its own by the mid-1980s—the first Arab country to have an atom bomb—Israeli newspapers and other media said nothing about Israel's own nuclear potential. Only one public figure— Moshe Dayan—came close to acknowledging Israel's nuclear capability when he said in an interview that Israel would be neither the "first nor the last" country in the Middle East to use nuclear weapons. Even after Israel destroyed the Iraqi reactor in June 1981, discussion of Israel's nuclear potential was minimal.

Israel does have censorship, but self-censorship is just as strong. Clearly, in matters relating to security, Israeli reporters often know a great deal more than they report. "I could make two hundred English pounds a week for six months selling items to London newspapers," one Israeli journalist said, "but I'm raising my children here, so I won't do it." Sometimes pressure is applied to journalists, none too subtly, to remind them that they are Israelis first and journalists second. "Raful [Chief of Staff Rafael Eitan] called us in," a journalist who covered military affairs recalled, "and told us simply, 'You're all soldiers in the army as well as being journalists and I expect that you'll remember that when you're writing your stories.' Now what the hell am I supposed to say to that?" Israeli reporters, especially military correspondents, who overstep the limits, can find themselves suddenly brought up short. Israeli reporters are dependent on the goodwill of the establishment in order to do their jobs. An Israeli military reporter who loses his accreditation is effectively cut off from his sources of information and finds it extremely difficult to do his job.

But even without these kinds of pressure and sanctions, Israeli journalists are more inclined to think of a story in terms of the country and the impact on the national interest than they are in the United States, where the prevailing tendency among the country's major newspapers is to publish rather than to suppress news.

An Israeli journalist informed me, after swearing me to secrecy, that he and several other journalists had been told by an Israeli government official of contacts between Israel and China to discuss opening trade relations. The contacts ultimately leaked and were reported, but not until months later, and even then in a quiet and discreet way.

An Israeli academic, who had just finished serving as a government official, described a request he had received from Israeli radio to go on the air to analyze a new wage and benefit package that had prevented the closure of El Al, Israel's state-owned airline. The plan had been presented to the public as a stringent program that would make severe cuts in El Al salaries and would require great sacrifices on the part of El Al employees. The action was among the first attempts—one of the most visible and certainly the most dramatic effort—by the government to curtail wage agreements and to encourage a spirit of self-sacrifice in order to bring inflation under control.

"The agreement was really a fraud," the former-government-official-turned-academic said. "The radio reporter knew that, and he was right. But he wanted me to analyze the agreement on the air and to expose it. I could have done it. It would have been true. But I said to him: 'Look, this is the first effort by the government to really try again to bring inflation under control. If we pour cold water on this thing, we could hurt the whole effort. Is that what you want to do?' He agreed with me. I convinced him and he dropped the idea."

Journalists in Israel can hardly be said to be tools of the government. Reporting of corruption and political scandals can be every bit as vigorous in Israel as in other countries, but Israeli reporters and the institutions for which they work clearly also have a sense of playing more than one role in the society. The hesitation of Israeli reporters (by no means universal) to print a story damaging to the country's national interest has to do with the smallness of Israel. Reporters are not able to put as much distance between themselves and the rest of society in Israel as American reporters can. The Israeli community is too small for a reporter to think about it abstractly and to construct some kind of greater philosophical good that might be served by printing a story damaging in a real way to Israeli security, especially when little imagination is needed to conjure up a picture of the threat.

This self-restraint has been institutionalized to some extent through an editors committee, which includes the editors of the country's major publications. The government can and does from time to time brief the editors on sensitive subjects, often with the understanding that the subject of the briefing will not be reported. Occasionally, the editors committee declines to be briefed in order to avoid the restriction on publishing. The Israeli press and the government also have established a formal Censorship Committee to hear appeals when the papers believe that the military censor has gone too far in the prohibition of publication of a fact or a situation. The committee can overrule the censor. Or if the censor believes that a security regulation has been violated by a publication, the censor can appeal to the committee, and if the committee agrees, the errant newspaper or magazine is fined. The law provides for stricter penalties, but the government prefers to use the voluntary approach with the milder penalty of fines since most transgressions are inadvertent or not so serious as to warrant criminal penalties.

The government, which is to say the Israeli cabinet, can also cloak its deliberations with a blanket security mantle by declaring itself to be a committee on security affairs. When that is done, any and every action taken by the cabinet is prohibited from publication, regardless of its content, importance, or relation to security matters.

"Obviously," one Israeli journalist observed, "much and probably most of what they discuss as a committee on security affairs has nothing to do with security. It's usually political stuff, since security matters already fall under censorship. If they constitute themselves a committee on security affairs, though, there's nothing we can do—or say—about what they discuss."

What prevents the government from abusing these rather wide discretionary powers it has to limit democracy in Israel? The press in Israel still is basically free and can complain publicly when not permitted to publish. Israel is still small enough so that a sizable number of people can be informed by word of mouth about a situation even when news cannot be printed or broadcast. But that does not guarantee that the truth will always win out in Israel. Ben-Gurion went down to defeat and ultimately quit the Mapai party over the infamous Lavon affair and his insistence that an independent board of inquiry be established to investigate the matter. The Israeli public has not to this day received a nonbiased explanation of the events behind the Lavon affair, nor was there a closed inquiry into it that would meet standards established for a judicial inquiry. Instead, the matter was handled to a large extent as an embarrassment to the Mapai party and swept under the carpet without the facts being fully known.

More recently, when charges of corruption were leveled against the minister of religious affairs, Aharon Abuhatzeira, the committee of the Knesset charged with the responsibility for lifting his parliamentary immunity temporized, even after the attorney general of Israel formally requested the committee's action so that Abuhatzeira could be tried in a court.

In both instances a kind of self-protective instinct among the ruling elite was at work, depriving the public of a full airing of facts in order to assess blame or to establish guilt or innocence. What the Abuhatzeira investigation demonstrated, among other things, was a widespread perception, especially among Oriental Jews, that the judicial system of the country could be manipulated for political reasons. It made little difference that Jews of European origin from the Labor Alignment had been tried and convicted for crimes committed while holding public office.

The Israeli government has other powers that also run against the grain of democratic tradition. The government can arrest and detain persons without disclosing to them the evidence against them. This administrative detention, which is used to protect "state security" or the "security of the public" rather than to punish a criminal after the fact, requires only that the state present evidence to a judge who then determines whether the administrative detention is justified. Neither the defendant nor his lawyer is entitled to examine the evidence. The material presented does not have to meet the rules of evidence that apply in standard court proceedings, but may be hearsay, intelligence reports, and other information that a court might not allow in a normal hearing. The judge is left with wide discretion to determine what weight to give this evidence. The defendant's rights in this procedure are largely restricted to appearing in his own behalf, and having his lawyer speak in his behalf. A person may be detained for up to six months, at which time the state can reapply for further detention of the person.

This administrative detention law applies in Israel, not in the occupied territories, and it can and has been used against Israeli citizens, including at least one Jew (Rabbi Meir Kahane). In the territories the military administration has even broader powers of arrest and detention, with much more restricted review by the Israeli Supreme Court over actions taken.

Within Israel the military can also, under regulations still in force from the British Mandate, restrict the movement of persons considered to be a danger to the state. Under these regulations the military governor of an area (especially the north, where Israel's Arab population is concentrated) can order Israeli citizens restricted to their villages and prohibited from leaving without his permission.

Everyone in Israel is required by law to carry official identification. Israeli citizens and Arabs from the territories must carry identity cards. Foreigners are required to carry their passports at all times. Citizens and foreigners may be required to show their identification by police officers or security officials without establishing a formal reason for the request.

The tolerance of Israelis for what are basically antidemocratic, antilibertarian methods and procedures seems rather high, even though the purported reasons for these measures seems clear enough. Israel still is a state under siege, and part of the threat, potentially, comes from the Arab minority within Israel. Acknowledging a threat to the state, however, does not dispel the danger that the security measures constitute to Israeli democracy. Although a small civil liberties movement exists in Israel, the public in general seems untroubled by the considerable powers that the government has at its disposal to maintain order and security.

Not only is the Israeli public tolerant of extraordinary and somewhat arbitrary powers exercised by its government, but a considerable segment of the population appears skeptical about the value of democracy at all. How strong Israeli democracy will remain in the face of record inflation, continued control of the West Bank, and other social problems is a question worth pondering. A 1981 public opinion poll in Israel, based on a representative sample of the Israeli public, found some striking attitudes toward the country's democratic institutions. When asked if they agreed or disagreed with the statement that the political system should be *fully* reorganized and a strong regime formed that was not dependent on political parties, almost 41 percent agreed, 41 percent disagreed and the rest—almost 20 percent—had no opinion. Viewed differently, almost 60 percent of the Israeli population either would support a change in the country's political system or is indifferent to such a change. More than half (55.5 percent) agreed partially or completely that the Israeli mass media damage the interests of the state, hurt national morale, and spread defeatism and "therefore, they should be limited and tamed." Only fourteen percent of those polled rejected the statement as being totally wrong.

The poll also found that antidemocratic attitudes were not concentrated in any single group of the population—ethnic, chronologic, or economic—but rather were spread across the spectrum. Although the poll does not necessarily mean that the threat to Israeli democracy is imminent, the continued well-being of democratic institutions—given external circumstances and these attitudes—is not something that can be taken for granted.

Indeed, considering the pressures on Israel—from within and without—what may seem remarkable is not how flawed democracy is in Israel, but that Israel is democratic at all. Other countries, faced with security threats less imminent than Israel's, have undertaken measures far more severe than those adopted by Israel. The American experience with the detention of Japanese-Americans during World War II is a case in point.

Within Israel, Arabs—as citizens of the Jewish state—enjoy a degree of political and personal freedom that far exceeds that of any other country in the region. Israeli Arabs have the right of free speech, free press, access to courts where they can adjudicate their grievances with assurance that they will be given a fair and impartial hearing under Israeli law.

And yet, to treat that as the end of the matter would be to ignore one of the most severe threats to the continuation of democracy in Israel. Besides the structural flaws of the Israeli political system, the faltering leadership, and weakening consensus, the single issue posing the greatest challenge to the future of Israeli democracy is the fate of more than one million Arabs living in Gaza, Judea, and Samaria—the occupied territories—who have no effective voice or control over their own government. Somewhere between the needs of Israeli security and complete suppression of civil rights and liberties for Palestinian Arabs lies a solution that will allow Israel to survive and also to be true to the progressive ideals that inspired the men and women who founded the country.

It seems unlikely that Israel can preserve its own democracy indefinitely while forced to maintain a repressive administration over a large, hostile, and growing Arab population that has the sympathy and support of world opinion.

Within months of the conclusion of the Six Day War, admonishing voices were raised in Israel arguing that retention of the territories posed a threat to Israeli democracy. "I would like to quote Abraham Lincoln," Yehoshua Arieli, an Israeli intellectual wrote in 1969,

> changing only one word, that: a democratic government cannot remain for a long time half democratic and half oppressive. It must change and become either the one or the other. I have no doubt what would happen to us.
>
> We would have to adapt ourselves to a state that was unwillingly turning into a police state, to a government whose need to maintain a special class with the responsibility for repression would affect its own mentality. We would have lost our souls for some additional territory.

This vision was no abstract prediction. Signs of erosion have already been observed—attempts to limit press coverage in the territories during operations to quiet disturbances and demonstrations, the arbitrary arrest and detention for questioning of Arabs for reasons of security, the use of collective punishment against whole towns or villages. "The problem for the Israelis," observed an American who had lived in Moscow for several years, "is that they can't make up their minds what they want to do. If the Russians were controlling the West Bank, it would be *quiet*. But the Israelis are torn."

As time goes on, as Palestinian nationalist sentiment grows, it is hard to foresee how Israel can avoid making the choice between its own founding principles of "liberty, justice, and peace" and maintaining control over more than one million unwilling subjects.

6/ARABS IN ISRAEL

We call upon the sons of the Arab people
dwelling in Israel to keep the peace and to
play their part in building the State on
the basis of full and equal citizenship and
due representation in all its institutions.

Israel's Declaration of Independence

"I am certain," Israel's first president, Chaim Weizmann, wrote on the eve of the establishment of the State of Israel, "that the world will judge the Jewish State by what it will do with the Arabs."

Weizmann's vision was prescient, but it was hardly based on guesswork. Weizmann had spent his entire adult life trying to convince statesmen all over the world that there was room enough in Palestine for two peoples—Jews and Palestinian Arabs—to realize their national destinies in an atmosphere of harmony, cooperation, and mutual benefit.

Weizmann, like Ben-Gurion, Berl Katznelson, Judah Magnes, Martin Buber, and thousands of other Jews who came to Palestine in the years before World War II, was a product of Western rationalism and humanism, a believer in progress and the idea that *ultimately* Jew and Arab would find a common ground of understanding in Palestine—or Eretz Yisrael, the Land of Israel, as they would have preferred to call it.

They were, perhaps, more than a little naïve in their belief—

unable to understand the depths of feeling of nationalism on the part of the Arabs and also unable to understand the likely direction that resurgent Jewish nationalism would take. But Weizmann, and other Israelis as well, understood clearly that the effort to build a new society based on humanitarian and democratic principles would be judged on the basis of whether those principles applied equally to all citizens of Israeli society, Arab as well as Jew.

The issue is still not decided. The conflict between Israel and her Arab neighbors, between Jewish and Arab nationalism, continues, and so the position of Arabs within Israel remains unsettled. Reading Arab and Jewish accounts of events and conversations over the last eighty to ninety years is like a venture into the realm of Pirandello, so different are the versions of the same facts. Each side, sincerely and profoundly believing itself to be in the right, has interpreted the past in a way that gives support to its position. The history of Arab-Zionist relations already has developed a mythology of its own, so that setting out the situation inevitably involves cutting through a thicket of misconceptions, distorted facts, and propaganda. The Arab-Israeli conflict is not, for example, "thousands of years old," as some observers would have it, or even hundreds of years old. Until the advent of Zionism in the late nineteenth century, Jews and Arabs in Palestine managed to live side by side in relative tranquillity. It may be, after all, that the conflict is incapable of solution, but all we have as evidence for that conclusion is the experience of less than a century.

The Arab-Israeli conflict is the product, on the one hand, of the inability of Arab nationalists to reconcile themselves to the return of a Jewish *political* entity to Palestine and, on the other hand, of the necessity for Jewish nationalists to find a home and safe haven for Jews whose place in a changing world was becoming more tenuous. Each side felt that any accommodation would mean giving up the essence of its position. Each side had absolute rights that were denied by the other. Each was impelled by pressing needs. Neither side was able to identify with the other's situation.

These considerations only make the tragedy more poignant. Zionists, despite the efforts of their opponents to depict them as such, were not traditional colonialists motivated by mere territorial aggrandizement but rather were idealists who sincerely believed that founding Israel was necessary to save the Jewish nation from extinction in an increasingly menacing world.

That the Jews of the early twentieth century faced a crisis was not denied by the more thoughtful of the Arab leaders and intellectuals. They simply demanded to know why it had fallen on the Arabs of Palestine to bear the brunt of the solution. "The relief of Jewish distress caused by European persecution must be sought elsewhere than in Palestine, for the country is too small to hold a larger increase of population and it has already borne more than its fair share," George Antonius wrote in *The Arab Awakening*.

> The treatment meted out to Jews in Germany and other European countries is a disgrace to its authors and to modern civilization; but posterity will not exonerate any country that fails to bear its proper share of the sacrifices needed to alleviate Jewish suffering and distress. To place the brunt of the burden upon Arab Palestine is a miserable evasion of the duty that lies upon the whole of the civilized world. It is also morally outrageous. No code of morals can justify the persecution of one people in an attempt to relieve the persecution of another. The cure for the eviction of the Jews from Germany is not to be sought in the eviction of the Arabs from their homeland; and the relief of Jewish distress may not be accomplished at the cost of inflicting a corresponding distress upon an innocent and peaceful population.

The concerns and principles that Antonius expressed were, as we shall see, shared by Jewish leaders, who were equally concerned that in seeking a refuge from injustice and a means of national expression, they should not deny what has come to be known in the loaded vocabulary of modern diplomacy as "the legitimate rights" of Arab Palestinians.

Zionism did not consciously embark on a collision course with

Arab nationalism. If anything—and the early Zionists may well be faulted for this failing—Zionism was not even conscious of Arab nationalism in the earliest days of the Jewish national movement. Zionist leaders reconciled themselves to the inevitability of conflict with the Arabs only when circumstance left them little alternative.

Musing over what might have happened if history had taken a different turn seems fruitless. Had it not been for the intervention of the British in 1917—issuing the Balfour Declaration and lending support to the creation of "a national home for the Jewish people" in Palestine—Israel might not exist today. But why stop there? Following the same line of reasoning, Jordan might not exist today, since Jordan also owes its existence to the British. Palestine might have fallen under the control of the Syrians, who might have been no more charitable and democratic in their treatment of Palestinian Arabs in Palestine than they have been toward Palestinians in Syria or Lebanon. History, after all, is not some laboratory experiment in which we can control the variables to test the results. Had there been no Balfour Declaration, it also seems pertinent to ask, what might have become of the hundreds of thousands of Jews who managed to make their way to Palestine before Hitler's madness was given its full expression.

Jews have a historic claim to Israel. Jews have lived continuously in Palestine (a name derived from the Philistines, who preceded the Jews in the area) since about 1100 B.C., after returning from Egypt. After 1000 B.C., Jews were the principal population of an area along the coastal plain—excluding Gaza—up to the modern city of Haifa and east twenty miles into what is now Jordan. The Jewish people lived in this area in a sovereign and semisovereign status until A.D. 70, when the Second Temple was destroyed and the main resistance to Roman rule in Palestine was crushed.

Although hundreds of thousands of Jews (perhaps as many as half a million) were killed by the Romans, and thousands more were sold as slaves, Jews remained the principal population of Palestine until A.D. 636, when Muslim Arab armies conquered the area. Jews were allowed to remain and did so, assisting the Arabs in the defense of the area when the Crusaders invaded and dealt more harshly with the Jewish population than the Arabs had. In 1291 Mamluks from Egypt defeated the Crusaders and ruled until 1517, when the Turks—Muslims like the Mamluks and the Arabs—defeated the Mamluks and made Palestine an outpost of the Ottoman Empire, which it remained until 1917. In that year the British took control of Palestine, after defeating the Turks.

Thus, the Jews have maintained a presence in Palestine for more than three thousand years, although prior to 1948 Jews had not been self-governing for roughly two thousand years and Arabs had not been sovereign for thirteen hundred years. Both the Jews and the Arabs who followed them established their presence in Palestine by conquest. Until the twentieth century the Jewish population in Palestine was relatively small. Although reliable population figures are hard to get, the Jewish population in 1880 is estimated to have been about 24,000 and the Arab population about 470,000. By 1914 an estimated 90,000 Jews lived in Palestine, compared to 500,000 Arabs.

The awakening of Jewish nationalism that was to become Zionism brought thousands of Jews to Palestine in the second half of the nineteenth century. They purchased land, usually from absentee Arab landowners and often at exorbitant prices. Even before this influx, by the end of the 1860s Jews constituted fifty percent of Jerusalem's population. By 1890 Jews were a clear majority in Jerusalem, the focus of two thousand years of prayers by Jewish exiles living in the Diaspora.

In the rest of Palestine the increase of the Arab population, by immigration and natural growth, had raised the number of Arabs to about 840,000, which represented eighty-one percent of the population by the end of the nineteenth century. Most of the Arab Muslims lived in rural areas and worked as farmers, while the majority of Christian Arabs lived in urban areas.

With the gift of hindsight, it is easy now to marvel at the blindness, naïveté, or lack of consciousness on the part of early Zionists to the presence of Arabs and their feelings about Jewish resettlement. One of Zionism's early slogans had been, A people without a land returns to a land without a people. The slogan was fatuous, but in fairness to the early Zionists it has to be said that the conventional wisdom of the late nineteenth century saw Palestine as empty. Literature confirmed this impression. Mark Twain reported after riding through the area of the Hula valley north of the Sea of Galilee: "There is not a solitary village throughout its whole extent—not for 30 miles in either direction. There are two or three small clusters of Bedouin tents, but not a single permanent habitation. One may ride ten miles, hereabouts, and not see ten human beings."

Few, if any, of the early Zionists have ever been to Palestine. Herzl himself did not actually visit until 1898, two years after publication of *The Jewish State.*

Nor was Arab nationalism at all well-defined in the early years of the Zionist movement. Concerned about repressive measures from the Turks, Arab nationalists met largely in secret in the nineteenth and early twentieth centuries. In the years before World War I certainly, Arab nationalism was not a movement of the masses. The experience of the earliest Jewish pioneers in Palestine was not such to force the conclusion that Arabs and Jews could not live together in peace in Palestine. Arab bandits attacked Jewish settlers, but such attacks were reasonably interpreted as an expression of lawlessness in an uncivilized area rather than as an expression of political hostility. Anyone who traveled the countryside in those days, Jew and non-Jew alike, had reason to fear for his well-being, and the wise traveler took along protection.

Still, there were signs that Jewish resettlement in Palestine would not be without problems. In 1899 a former mayor of Jerusalem—Yussef Ziah el-Khaldi—wrote to Zadok Kahn, the chief rabbi of Paris, expressing concern with the intent of Zionists to resettle in Palestine.

El-Khaldi conceded the historic right of Jews to be in Palestine. "But unfortunately," he wrote,

the destiny of nations is governed not only by abstract concepts, however pure and noble they might be. One must

241

consider reality and respect established facts, the force, yes, the *brutal* [el-Khaldi's italics] force, of circumstance. The reality is that Palestine is now an integral part of the Ottoman Empire and what is more serious, it is inhabited by others than Israelites.

If Zionism were to succeed, el-Khaldi wrote, it would take more than money. Zionists would need force. His advice was that the Zionists should find some other place for their homeland.

The letter was passed on to Herzl, who replied directly to el-Khaldi. Besides underestimating the capacity of Jews to learn martial arts, Herzl's response reveals the same erroneous assumption that was repeated by generations of Zionist and Israeli leaders that followed him—that Arabs in Palestine would prefer material progress to sovereignty and the expression of their own nationalism. This assumption represented a fundamental misreading of Arab psychology and an inability to ascribe to Arabs the same desires and aspirations as a people that the Jews had. It is a failing of profound proportions, and one that continues—in other manifestations—to the present day.

"As you yourself said," Herzl wrote, "there is no military power behind the Jews. As a people they have long lost the taste for war, they are a thoroughly pacific element, and fully content if left in peace. Therefore there is absolutely no reason to fear their immigration." Herzl assured el-Khaldi that the holy places would be left untouched.

You see another difficulty in the existence of a non-Jewish population in Palestine. But who wishes to remove them from there? Their well-being and individual wealth will increase through the importation of ours. Do you believe that an Arab who owns land in Palestine, or a house worth three or four thousand francs, will be sorry to see their value rise five- and tenfold? But this would most certainly happen with the coming of the Jews. And this is what one must bring the natives to comprehend . . . if one looks at the matter from this viewpoint, and it is the right viewpoint, one inevitably becomes a friend of Zionism.

The pioneering generation, the *halutzim* ("pioneers") of the Second and Third Aliyahs also had a profound and sincere belief in their own humanity, in their own intention to create a new and just society that would deal fairly with all people. That purpose might be seen today as presumptuous on their part, but those Jewish pioneers were also revolutionaries, and they brought their ideological zeal with them.

"Palestine," Ben-Gurion wrote in 1918,

> is not an unpopulated country. Within the territory that may be regarded—historically, politically, ethnographically and economically—as *Eretz* Israel, and which covers an area of 55,000–60,000 square kilometers on both sides of the River Jordan, there is a population of slightly over one million. In Cisjordan alone there are about three-quarters of a million. *By no means and under no circumstances are the rights of these inhabitants to be infringed upon* [emphasis in the original]—it is neither desirable nor conceivable that the present inhabitants be ousted from the land. That is not the mission of Zionism. The true aim and real capacity of Zionism are not to conquer what has already been conquered, but to settle in those places where the present inhabitants of the land have not established themselves and are unable to do so. . . . The demand of the Jewish people is based on the reality of unexploited economic potentials, and of un-built-up stretches of land that require the productive force of a progressive, cultured people. The demand of the Jewish people is really nothing more than the demand of an entire nation for the right to work.
>
> However, we must remember that such rights are also possessed by the inhabitants already living in the country—and these rights must not be infringed upon. Both the vision of social justice and the equality of all peoples that the Jewish

people has cherished for three thousand years, and the vital interests of the Jewish people in the Diaspora and even more so in Palestine, require absolutely and unconditionally that the rights and interests of the non-Jewish inhabitants of the country be guarded and honored punctiliously.

In principle, the Zionist program promised to respect the rights of the Arab "natives" in Palestine, to avoid conflict and usurpation, and to bring the benefits of progress and enlightenment to a backward area. The socialist pioneers, like Ben-Gurion, envisioned an alliance of workers—Jewish and Arab—against capitalist oppression. That this credo could not be reconciled with the demand of Jewish workers that Jewish employers would hire only Jewish labor was another shortcoming of their own self-awareness.

By the end of World War I unmistakable signs of Arab hostility to the Zionist program had appeared. Ben-Gurion recalled years afterward his initial firsthand encounter with Arab nationalism. He recounted that when he was detained by the Turks after the outbreak of World War I, he was walking about the compound in Jerusalem where he was being held. He met an Arab friend:

> "What are you doing here?" I asked him.
> "I've got affairs with the government," he answered.
> "And what are you doing here?" he asked.
> "The government's got affairs with me," I answered, telling him that we were prisoners and why and that there was an order from Jemal Pasha to deport both of us (Itzhak Ben-Zvi and myself) from the Turkish Empire—"so that we should never come back." And then he replied to me:
> "As your friend, I'm sorry. As an Arab, I'm glad." And I know that both things were sincere. We spoke Turkish and that was the first time I had heard a sincere answer from an Arab intellectual. It is engraved in my heart, very, very powerfully.

Following the issuance of the Balfour Declaration by the British government in 1917, with the prospect of a Jewish homeland in

Palestine, the Zionist leadership had reason—briefly at any rate—
to be hopeful that Arab and Jewish interests could be accom-
modated in Palestine. The Emir Feisal, head of the Arab delegation
to the Paris Peace Conference after World War I, wrote to Felix
Frankfurter, a dedicated Zionist who was also present at the conference, on March 3, 1919:

> We feel that the Arabs and Jews are cousins in race,
> suffering similar oppressions at the hands of powers stronger
> than themselves, and by a happy coincidence have been able
> to take the first step toward the attainment of their national
> ideals together.
>
> We Arabs, especially the educated among us, look with
> the deepest sympathy on the Zionist movement. Our deputa-
> tion here in Paris is fully acquainted with the proposals
> submitted by the Zionist organization to the Peace Con-
> ference, and we regard them as moderate and proper. We
> will do our best, in so far as we are concerned, to help them
> through; we will wish the Jews a most hearty welcome.

Obviously, the spirit that informed that letter did not prevail.
Within two years the British separated the eastern part of Palestine that lay across the Jordan—Transjordan—from the area designated as the Jewish homeland in an effort to placate King
Abdullah, the Emir Feisal's brother and son of King Hussein ibn-
Ali, the Grand Sharif of Mecca. The full import of the British
move was not immediately grasped by Zionist leaders, who failed
to see that the separation of Transjordan from the rest of Palestine
was not a mere administrative change but a move that effectively
closed the area to Jewish settlement. Within the area left for Jewish settlement friction between Arabs and Jews increased. In 1929
Arabs attacked Jews in Hebron, Jerusalem and several other places
in Palestine. When the fighting subsided 133 Jews and 87 Arabs
were dead; 399 Jews and 91 Arabs were wounded. From that
point, with occasional periods of quiet, the relations between Jews
and Arabs in Palestine were in a state of fairly steady decline. The
British tacked back and forth over the years with the political

winds, attempting to appease the Arabs, then the Jews, then the Arabs again.

The principal Zionist effort in those years following the Balfour Declaration was spent persuading the Western powers of the justice of the Zionist cause and the benefits for the West. Why, one prominent Arab asked a group of Jews in 1930, did Zionists spend so much time talking about Zionism to everyone but the Arabs? "If only even the thousandth part of this effort were expended to clarify Zionism to the Arabs," said Muhummad Achtar, editor of the largest daily, *Falastin*, in Palestine.

> I suspect that you will not find a single leaflet in Arabic in which Zionists explain their needs, their rights, their claims—absolutely none. You yourselves know better than I the extent to which this was explained to the Americans, the English, the French. Although they must live among the Arabs, the Zionists did not care whether or not the Arabs understood. They thought it more essential for someone in Vienna or in Paris to know what Zionism desired.

This criticism was not without foundation. In one respect, at least, this view is the mirror image of Chaim Weizmann's position that the conflict between Arabs and Jews was all somehow a misunderstanding. More communication, a better explanation, Weizmann maintained, and the Arabs would come to appreciate that the Zionist program posed no threat to them. Ben-Gurion had a series of talks over the years with Arab leaders in a futile attempt to open a dialogue and reconcile differences. The problem ultimately was not that the Arabs failed to understand Zionism. The Arabs understood Zionism only too well. The Zionists wanted as many Jews as possible to come live and work in Palestine. The Arabs saw clearly that they were being supplanted as the principal population in Palestine with the increase of Jewish immigration.

"At the rate at which [Jewish] immigrants had come in during 1935," George Antonius wrote in *The Arab Awakening*, "the Jews who had formed 8 per cent of the total population in 1918 might

acquire a majority in another 10 years." Antonius, whose book was
first published in 1938, proved prophetic. In 1948—or soon there-
after—Jews were indeed a majority in at least part of Palestine—
Israel.

Arab nationalists could hardly help but be alarmed by the
influx of Jewish migration and what it portended for their own
aspirations to self-determination throughout the *entire* Arab
world. Zionists looked on their desire for a Jewish homeland as
requiring only a tiny fraction, a small corner, of the vast area that
was Arab. From the Arab point of view, the Zionist presence was a
blemish that reminded them of a colonial past and also threatened
to dislodge Palestinian Arabs from their land. Regardless of their
public political stance it was clear to even moderate Zionists that
ultimately nothing less than Jewish sovereignty in their homeland
would suffice for them to accomplish their purpose.

In contrast to this position a small group of Jews living in Palestine, calling themselves Brit Shalom (Covenant of Peace), ex-
plored the possibilities of establishing a binational, Jewish-Arab
state in Palestine. Answering one of the advocates of a binational
state, Yosef Sprinzhak, at a meeting of Brit Shalom in 1924, Ben-
Gurion explained why the binational proposal was unacceptable:

> What is meant by the formula, a bi-national state? Sprinzhak
> says we don't want to become a majority, but only to become
> many. How much is many? A hundred thousand? A hundred
> and fifty thousand? Many in relation to whom—to the Arab
> community in Palestine, or to the Jewish communities in the
> Diaspora? Does it imply a restriction on our increase to be-
> come a majority in the country? Yes or no? Will we agree to
> such a restriction? For me, an Arab question exists only when
> I adopt a Zionist stance, when I want to solve in Eretz Israel
> the question of the Jewish people, that is, to concentrate it
> in Eretz Israel and make it a free people in its land. Without
> this Zionist basis there is no Arab question in Eretz Israel
> but a Jewish question, just as there is a Jewish question in
> all countries of the Diaspora, even where we are many. We

are many in Russia, in Poland, in America. There are millions of us there—and yet the Jewish question exists. There are vital historic needs of the masses of the Jewish people that are the foundations of Zionism, and the Jewish people will not hear of this. The Jewish people wants to be a free people in its land, to be its own master, and that means—a Jewish State.

What the Zionists wanted, Ben-Gurion said in 1929, "is only a small district in the tremendous territory populated by Arabs— most sparsely populated, I might add." But for the Jewish nation, "this is the one and only country with which are connected its fate and future as a nation."

Given this posture, conflict hardly seemed avoidable with the Arabs, who had an agenda of their own. Following the riots of 1929 it became increasingly clear to Zionist leaders that the two nationalisms were on a collision course. "The Arab in the Land of Israel need not and cannot be a Zionist," Ben-Gurion wrote in 1929. "He cannot want the Jews to become a majority. Herein lies the true conflict between us and the Arabs. [Both] we and they want to be a majority."

Ben-Gurion searched for a "reasonable" Arab with whom to carry on discussions. He spoke with Musa Alami, a wealthy landowner, attorney general of the Mandatory administration, and a confidant of the powerful Grand Mufti of Jerusalem. Ben-Gurion tried the same approach that Herzl had tried years earlier, appealing to the Arabs' economic self-interest as a reason why they should support Zionism. The Jews, Ben-Gurion argued, would bring the money and muscle to develop the land.

"The prevailing assumption in the Zionist movement then was that we were bringing a blessing to the Arabs of the country and that they therefore had no reason to oppose us," Ben-Gurion wrote.

In the first talk I had with Musa Alami . . . that assumption was shattered. Musa Alami told me that he would prefer the land to remain poor and desolate even for another hundred years, until the Arabs themselves were capable of developing it and making it flower, and I felt that as a patriotic Arab he had every right to this view.

From the Arab perspective, as another Arab leader made clear in a later conversation with Ben-Gurion, the Zionist enterprise was an economic catastrophe. Jews were buying the best land, dispossessing Arabs. Some Arabs became rich, but the lot of the common Arab had become worse. Land speculation had driven the price of land to exaggerated levels, the Arab told Ben-Gurion. Ben-Gurion tried to argue that Jewish settlement had helped Arab farmers learn new techniques and to increase their yields. The Arab disputed Ben-Gurion's assertion, maintaining "that in any case the land was being transferred to the Jews, and even though the Arabs might not need it at the moment, they would require it in a generation or two, when their numbers would be greater."

Hitler's rise to power in Germany in 1933 underscored the darkest visions of Zionist leaders and gave a new sense of urgency to their efforts to bring the maximum number of Jews to Palestine. The inevitability of conflict with the Arabs was becoming clearer all the time, even among the most moderate and conciliatory Zionists. Jews had to have a state ensure adequate immigration to Palestine, they reasoned. To have a state, they had to be a majority. And if they were to be a majority, it was certain that the Arabs would intensify their opposition to Zionist efforts.

It is instructive to consider the odyssey of Arthur Ruppin, a German Jew who became the first administrative head of the Jewish National Fund—the land purchasing agent in Palestine. Ruppin was one of the founders of Brit Shalom, a man deeply committed to Zionism but also profoundly concerned about the effect that Zionism would have on the Arabs of Palestine. It became clear, Ruppin wrote after a conversation in 1928,

how difficult it is to realize Zionism and still bring it continually into line with the demands of general ethics. I was well and truly depressed. Will Zionism indeed deteriorate into a pointless chauvinism? Is there in fact no way of assigning, in Israel, a sphere of activity to a growing number of Jews, without oppressing the Arabs? I see a special difficulty in the restricted land area. Surely the day is not far off, when no more unoccupied land will be available and the settlement of a Jew will automatically lead to the dispossession of an Arah *fellah?* What will happen then?

Eight years later the question was, if anything, more poignant. "Since our immigrants, for the vast majority, are people without means," Ruppin wrote, "the possibility should not be ruled out that these immigrants would take away the livelihood of the Arabs."

By 1936, as the position of Jews in Europe, especially in Germany, was becoming more untenable, Ruppin was still torn by the same question; but now the priorities had shifted in favor of Jewish immigration. He found himself at odds with other members of Brit Shalom, who, he wrote,

> thought that economic advantages, and certain political guarantees, would in themselves be calculated to persuade the Arabs to accept the Jewish national home. There was nothing new in this concept. It was, in fact, just a continuation of the false approach towards the Arabs, which had prevailed in the Zionist movement from the beginning. . . . All the economic advantages, and all the logical considerations, will not move the Arabs to give up the control of Eretz Israel in favor of the Jews, after they consider it was handed to them, or to share this control with the Jews, as long as the Arabs constitute the decisive majority in Eretz Israel.

From his perspective, Ruppin summed up the situation succinctly: "What we can get today from the Arabs—we don't need. What we need—we can't get."

But obviously that was not the end of it. Following the Arab riots of 1936 Ruppin looked at the present, the future, and drew what seemed the unavoidable conclusion:

It is only natural and inevitable, that Arab opposition to Jewish immigration should find an outlet from time to time in outbreaks of this sort. It is our destiny to be in a state of continual warfare with the Arabs, and there is no other alternative but that lives should be lost. This situation may well be undesirable, but such is the reality. If we want to continue our work in Eretz Israel, against the desires of the Arabs—then we shall be compelled to take such loss of life into consideration!

When the first attempt at partition was broached by the British in the mid-1930s, Ruppin studied it and found that the three hundred thousand Arabs envisioned to live in the proposed Jewish state were more than the state could absorb. Better to have a smaller state and fewer Arabs than to have so many, he wrote. Ruppin had reconciled himself to a situation of conflict into the indefinite future.

With the outbreak of World War II, of course, the worst fears of Zionist leaders were realized and exceeded. One by one, the countries of the world shut their doors to Jewish immigration. Palestine was no exception. The British, reacting to Arab pressure, imposed strict immigration quotas on Jews coming to Palestine. The British turned Jews away from Palestine, sending many back to their death. When the war actually began, the number of Jews coming to Palestine dropped to a trickle. During the war, as stories came back to Palestine about the Nazi death camps, the Jews of Palestine searched desperately for ways to bring Jews out of Europe. Nothing done was equal to the task, and in the end the Jews of Palestine were helpless to stop the slaughter of six million Jews in Nazi death camps.

The experience of the Holocaust only strengthened the belief of Ben-Gurion and other Zionist leaders that the creation of a Jewish state was essential. In 1942 the Zionist movement officially declared that Jewish statehood was its goal. The political ground-work had already been laid for a partition solution in Palestine that recognized the right of the Arabs and Jews to separate states. Under the pressure of coping with a million Jewish refugees, languishing in displaced-persons camps all over Europe, the United Nations approved the partition plan in November 1947—over the objection of Great Britain and with the support of both the United States and the Soviet Union.

The plan proposed a Jewish state in three tenuously connected segments—the bulk of the Negev in the south, a strip of land roughly 10 miles wide running from a point about 15 miles south of Tel Aviv to a point 10 miles north of Haifa (directly south of Acre), and a strip north of Samaria, including the eastern Galilee and the Sea of Galilee (the Kinneret). The western Galilee, the West Bank (Judea and Samaria), Gaza, and a strip of the Negev south of Gaza would have been an Arab-Palestinian state. Jaffa, which lay within the boundaries of the Jewish state, was to have been an Arab enclave.

The UN proposal, though far less than what the Jews of Palestine wanted, was accepted by them. The Arabs rejected the proposal out of hand. The Arabs, as it turned out, had seriously miscalculated in their diplomatic and military preparations. Diplomatically, the Arabs failed to make their case to the governments of the various countries who were members of the United Nations. The Arabs treated the UN effort itself with scorn, realizing only at the last moment that the Zionists had carefully and persistently made their case wherever they thought it would help their cause. One UN delegate, initially opposed to partition, explained after the General Assembly vote why he had supported it. "We found the Arabs, whose case we had considered to be a very strong one, to be in a weaker position than the Jews, partly because [the Arabs'] attitude of non-cooperation deprived them of many opportunities to influence the course of events."

The partition formula, among other things, was an effort to avoid a war over sovereignty over the land. As envisioned by the UN plan, the Jewish state would have had a majority of Jews but a substantial number of Arabs living in it, while the Arab state would have had a clear Arab majority and a minimal number of Jews.

The UN partition plan did not prevent war. Guerrilla warfare broke out almost immediately after the November 29, 1947, vote. When Israel actually declared her independence on May 14, 1948, the announcement was greeted with the simultaneous invasion of the land designated to be Israel by the Egyptian army from the south, the Iraqi and Syrian armies from the north, and the Jordanian army from the east. Local Palestinian forces also took up arms. Although badly outnumbered and poorly equipped, the Israelis were fighting separate armies that did little to coordinate their strategies and whose equipment often was little better than what the Israelis were using. The War of Independence continued in stages, with brief truces in between, until January 9, 1949. Although Israel had to fight desperately to survive in the initial part of the war, it gradually gained the upper hand, exploiting the lack of cooperation and coordination among the armies opposing it.

In resisting the partition plan, Palestine's Arabs participated in the dismemberment of what had been planned as the Palestinian state. The bulk of the proposed Arab state was seized by Jordan during Israel's War of Independence. Israel captured the Western Galilee and Jaffa, and Egypt took Gaza.

The War of Independence left Israel with about twenty percent more land than it would have had under the partition plan the Arabs rejected. The total land area of the new state was about eight thousand square miles. The Arab assumption had been that the Jews would be defeated and the Jewish land could be carved up along with the Arab part of Palestine. Following the War of Independence, nothing prevented Egypt or Jordan from allowing the establishment of a Palestinian state out of the territory of the Palestinian entity that had come under their control. But neither Egypt nor Jordan showed any disposition to do so. In fact, historical evidence suggests that Jordan was opposed to the establishment of an independent Arab state between itself and the Mediterranean because such a state would be inherently unstable and ultimately threatening to the well-being and future of the Hashimite Kingdom of Jordan.

Of approximately 650,000 Arabs living in the area that came under Israel's control, all but about 150,000 of them fled. Whether they fled voluntarily, under prodding from Jewish forces, or at the urging of Arab leaders is a matter of some contention. At least one historian sympathetic to Israel has concluded, after searching the available evidence, that he could find nothing to support the Israeli claim that the Arabs fled at the urging of their leaders. "Rather," Howard M. Sachar writes in *A History of Israel*,

> the evidence in the Arab press and radio of the time was to the contrary. By and large, except for towns like Haifa, already captured by the Jews, the Arab League ordered the Palestinians to stay where they were, and stringent punitive measures were reported against Arab youths of military age who fled the country. Even Jewish broadcasts (in Hebrew) mentioned these Arab orders to remain. [Arab leaders] and the various "national committees" appealed repeatedly to the Arabs not to leave their homes. The Ramallah commander of the Arab Legion threatened to confiscate the property and blow up the houses of those Arabs who left without permission. At one point the Lebanese government decided to close its frontiers to all Palestinians, except for women, children, and old people.

On the other hand, one prominent Israeli directly involved— Yitzhak Rabin—has claimed that he acted under orders from Ben-Gurion to drive Arabs from the territory under Jewish control.

Certainly thousands of Arabs fled from Jewish-controlled areas voluntarily, out of fear, especially after the Deir Yassin massacre outside of Jerusalem in April 1948 when more than two hundred Arab men, women, and children were slain and mutilated by forces of the right-wing Irgun Z'vai Le'umi and the Lech'i. The incident was quickly disavowed by the Haganah and condemned by the Jewish Agency, but it left an indelible stain on the Jewish war effort.

Despite the creation of an Arab refugee problem by the War of Independence, the inescapable fact is that the war was initiated by the Arabs, who—following Clausewitz's maxim—were continuing diplomacy by other means. The Arabs exploited the atrocity at Deir Yassin to its maximum advantage, but their own conduct in the war was hardly exemplary. Prior to Deir Yassin a force of Arab irregulars had ambushed a Jewish convoy coming to Jerusalem from the besieged settlement at Kfar Etzion, located between Hebron and Jerusalem. Many Jews were killed, and the Arabs mutilated their bodies.

Less than a week after the Deir Yassin incident the Arabs retaliated by ambushing a convoy of two ambulances, two buses, four trucks, and two armored car escorts carrying doctors, nurses, hospital patients, and assorted scientists across Jerusalem to Hadassah Hospital on Mount Scopus. More than seventy-five Jews were killed in the ambush, while British forces stood by and did nothing to prevent the slaughter.

A month later at Kfar Etzion, which had held out against Arab assault for months, eighty male and female defenders who surrendered were gunned down in cold blood by Arab irregulars.

In Jerusalem the Jewish part of the city was subjected to merciless, indiscriminate shelling by Arab artillery. Arab snipers shot scores of unarmed civilians who ventured outside.

After the War of Independence, Israel insisted that it would settle the claims of Arab refugees only within the terms of a comprehensive peace agreement that would include settlement of the claims of Jewish refugees who were forced to leave Arab countries, abandoning their homes, businesses, and other property.

Although admittedly most Israelis do not spend much—if any— time agonizing over the Jewish displacement of Arabs, the irony of the situation arouses complicated feelings of guilt and isolation, simultaneous attraction, fear, and revulsion among Jewish intellectuals. Clearly a minority in Israel, intellectuals are nonetheless an influential minority. As Amos Elon points out in his own book, *The Israelis: Founders and Sons,* feelings of guilt over the misery that the Jewish return caused Palestinian Arabs is a principal theme in the works of several Israeli writers. No feeling person could look at the plight of the Palestinians without feeling sympathy for their suffering. Yet at the same time, there is a sense that the Jews who came to Israel had little choice. For many, circumstance rather than desire sent them back to their ancient homeland. It was either that or annihilation. Given that situation, few if any Israelis have a problem deciding what the proper course was.

"If the alternative is between a) the Jews having their own roof overhead at the price of uprooting hundreds of thousands of Palestinian refugees from their land and resettling them in some other part of the *same* Palestine, and b) the Arabs of Palestine continuing to live on the land while the Holocaust refugees remain homeless—then the moral price of setting up the state is justified," Israeli Professor Shlomo Avineri said in a 1966 interview. "Between the lack of a Jewish homeland following the Holocaust and the uprooting of part of the Arabs of Palestine to another region in the same country—the moral alternative is clear."

A majority of the residents of Jordan, it is true, are Palestinians. The land area of Jordan, which was carved out of Mandatory Palestine by the British in the 1920s to provide a kingdom for the Hashimite dynasty, is greater than Israel's. In principle, it does not seem illogical to argue that if the Arabs are one nation, that displaced Palestinians—admittedly displaced at great hardship—could be absorbed elsewhere within the Arab nation. Many of the Arabs displaced by the Jewish return were, after all, migrants—or the sons and daughters of migrants—who had come to Palestine from other parts of the Arab world because the prospect of a better life had been opened up with the British Mandate and the support for a Jewish homeland.

Facts, however, never mitigate a tragedy for its victims. The tragedy of this situation is not simply that Jews displaced Arabs,

but that—given the continuing demand of the Palestinian Liberation Organization (as the generally recognized voice of Palestinian
nationalism) for a complete return to *all* of Palestine—no solution
is possible that will not compound the tragedy. If the Palestinians
are unbending in insisting that they be permitted to return to
their former homes and land, then the State of Israel as the world
knows it will cease to exist—and ultimate civil war among the
country's Jewish and Arab residents would be a likely eventuality.

As a result, even the most sensitive and sympathetic Israelis—
unless overwhelmed by guilt-motivated self-hate—cannot allow
themselves to go too far in their feeling for the Palestinian cause.
Why, an American journalist wondered in a conversation, do Israelis have such difficulty in appreciating the depth and sincerity
of feeling in Palestinian Arabs? On the contrary, I answered, many
Israelis—consciously or subsconsciously—understand only too well
how deeply and intensely Palestinians feel. Those feelings are an
obvious threat to the feeling of security that Israeli Jews would
like to have. Denying the sincerity of the feelings is only one
way—not very efficient or logical perhaps, but nonetheless human
—of denying the threat. Israelis, another American journalist
remarked, see their conflict as a zero-sum game—one side cannot
gain without the other losing something, perhaps everything.

It is true, of course, that some of the Israeli denial of Palestinian
sincerity in longing for their old homes and land reflects a fundamental difference in outlook and attitude as well. For the Zionists,
reclaiming the land—working it, building on it, developing it—
was a symbiotic process. In rebuilding the land the Jewish nation
would also be rebuilt. With so many Jews anxious to come to
Eretz Yisrael, leaving a patch of ground untilled was considered an
utter waste. During a trip to the prosperous development town of
Carmiel in the Galilee, I was taken for a ride around the area by
the town's mayor. As our car went up the side of an adjacent
mountain, the mayor pointed to landmarks of interest. This area
had been proposed by the UN to be part of the Arab state. The
mayor pointed out a nearby Arab village whose inhabitants had
fought the Jews during the War of Independence but since had

become more or less reconciled to the Jewish state. He called my attention to the industrial zone, to kibbutzim and moshavim in the area that were working the land, to homes and apartment buildings going up. "When the Arabs were here, they didn't do anything with the land," the mayor told me, by way of justifying the Jewish conquest of this area. "We've built it up."

The Arabs who remained in Israel after 1948 were concentrated in the north, in the Galilee, where they lived in villages dotting the hilly landscape and worked the land. Several thousand Bedouin also lived in the north, although a greater number lived in the south, in the relatively barren lands of the Negev. It is the Arab population of the north, relatively isolated from the rest of the country with its different culture, customs, language, educational levels, and the ever-present danger of irredentism it represents that poses a challenge to Israeli democracy and a simultaneous threat to the security of the Jewish state. The circumstance of Israeli Arabs—citizens of the state—is a situation of reciprocal ambivalence and ambiguity, neither side fully trusting or accepting the other, coexisting in a kind of nervous limbo, while events in the region create new strains on the relationship.

In principle, Israeli Arabs—who now number about 630,000— have all the rights of Israeli citizens. They vote in Israeli elections, they have full access to Israeli courts, their children are educated in state-supported schools, and they are eligible for membership in the Histadrut. The actual situation of Israeli Arabs, however, is considerably different from that of the Jewish population. Israel's Arabs continue to be, practically as well as figuratively, a nation apart, separated by culture, language, and living standards from the rest of the population. On the other hand, considerable changes have occurred in the conditions of Israeli Arabs since the establishment of the state. In 1948 only 15 percent of Arab women received any education. Thirty years later 80 percent were finishing high school. In 1954 more than half of Israel's Arabs were engaged in farming. Ten years later the number had dropped to 39 percent, and by 1980 only 13 percent of Israeli Arabs worked as farmers.

Of the Arabs who did not flee during the War of Independence, few left after the establishment of the state. As Israeli citizens and workers, the benefits of Histadrut membership are available to them. Israeli Arabs, as a result, enjoy a higher average standard of living and better social and medical services than Arabs in any other Middle Eastern country. By 1975 almost 100,000 Arabs had joined the Histadrut. Arab workers employed in factories organized by the Histadrut receive the same pay scale and benefits paid to Jewish workers. By 1975 sick fund dispensaries operated by the Histadrut (Kupat Holim) were operating in ninety-five Arab villages in Israel, serving 250,000 members.

Israel's construction trades are now almost exclusively manned by Arab workers—either from Israel or the occupied territories. Aside from an occasional Jewish foreman, it is rare to find Jewish laborers in skilled or unskilled construction jobs. Roughly 40 percent of the Arab labor force is now classified as being skilled workers in industry or construction. The number of Arabs in construction and industry is disproportionate to their number in the population. Although only about 7 percent of the entire population of Israel work in construction jobs, 24 percent of all Arab workers work in construction trades. At the same time, almost 43 percent of the total population of roughly 3.9 million persons hold jobs classified as service positions, but only 24 percent of Arab workers hold service jobs. The overwhelming majority of Arab workers—almost 75 percent—work as employees, although it is difficult to determine how many work for Arab employers. Less than 1 percent of the Arab working population is employed as administrators and managers, compared to 4 percent of the Jewish work force.

A factory manager said that he once had tried employing an Arab as a foreman but that it had not worked out because the other Arab workers failed to understand why one of them should be "honored" and not any of the others. Finally, he said, the Arab foreman asked to be given his old job back as an ordinary worker. On the other hand, another factory manager interviewed had an Arab foreman whom the manager considered to be one of his best employees. The Arab foreman in this factory had no problems with other workers, most of whom were Jewish, although some were Arab. The difference, it seems, had to do with the climate established in the factory by the manager, who made it clear from the outset that efficiency and hard work would be rewarded and that everyone would benefit from management based on merit.

The broad situation that emerges, however, is of a vast economic separation between Jews and Arabs, confirming the worst apprehensions of the early Zionists who had insisted on the principle of Jewish labor. In a talk with Musa Alami in 1934, Ben-Gurion had explained why Jews were insisting on the principle of Jewish labor. Recalling what he had told the former British high commissioner of Rhodesia, Ben-Gurion said:

> I told him that we did not want to create a situation such as existed in southern Africa, where the Whites were the lords and masters while the Blacks were the workers. If we remained merely the owners of the land, without doing all the necessary work with our own hands, easy and hard, skilled and unskilled, this would not be our homeland. I told Musa Alami about the builders of the first villages—Petah Tikva, Rishon Le-Zion, Zichron Ya'akov and Rosh Pina—and about the Bilu settlers. They had come here driven by the impulse to revive our homeland and independence, but in the course of time many of them had forsaken these ideals and employed only Arab laborers, who were cheaper (because they had fewer needs) and more subservient, whereas the Jewish workers, most of whom had come with a vision of redemption, regarded themselves as no less important than the farmers. I explained that in the Diaspora we were cut off from the land and were accused of living on the toil of others. . . . I explained why we regarded work as the basis of life and the foundation of national renascence.

For better or worse, Israeli Jews have again "forsaken these ideals." In the fall of 1980 Beersheba's Soroka Hospital, which serves the entire northern Negev area, was forced to cancel all surgery save for emergency cases. The reason given was that the hospital had an insufficient supply of sterile linen to maintain its normal surgery schedule. The laundry that did the hospital's linen was temporarily unable to function: its Arab employees had not come to work because of an Arab holiday of several days' duration.

The gravitation of unskilled and semiskilled Arab workers to lower-paying, less-demanding jobs of a menial and manual nature, while better-educated more highly skilled Jewish workers opt for more demanding jobs or white-collar work, no doubt represents the victory of universal economic laws over Zionist principles. Workers the world over dream of escaping the monotony and relatively low pay of manual work, especially in factories, for the better pay and higher prestige of white-collar employment. Nevertheless, Israel stands in jeopardy of creating the sort of permanent underclass that Ben-Gurion told Musa Alami the Zionists feared.

Disparities in positions held by Arabs and Jewish Israelis can, of course, be attributed to cultural and educational differences. Israeli Arabs, emerging from an agrarian, semirural culture into an industrial society lack the skills and talents of a modern society. Much the same gap separates Israeli Jews from Oriental countries —who hold a disproportionately high percentage of blue-collar jobs in Israel—from Israeli Jews of European or American origin.

On the average the income of Arab families in Israel is roughly eighty-three percent of the income of Jewish families. The average income of an Arab family is roughly the same as the average income of an Oriental Jewish family—even higher in some years— but is considerably lower than the average Jewish family of Western origin. Comparisons are somewhat difficult, since Arab farmers have less income to report because they consume much of what they produce. Besides that, Israeli government officials continually complain that Israeli Arabs underreport their income to avoid paying taxes.

Arabs, 16 percent of the population, represent only 6 percent of the Knesset's members. None of the Supreme Court justices is an Arab. No cabinet minister or deputy is an Arab. No major official of the Histadrut or any prominent business or financial institution is an Arab. Israel's defense industries, which are a major Israeli employer, are closed to Arabs.

A casual visit to any number of Arab villages in Israel suggests that the level of public services in these areas is lower than in areas of Jewish settlement. According to an Israeli government survey, one out of every three classrooms in the state-supported Arab school system is in a converted residential flat or building. Many of these classrooms lacked heat, electricity, and adequate bathrooms, according to the survey, released in late 1980.

One explanation given by Israeli officials for the higher level of improvements in Jewish towns as compared to Arab villages is that the Arab municipalities do not choose to levy taxes to provide for paved streets and proper sewage disposal. Arab villages also do not, however, qualify for development funds provided by the Jewish Agency, an extragovernmental body whose budget is derived from the contributions of Jews living outside of Israel. Despite the extragovernmental nature of the Jewish Agency, there is no doubt that it works hand in glove with the Israeli government and can be considered, for all intents and purposes, an extension of the state. Thus, the distribution of Jewish Agency funds to *Jewish* Israelis only serves to underscore the preferred positions that Jews hold in Israel, despite the Israeli Declaration of Independence's assertion that Arabs will participate in the state "on the basis of full and equal citizenship."

Arabs living in Israel are eligible to vote in local and national elections without restriction and to hold elective office. A number of Arabs serve in the Knesset, elected on lists associated with the major parties—especially the Labor Alignment—or on the Rakah (Communist) party list.

The existence and use of these formal rights and the relative prosperity that Israeli Arabs enjoy, however, do not alter the basic ambivalence of their status in Israel. The question, Who am I? has special poignance for Israel's Arabs, living in the midst of a Jewish state, surrounded by Arab countries hostile to the country where they are living. Many of Israel's Arabs have family and close relatives living in neighboring Arab countries. Israeli Arabs are not inducted into the Israel Defense Forces for the stated reason that asking Arabs to serve would force many of them to choose between family and country. Thus, the sine qua non of Israeli citizenship, participation in the army, is closed to Israel's Arabs (although some of Israel's Bedouin do serve, along with Circassians and Druze).

After the 1948 War of Independence the rights of Arabs in the Galilee were severely limited. They were kept under the control of a military governor. They were prevented from traveling from their villages without permission of the military governor. Arab property in the Galilee was seized, and it was years before the Israeli government provided compensation. In some cases the expropriation of land—nominally done for security purposes—amounted to little more than a land grab by the government for Jewish settlements. Not until 1963, under pressure from both Arabs and Jews in Israel, were the restrictions on free Arab movement in Israel eased. Military government was abolished in 1966. By then the very real security threats that had brought the government to impose the restrictions had eased. But the government, acting through the northern military commander, still has emergency powers that it can and does invoke from time to time to limit the movement of individual. Arabs and to prohibit meetings, conferences, and conventions it considers a threat to the security of the state. That these powers can also be used against Jews hardly alters the point that they are almost always used against Arabs, and it is Israel's Arabs, not Israel's Jews, who remain an undigested segment of the society.

More than fifty percent of Israeli Arab workers leave their villages during working hours to travel to their jobs, but when they return home at night, they recede into a world separated by custom, religion, and language from the rest of Israeli society. The population of the villages is almost always totally Arab. Israel offers Arab-language radio programs throughout the day, and two hours or more of Arab-language programs are televised each evening. Israeli Arabs are not limited to the listening or viewing offered by Israeli radio. More than a score of Arab stations, broadcasting from Jordan, Syria, Iraq, and Egypt are available to and are popular among Israeli Arabs. Some of these stations are a constant source of anti-Israeli propaganda and invective.

Arab children attend Arab schools where they are taught by Arab teachers. In deference to their sensitivities Arab children may not be taught much, if anything, about Zionism, but neither are they given a very strong dose of Arab nationalism in the classroom—at least not in the officially sanctioned curriculum. Arab children learn Hebrew, but since they live in an atmosphere where Arabic is spoken, they have less chance to use it than they need to become proficient in the language. As a result, Arab children who speak and read Hebrew do so with far less ability than Jewish children, putting Arab children at a disadvantage when they come to enter Israeli universities.

Socially, the two populations hardly mix. Fewer than one thousand marriages have occurred between Arabs and Jews since 1948. It is not unprecedented for Jews and Arabs to entertain one another in their homes, but it seldom happens. Jews and Arabs come into contact with each other in business dealings, and sometimes these business relationships are extended over long periods of time and do take on an almost social aura. One Israeli told how he is greeted with kisses by the Arab mechanic who fixes his car. Another Israeli makes a point of spending an hour or two every week sipping Turkish coffee and exchanging small talk with Arab merchants in the Old City of Jerusalem. But these individual instances are the exception rather than the rule. Only a comparatively small percentage of Israelis speak Arabic, for one thing. For another, Arabs who venture into Jewish areas are often treated with suspicion, causing them discomfort and discouraging them from making the effort. An Arab with whom I had become friendly told me that when he stopped people on the street to ask directions to my house, the first response he invariably received was, "Why do you want to go there?"

Israeli attitudes and feelings toward Arabs run the gamut from a deep-seated desire to establish warm and close personal relations with Arabs on a basis of full equality to a profound hatred and contempt for Arabs that borders on racism. A survey of Jewish attitudes toward Arabs found that only 13 to 14 percent held views at either extreme—positive or negative. The vast majority of Jewish Israelis—roughly 70 percent—had a mixed attitude, positive and negative, toward Israeli Arabs. About 69 percent of those surveyed, for example, thought Arabs were devoted to their families, but 36 percent thought Arabs were dirty. Some 42 percent thought Arabs *did* value human life, while 33 percent thought Arabs did *not* value human life. Roughly 45 percent agreed that Israeli Arabs are torn between loyalty to Israel and loyalty to the Arab people. Only 16 percent thought most Israeli Arabs are happy when Israel is hurt. About 40 percent believed Israeli Arabs were entitled to full equality in Israel; security grounds were usually cited as the reason for opposing equality. More than half were willing to establish social contacts with Arabs. And 40 percent were willing to live in the same building with Arabs.

These attitudes on the part of Israelis indicate that from the perspective of Israeli Jews the situation is not hopelessly hostile. Far from being completely negative, Israel has strong pockets of friendly feelings and affection for Arabs. A separate survey of Israeli Arabs, asking different questions, found that only about a third of the Arabs surveyed were satisfied with Israeli democracy, with the Knesset, or with freedom of speech. Almost 60 percent were satisfied with Israel's legal system, however, and 90 percent expressed satisfaction with medical services.

Measured by the performance of political parties, Jewish attitudes toward Arabs confirm the poll's findings. The most conciliatory political party in the 1977 elections (other than the Communists) was Sheli, which advocated unilateral concessions to the Arabs in an effort to achieve peace. Sheli won only 2 seats (out of 120) in the Knesset. On the other hand, Rabbi Meir Kahane, the right-wing American Israeli, ran on a platform advocating the unbridled use of force if necessary to expel Arabs from Israel and the occupied territories. Kahane won no seats at all—which is to say he received less than one percent of the vote.

Considering the history of Israel, it should hardly be surprising that Jewish attitudes toward Arabs are complicated. Roughly half of Israel's Jewish population came—or are the children of parents who came—from Arab countries where they felt less than welcome. "All the time, they told us in Tunis, 'Go to Palestine, go to Palestine. We don't want you here,'" a Tunisian Israeli said. "So now we're here and we shouldn't give them anything back. The hell with them."

Israelis have a particularly contemptuous way of describing someone or something as being beneath them. "They live like Arabs," an Israeli Jew might say of other Jews. Or work may be described as "Arab work." In both instances the clear meaning of the description is that Arab culture is of a lower order than Jewish culture. This contemptuous attitude is reinforced by the manner in which Israel's Jews, using modern technology and the advantage of superior communication and coordination, were able to defeat Arab armies in five wars.

Considering the past success Israel has enjoyed on the battlefield despite the overwhelming numerical superiority of the Arabs, it is not difficult to understand why many Israelis should have felt superior to Arabs, the more so since Arabs have proved less adept at a skill in which Israelis take particular pride. "What," an Israeli asked following the rout of the Arab armies in the 1967 war, "did the Israeli army and the Egyptian army have in common? When the war broke out, they both headed for Cairo."

After the shock of 1973, however, this feeling of superiority has been tempered with the realization that the Arabs have access to the same modern technology that Israelis depend upon to defend themselves. Without feeling any less intellectually superior to Arabs, Israelis again are aware that they are surrounded by hostile Arabs who are, in theory, and not infrequently in practice, dedicated to the destruction of Israel.

Hardly a day goes by in Jerusalem, Tel Aviv, Beersheba, Haifa, or somewhere else in the country that a bomb isn't found. Usually these explosives are disarmed before they can harm anyone, but life in Israel is a constant reminder for Israelis that they cannot afford to relax even for a moment. Signs everywhere alert bus passengers to watch for suspicious objects. Television spots and notices in the newspapers also constantly exhort readers to be on the alert. An Arab seen in a Jewish neighborhood after working hours is a source of suspicion.

An Israeli woman recounted how she returned home from an errand on a day when she expected her Arab gardener to appear. She did not see the gardener, but she found a plastic shopping bag—which she recognized as his—filled with packages and wires. Although she had a long and close relationship with her gardener, she could not help feeling alarmed and frightened by the package. She was considering calling the police when her gardener appeared.

"Is this yours?" she asked.

"Yes, of course," he answered. "Why?"

"I didn't know what it was," she said, not quite able to conceal her anxiety from him.

"And you thought I might have left a bomb here?" he asked her. "How could you think that? I'm your friend."

"I knew he was a friend," she said afterward, "and I was embarrassed by the whole incident. I felt very bad for being suspicious. But, still, you can never be sure."

For the average Israeli there is an undercurrent of anxiety that is constantly present in dealings with even the most moderate of Arabs. That these fears and anxieties are normally groundless may well be. But survival and avoiding injury in Israel depend not on assumptions of goodwill but just the opposite. Enough incidents occur to justify the anxieties and to encourage the precautions.

Shortly after the opening of the public beaches in Haifa during the summer of 1980, a Jewish kiosk operator noticed three Arabs arrive at the beach, settle themselves in as if to stay, and then leave hurriedly after burying something in the sand. The kiosk operator chased the Arabs, who were eventually caught by the police. The three had left a bomb buried, in what would have been within hours a crowded beach.

When a new immigrant to Israel from America complained to another American Israeli who had lived in Israel for several years about the indignities Arabs suffered because of security precautions, the veteran Israeli listened patiently until the newcomer had finished. "Them's the facts of life," the veteran commented succinctly. For him as for many other Israelis the desire to keep life and limb intact superseded any sensitivities he might have about embarrassing or humiliating Arabs.

Obviously, these precautions and searches are unpleasant for Arabs. Approaching Jerusalem on the highway, one often sees long lines of Arab cars pulled over to the side of the road while Jewish cars are allowed to pass without even stopping. Arabs entering Jerusalem occasionally are delayed forty-five minutes or more, depending upon how heavy the traffic is, while their cars are searched by security forces.

Israeli Arabs who fly abroad from Israel on El Al encounter much the same situation. A woman flying abroad from Israel described how an Israeli Arab family was asked by El Al security officials to unpack each of the suitcases they were carrying so that the contents could be inspected before the bags were checked through and loaded on the plane. The entire inspection of the baggage was carried out with courtesy and respect by the El Al security officials. "But you could see," the woman said, "that no matter how courteous the officials were, the whole experience was a tremendous embarrassment for the Arab family. Even though the tight security was as much for their protection as anyone else's, that thought hardly compensated for the humiliation of the experience."

The failure—or at least the inability—to integrate Arabs into the life of the larger society renders Israel a country with two major cultures living next to each other, peacefully perhaps, but without the kinds of permanent bonds that cement a population to the state. The contradiction in Israel is not so much between the ideal and the reality as it is embedded in the ideal itself. Israel is a Jewish state. The national holidays of the country are Jewish holidays. The only secular holidays celebrated in Israel—Memorial Day and Independence Day—hold no joy or meaning for Arabs, unless the meaning is a negative one, since both holidays commemorate the creation of the Jewish state. Israel does not exist for the benefit of non-Jews. Its doors are not open without question, as a matter of birthright, to non-Jews as they are to Jews. No one supposes that Israel's Arabs have the slightest interest in whether or not the Jews of Soviet Russia are allowed to come to settle in Israel, or whether they actually do so. Israel's Arabs live in a kind of netherworld, reflected in their Israeli identity cards, which classify them as Arab nationals but Israeli citizens. "My people are at war with my country," one Israeli Arab lamented in 1967 when the Arab countries of the Middle East took on Israel.

The ambivalent attitude of Israeli Arabs is only a mirror image of Israel's attitude toward them. And nowhere is this ambivalent attitude more poignantly demonstrated than in the Galilee where Jewish concern about the Arabs of the country is expressed in a quiet, nonviolent struggle to determine who will control the area. From the northern border to Nazareth, Jews are a minority in the Galilee, concentrated in urban centers, while Arabs live in dusty villages in the hills. The entire area covers about 300,000 acres, and the state owns about 158,000 acres. According to official estimates Arabs are illegally using more than half of the state land, either farming it, grazing livestock on it, or building on it. Although the government now concedes that it is probably no longer possible for Jews to be a majority in the Galilee, Jews are encouraged to settle in the north in order to maintain a solid Jewish "presence" to foreclose the future possibility that Arab irredentism will result in a secessionist movement to attach the area to some kind of Palestinian state or entity.

As part of the campaign, promoted with posters and television advertisements encouraging young Israeli families to move to the Galilee, settlements are being started at carefully selected sites in the north to plant Jews in the midst of Arab concentrations. The settlements are relatively self-sufficient units, planned with industry as well as housing, schools, and a regional service center to provide for needs other than the most basic.

Besides the settlements, the government has built a series of "lookouts" in the Galilee for the primary purpose of permanently locating Jews in the area in places where they can observe—and report when necessary—the activities of Arabs so that the government can act quickly to check illegal efforts by Arabs to move onto state-owned land.

In many instances Arab villagers dispute the government's claim to the land, arguing that the villages have used the land for generations preceding the establishment of the state. In any case, they argue, if the land is not being used, why shouldn't they, as Israeli citizens, have the right to use it. "I am Israeli, too," one Arab Israeli said. "If the government wants the land settled, what's wrong with my settling it?"

The answer, rarely expressed openly by government officials, is that the country's Arab population is still viewed with apprehension, as a potential fifth column within the country. When the northern Israeli military commander told a group he was addressing in 1979 that the Arabs of the Galilee were a "cancer" that had to be checked, he was officially reprimanded for his statement. The government was embarrassed by it. Yet the military official said what many Israelis think, and the Israeli government keeps a nervous eye on Arabs in the Galilee.

From the perspective of national identity, citizenship in Israel is a dead end for Arabs so long as the end point of the Jewish state is the expression of Jewish ideals and the construction of a Jewish homeland. Arabs may be able to prosper economically in such a place. They may even enjoy rights and advantages that they would not enjoy in Jordan, Syria, or Egypt. One Israeli Arab, a school principal living in a large Galilee village with a Communist town council, said that he had traveled to Jordan for a visit in 1977, his first trip there since 1948. He said he was shocked at the difference in atmosphere between Amman and Israel, between the relative freedom that Arabs have in Israel and the strict limitations on them in Jordan. "Here," he said, "I can stand up in the middle of the street and say that Menachem Begin, Moshe Dayan, Yitzhak Rabin, and Shimon Peres should all go to hell and nothing will happen to me. If I said the same thing about King Hussein in Jordan, I'd be in jail."

But it is far from clear that Israel's Arab population has recon-

ciled itself to living forever under the rule of a Jewish government. The underlying tension between Israel's Jewish and Arab
population is more evident in recent years, with the growth of a
Palestinian nationalist movement outside Israel and in the occupied territories, than it was in preceding years. Prior to 1967 Israeli Arabs were cut off from the rest of the Arab world and the
main currents of Arab nationalism. Following the 1967 war, however, the Israeli government pursued a moderate policy of "open
bridges" with Jordan, allowing Arab goods from the West Bank to
be trucked to Jordan and permitting Arabs to move back and
forth across the bridges in both directions. As a result, families
that had been separated for years were able to reunite. And Israel's
Arabs once again came into contact with Arabs outside of the
country.

There are almost no signs that Israeli Arabs would prefer to live
outside of Israel. In the years since 1948 only a small number of
Arabs have left Israel. In 1978, according to a survey of 900 Arabs
who left the country during the year, 890 returned. And though
few signs indicate that Palestinian terrorist organizations have
been able to recruit any more than a handful of Arabs from inside
Israel, other signs suggest that sympathy for a Palestinian state is
growing. A poll of Israeli Arabs in 1979 found that 50 percent of
those polled questioned Israel's right to exist; 48 percent—less
than a majority but a large minority—called themselves "Palestinians" rather than Israelis; 87 percent favored a return to Israel's
1967 borders; and 57 percent favored the 1947 United Nations
partition borders, which would leave many Israeli Arabs outside
Israel and inside a Palestinian entity of some kind.

Support for the Communist party, the only anti-Zionist party
offering candidates for the Knesset, has increased considerably
since 1967. Although the line that Rakah, the Communist party,
must tread is a narrow one, it advocates the establishment of a
Palestinian state and recognition of the PLO. In Israel's earliest
elections, from the first through the sixth Knesset, the majority of
Arab voters supported either Mapai or one of the Arab lists associated with it. In 1951, the high point for Mapai, 72 percent of
Arab voters cast ballots for Mapai, Mapam (which at one time

favored a binational rather than a Jewish state), or for one of their Arab lists. After that, the percentage fell, so that by 1969 Jewish left-wing parties—or Arab parties associated with them—received only about 55 percent of the vote, and by 1977 the percentage had dropped to only 27 percent.

The main beneficiary of the declining Arab vote for Jewish parties was Rakah, which increased its share of the Arab vote from about 23 percent in 1965 to almost 50 percent in 1977. In 1981, Israeli Arab voters followed the national trend by concentrating on the major parties. Rakah's strength in the Knesset was diminished by one seat—going from five to four—as some Arab voters moved back to the Labor Alignment. Political commentators were quick to seize on this move as proof that Arab voters were disenchanted with Rakah. Virtually no one commented, however, on the absolute decline in the number of Arab votes cast, an indication that many Israeli Arabs had concluded that the entire electoral process was irrelevant and unresponsive to their needs.

The position of Rakah in the Arab political spectrum is relatively moderate, given the emergence of a radical, pro-Palestine Liberation Organization movement among young Israeli Arabs. Muslim fundamentalism, sparked by the Iranian revolution, appears to be increasing. In addition, a movement calling itself Sons of the Village is attracting a small, but apparently growing, following among younger men in Israel's Arab villages and among Israeli Arab university students. Tension on university campuses among Arab and right-wing Jewish students has increased, leading to violent clashes—an unheard of occurrence in the late 1960s and mid-1970s.

The position of the university-educated Arab in Israel is particularly difficult. According to one official of the Hebrew University:

The Israeli Arab student comes from a highly conservative, traditionalist, land-oriented society. Up to 1967, as an Arab in a Jewish state at war with its Arab neighbors, he suffered from an identity problem. Today, the crisis of identity is over; all Arab students readily and totally identify themselves as Palestinians.

Although it may be something of an exaggeration to say that all Arab students identify themselves as Palestinians, it seems clear that they are in an ambivalent position in Israel. "We are made to feel like strangers in our own land," one radical Arab student said.

Not more than two thousand Arabs attend Israeli universities. Those who make it to college in Israel more than likely are having their first exposure to Jewish Israeli society and culture. Arabs in Israel, save for those living in Jerusalem, can go for months or even years without having any prolonged contact with Jews or with things Jewish. Living in Arab villages in a predominantly agrarian society, listening to the twenty or more radio stations broadcasting from neighboring Arab countries, watching Jordanian, Egyptian, or Arab broadcasts on television, Arabs can easily disregard that they are in Israel.

Once Arab students enter the university, however, they find themselves in an atmosphere where they are suddenly in a minority among people speaking Hebrew or English. Once their studies are completed, the number of job opportunities open to them is limited. They can become schoolteachers, teaching in Arab schools, or they can try to find a job in the Israeli labor market. Most Israeli firms, however, are not interested in hiring an Arab college graduate to work for them. With a degree from an Israeli university, getting a job in an Arab country is next to impossible for an Arab.

Few dangers to the continued domestic calm of Israel could be greater than the growth of a disaffected class of educated Arabs who find no creative outlets for their abilities. The existence of a radical Palestinian movement, taking deep root in the territories occupied in the 1967 war, only aggravates the problem for Israel, suggesting to Israeli Arabs that a Palestinian state will somehow enable them to lead more complete and satisfactory lives.

The growth of a Palestinian nationalist movement is a comparatively recent phenomenon. Prior to 1967 the Palestinian problem was expressed as a matter of refugees rather than of a homeland or a state. The territory that had been designated in the United Nations partition plan of 1947 as an Arab state had all been captured by outside forces, and primarily Arab forces at that.

Israel had captured the portions of the western Galilee that were to have been part of the Arab state. Egypt was in control of the Gaza Strip. And Jordan was in control of the West Bank and East Jerusalem.

Under these circumstances the question of Palestinian nationalism did not arise. Neither Egypt nor Jordan was willing to grant independence or autonomy to the Palestinian Arabs under their control. Jordan had made no secret of its apprehension of an independent Arab state on its western border. Jordan's entry into the 1948 Israeli War of Independence was aimed at eliminating the possibility that an Arab state would be created according to the United Nations partition plan. Once that goal had been reached, Jordan lost interest in pursuing the war against Israel further.

The Arabs of the West Bank, though allowed to participate in the governing of the Hashimite Kingdom of Jordan, were not permitted to express their separateness. Jordan, while asserting that its action did not foreclose "final settlement of Palestine's just cause," annexed the West Bank in 1950, despite opposition from Palestinian Arabs. Arabs of the West Bank were Jordanian citizens —unlike refugees in Lebanon and the Gaza Strip, who were stateless. But attempts to express their nationality were discouraged and suppressed by the Jordanian regime of King Hussein.

The question of Palestinian nationalism was largely moot during the years from 1948 until 1967 because it had no territory on which to focus. Whatever the United Nations 1947 partition plan had called for, Israel's new borders were a *fait accompli,* recognized in fact, if not in international law. (Technically, until all the countries at war with Israel sign a peace treaty with her, as opposed to the armistice agreements they have signed, Israel does not have defined permanent borders.) The Galilee was in Israel's hands and there seemed little prospect that it could be dislodged.

In any case, the Galilee alone would not be enough to constitute a Palestinian state. Outside the Arab world, there was no sentiment for taking the Galilee away from Israel. Israel, after all, had been willing to accept the UN partition plan and to live with it. It was the Arabs who had rejected the plan because they could not accept any proposal that provided for a Jewish state. In the subsequent fighting the Palestinians were the major losers and the cause of Palestinian nationalism became a dormant issue.

Dormant, but not entirely dead. In the years between 1948 and 1967 the problem of terrorist raids from Arab countries into Israel was a serious but not overwhelming problem. On several occasions, when the problem threatened to get out of hand, Israel conducted reprisal raids into Jordan to discourage Jordan's support for the terrorist attacks on Israeli border settlements. From the perspective of security Israel had been left with borders that, at their narrowest points—north of Tel Aviv—were only ten miles from the seacoast to the Arab West Bank. This entire border area along the West Bank, which meandered for more than 200 miles, was difficult to defend. The strategic advantage was with the Jordanians, who occupied the high ground of the Judean and Samarian hills, while the Israelis were forced to defend a long border from the lowlands of the coastal plain. Holding the strategic advantage, the Jordanians could—if they chose to do so—invade Israel from any of a number of points along the border, tying down Israeli forces.

The 1967 war obviously changed the entire equation for Israel and the Palestinians when it ended with Israel holding the high ground facing Jordan. Any Jordanian attempt to attack Israel would require Jordan first to cross the Jordan River and then to come over the north–south chain of mountains that traverse the West Bank. In addition, the border between Israel and Jordan had been shortened to about one fifth of its former length, and the narrow neck north of Tel Aviv, at Natanya—where the danger had existed that Israel could be cut in two—was eliminated.

But the 1967 war raised other problems for Israel. Overnight, approximately one million more Arabs came under the control of

Israel. Initially, Arabs on the West Bank lived under an Israeli military occupation that was widely described as one of the most liberal and humane in history. Israel kept the bridges to Jordan open so that produce from the West Bank might continue to move into Jordan. Public employees on the West Bank continued to receive salaries from Amman and to travel there periodically.

In Gaza, a hotbed of terrorist activity against Israel, strict measures were enforced to stamp out violence against Israelis. In the Golan Heights the Syrian population fled, leaving behind only Druze villages whose inhabitants had little trouble accommodating themselves to Israeli rule and in some cases even preferring it.

Clearly, though, Israeli control of Palestinian territory formerly occupied by Arab countries gave a boost to the Palestinian movement. The refugee problem had become worse. Thousands of refugees who had been living in camps on the West Bank fled to Jordan, Lebanon, and elsewhere in the Arab world. The task of dramatizing the "homelessness" of these refugees became easier for Palestinian nationalists now that a non-Arab country was in control of the territory that had been designated by the United Nations in 1947 to be an Arab state. Obviously, Palestinian Arab nationalism could not be expressed or satisfied within the borders of a Jewish state. All the land that was to have been that state was now in the hands of one country, and a non-Arab country at that.

Israel, an open society with a free press and free speech—allowing journalists relatively free access to all parts of Israel and the territories—was more vulnerable to international pressure and criticism when pursuing repressive measures against the Palestinians than the authoritarian Egyptian and Jordanian regimes had been. Democracies are always weakest when pursuing antidemocratic policies, and Israel was no exception.

As time passed, the Palestinians became more adept at public relations, presenting the perceived justice of their cause against a backdrop of the misery of the refugees who had fled first from Israel and later from the West Bank.

Israel, to a large extent, was a victim of her own success. No longer helpless in the face of attacks, Israel was able to move ruthlessly against terrorists, clearing out their bases on the West Bank and delivering menacing blows in the neighboring states that gave aid and comfort to them.

Under the direction of Israeli Defense Minister Moshe Dayan (1967–74), who kept a close watch over the military government of the West Bank and Gaza, relations with the Arabs in the territories remained relatively calm. Israel's victory in 1967 had been so decisive that the likelihood of another war anytime soon seemed remote, and the likelihood of an Arab victory in such a war seemed even more so.

The 1973 war, however, altered the equation again. Although Israel avoided a military defeat (something that the Arabs do not concede), she suffered enormous casualties and proved unprepared when the war began. Israel had counted on her strength to deter a war, and certainly to contain it quickly should war break out. Israel failed in 1973 to deter the Arabs and it took an enormous, desperate effort to turn the situation in her favor. In addition, Israel's image and status in the territories was greatly diminished by the 1973 war. The Arab oil boycott increased Western pressure on Israel and focused greater attention on the Palestinian cause. The Arab oil boycott gave Arab oil customers a direct stake in the resolution of the question. The United Nations, which had once made possible the creation of Israel, had become over the passage of time and the admission of scores of Third World countries a forum for airing Palestinian grievances against Israel. So long as Palestinian grievances were directed against Israel rather than against an Arab country, no Arab state had an interest in suppressing Palestinian nationalist aspirations.

Jordan, always the weakest link in the pan-Arab movement, was dislodged as the representative of Palestinian nationalism and replaced by the Palestine Liberation Organization at the 1974 conference in Rabat. The net effect of the Rabat conference, from Israel's point of view, was to interpose the more radical PLO instead of the more moderate Jordan as a potential negotiating partner in reaching some sort of agreement concerning the West Bank.

Israeli policy under the Labor Alignment government treated the West Bank, the Golan Heights, and Gaza as strategic assets that could be the subject of negotiations in exchange for a "real" peace. Israeli settlement policy, pursued with a minimum of fanfare in the period prior to 1977—when the Labor government was replaced by the right-wing Likud government of Prime Minister Menachem Begin—stressed the strategic value of settlements on the West Bank. As a result, settlements were concentrated along the Jordan River facing Jordan, in the hills and mountains above the Jordan valley, and not, for the most part, near the population centers in the western part of the West Bank.

Without ever formally adopting it, the Labor government followed the broad outlines of a plan proposed by Yigal Allon, then education minister but also a former high-ranking officer in the Israel Defense Forces. Support in principle for Allon's plan came from Moshe Dayan, who proposed in 1971 that Israel should proceed with plans for the territories on the assumption that peace might be long in coming. Israel, Dayan said, should "create facts," a concept not unknown to Israelis. "If the Arabs refuse to make peace," Dayan said, "we cannot sit still. If we are denied their cooperation, let us act on our own."

Yet these settlements were not, as already mentioned, near population centers. The sole exception was a religious enclave outside Hebron called Kiryat Arba (Town of the Four), the site where Abraham purchased a cave to bury his wife, Sarah, and where Jews and Arabs believe Abraham, Isaac, and Jacob are also buried.

After the 1973 war and 1974 Rabat conference the centrality of the Palestinian issue as an Arab cause and as the focal point of anti-Israeli policy emerged clearly. Israel was committed in principle to returning an unspecified portion of the territory captured in 1967 as part of an overall peace settlement. Since the end of the 1967 war Israel had accepted the principles of United Nations Resolution 242, calling for withdrawal of Israeli military forces "from territories of recent conflict" and calling for an end to the state of belligerency with "acknowledgement of the sovereignty, territorial integrity and political independence of every state in the area and their right to live in peace within secure and recognized boundaries."

In 1977, however, Israel's stated policy took a pronounced shift with the advent of the Begin government. Prior to Begin the Israeli government had always conceded in principle that it would withdraw from some part of the West Bank and other territories occupied in 1967, but now the Israeli government intimated that it intended to maintain a permanent presence—at least on the West Bank. Under Begin, who believed that Israel had a historic right to the West Bank, Israel began establishing settlements near major population centers, not for strategic reasons so much as to assert the *right* of Jews to occupy land on the West Bank under Israeli control.

No other policy of the Israeli government is as potentially subversive of the original Zionist ideals, as expressed by Herzl, Weizmann, and Ben-Gurion, as is the continued occupation of the West Bank and Gaza. No other policy threatens to undermine Israeli democracy or to deflect the energies of Israel in the way that a continuation of the occupation does. As a domestic political issue within Israel, the continued occupation is clearly one of the most explosive confronting the body politic. Quite apart from the damage that Israel's continued occupation of the West Bank has done to its international position is the cost that Israel has had to pay in compromised principles and values. More than that, the Israeli occupation reopens the long-dormant question of rights over territory, a debate long thought to be settled.

The settling of the West Bank by Israelis began under the Labor Alignment government after the 1967 war as part of an effort to fortify Israel against attack on its eastern border with Jordan. In addition to the security settlements that were placed in the Jordan valley, another effort—without official sanction—was begun less than a year after the conclusion of the Six Day War.

Shortly before the Passover holidays in 1968 a small group of "Swiss tourists" checked into the Park Hotel in Hebron, one of the four holy cities of the ancient Land of Israel. Once in their rooms, the "tourists" announced that they were, in fact, Israelis and that they had returned—permanently—to Hebron. This objective was in direct contravention of Israeli government policy, which sought to prevent Jewish Israelis from moving into Arab population centers on the West Bank. In fact, at that early date, the government still had in mind the vague intention to return the West Bank to Jordan as part of a peace agreement.

Eventually, a compromise was worked out between the settlers and their government. The settlers were allowed to move out of Hebron to an adjacent site in an Israeli army base, where they were given permission to establish a yeshiva, or school for Jewish studies. Twelve years later the yeshiva at Kiryat Arba had become the centerpiece of a town with permanent high-rise apartments, a community center, schools, grocery stores, gardens and five thousand occupants. True to the Israeli tradition, the settlers had presented the government—which, in this case happened to be their own—with a fact.

Kiryat Arba was not the first of the Jewish settlements on the West Bank after the 1967 war. The first settlements were located somewhat north of Kiryat Arba and Hebron at a site called Gush Etzion, where a religious kibbutz's fall in the 1948 War of Independence, two days before the declaration of the state's independence, had caused a trauma in the nascent Jewish state.

The reestablishment of a Jewish presence in the Etzion bloc, as it is known, was almost as inevitable as the reunification of Jerusalem under Israeli sovereignty. But the establishment of Kiryat Arba was not inevitable. In the next nine years other settlements along the western edge and the interior of Judea and Samaria were established as the Labor government, suffering from internal divisions and decreasing support from the Israeli public, gradually acceded to growing pressure from religious groups and permitted them to occupy land.

Little was said about the security value of these settlements before 1977. The *security* settlements were located in the Jordan valley and in the highlands overlooking it, guarding against a potential invasion from Jordan. The motivation for the settlements in the interior and western edge of Judea and Samaria had less to do with security than with the belief of the settlers in the fulfillment of the biblical promise God made to Abraham thousands of years before. ("As an everlasting possession I will give you and your descendants after you the land in which you now are aliens, all the land of Canaan, and I will be God to your descendants" [Genesis 17:8]).

Until 1977 only a handful of settlements were established by religious zealots, who formally organized themselves into a group called Gush Emunim (Bloc of the Faithful) in 1974. The Labor government was essentially unsympathetic to the program of Gush Emunim, generally resisting its efforts and arguments. (Gush Emunim was not totally without support in the Labor Alignment. In 1968 the settlers of Kiryat Arba were visited by then Minister of Labor Yigal Allon, who had aspirations to greater political position. "You have earned for yourselves the right of the 'firstborn' in the renewal of Jewish settlement in Hebron," Allon told them. "There have always been Jews in this city, which is the city of our forefathers and the cradle of the nation. . . . It is inconceivable that Jews would be forbidden to settle anew in the ancient city of our forefathers.")

In the waning days of the Labor government, during the prime ministership of Yitzhak Rabin, as the Labor Alignment's grasp of power weakened and its relations with the National Religious Party grew more strained, the government's ability to enforce its proscription against settlements in populated areas grew more difficult. Labor was dependent on the NRP for the survival of the government, and the NRP's old-guard leadership was being challenged from the right, ironically enough, by younger, more militant party members who supported the settlement program of Gush Emunim. Yet the handful of religious settlements that had been established, as the United States pressured Israel to make territorial concessions for peace, were primarily political statements rather than viable residential sites. The settlements initially were small, isolated, and in many cases occupied only on weekends when the settlers left their permanent housing in Jerusalem and Tel Aviv to come live in the spare, temporary quarters they kept in the hills of Judea and Samaria. Rabin more or less successfully resisted the entreaties of his sometime security adviser Major General (Res.) Ariel Sharon, who advocated full-scale settlement of the West Bank interior and its western edge as well as the Jordan valley.

The melding of power and program came in 1977 with election of the Likud party to power. As a Zionist Revisionist, Prime Minister Menachem Begin and his fellow Herut party faction members believed profoundly that all of Mandatory Palestine belonged to the Jewish people (including the portion that lay on the east bank of the Jordan, in Jordan proper). As part of the ancient Land of Israel, Begin believed, Judea and Samaria were part of the land promised to the Jewish people through Abraham so many years before and were part of the ancient land Zionism sought to restore. Under Begin the policy of establishing settlements began in earnest. In the early days of the Begin government little effort was made to explain the new settlement policy as being anything other than a fulfillment of the Jewish rights in Judea and Samaria. The argument that the settlements somehow fulfilled a security need for Israel proper was a secondary explanation, when it was offered at all.

The principal architect of the government's settlement policy was Ariel Sharon, making his first appearance as a member of a government. One of the heroes of the 1967 and 1973 wars, a brilliant tactician in combat, and a charismatic figure in Israel, especially among the Oriental Jewish population, Sharon proved to be every bit as much the tenacious bulldog in the cabinet as he had been on the battlefield. Propelled by seemingly unbounded energy, unrestrained by the niceties of diplomacy or even by internal political considerations, Sharon—in his capacity as minister of agriculture in the first Begin government—assumed the chairmanship of the government's settlements committee, putting him in the key position to make decisions about when and where to place new settlements.

Offended by his often coarse manner and a single-mindedness

approaching fixation, Israelis of a contrary persuasion tended to underestimate Sharon. The brusque manner and the blunt speech concealed a first-class mind, capable of analyzing complex situations and devising innovative solutions. This analytic ability, combined with Sharon's toughness and tenacity, had served him well in the army and made him a formidable figure in government.

During the first Begin government Sharon became accustomed to explaining the government's settlement policy to visiting diplomats, wealthy Jewish contributors to Israel from abroad, journalists, and other public figures. Holding a map specially prepared for the benefit of his audience, Sharon explained the "problem" with which Israel had to contend. Roughly sixty percent of the Jewish population of Israel lived along a narrow band of land bounded by the Mediterranean to the west and the hills of Judea and Samaria to the east. This was the heartland of Jewish settlement within Israel and it lay within six to fifteen miles of a concentrated Arab population (which included Israeli Arabs living inside Israel). The Arab population, Sharon explained, was growing and expanding across the land, making the Jewish corridor along the seacoast even narrower. (About seven hundred thousand Arabs lived on the West Bank alone.) Equally important, the major population centers of Israel on the coastal plain lay within sight and easily within artillery range of the hills of the West Bank.

The other problem, Sharon explained, was "how to secure Jerusalem as the capital of Israel forever." The city, he recalled, had been divided from 1948 until 1967, when the eastern part, including the Old City, was in Jordanian hands and the western part was under Israeli rule. To ensure that Jerusalem is never again similarly divided, the Israelis have ringed the city with a series of new communities—Gilo on the south, Ramot Eshkol and French Hill on the north, Ramot to the northwest, and the old campus of the Hebrew University on Mount Scopus to the east.

The Begin government initiated a second ring of development, circling Jerusalem from the south, east, and north with another layer of Jewish settlements. (Since Israel proper lay to the west, it was unnecessary to build new communities in that direction.) In addition to these settlements around Jerusalem the Begin government initiated a string of settlements along the western edge of the West Bank—the eastern border of Israel—from the northern to the southern end. A second line of settlements, running in an irregular line along the dominant interior highlands of the West Bank, also was started on a north-to-south axis. These two lines of settlements complemented those set up by the Labor government in the Jordan valley as part of Israel's border defense system.

On Sharon's map large blocs of land on the West Bank surrounding the Jewish settlement sites were colored in purple. These areas were considered by the Begin government to be "important security areas." Roughly two thirds of the land area of the West Bank was so designated on Sharon's unofficial map. This plan, rejected by the Labor government of Prime Minister Rabin, had become the blueprint for the Begin government's settlement policy. Sharon said he looked forward to the day when three hundred thousand Jews would settle on the West Bank. By 1980, roughly twenty thousand had settled. Several of the towns founded on the rocky hillsides had a temporary air that was inevitable when prefabricated structures are used for housing. But more permament, high-rise apartment buildings were being constructed in several of the larger settlement towns, and an extensive road network was being built along the length of the West Bank and crossing it at several points. Water pipes were being laid to bring water from Israel proper, and local industries were being started to provide some employment on the spot for Jewish settlers.

Unlike settlements started in the years before the founding of the Jewish state, these new settlement towns were not primarily agricultural. With only a few exceptions the settlements were either bedroom communities—with the working inhabitants commuting daily to Tel Aviv, Haifa, Jerusalem, or elsewhere for employment—or industrial—with small factories on the site.

Housing in the settlements was available to the settlers at preferential prices—subsidized by the government—to encourage Jews to leave the crowded urban centers where they might not be able to find adequate housing at prices they could afford. The temporary housing provided, usually either mobile homes or simple, prefabricated modular units, was spare, providing only minimal shelter, with few comforts. The permanent housing was more elaborate, but not luxurious—comparable to other middle-class housing being built in Israel.

Exempt from reserve duty in the Israeli army, settlers participated in a regional defense system. Settlers were armed and theoretically were trained and prepared to defend themselves against attack if necessary. The strategic theory behind the settlements purportedly was that the settlers would be able to hold the line long enough for the Israeli army, which has a twenty-four-hour mobilization plan, to come to their defense. Although reluctant to discuss details, government officials said that the settlements had been provided with "sophisticated weapons" that they would be able to use in the event of war. The assumption was that the men who normally work outside the settlements would be home if a war should start.

The settlements, in Sharon's words, were "the strongest answer to the establishment of a second Palestinian state." (He considered Jordan to be a Palestinian state.) Under the Labor government the settlements started by the religious groups represented more of a political statement than real communities. The same could not be said of the settlements during the Begin government's tenure. Deep roots had been planted. Sharon, and the thousands of Israelis who settled on the West Bank, did so with a firm conviction that they had come as a matter of right—and to stay. Working feverishly against the clock, Sharon made no secret of his intention to make it difficult, if not impossible, for future Israeli governments of any political stripe to undo what he had worked so hard to build. "We will leave an entirely different map which no one will be able to ignore," Sharon said. Asked if he foresaw a day when there would no longer be a Jewish presence on the West Bank, Sharon answered simply and without elaboration, "No."

No natural barrier separates the West Bank from Israel. Except that the land becomes hilly—mountainous in parts—as one leaves the coastal plain of Israel and moves inland into Judea and

Samaria, one has no sensation of entering a different country at all. The term "West Bank" itself suggests some remote area, but the newly arrived visitors to Israel, standing on the Tarmac at Ben-Gurion Airport need only lift their gaze slightly to the east to see the hills of the West Bank less than five miles away.

Similarly, no clear physical distinctions mark the differences between Arab and Jew, to the point where one group is sometimes unable to identify members of the other. Not long after the Six Day War in 1967, when Jerusalem had been unified under a single municipal administration, a policeman stopped an Arab cabdriver who had driven through a red light. Speaking fractured Hebrew, the cabdriver told the policeman to ignore the offense. "I work for your security service," the cabdriver said.

"Could be," the policeman replied in Arabic, continuing to write the ticket, "but I'm an Arab."

These physical similarities and lack of natural geographic barriers ought not to obscure the vast gulf separating the Jews of Israel from the Palestinian Arabs of the West Bank. They are different nationalities, with different agendas and an entirely different perspective.

The settlement policy of the Begin government annexed the West Bank in all but name, leaving its Arab inhabitants politically and economically tied to Israel but without the rights of Israeli citizens. Begin's autonomy plan, drafted as part of the peace process under the Camp David accords, left the future status of the West Bank open. Yet the combined efforts of Begin, Sharon, and Gush Emunim seriously limited the range of choices open to any successor government in Israel.

The settlements that had been constructed for and populated by Israelis committed to Israel's continued presence on the West Bank could not be dismantled easily. Any attempt by the Israeli government to dislodge Israeli settlers on the West Bank would, at a minimum, create a political furor in Israel and, in the most extreme eventuality, would lead to violence—Jew against Jew. The continued presence of Israeli citizens on the West Bank would require adequate measures by the Israeli government to ensure their security and free movement. Without ceding sovereignty over the West Bank, Israel could not hope to conclude any kind of an agreement with Jordan for transfer of responsibility for the West Bank.

Continuation of Israeli authority over the West Bank holds out the prospect of continuing conflict with Palestinian nationalism on the West Bank, increased tensions with Israeli Arabs inside Israel, and increased opposition to Israeli policies from abroad.

Palestinian nationalism, kept carefully in check by King Hussein when the West Bank was part of Jordan, has flourished under Israeli rule. When the Israeli government moves to suppress Palestinian nationalist efforts, the action takes place in the goldfish bowl of international media coverage. As tensions increase, the need for the Israelis to take increasingly repressive measures also increases. An Israeli who serves at least one month a year with the Israeli border police (as his army reserve duty requirement) patrolling towns on the West Bank, said that the customary practice of patrols is to stop and question Arabs on the street arbitrarily as part of a calculated campaign of harassment of the population. "It's the only way you can do it," he explained. "If you don't harass them, they'll harass you. But every time I go, I feel like a Nazi. They pick up people for questioning for no good reason, hold them for a few days without notifying their families, and then let them go, after getting them to do a little work around the police encampment."

Israeli rule on the West Bank has brought the area unprecedented prosperity, although the prosperity is largely dependent upon Israel for its continuation, since it has not led to the formation of a local economic infrastructure on the West Bank. West Bank Arabs, despite their prosperity, are not mollified. As Israeli journalist Danny Rubenstein wrote:

Viewed from the perspective of Nablus, East Jerusalem, Ramallah and Bethlehem [all Arab centers of population], the Israeli military government is a foreign regime which hurts their national pride and humiliates them. Such a regime encourages nationalist feelings, impels violent conflict and arouses the need for attachment to PLO formulas which are harsh and militant. They do not identify the Israeli regime as having brought them economic welfare nor as having proposed to them an unclear form of home rule, but rather as the regime which robbed them of East Jerusalem and has surrounded it with Jewish neighborhoods, the regime which harms nationalist attributes, expropriates land, establishes settlements, scorns what is holy to them, and so forth.

Over the 13 years [since 1967] the number of youths and adults from the West Bank who have joined the PLO and identified with it has increased incessantly. This is the most concrete expression of the tendency caused by the continued Israeli rule, which has sought coexistence with the Arabs living under its jurisdiction, that has stirred the development of national, radical and hostile anger. Such anger was not prevalent before 1967 along the entire (West Bank) mountain range from Jenin to Hebron.

The policy of allowing Jews to settle near Arab population centers on the West Bank has increased Jewish traffic and Arab-Jewish friction. When Israeli security forces prove unable to provide adequate protection for Jews settled on the West Bank, the Jewish settlers provide self-protection. On several occasions armed Jewish settlers have assaulted Arabs and destroyed Arab property in retaliation for incidents when Arab youths threw rocks at Jewish vehicles. On other occasions Jewish settlers have harassed Arabs and destroyed their property for no apparent reason other than bullying them.

As Israelis increased their demands on the West Bank, a reactive radicalization occurred among West Bank Arabs. An indigenous, radical leadership developed despite periodic efforts by the Israeli government to nip the leadership in the bud by deporting the more radical and outspoken leaders. But others emerged to take their places. Ironically, although the PLO is kept under tight con-

trol in Egypt, Jordan, and Syria, it flourished in the West Bank.
"In the past," Rubenstein wrote,

> there were traditional strata in the West Bank that were loyal
> to Hussein and there were many without a political label.
> Today the loyal support for the PLO is so deep and broad
> among the entire population that it seems that any area of the
> country where Arabs live belongs to the PLO.

There was a time when Israelis prided themselves on administering what they were pleased to describe as the most humane occupation in history. Whatever the accuracy of the characterization, it is one rarely used in Israel any longer since it hardly captures the spirit of a time when the entire male population of a town or village is rounded up in the middle of the night and forced to stand in the rain to counter an organized protest strike, or when the families of boys accused of throwing rocks at passing cars have been forcibly moved from their homes to deserted refugee camps, or when instances of Israeli soldiers looting Arab homes have been officially reported.

An erosion of standards and conduct has occurred on the part of the Israelis administering the West Bank, hardly surprising when democratic tradition holds as a basic principle that power must be responsible to the people governed if it is not ultimately to become corrupted. The accidental fatal shooting of a nineteen-year-old Arab girl from Bethlehem by an Israeli border patrol officer in mid-1980 prompted Yehuda Litani, the highly respected correspondent for Israel's morning paper, *Ha'aretz*, to remark on the lack of outrage within Israel at the killing, albeit that it was an accident. "One can imagine the scandal," Litani wrote, "that would have broken out had a Border Patrolman accidentally shot an Israeli girl in Ramat Gan or Natanya. But Tagid al-Batma was a resident of Batir, an Arab resident of the West Bank, and her fate seems to be of interest only in the administered areas and East Jerusalem." Litani had no doubt that if the patrolman responsible was found to have been negligent, that he would be tried. What the killing, and other similar incidents showed, he wrote, was how the tone and conduct of the Israeli administration had changed.

"There were times," Litani said,

> when members of the military government would see themselves as representatives of the West Bank residents to the Israeli government. There were those in the military government who fought arduously against the expropriation of land for one or another settlement. . . . The Israeli government did not regard the local population as mostly hostile, as it appears today. The polarization which has developed over the last years between the Palestinians of the territories and the Israelis did not exist at that time.
>
> Under present circumstances in Israel residents of the territories are third-class citizens, following the Israeli Arabs and the Jewish residents of Israel. For many years the residents of the areas sensed that, despite the occupation . . . they were defended by the people in the government and were not under the jurisdiction of a hostile regime.

What has changed over the years, especially under the Begin government, is the Israeli government's attitude toward the West Bank—from an area being held temporarily, pending a peace agreement, to an area ripe for Israeli settlement and control, more or less permanently. The settlements that have been initiated during the Begin government's tenure—approximately eighty in all—are clear and concrete evidence of that change.

The restiveness of the Arab population of the West Bank, as it reacts to the change in Israeli policy, produces a predictable counterreaction within the Israeli government. The liberal and humane policy, the purposely low profile maintained by Israeli forces on the West Bank has gradually stiffened. Ironically, the new, tough policy followed the first open and free elections ever held on the West Bank under any administration—Israeli or Jordanian—allowing the population to elect local leadership. The election swept out the old, moderate, pro-Jordanian leadership and allowed a younger, more militant and pro-Palestine Liberation Organization leadership its first taste of power.

The Israeli government, so long as it pursues a policy of settling the West Bank, may be faced with a largely hostile (and growing) population that will be kept quiescent only by maintaining a large military presence. The prospects for Israeli democracy are not sanguine. It is difficult to practice democracy on one side of a line for an extended period of time while five miles away, on the other side of the line, the native population is dominated by a government it neither chose nor wants. (On the other hand, if the Israeli government did not continue to support the settlements, especially those populated by members of Gush Emunim, it faces strong resistance—or worse—within Israel. See Chapter 9.)

Israeli democracy will not be affected only by the nature of the occupation itself. The Arab population—in Israel and the occupied territories—is growing at a rate more than fifty percent that of the Jewish population of Israel. By the year 2010, according to careful calculations of Israeli demographers, Jews will be a minority in Israel and the territories. Even with "autonomy" the territories would lack full self-determination and the Arab population would continue to live under the ultimate control of a government they had no hand in choosing. Israeli democracy would be in a quandary—to give Arabs on the West Bank full voting rights and allow Jews to become a minority in the Jewish state, or to continue to deprive Arabs in the territories of full civil rights, maintaining a Jewish voting majority by denying the benefits of democracy to a substantial part of the population.

In any case, by the year 2000 Israeli Arabs—who do have the right to vote—will constitute roughly one quarter of the Israeli population. They will be a political force to be reckoned with under Israel's political system of proportional representation. Continued friction with West Bank Arabs can only complicate relations between Jews and Arabs within Israel, sharpening the opposite forces that make the position and identity of Israeli Arabs so ambiguous and ambivalent in the first place.

Any arrangement that Israel might make to treat the Arabs of the territories as a separate population still under the sovereignty of Israel—such as autonomy—opens the possibility that Israeli Arabs, especially those in the northern part of Israel, would demand some similar arrangement for themselves. On the other hand, a separate Palestinian state on the West Bank (and perhaps including Gaza) could also probably increase the ambivalence of Israeli Arabs. Unless a Palestinian state were part of an overall peace settlement in which the major Arab states of the region (Syria, Egypt, and Jordan) recognized Israel's right to exist—thus foreclosing the prospect of dismemberment of Israel—Israeli Arabs will not reconcile themselves, once and for all, to the fact of Israel.

Continued development of the West Bank as a place for Jewish settlement also would mean that development of Israel proper—especially the Negev and the Galilee—would be impeded. With resources limited, settlement of the Negev—which Ben-Gurion saw as holding the promise of Israel's future—could not proceed. Similarly, settlement of Jews in the Galilee, considered necessary in the eyes of many Jews to prevent northern Israel from becoming an Arab enclave in the midst of the country, would be severely restricted.

The most serious, if somewhat less tangible, effect of the Begin government's settlement policy has been to bring the entire issue of Jewish and Arab claims in Palestine full circle. Sensing that a formal annexation of the West Bank would have unleashed a hostile storm in the world at large and would have created profound changes in Israeli society, the Labor government had avoided formal action that would have brought the Arabs of the West Bank permanently under Israeli sovereignty.

The Labor Alignment's position (and the position of Mapai before creation of the Alignment and even before the creation of the state) was basically pragmatic regarding the issue of a Jewish "right" to Palestine. Labor tacitly conceded that both Arabs and Jews had rights in Palestine, and therefore Labor (then Mapai) accepted, despite internal dissension, partition as a solution to the problem, satisfying both parties' claims to the land by dividing it between the two parties. Neither was totally satisfied, but both received some portion of what they were seeking. Even after Israel came into control of the West Bank after 1967, Israel did not, under Labor, assert a *right* to the land. The Labor government's position saw the West Bank as a strategic asset rather than as a domain for settlement.

Begin, however, did assert the right of Israel to all of the ancient Land of Israel (which included the West Bank, but not the Sinai, the Golan Heights, or Gaza). In so doing, he revived the dormant debate about rights in Palestine. Almost any argument that Israel can make in claiming *all* of Palestine can be made by Palestinian Arabs as well. Both Jews and Arabs can point to a period in the distant past when they were sovereign in Palestine. Both have centuries-old ties to the land. For both, Jerusalem has religious significance. Both have populations that were rendered rootless by their dispersion from the land.

The one claim that Israel can make that the Arabs cannot, that the land was promised by divine covenant, is the one claim that carries the least weight among non-Jews. As an arguing point Israelis pressing the Jewish claim to the West Bank suggest that if Jews have no claim to Hebron or Nablus—the two principal population centers on the West Bank, but also towns of significance in the Jewish religion—then they have no claim to Tel Aviv or Haifa. It is an argument that Arabs are only too happy to accept, since Arabs deny the Jewish claim to any of what they still call Palestine. In pressing their claim to *all* of the ancient Land of Israel, Begin and his supporters reopened the old question of whether Jews have a rightful claim to *any* of it.

The Israeli occupation of the West Bank served to tarnish Israel's moral stature. "In our situation," Israeli historian Jacob Talmon wrote in 1980,

> in contrast to what generations have considered our unique gift to humanity—the idea of the rule of the spirit rather than the rule of force—we are using that rule of force. We now are using the rule of force to implement our historic

rights; rights that, in their present interpretation, are holy neither to the gentiles nor to most Jews. And so we no longer can expect the world to look upon our rights as so pressing that they ought to cancel out the rights of the Palestinians to self-determination. Without the foundation that is represented by the writings of our prophets, we are nothing but a peculiar band of tribes that has given nothing to humanity except a lot of trouble, that is now asking to expand at the expense of another people and to subordinate this other people's freedom to its own security needs, real or imaginary, as well as to self interest.

Not a single other country recognized Israel's right to maintain permanent control or sovereign rights over the West Bank. One of the most outspoken critics of the Begin government's settlement policy was a former adviser to Begin on Arab affairs, Professor Yehoshafat Harkabi. Harkabi characterized the national impulse that gave rise to the Begin government's settlement policy as "vainglorious," a throwback to a vanished past in which colonial nations could pursue a policy of imperialism.

"To me, personally," Harkabi wrote,

this is the most disquieting fact of all. Israelis are hardly aware of the extent to which Zionist enterprise was made possible by external moral support. The Jews could not have translated their potential into action without the support of the enlightened world; and now the majority of the enlightened world shows disdain toward Israel's policy in the West Bank.

Israelis are not sufficiently aware of the extent to which, without such moral support, our actual material and military strength would be reduced. Why should others give us arms and money in order to implement a policy to which they are opposed?

There was a time when the enlightened circles in the

world were proud of us. But we are fast becoming for the world—and the present Israel Government has given this process a push—a loathsome country. It is very painful for me to have to say this, but I think it is true. And it is not an abstraction but something most tangible.

7/SECURITY

"The Jewish State," Herzl wrote, "is conceived of as a neutral one. It will therefore require only a professional army, equipped, of course, with every requisite of modern warfare, to preserve order internally and externally."

Prophet though he was, Herzl's optimistic vision fell somewhat short of the mark in his cursory treatment of the Jewish state's security needs. Herzl probably cannot be faulted for not forecasting the Cold War and the choices it forced upon Israel, nor even perhaps for not anticipating the opposition that the Jewish state would arouse in its Arab neighbors. In any case, the problem that Herzl saw fit to dismiss in two sentences is a consuming preoccupation of the State of Israel. The burden of equipping Israel's army "with every requisite of modern warfare" has become the central focus of Israeli diplomacy as well as a drain on her treasury and the source of employment for a large segment of her civilian work force.

Although puny in comparison with the armies of the United

States or the Soviet Union, and some other countries, Israel's defense force is a colossus in comparison to the size of the country. In proportion to the country's population, the Israel Defense Forces (IDF) are the largest in the world. Women, as well as men, must serve.

In sheer weight of numbers, the amount of money spent by Israel for security is staggering. In the ten years from 1970 until 1980 defense expenditures accounted for an average of 40 percent of the government's spending (and almost 64 percent if American military aid is included). In the entire range of goods and services produced in Israel, defense spending accounted for more than 27 percent of the gross national product (approximately five times the comparable amount for the United States during the 1970s). The revenue needed to support these expenditures made Israelis the most heavily taxed people in the world.

Security exacts costs in other ways as well—in the production lost by factories and businesses whose workers perform their obligatory annual army reserve duty, in the requirement that public and private buildings construct air raid shelters, in the need for private citizens to serve as guards outside schools, and in the use of paid employees at the doors of public institutions and heavily frequented stores to inspect handbags and packages of customers coming in.

It is virtually impossible to be unaware of security measures in Israel. Israelis have long since become inured to the crash and shudder of sonic booms from fighter planes training overhead. Off-duty soldiers, often required to carry their weapons while on leave, are ever-present on buses, hitchhiking along the highways or strolling the streets of Israel's large cities and small towns. Heavily armed jeeps patrol the country's beaches, winding their way among sun-worshiping Israelis who pay scant attention. Barely visible on the horizon are fast Israeli navy boats, part of an extensive electronic network that keeps its eyes and ears on the horizon for signs of impending danger. Tanks and armored personnel-carriers, transported on special trucks, move up and down the country's highways.

The initial reaction of an outsider unused to rubbing up against all this weaponry is a feeling of having walked into what looks and feels like an armed camp under siege. The wife of a foreign journalist who had moved to Israel found herself in a movie theater on one of her first nights in Israel. During the customary intermission, when the film is abruptly stopped so the audience can go out to smoke or buy refreshments, she decided to leave her seat. As she started to get up, she found that her dress was snagged on something. "Excuse me," she said, turning to the Israeli soldier sitting next to her, "but I think my dress is caught on your machine gun."

It would be too easy, though, to characterize Israel simply as a garrison state or an armed camp or as a kind of Middle Eastern banana republic. Israel is not any of those things despite appearances. The Israel Defense Forces are, it is true, a prominent institution in Israeli life and society rather than the skeleton force Herzl had contemplated. What is remarkable though, considering the relative size of the army and the resources devoted to it, is that the country has been able to resist allowing the economy, politics, and culture to become subordinate to the demands of security.

The danger is not one to which Israelis are insensitive. During the period he served as Israel's defense minister (1977–80), Ezer Weizman warned repeatedly that Israel had to take care to avoid becoming not a state with a great army but a great army that has a state.

Despite this wariness, the Israeli army is an organic part of Israeli society, an institution integrated into the life of the country, touching the lives of all those who consider themselves citizens and many who do not.

The IDF consists of three main components—the ground forces, the navy and the air force. In terms of size the ground forces are easily the largest, although the air force—because of the cost of modern weapons—commands a disproportionately high percentage of the defense budget. All three components are unified under the single command of the IDF chief of staff.

Israeli military planners must keep in mind three salient factors in mapping strategy: the size of Israel's potential enemy, Israel's own limited manpower, and her small geographic size.

With a total population of about 3.7 million, Israel has to plan for a potential threat coming from countries with a combined population of more than 50 million. Israel's 750,000 Arab citizens are not considered eligible for service in the IDF for security reasons, although Bedouin, Druze, and Circassians do serve in the Israeli army. Israeli women must, unless married or exempted for religious reasons, serve two years in the IDF, although they are barred from combat roles. All adult males, except those who seek exemption for religious reasons, are expected to serve three years in the IDF—usually between the ages of eighteen and twenty-one or generally following completion of high school.

Although exact numbers are classified, according to one authoritative and reliable source (the London-based Institute of Strategic Studies), the Israeli army in 1980 had a regular army (army and air force included) of 44,000 with another 125,000 conscripts performing their three-year mandatory national service. The permament regular army consists almost entirely of officers with a small number of career senior noncommissioned officers. Aside from these Israel has no standing army. The bulk of the army's manpower comes from the 400,000 reservists who are required to serve three to six weeks a year in the army until age fifty-five. Yigael Yadin, the second chief of staff of the Israel Defense Forces (and later deputy prime minister), described the male population of the country as being "soldiers on leave eleven months of the year." Israel has the highest ratio of soldiers to civilians—1 to 22—of any country in the world. (The ratio for the United States is 1 to 100 and for the Soviet Union is 1 to 71.)

In the 1973 war the Israeli army faced a combined force of roughly one million Arabs, who were armed with several times the number of tanks, artillery, and aircraft at the disposal of the Israelis.

Despite this numerical disparity the Israeli army has been able to perform its mission of protecting the country and its population. The greater number of the Arab forces clearly imposes the necessity for the size of the Israeli army's reserves and the extended length of service. But this necessity to press all able-bodied men into service also shapes in a very direct sense the content of the Israeli army's doctrine, strategy, and tactics.

When fully mobilized, the Israeli army deprives the country of the main part of its civilian work force. When the army is standing at full strength, Israel's factories, farms, and businesses come to a virtual standstill. As a result, Israel cannot afford to mobilize and keep its army on alert indefinitely—a fact that partially explains the 1967 war and the near disaster of the 1973 war.

A second consideration for strategic planners is Israel's small size which makes it especially vulnerable to attack. The industrial plant and population center of Israel is concentrated on a sixty-mile coastal strip not more than twenty miles wide from south of Tel Aviv to north of Haifa. An Israeli military expert outlined a "worst case" scenario that Israeli military planners must keep in mind. "Let's say that sixty planes come at us from the east," the military expert said. "It takes only two and a half minutes once they're over Jordan to reach Tel Aviv. Let's say sixty F-15's take off from Saudi Arabia. The F-15, which Saudi Arabia has, can carry thirteen separate types of armament. Now, of those sixty planes, let's say only ten get through. With our industry and population concentrated on the coastal plain, they can do an enormous amount of damage. If they hit the Haifa refinery and the factories near Tel Aviv and Rishon Le-Zion, and they'll probably go for the Israel Aircraft Industry which is in the same vicinity, we're out of business. Our industrial plant is ruined. Or if they just hit Tel Aviv and we suffer five thousand or six thousand civilian casualties—devastating."

In the past Israel has had to plan for a war on three fronts—the southern border with Egypt, the northern border with Syria, and the eastern border with Jordan. The peace treaty with Egypt eases Israel's strategic problems considerably by removing a principal Arab enemy, one without whom the other Arab states would be hard-pressed to mount another war. Whatever the outcome of the treaty with Egypt, Israel still has to maintain a defense force that can meet the combined resources of Iraq, Saudi Arabia, Syria, Jordan, and Libya—which have the financial resources to buy modern weapons in large quantities and have ready access through France, the Soviet Union, and the United States to what they want.

Three factors, then, determine the shape of the doctrine Israel has fashioned to meet the external threat: small population, small area, and a potential enemy numerically stronger and possessing greater material resources with which to buy weapons.

The concept of the whole nation being Israel's army is the starting point of the doctrine and strategy of the IDF. According to IDF doctrine, as outlined by Major General (Res.) Israel Tal, war has to be carried to the enemy "with all possible speed." Israel, Tal points out, has no strategic depth geographically. Any initial success on the part of an invading force could mean the destruction of Israeli population centers and industry.

Because the great powers are likely to intervene in any conflict involving Israel, Israeli doctrine holds, it is "doubly vital" that military results be quick and decisive. In addition, protracted conflict will drain resources. High casualties must be avoided.

In order to strengthen her position in the postwar negotiations, Israel must see to it that the Arabs "lose" in order to leave Israel with something to offer as a settlement.

The principles laid out by Tal help explain Israel's approach to the four active wars it has fought since gaining independence in 1948. The 1973 war, which was not fought on a schedule determined by Israel, demonstrated the logic of Israeli doctrine. Although the war lasted only three weeks, much of the army remained mobilized for six months. This situation had a devastating effect on Israel's economy, which was forced to pay for replacing expensive weapons while much of the civilian work force had to remain in uniform. Worse, because of the high casualties suffered by Israel as well as its general lack of preparedness, the morale of Israeli society, a factor that Israeli military planners also have to take into consideration, was severely affected.

The enormous stress on security and self-protection in Israel is also obviously a product of the experience of the Jewish people over several centuries, and more recently in Palestine and Israel. The cultivation of toughness, self-defense, and self-reliance runs deep in Israel. The horror of the Holocaust, coming after generations of humiliation and terror suffered by ghetto-dwelling Jews in Europe and Islamic countries, inspired a determination among the early Jewish settlers in Palestine to reject what they saw as the weak, unmanly behavior of the Diaspora Jew. The new Jew would stand his ground. "Our aim has been," wrote one of the founders of the first Jewish self-defense organization in Palestine, "to inculcate in the farmers and workers the feeling that they, and only they, can defend themselves and property." This emphasis on self-sufficiency ultimately has evolved not only into the Israel Defense Forces but also into a complex network of defense industries established to supply the Israeli army with the modern weapons it needs.

Self-sufficiency has meant that the Israeli army is largely self-taught, although many of its early officers served with the British army during World War II, and Israel continues to send career officers abroad to attend staff colleges of friendly countries. The self-taught nature of the Israeli was wasteful in the sense that hundreds of hours were spent learning by experience what a skillful teacher might have taught in a fraction of the time. But it also meant that Israelis fashioned solutions that were tailor-made to their own situation rather than adopting approaches designed by other armies for an entirely different set of circumstances.

Ezer Weizman, largely responsible for shaping the Israeli air force that made Israel's lightning-swift victory in 1967 possible, was a firm advocate of examining each situation afresh without regard to what "the book" said. "We mustn't ape others," Weizman writes in his memoirs, "whether in organizational matters, in military theory, or in operational tactics, for all these stem from the character of the men who have to apply them. . . . What counts is your originality, your improvisation and your inventiveness."

Over time, through a process of trial and error, the Israeli army developed tactics, strategy, and a doctrine suited to the circumstances confronting the country. Since its earliest days it has succeeded in fulfilling its missions by finding unconventional approaches to problems. The Israeli army has preferred the "indirect approach" outlined by British military analyst B. H. Liddell Hart. Rather than losing precious men and resources in costly frontal assaults, the army has preferred to find ways of disrupting, confounding, and then overwhelming its enemies. In practice, this approach requires discarding conventional, time-honored theories of warfare that are more conservative but unsuited to Israel's situation.

The Israeli army has been at its best at those times when it has had to rely on its own ingenuity, rather than superior equipment, in order to carry the day. During the 1956 Sinai campaign General Moshe Dayan (chief of staff at the time) noted that Israeli pilots had been assigned the job of neutralizing Egyptian telephone lines to prevent communications near an important objective. When the hooks suspended from the Israeli airplanes failed to do the job, the Israeli pilots—rather than returning to base unsuccessful —cut the wires using the wings and propellers of their planes even though the wires were only twelve feet above ground.

The decision of the pilots to improvise on the spot to complete their mission exemplifies the kind of initiative and determination that is a trademark of the Israeli army. A strategy that relies on speed and aggressiveness because of a need to carry the battle to the enemy cannot succeed if all decisions have to be referred back to the central command first.

In the 1967 Six Day War the Israeli air force was able to neutralize the Egyptian, Syrian, and Jordanian air forces on the war's first day even though Israel had far fewer planes at its command and its equipment was inferior to the Arabs'. Israel employed careful planning, precision flying, and the unconventional approach to succeed. Rather than striking at dawn, when an attack would be most expected, the Israeli air force struck after breakfast as Egyptian commanders were on their way to their offices to begin their daily routine, comfortable in the knowledge that the likely hour for an Israeli attack had already passed. Catching the planes on the ground, the Israeli air force staggered its sorties so that its planes could deliver their loads and return to their bases for refueling and more bombs without leaving the skies over the Egyptian bases clear long enough to permit recovery from the attacks. Simultaneous attacks were conducted on nine Egyptian airfields, the first wave destroying runways, while the second and third waves destroyed aircraft on the ground. The bombs used to destroy the runways were carefully modified to ensure that they would explode on impact with the surface rather than skidding off the concrete. Israeli planes had been modified to use relatively slow-firing but highly accurate cannon fire in order to maximize the destructiveness of each sortie. The first air bases hit contained fighters. Subsequent attacks destroyed bombers, and in the afternoon of the first day the air forces of both Syria and Jordan were also destroyed.

In 1973, after the Syrians attacked Israel in the north while the Egyptians attacked simultaneously in the south, the Israeli army was confronted with its greatest crisis since the War of Independence in 1948. Israeli strategy had been based on two assumptions: that intelligence would provide a forty-eight-hour warning of an impending attack so that reserves could be mobilized and deployed, and that the air force could stave off an assault until the reserves could be brought to the fronts to push back an attempted invasion or assault.

In 1973 Israeli intelligence gave a warning of less than twelve hours before the war started—and not a clear warning at that. The Israeli air force, in the initial stages of the war, was able to keep the skies over Israel clear but was seriously hampered at the fronts, suffering enormous damage from Soviet antiaircraft missiles operated by the Syrians and the Egyptians.

In the opening stages of the 1973 war almost nothing went according to Israeli plan. What saved the day for Israel was the determination and resourcefulness of a small, heavily outnumbered corps of well-trained officers and enlisted men in both the north and south. The Syrian attack in the north—led by a force of eight hundred tanks—was held in check by less than two hundred

Israeli tanks, a number that dwindled rapidly down to a literal handful that stood between the Syrian army and the northern settlements of Israel.

In the south a premature, faulty counterattack by the Israeli army left its forces seriously depleted. Had the Egyptian army not hesitated after the abortive Israeli counterattack, the battle in the south might have turned out far differently. As it was, the Israeli army recovered, spotted a gap between the Second and Third Egyptian armies, penetrated the gap, crossed the Suez Canal and succeeded in encircling the Third Army. The operation was daring and highly unconventional, exploiting the Egyptian army's weaknesses as the Egyptians had earlier exploited Israel's. The canal crossing by the Israeli army was a prime application of carrying the war to the enemy.

From a political point of view, the encirclement of the Third Army was vital to Israel, giving it the necessary wedge to use with Egypt in the cease-fire negotiations. From an operational point of view, the battle relied heavily on the judgment of commanders on the scene. The timing of the operation was determined by the army's higher command. The details were largely worked out on the spot, under fire.

Clearly, a strategy that stresses flexibility must be prepared to pay a price in terms of discipline and orderliness. Since initiative is encouraged, the danger always exists that orders may be exceeded, modified, disregarded, or otherwise disobeyed. In 1956 the Israeli army suffered heavy casualties when field commanders near the Mitla Pass in the Sinai circumvented an order barring Israeli troops from attempting to capture the pass. Another field commander in the 1956 Sinai campaign disregarded orders and attacked twenty-four hours earlier than he was supposed to because, he later explained, he feared intervention by the great powers to restrain Israel before it had achieved its objectives.

In 1967, Moshe Dayan—then minister of defense—ordered Chief of Staff Yitzhak Rabin to capture the Golan Heights. According to Rabin he passed the order to the northern commander, David Elazar. When Dayan subsequently attempted to curtail the

Golan campaign, Rabin reports, he was unable to call off the attack because Elazar—who was eager to press the attack to victory—falsely reported that it was too late to stop the decisive action.

The 1956 Mitla Pass operation cost Israel 38 dead and 120 wounded. Once the objective was captured, Israeli forces pulled back from it, rather than attempting to hold it. Dayan, the chief of staff whose order were disobeyed, was surprisingly forgiving over what he describes as a "breach" of his orders.

"The truth is," he wrote in his *Diary of the Sinai Campaign,* "that I regard the problem as grave when a unit fails to fulfill its battle task, not when it goes beyond the bounds of duty and does more than is demanded of it." Dayan's philosophy, succinctly stated in explaining his similarly forgiving attitude toward the premature 1956 attack gets to the heart of much of the Israeli experience: "Better to be engaged in restraining the noble stallion than in prodding the reluctant mule."

This clash between the need for orderliness and discipline on the one hand and the spontaneous, creative impulse on the other is not limited to the Israeli army. It is an issue that presents itself frequently in Israeli life, where both the welfare of the group and accomplishments of the bold individualist are prized. The figures whom Israelis have most admired have been colorful, even swashbuckling types like Dayan, Weizman, General Ariel Sharon, and David Ben-Gurion (though he is not commonly thought of as a swashbuckler)—all essentially loners whose personal charisma attracted other Israelis to their views. Each of them in his own way embodied part of the heroic image that was the prototype of what an Israeli was supposed to be.

In fact, the issue of spontaneity versus organization is not limited to the army in Israel because the army does not exist in absolute or even relative isolation to the rest of Israeli society. The army, save for the possible, though doubtful, exception of the cadre of career officers, does not have a value system different from that of the rest of the population. The army in Israel *is* the population. Understanding this identity is important to understanding what happened to the army between 1967 and 1973, leaving the

IDF and Israel unprepared for the most serious and costly challenge to Israel's existence since 1948.

Prior to the 1973 war admiration for the military was widespread in Israel. Because of Israel's past successes, military figures like Rabin, Dayan, Sharon, Mordechai Gur (who led the battle for the capture of the Old City of Jerusalem) and others were venerated. By celebrating the military, Israelis were also celebrating themselves. Everyone had his own story to tell about the 1967 war—where he was, what she did, what another saw.

From the Israeli army's perspective, the 1967 war had been a classic example of accurate intelligence, appropriate strategy, brilliant tactics, and well-coordinated execution. As a result of 1967, however, Israelis and the IDF came to think of themselves as invincible. The Israeli public had absolute confidence in the military's preparations to prevent another war and had no doubt that if a war came, Israel would be able to win it quickly and decisively—as Israeli doctrine dictated.

The great pitfall for military planners, though, is to assume that the war for which they are planning will be like the last war they fought. This failing assumes that one's enemy will fight according to the suppositions that one has made about the enemy. Israel's near disaster in 1973 contained elements of both mistakes. Taking its great success in 1967 as a lesson, Israeli military planners proceeded to emphasize its long suits—beefing up the tank corps, stripping the armor of infantry assistance that would slow it down in war, and continuing to improve the quality of aircraft. Israeli military planning after the 1967 war showed a curious lack of coordination between intelligence and planning. The Israeli army knew, from intelligence reports, that both the Egyptians and Syrians had new weapons—antitank missiles and bazookas, antiaircraft missiles, night-fighting equipment—that would enable it to adopt a new approach in another war with Israel. Israel also knew that Egypt had been practicing a crossing of the Suez Canal using Soviet bridging equipment. The Israeli army had been able to observe an Egyptian army exercise along one part of the canal (where the Egyptians could cross from their side on the west bank to an island in the waterway) and had a preview of the techniques the Egyptians would use in 1973.

The Israeli army prepared a detailed plan to counter the Egyptian crossing techniques it had observed. When the Egyptians crossed the canal on October 6, 1973, crucial elements of the plan were delayed in their implementation. The Egyptians were able to cross more quickly, with fewer casualties than they had anticipated. The Israeli plan to counter the Egyptian invasion was not implemented for reasons having to do with faulty intelligence and faulty execution based on the intelligence. Even with the knowledge of the new Arab weapons, the Israeli military did not, apparently, assume that the Arab armies would look at their 1967 performance and develop new strategies based on new weapons.

The defects in Israeli preparations can be traced ultimately to a wave of overconfidence that swept over Israel following 1967. Israeli intelligence refused to believe up until the time the war started that the Egyptians and Syrians were preparing for war. Operational officers believed that they would be fighting the same enemies they had faced in 1967, using much the same tactics, even though the Israelis knew of the new weapons the Egyptians and Syrians had. Part of the heavy losses suffered by the Israeli army in the initial period of the 1973 war were a result of Israel's failure to comprehend that it needed new tactics against the Arabs. The Israeli air force, which had been decisive in 1967, was neutralized to a large degree in the early stages of the 1973 war. The air force was able to prevent infiltration over the skies of Israel, but not until later in the war could it provide support for ground operations in the Sinai or in the Golan Heights.

The army was not properly equipped or ready for combat when the 1973 war broke out. Equipment had not been properly maintained. Ammunition stocks were low. Tank units were sent into battle without binoculars and machine guns because not enough could be found.

In contrast to 1967, when the Israelis had maintained their silence while the Arabs boasted about the destruction they were about to bring on Israel, the Israelis in 1973 had come to believe in their invincibility and, worse, from Israel's point of view, to believe that the image of strength would be enough to deter the Arabs from attacking. When that image was not enough to prevent attack—because Israel failed to understand the essentially political logic of the Arab strategy—Israel was not prepared and suffered heavily before gaining the upper hand.

But the final outcome of the 1973 war, which found the Israeli army within artillery range of the Syrian capital and on the road to Cairo, did not restore the Israeli public's confidence in the men directing the military. In fact, the military's confidence in itself was severely shattered by the war. In the wake of the war an unseemly and destructive debate broke out, first in private and then in public, between high-ranking officers over who was responsible for the army's poor initial performance and for the strategies adopted. The failure had not been on the part of the soldiers fighting—which is to say the civilian population in uniform—but on the part of those whose career and job it was to think about and prepare the country's defenses. As an institution the army had failed Israeli society, and the army and political leadership stood discredited in the eyes of the public.

The horrendous casualties in 1973—2,550 Israelis killed (the equivalent of 160,000 Americans)—also erased any lingering glorification of war as an activity. The 1973 war established that Israel probably would not again enjoy another relatively easy victory like 1967. The Arabs, using their superior numbers to good advantage, supplied with high-quality equipment by the Soviets in seemingly unlimited amounts, and better-trained than in 1967, were able to deliver a crushing psychological blow to Israel.

Israelis understood after 1973 that the Arabs might not wait to start a war until sure of victory. In other words, Israeli strength would not be enough to prevent a war. Israel would have to look forward to fighting periodically on a timetable over which it had no control. Compounding the trauma of the war for Israelis was the widespread feeling that they had been misled by their government before the war started and had not been told the truth while it lasted.

Something fundamental—a bond of trust—was broken by the 1973 war. "The effects of the 1973 war were mainly in the very severe shock it gave to our sense of security," a young Israeli told psychologist Amia Lieblich.

During the years before 1973, we lived through different phases of the Israeli-Arab conflict with the fear of war, which is a very rational fear. But, basically, we felt secure. It was clear to me, as to other people with whom I spoke, that even if another war were to break out, which would certainly be disastrous, with many people being killed and wounded, there was no doubt that we would come out on top. In other words, we couldn't imagine that the State of Israel would be destroyed.

I feel that this basic confidence has been shattered by the Yom Kippur War. It suddenly dawned on us that if all the Arab states open fire one day, catching us unprepared, they could destroy us as a national-political entity and, perhaps, on a personal level as well. Who can imagine the outcome for women and children, let alone the soldiers, if the Arabs were victorious and entered our cities and towns? Actually, this didn't happen—the war was still far away from the population centers—but there was a feeling that it had almost happened, that by sheer luck, or thanks to a miracle, a small tank unit was able to stop the Syrian forces at the edge of our settlements. Maybe the Syrians themselves didn't advance as far as they could have, since they didn't know how unprepared we were for attack and therefore how open we were for it. So, the last war has undermined our sense of security as a nation for a long time to come.

On an official level as well the war was devastating. As a result of an official inquiry after the war, brought about by popular pressure, several high-ranking officers including the army chief of staff were forced to resign. Defense Minister Moshe Dayan also resigned as an indirect result of the 1973 war and Prime Minister Golda Meir retired.

These changes and the bitterness felt by the population toward the army and the top government officials hardly served to erase the trauma of the Yom Kippur War. Because the army is an organic part of Israeli society—not some remote appendage of it—the army's failure is the society's failure. The Israeli army presumably represents the best effort that Israel could make. The army was generally believed to comprise the men best qualified to provide for Israel's security. And in 1973, either the best failed to put forth an adequate effort or the best were not quite good enough. The failure in 1973 was not simply the army's, although to be sure anger was directed at the army, but was also understood by Israelis in a more profound way to be a failure of Israeli society as a whole.

In many respects, in the years preceding the 1967 war, the army represented what was best about Israel—abstemious living, self-sacrifice, devotion to self-defense restrained by humane principles and discipline. Army units not engaged in training or actual defense work were used to begin new agricultural settlements, and to help in the construction and improvement of development towns, in education of new immigrants, and in other social welfare projects. The army was a social resource as well as a defense force.

Immediately after the 1967 war Israelis found in the army's stunning victory tangible proof and confirmation of Israel's purpose and moral rectitude. The army's chief of staff, Yitzhak Rabin, found the secret of victory in the "power of moral and spiritual values" that the army possessed. The Israeli army was the population of Israel in uniform, but also transformed—hard-working, alert, united, and purposeful.

The Israeli public turned to the army to fill a void that was beginning to be felt in the country as a whole. Weak political leadership was failing to give the country a sense of direction. Military officers became celebrities, darlings of café society. The Israeli public hung on the pronouncements of her military leaders, who had acquitted themselves so brilliantly in the Six Day War.

But the army could not be better—at least not indefinitely, if ever—than the society that spawned it. Nor could the army maintain its vigilance and high standard when it came to believe in its own brilliance. The orgy of relative affluence and self-indulgence that began overtaking Israel after the Six Day War did not leave the army unaffected. Senior officers began cultivating habits that would have been considered absolutely corrupt in the days before 1967. Enlisted men assigned as drivers to high-ranking officers became personal servants to the officers' families.

"Another grave development," according to Ya'acov Hasdai, a career Israeli army officer,

> is the way so many IDF officers became publicity hounds and show-offs. The dam burst after the Six Day War. A publicity race began between many officers, and the newspapers were flooded with interviews and articles, and book after book appeared—war diaries, first-person accounts and books written by journalists based on interviews—emphasizing the personal part that one or another commander played in the victory. . . . The pursuit of public prestige even caused some senior officers to start surrounding themselves with "social lions" or gossip-columnists. As a result, a permanent link was established between the officers as a class and the *bon vivant* high-society class, which is not exactly characterized by high moral standards and lifestyle.

The Israeli army was rearmed after the 1967 war. Defense spending was increased to buy new equipment—tanks, artillery, and especially planes. An extensive system of fortifications—the Bar-Lev Line—was built along the Suez Canal to guard against an invasion by the Egyptian army and to protect Israeli soldiers on the line from bombardment. The enormous investment in constructing the Bar-Lev Line along with other military installations in the Sinai—something in excess of $500 million was spent—produced a new class—Israeli millionaires—made wealthy by the country's investment in its physical security. North of Tel Aviv, in

Herzliyya and Herzliyya Petuah, expensive new homes evidenced the new life-style. In Ramat Aviv, Ramat Hasharon, Zahala, and Afeka—all suburbs north of Tel Aviv—it was clear that the military was joining in the affluent lifestyle of the nouveaux riches.

It would have been unrealistic and perhaps even unfair to expect that the military would be unaffected by the spread of the good life in Israeli society as a whole. The military, after all, *shares* the value of Israeli society. Unlike the military in other countries the military leadership of Israel is not a separate class. If the military could reflect positive aspects of Israeli life, it could also reflect the negative.

The political leadership of the country in the period after 1967 evinced a rigidity in their approach to Israel's foreign policy. Even after the Egyptian president Gamal Abdel Nasser's death in 1970 and the appearance of an apparently more moderate Arab leader in Anwar el-Sadat, Israel continued to turn a deaf ear to entreaties to take a more flexible line. The Israeli military's position in this period was one of smugness and self-satisfaction. Nothing that happened in the Arab world following 1967 caused the Israeli military to change its estimation of its Arab enemy as a poorly trained, poorly motivated, poorly led fighting force. For its part, the Israeli army came to rely more on muscle and less on ingenuity to deal with its security problems. Self-confidence prior to 1967 had led to boldness in the Six Day War. Enormous success had increased that self-confidence in the subsequent period and led to arrogance and complacency after 1967.

Discipline slipped in army units. The tendency to permit expressions of a natural Israeli resistance to authority became more pronounced. Vehicles were not properly maintained. Supplies of essential items were allowed to dwindle. Rather than being unique to the army or isolated within the military, this trend was symptomatic of what was happening in Israeli society as a whole. Israelis believed after 1967 that they had entered a new era where they no longer had to worry about the country's destruction. Or at least, they believed, they had won an extended breather from the pressure that they had lived under from 1948 until 1967.

Israeli military intelligence continued to gather and evaluate information on Arab military moves. The intelligence gathering, according to authoritative accounts, continued to be thorough. Evaluation of the intelligence gathered, however, was filtered through a basic "concept." Simply stated, the concept was that the Arabs would not attempt to start a new war with Israel until they were ready to challenge Israeli air supremacy. In 1973 Israeli intelligence confidently—and correctly—predicted that the Arabs were not ready to challenge Israeli air superiority and would not be until at least the mid-1970s.

This analysis was apparently based on the thinking of Egyptian army commander in chief and war minister Mohammed Sadeq, who was dismissed by Sadat in 1972. Sadeq's thinking had run in terms of an ambitious plan including a cross-canal invasion of the Sinai, a storming of the strategic passes, and a movement toward the Israeli border. Sadat wanted a more limited operation, in order to break the political stalemate. When Sadeq was dismissed by Sadat, however, Israeli intelligence did not reassess the strategic conclusions that had been based on Sadeq's thinking. As a result, Sadat—as he outlined in well-publicized interviews—saw war with Israel as inevitable sooner than Israel believed, a shift that was not reflected in Israel's analysis. Sadat, it turned out, was not interested in military victory, but in using war to achieve a political victory.

After the fact, one well-placed career officer said that the 1973 war has been a blessing to Israel, a blessing secured at a terrible price. "We were lucky that it happened when it did," he said. "If it had come later, it would have been worse. It shook us up, made us change things."

Following the 1973 war a wave of reaction and resentment was directed toward the military leadership. The wife of an Israeli general, a career officer, said that when she and her husband appeared in public after the war, she encouraged him to wear civilian clothes or at least to remove his rank insignia from his uniform to avoid harsh looks and unpleasant comments from civilians. This reaction obviously reflects the feeling that the permanent military establishment failed to do the job and to live up to the expectations that the public had of it.

The depths of this feeling cannot be exaggerated. One woman, in discussing Moshe Dayan's responsibility as defense minister for the 1973 war, referred to him as a "murderer." Another woman, also discussing Dayan, suggested calmly that the only honorable course for him to have followed after the 1973 war was suicide. Still a third Israeli suggested during another conversation that he should have been hanged.

These reactions, though without question severe, are directed toward the *performance* of the military as an institution and not toward the existence of the military. The need for the military, for discipline, and even for extensive training—though examples of waste of time and money are widely perceived and criticized—is generally not questioned.

The peace treaty with Egypt, paradoxically, has not permitted Israel to decrease its defense spending but rather has increased the burden. The Israeli army and air force, occupying forward bases in Sinai constructed at a cost approaching $1 billion, has been forced to dismantle them and to construct new ones within Israel to accommodate the forces formerly stationed in the Sinai. Part of these expenses has been offset by American military assistance—principally $3.2 billion to build a new air base in the Negev.* In addition to the air base, ground force units also have been moved out of the Sinai and redeployed.

These expenses exacerbate one of the Israeli military's most urgent problems in the coming years. The serious financial situation that Israel found itself in by the end of the 1970s—with its foreign debt increasing and inflation running at a rate well over one hundred percent—could not be eased without deep cuts in government spending. Unless Israel's economic situation were improved, Israeli economic experts warned, the country would ultimately find itself in the predicament of Turkey, Rhodesia, and

* American aid for the Negev base includes a grant of $800 million and a loan of $2.4 billion.

other financially pressed countries. Lacking raw materials of her own, Israel is dependent on imports to manufacture the finished products it exports. But without a change in her financial position Israel would find it increasingly difficult to import raw materials.

The first priority for the government, these experts argued, was to cut her own spending, since it was such a major portion of the Israeli economy. After a year or so of reducing nonmilitary items like subsidies on food and social services, without making much impact on the dismal financial picture, the government was told that reductions in government spending would be meaningless without cuts in the largest portion of its budget—defense spending.

The amount of waste in the Israeli defense budget was generally conceded to be significant. As Israeli defense spending increased following the 1973 war (from 21 percent of the gross national product to a high of 35 percent), it was inevitable that the amount of waste would also increase. Reservists returned from training with stories about wasted food, wasted equipment, and wasted time. These stories were true enough, and the army's controls were more than likely insufficient. But the waste fell far short of the cuts demanded, and made, in the military budget. Nor could the cuts in defense spending have come at a worse time for Israel in terms of maintaining her defense posture.

In the late 1970s, the Israeli air force embarked on an extensive program to replace its aging and increasingly obsolete stock of A-4 Skyhawks and Phantoms—bought in the late 1960s and early 1970s —with American F-15's and F-16's. The price tag of a Phantom was in the neighborhood of $6 million. The cost of an F-16, including spare parts, training, and other subsidiary costs, is estimated at $12 million. An F-15 costs $20 million. Israel is replacing an estimated 170 Phantoms with 48 F-15's and 75 F-16's. These acquisitions, along with 250 to 300 more planes Israel would buy or produce herself, would not enlarge Israel's air force, only maintain it at its present size. The cost of this effort, even with American military aid, constitutes an enormous burden on the Israeli economy. The cost of operating these new weapons will also be greater than for the weapons they replaced. Maintenance, though simpler, is more expensive.

At the same time that Israel has been replacing her air arsenal with newer weapons, the Arab countries surrounding Israel have embarked on a similar campaign. Iraq, Saudi Arabia, Jordan, Libya, Syria, and Egypt have all been purchasing new weapons. Saudi Arabia, Iraq, and to a lesser extent Libya—all flush with oil revenues—have had no financial problems in obtaining sophisticated weapons. Egypt, Jordan, and Saudi Arabia have been able to buy much the same equipment from the United States that Israel has been getting. Iraq, Libya, and Syria have been able to purchase weapons from the Soviet Union and France.

The nature of these new weapons is such that they are not more but less difficult to handle—both to maintain and to operate. One of the reasons for the relative success of the Syrians and Egyptians in 1973 against Israel was that the weaponry they employed—though highly sophisticated and extremely effective—had been simplified so that the soldiers using the weapons did not have to be well-educated or highly intelligent to use them properly.

Israel is caught in a very real dilemma and faces a situation that is extremely risky, regardless of the decision made. Not to cut defense spending means endangering the entire economy and ultimately the country's well-being and perhaps even survival. Cutting defense spending means much the same thing by running the risk of putting Israel at a quantitative disadvantage—which is nothing new—but also a qualitative disadvantage—which is—in preparing for a future confrontation with hostile Arab states.

The army has been forced to cut training time in order to reduce its outlays. Air force pilots have been given less flight time. Live-fire exercises have been reduced. All these measures have cut expenses but also have alarmed career officers and private citizens alike, since the IDF's ability to offset superior Arab numbers has traditionally relied on being trained to a fine edge.

The IDF has faced other problems besides money. Following the 1973 war, the army's combat potential was greatly increased. Knowledgeable Israelis estimate that the army's fighting units are now roughly twice the size of the pre-1973 army. In order to increase its fighting ability the army has taken in groups of men it previously rejected. Persons with criminal records and Israelis of lower intelligence who would have been screened out of the army before 1973 are now accepted. Discipline problems for the army have increased as a result. Retaining good officers, a perennial problem for the IDF, has become more difficult.

Yet none of these problems has changed the basic character and role of the Israeli army in Israeli society. If anything, the need to lower its standards and to accept persons from the margin of Israeli society has enhanced the role the army has traditionally played as the integrator of disparate groups in Israel. Regardless of other differences, service in the army is the one experience that Israeli men have in common. The legal requirement to serve reflects an overwhelming consensus in the country supporting the necessity of army service. Army service is seen as simply part of Israeli life, an onerous but essential obligation that cannot be avoided. The army represents on one level a tangible symbol of the interdependence of Israeli society. That Israelis accept the obligation is indicated by the spirit of voluntarism within the army, where a significant part of the combat units are manned by volunteers.

For Israeli men (excluding the ultrareligious), army service is a rite of passage—an accepted part of life along with going to school, getting married, and having children. The higher one's socioeconomic status in Israeli life, generally speaking, the stronger are the social pressures not only to serve but to do so with distinction. Not to serve in the army, without a legitimate excuse, is to doom oneself to a life on the margin of Israeli society. The Israeli who avoids this obligation is not regarded as clever or smart, but as a shirker who is increasing the burden for everyone else.

The requirement of three to six weeks' service in the army reserves every year evokes an ambivalent reaction from Israelis. For some, obviously, the army affords a welcome relief from the pressures of job and family life. Others enjoy being reunited with their army buddies. But most Israeli men find reserve duty an enormous disruption and inconvenience, a constant reminder that they lack total control over their lives. At the same time, though, while resenting the intrusion and disruption, they take quiet pride in being able to participate in the defense of their homes and family. Military service is a sign of continuing virility and youthfulness. Israelis who "missed" one or another of the country's wars by being out of Israel at the time often mention the experience more with a tinge of guilt than as a proclamation of good fortune.

"Reserve duty is an enormous pain in the neck for me," an Israeli who works as a radio technician in the armored corps said. "I'm away from home. It disrupts my work. It's dirty and uncomfortable. The food isn't all that great. But if they told me that they didn't need me or that I was too old to do my job in the army anymore, I'd feel terrible."

Another Israeli, who at thirty-five is past the normal age for service in a field unit of the paratroops, said with some pride that he and the other—similarly aging—members of his unit wage a continuing battle with the army to keep the unit intact rather than to accept a transfer to a less-demanding noncombat unit.

Both of these Israelis, it so happens, are strongly critical of Israel's continued occupation of the West Bank and are strong supporters of attempts to reach a peaceful accommodation with Israel's Arab neighbors. But these political views have no effect on their feelings about army service. In general, army service and political affiliation have no correlation. The army has left-wing socialist officers who take a hard-line position in battle and right-wing officers who are less aggressive (as well as the other way around). Moshe Dayan related that during the 1973 war the second-in-command of a unit sent to defend Sharm al-Sheikh was a member of the left wing on issues regarding peace with the Arabs. This officer pressed the unit commander to vigorously ferret out Egyptian commandos sent to sabotage Israeli positions in order to "teach the Arabs a lesson." The politically right-wing commander took a more relaxed attitude, assuring his deputy that if the commandos attacked, there would be ample time to deal with them.

The peace movement in Israel comprises Israelis who serve in the army along with everyone else. The peace movement is not directed against the military, but against the political position of the Israeli government regarding retention of the territories occupied since the 1967 war. In fact, several prominent high-ranking reserve and retired officers serve as spokesmen for groups favoring a more flexible and conciliatory policy toward the Arabs.

To a large extent, the widespread support for the army in Israel is a result of its well-integrated position in the society. Little difference exists between the military's perception of Israel's strategic situation and that of the population. Nor has Israel developed a separate officer-class. Not only are a heavy percentage of officers in the reserves, moving back and forth from civilian routine to the military, but also officers almost always retire by age forty-five or fifty in order to pursue a second career.

Furthermore, the gap between officers and enlisted men is narrowed considerably by the nonprofessional character of the Israeli army. Officers are trained to lead by example rather than by order and the casualties suffered by officers in Israel's wars is unusually high. Though clearly not democratic in procedure, the Israeli army remains highly democratic in spirit. One of the strongest reasons why Israel is not a garrison state or militarist, despite the pervasiveness of the military, is simply because the military continues to be dominated by civilians. Where martial values are encouraged, it is for the practical reason that such values are needed to ensure an efficient army that, in turn, is needed to protect Israeli society. The sort of Spartan philosophy advocated by professional military men in larger countries has never attracted much of a following in Israel, where military duty is generally regarded as a disagreeable but necessary job that needs to be done. If anything, Israelis submit to the discipline of the army reluctantly, accepting it as essential but not reveling in it in the slightest. The Israeli army is notable for its lack of fancy uniforms. Ordinary soldiers receive only an olive-drab working uniform, no dress uniform for formal or business occasions. Career officers occasionally wear a slightly dressier uniform. But the gold-braid, medal-encrusted dress uniform favored by most armies has no counterpart in Israel. At his most spectacular, the Israeli army officer appears to be wearing a suit borrowed from a friend who bought it on sale from a Sears catalog.

In recent years the army has been a major source of political leadership. Moshe Dayan, Yitzhak Rabin, Ezer Weizman, Haim Bar Lev, Ariel Sharon, Meir Amit, and Aharon Ya'ariv all were generals in the Israel Defense Forces before entering politics. Each of them distinguished himself in some way during the Six Day War and achieved national prominence. During this same period, however, the political leadership of the ruling Labor Alignment was dominated by an aging group of Russian- and Polish-Jewish Israelis who were increasingly out of touch with the younger generation of Israelis. Since the party structure in Israel was too rigid to allow bright young faces to emerge without the acquiescence of the top leadership, the military provided one of the few alternative systems where leadership could develop and achieve national prominence.

Even with the emergence of the military as a source of political leadership, the results have been mixed. Military figures have become prominent, but far from dominant in politics. Rabin was relatively weak as prime minister and had to resign because of a financial scandal. Dayan, though a charismatic figure, was never able to command enough support to win the top position in Israeli politics. Ya'ariv resigned from the Labor party to join the Democratic Movement for Change as a protest to the inertia and corruption of Labor. Weizman, though a popular figure, was viewed with suspicion by other politicians who found him too mercurial, unpredictable and independent. Sharon, a field commander who distinguished himself in three wars (1956, 1967, and 1973) failed to win more than 2 percent of the vote in 1977 when he ran for the Knesset on his own party list.

As an institution in Israeli life the army also has not, for the most part, feathered its own nest in the manner that well-established armies normally do. Israeli military bases remain spare, almost purely functional. Except for the air force, which is on twenty-four-hour alert, housing is not provided for military families. Families of officers in the regular army live among the rest of the Israeli population. Military children go to the same schools that other children in their community attend. Attempts to start officers clubs have generally been unsuccessful. Where officers have to live on their bases during the week, their quarters are often no better than what an enlisted man in the American army would have. The commander of one base I visited—a lieutenant colonel —slept on a cot in a room with another lieutenant colonel and a major. His clothes were kept in a two-foot square cupboard. The only source of heat during the cold nights was a single electric space heater. The shower and toilets, shared with another twenty or so officers, were at the end of an outdoor passageway.

The stress on self-reliance that prodded early Jewish pioneers to form their own defense units remains deeply ingrained in Israel. Following the 1967 war, Israel found herself without an assured supply of weapons. France, which had sold airplanes and other weapons to Israel in the 1950s and early 1960s, imposed an embargo on further sales to Israel. French president Charles de Gaulle did not permit Mirage fighter-bombers and light missile-boats already paid for to be turned over to Israel. Although the United States was a possible and promising source of arms for Israel, the experience with France strengthened the feeling of Israeli officials that the country had to develop its own capability for manufacturing weapons, despite the enormous investment required, in order to ensure that arms would be available when needed.

Aided by a sympathetic Swiss engineer, and also by French technicians, Israel clandestinely obtained detailed blueprints for the manufacture of the Mirage engine and frame. The plans were extensively modified, and beginning in 1971 a series of planes was produced. The ultimate product of the evolution was the Kfir, a substantially altered and improved version of the Mirage fighter-bombers Israel had hoped to purchase from France.

The Israel Aircraft Industry also developed its own missile boats, equipped with Israeli-designed and -built missiles; a light cargo plane that can be used for military or civilian purposes; an executive jet (based on an American design purchased by Israel) that can be modified to serve as a high-speed reconnaissance plane; ground and airborne radar and electronic surveillance systems;

and a variety of supporting smaller companies to provide component parts for the final product. The Israel Aircraft Industry alone employs twenty-two thousand Israelis. In addition, in the 1970s Israel began production and deployment of its own tank, the Merkava.

In order to recoup some of the money invested in developing its arms industry, Israel has been anxious to develop overseas markets, especially for the Kfir. Since the Kfir (and the Merkava tank) are powered by American-made engines (or engines made in Israel under license from American companies), the permission of the United States government has been necessary to sell Kfirs to interested countries. Efforts to sell Kfirs to Ecuador and Taiwan were blocked by the Carter administration, which had adopted a policy of attempting to restrain arms sales generally. (Shortly before the 1980 election, the Carter administration lifted the ban on sales to Ecuador.)

Israel has not, however, been restricted in selling light weapons of Israeli design and manufacture to other countries. It is a source of pride to some Israelis and of embarrassment to others to know that their country has become one of the world's more active, if small-scale, supplier of small armaments and weapons, with sales now in excess of one billion dollars a year—a major export item for Israel.

Although the military industries may not be profitable, despite these heavy exports, their existence has created a growing complex of high-technology electronic industries in Israel that also promise to become major exporters. Still, the cost of designing, testing, and producing combat aircraft and armor is hardly cost-effective. Whatever profit comes from the military industries goes to the government, which owns almost all of the stock in the companies.

Israel has a well-deserved reputation for military proficiency, having overcome numerically superior and better-equipped armies in 1948–49, 1956, 1967, 1968–70, and 1973. The training given Israeli soldiers is hard. The quality of leadership in the army is generally high. In contrast to centuries of oppression the Israeli army provides certain proof to Israelis that they have reversed the trend of history and are able to defend themselves through ingenuity and courage. But despite the cultivation of martial arts in Israel, the universality of military service, the omnipresence of security personnel, and the prominence of former high military officers in Israeli politics, Israel has largely resisted the glorification of battle. Particularly since 1973, the taste for war has ebbed and the desire for peace has grown. Prior to 1973 it was virtually unthinkable for any Israeli who considered himself in the mainstream of political society to entertain the idea of negotiations or compromises with Israel's Arab neighbors.

The requirement that all able-bodied men serve in the army from ages eighteen to twenty-one and then to give three to six weeks every year until age fifty-five is a necessity considering the array of forces opposing Israel. But this universality of service is also an effective check against adventuristic, unnecessarily belligerent policies on the part of the Israeli government. Military service is, at best, an enormous personal nuisance and inconvenience on an individual level. At worst, it is a personal and national tragedy on an incalculable scale.

"Why is there such strong support for peace in this country?" a veteran of the 1973 war asked rhetorically. "Because I don't know anyone who wasn't affected by the Seventy-Three war!" No one is left untouched by war in Israel. One percent of the Israeli population died in the 1948 War of Independence (the equivalent of 2.2 million Americans). In the 1967 war less than 700 Israelis were killed (the equivalent of 50,000 dead for the United States). Another 700 Israelis were killed during the war of attrition Egypt waged between 1968 and 1970. And 2,550 Israelis were killed in the 1973 war.

Whether or not Israel can "afford" losses on this scale—a point of contention among some observers (see Luttwak and Horowitz, *The Israeli Army*)—it is clear that Israelis will not tolerate such casualties. It is safe to say that every Israeli has a relative or friend who was killed in a war. The country's cemeteries are filled every year on Memorial Day when tribute is paid to soldiers killed in action. The wounded, who far outnumber those killed, can also be seen everywhere in Israel, men—and women—maimed for life, walking on artificial limbs, offering a left hand for an introductory handshake because the right arm has been blown off in a never-to-be-forgotten battle.

The price Israelis pay for their security isn't only economic. My wife mentioned to an Israeli during a conversation that a divorced woman in Israel whom we knew was having trouble finding a single man, either to date or to marry.

"There aren't any," the Israeli said.

My wife indicated that she didn't understand why.

"It's not so hard to explain," the Israeli said, "we have a shortage of men her age. They were killed in the wars. That's why."

The psychological price of this burden cannot be estimated. "The horrible thing" a widow of the 1967 war said, "is that we were prepared to make sacrifices—our own lives if necessary—in order to make things peaceful for our children. My son will be going into the army next year. It begins to look as though our children will have to make the same sacrifices. There's no end to it."

With all of its brutality and horror war is too familiar an experience for Israelis to have any romantic conceptions about it. Young men and women in Israel do not dream about marching off to battle. In fact, an Israeli paratrooper observed, the marching songs of the Israeli army describe not a lust for combat but a longing for peace and solitude. During a visit to an Israeli army base where artillery officers were being trained, I mentioned to the commanding officer of the course that the instructors and students seemed extremely intelligent. His reaction was not, as I had expected, a swelling of pride.

Yes, he agreed ruefully, they were very bright. "Just think what an enormous waste all of this is, to have bright kids like this learning how to project a load of explosives from point A to a precise point B five or ten miles away, to kill some people they've never seen. We have more important things that we ought to be doing with our time—if we could."

The closeness of the army to the population, the smallness of the country, the real trauma experienced when any Israeli soldiers are killed in combat—these are factors that discourage adventurism on the part of the Israeli army. On the other hand, there is an implicit recognition in the army and in Israeli society that circumstances have demanded that Israelis sacrifice their lives in the past and, more than likely, again in the future.

Despite Israel's clear supremacy in the past and her ability to overcome greater Arab forces, there are indications that the balance of power is beginning to tilt away from Israel, toward its Arab adversaries. The increasing cost of weapons as well as of buying oil on the world market at premium prices and maintaining a high standard of living is beginning to strain Israel's capacity. Despite superior Arab numbers Israel traditionally has been able to defend herself by maintaining a qualitative edge. The nature of the new weapons, the greater number of them and the Arabs' ability to use them as well as the increasing financial restraints imposed on Israeli weapons procurement and training all mean that the qualitative edge Israel has enjoyed in the past may be narrowing.

In 1956 and again in 1967, seeing itself as the clearly intended victim of an Arab attack sooner or later, Israel chose to launch a preemptive strike while it held the upper hand. So long as Israel continues to see itself in control, it seems unlikely that it would precipitate an attack. Should Israel's strategic position erode to the point where its leaders and population saw the country again in jeopardy, the outlook would be less sanguine.

8 / THE KIBBUTZ

> If we may judge each man by the contribution
> he makes to the community, we are equally
> right to ask of the community what it is
> doing for this man. The greatest happiness
> will not be realized by the greatest or any
> great number unless in a form in which all
> can share, in which indeed the sharing is for
> each an essential ingredient.
>
> Leonard Hobhouse

Probably no other institution is as quintessentially Israeli as the kibbutz—the unique communal farm that played a critical role in the Jewish settlement of Palestine, and later in the establishment and development of the Jewish state. The kibbutz is the ultimate symbol of pioneering Labor Zionism, the institutional embodiment of the dream of returning to the land, working it, receiving sustenance from it, and reviving an ancient culture in the process.

The kibbutz also represents a distinctly Israeli blend of pragmatism and idealism in solving problems confronting the wave of Jewish settlers who came to Palestine in the early twentieth century.

Most of the earliest Jewish agricultural experiments in Palestine in the late nineteenth century foundered. Poor land, inexperience, disease, and the hostility of the native Arabs—all took their toll. The individual farmer stood little chance of success. The single family farm familiar to Americans is not totally unknown in Israel, but by and large, agriculture in Israel developed as a group, rather than as an individual, enterprise. Under the conditions collective farming simply made more sense.

The first kibbutz was started in 1910 on the shores of Lake Kinneret (the Sea of Galilee) almost as an act of desperation after the failure of an earlier, conventional effort sponsored by the Jewish National Fund. A group of settlers petitioned the JNF to allow them to farm the land on a collective basis, without supervision by the customary overseer. The request was granted and the first kibbutz (or *kvutza* as it was then called) was created—Kibbutz Degania.

The basic principles of kibbutz life quickly took shape: community ownership of all property, absolute equality of members, democratic decision-making, the value of work as an end as well as a means, communal responsibility for child care, and primacy of the group over the individual interest. These principles have remained more or less intact during the three quarters of a century that have passed since the founding of Kibbutz Degania, as more than 230 kibbutzim have been established. Members of a kibbutz "own" no part or shares in the enterprise. They buy nothing when they join, and they sell nothing if they choose to leave. They receive no pay or salary for their work. All essential needs—food, clothing, shelter, medical care, and education—are provided by the community. Children usually, but not always, are raised with their peers, visiting their parents for a portion of the day after school and working hours. Meals customarily are eaten in the kibbutz dining hall rather than in the private homes of the members. The kibbutz members meet once a week—usually on Saturday night— to discuss problems and to vote on issues that are brought before it by the kibbutz secretariat for decision. The questions might range from deciding on the construction of a new factory to permitting a member a year's leave to work or study abroad.

Jobs on kibbutzim rotate among members. The chief executive of the kibbutz, the secretary, changes every one or two years, as do factory managers, supervisors, and others holding positions of authority. Power is not permitted to accumulate in the hands of an individual or an elite by virtue of position.

Clearly, the financial security the kibbutz offers its members is one of its most attractive features, especially for persons with moderate material needs and desires. A kibbutz is not, however, a kind of glorified hippie commune. The mores of a kibbutz are strict and rather puritanical: drug use is absolutely prohibited; the indolent are not welcome; the dishonest are expelled.

The kibbutz cannot be understood simply as a financial arrangement between the individual member and the group. The lack of private property or wages paid to members is an important aspect of kibbutz life, but these are manifestations of a more central phenomenon—the emphasis on the bond between the individual and society and the reciprocal obligations that this relationship entails. The kibbutz is a community and a way of life in which each member invests a fundamental part of himself in the well-being of the group and in turn, derives his own sense of well-being from the success or failure of the group. The group is small enough so that the individual's stake and role in the community is visible and tangible. In place of the anonymity and alienation of mass society, the kibbutz gives the individual a sense of having a place in the community and a role in the general welfare, and of the community's responsibility to him should personal tragedy or hardship befall him.

Because of its innovative practices, its radical alteration of conventional modern institutions, and its relative success as a social, political, and economic enterprise, the kibbutz has attracted enormous attention outside Israel. Scores of books and articles have been written on the kibbutz, and, more than any other institution of the prestate or poststate era, the kibbutz has endured as a symbol of the new society Zionism sought to build.

Yet the kibbutz is far from representative of what Israel as a whole is like. Less than four percent of the Israeli population lives on kibbutzim. Nor does the kibbutz represent a growing trend. Although kibbutz society in Israel is stable and relatively prosperous, the influence of kibbutzim appears to be waning, rather than growing. The kibbutz is interesting not so much from the power that the institution or its members yield in Israel today but rather because of the insight into the Israeli character one gains from an analysis of it. It's analogous to looking at the family farm and small-town America to try to understand contemporary America. The kibbutz is more useful to our understanding of the mythology from which Israelis draw their self-identity than it is for an understanding of how things "really" are.

In this sense, the kibbutz represents for a significant number of Israelis, how—in the best of all possible worlds—they would like things to be. The essentially agrarian character of early Zionist settlements in Israel is preserved in the kibbutz, along with the continued devotion to the relatively ascetic principles of rural life. In its dedication to promoting the general welfare through humane individual self-sacrifice and self-restraint, its dedication to hard work, its commitment to democratic principles, its relative openness to change, its continued contact with the land, and the comparatively simple life of the small community away from the corrupting influences of the city and mass society, the kibbutz continues to represent for tens of thousands of Israelis the ideal existence and the "true" spirit of Zionism.

In its early years the kibbutz was an ideological battlefield, especially for those settlers who were interested as much, if not more, in socialism than in Zionism. In the earliest years of kibbutz life *no* property was private. Clothing was community property along with everything else. The pants or shirt one member wore this week might be worn by another the next. Men and women showered together communally. Marriage was disparaged. Early discussions among kibbutzniks reflected doubts about the wisdom of having children, since they would draw the parents away from the group. When, inevitably, children were born, arrangements were made for children to be cared for collectively so that the mothers could continue to work outside the home. Meals, of course, were eaten collectively.

Some students of kibbutz life see in its customs and rituals a subconscious (or conscious) attempt to depart clearly from the life of the Jewish ghetto. The collective life of the kibbutz, with its emphasis on the group, represented an ideological rejection of the ghetto life with its stress on the nuclear family. The kibbutz looked to the creation of a society in which the "new Jew" could emerge. While family meals were the centerpiece of ghetto life and served a psychological as well as a functional purpose, in the kibbutz the members eat their meals in a common dining hall where husband and wife may or may not eat together and children are excluded save for special occasions. (Children usually take their meals with their peers in the children's house, where they live until their teens when they begin eating in the dining hall.) The private preparation and consumption of food on a kibbutz was regarded as a rejection of the group, a matter of shame, since it was considered a reversion to the bad, old days of the ghetto that, according to Stanley Diamond, "reawakened memories of the old discarded family relationships which had produced what was conceived to be the weak, unmanly, fearful, incapable Jew of the *Galut* [exile]."

The ideological rigidity of the first generation has eased considerably. If it is true that some of kibbutz practices represent a reaction to memories of a former life in the ghetto, fading memories and a new generation with no experience of the ghetto has begun making changes as the kibbutz adapts to a changing world.

An Israeli who lived for several years on a kibbutz remembered that at the end of World War II, when Jewish soldiers returned to the kibbutz where they had been living, veteran kibbutzniks despaired at the damage that would be done to community life by two items the soldiers were bringing back with them—radios and coffeepots. Both items, the veteran kibbutzniks said, would destroy the communal integrity of the kibbutz by permitting members to sit in the privacy of their rooms, drinking coffee and listening to the radio—which had been group activities in simpler times.

The kibbutz has managed to survive the radio and coffeepot, as well as the television, refrigerator, stove, and dining table, all of which can be found in most kibbutz homes today. Men and women now shower in the privacy of their own homes. Women bake cakes in their own kitchens. Children occasionally live with their parents rather than their peer groups. Although some older members of kibbutzim despair at the disintegration of the group cohesiveness that these changes represent, many more members—especially younger ones—see these developments as reasonable and sensible adjustments to changing circumstances.

Along with color televisions, Danish modern furniture, vacations abroad for members, mid-life career changes, weekly facials for women in the kibbutz beauty salon, trips to theaters in Haifa, Jerusalem, and Tel Aviv, and scores of other modifications in the kibbutz life-style as life becomes more prosperous, other dramatic shifts are occurring. In 1950 agriculture was the dominant enterprise of kibbutzim. Only 50 factories were located on kibbutzim. By 1965, 134 factories were located on kibbutzim. By 1979, the number was 332.

Considering the limitations on it, Israeli agriculture had been enormously successful. Israel grows or raises 90 percent of the food it consumes and Israeli agricultural exports—amounting to more than $500 million worth in 1979—more than cover the cost of the food the country imports. Agricultural exports amounted to 12 percent of Israeli exports in 1979. (Although Israeli agricultural exports have grown enormously in the past decade—from more than $100 million to more than $500 million—their percentage of total exports has declined relatively because industrial exports have grown at an even greater rate.)

But Israeli agriculture may have reached its upper limit. The problem is not so much available land, which is abundant in the Negev, in the south of Israel, but water. According to an authoritative estimate, by 1980 Israel was using *all* of its known replenishable water supply as well as additional marginal and unconventional sources. Some authorities maintained that abundant —if somewhat brackish—water was available in the Negev, but this water source was unproven and constituted a one-time only supply rather than a replenishable source. The annual demand for water in Israel by 1980 was 200 million cubic meters more than the conventional supply. Half of this gap was filled by using groundwater, brackish water, and waste water. The projected gap by the year 2000 was estimated to be between 400 and 500 million cubic meters annually. Desalination, once widely expected to be a technology that would provide plentiful fresh water from the sea at a reasonable price, has proved so far to be an extremely costly source, with the cheapest rates for desalinated water costing ten times the average of agricultural water in Israel (which is government-subsidized).

"Unless a policy of further reduction of agricultural use of water greater than presently planned for is instituted," one expert warned, "there will be a severe water shortage which will hinder further urban and industrial growth vital for the country's development."

Consumption of water is tightly controlled in Israel. Even kibbutzim that pump water from their own wells, rather than using water from the national system, have their consumption regulated in order not to draw excessively on the groundwater table and allow seawater to penetrate and contaminate the underground fresh water.

Further expansion of agriculture seems to be out of the question. According to Hillel Shuval, an Israeli ecologist, the reverse seems likely.

> Although, in the past, agriculture has been the dominant consumer of the country's water resources, there appears to be little doubt that as the population grows to five million or more by the year 2000, all of the water resource development effort will have to be devoted to meet growing urban needs as well as the needs of industry, which is the sole anticipated mode of employment for the new immigrants and increasing population. This will most likely involve further cutbacks in agricultural allocations.

It seems fair to say that as a result of the increasing scarcity of water, agriculture is not the wave of the future for Israel or for kibbutzim. Intensive land use, energetic experimentation, and enthusiastic application of scientific innovations have made Israeli agriculture among the most efficient and productive in the world. Not only kibbutzim but also moshavim, as well as the relatively few privately owned Israeli farms, have achieved considerable success through application of modern techniques and technology to increase their yields without using more labor. (Israel has a variety of moshavim, ranging from those that are virtually indistinguishable from kibbutzim to others that are basically private farms with equipment owned in common. Of the million or so acres of farmland in Israel, 35 percent is farmed by kibbutzim, 33 percent by moshavim, 10 percent by private Jewish farmers, and 22 percent by Israeli Arab farmers. Although important agriculturally, politically, and economically to the life of the country, Israel's moshavim hardly represent the innovative departure from conventional social arrangements that the kibbutzim do.)

Steady advances in agriculture have allowed kibbutzim to increase production without adding to the work force, freeing workers for industrial development. In 1969 about 30 percent of kibbutz workers (outside those involved in education and service jobs on the kibbutz) were employed in industry and 70 percent in agriculture. Ten years later 55 percent of those workers were involved in agriculture and 45 percent in industry. About 85 percent of all kibbutzim already have at least one factory, and many have more than one.

The future of kibbutz life, like the future of Israel, almost certainly lies in industry rather than agriculture. What this will mean for the vitality of the kibbutz as an alternative life-style is hard to predict. Kibbutzim have generally been successful in their industrial efforts. But the movement toward industry and away from agriculture has not been easy. A member of one kibbutz, which has been extremely successful in manufacturing and marketing irrigation systems, said that a certain tension has developed between kibbutz members who work in agriculture and members who work in the factory. "The factory members are always telling the agricultural workers: 'Look, why don't you come work in the factory? That's really where the future of the kibbutz is.' But the agricultural workers don't want to work in the factory. They think the work is boring, and one of the reasons why they want to live on kibbutz is to be able to farm."

Kibbutzim have become multi-million dollar enterprises, serving not only the local market, but exporting products as well. The transition from an agrarian to an industrial economy has brought other changes and problems for kibbutzim. Although a few kibbutzim have 1,000 or more members, most are considerably smaller—with about 450 to 600 or so members. One of the principal features of a kibbutz is its relatively small size, which allows all of the members to know each other personally. Small size, however, limits the kind of industries that can develop on the kibbutzim, since many industries require larger labor pools and larger-scale production than an individual kibbutz can manage. As a result, kibbutzim have banded together to man and manage factories jointly, pooling labor in a regional factory. These larger-scale operations, however, cannot be as firmly controlled as a factory located on an individual kibbutz. Also different kibbutzim have different attitudes and philosophies, and problems can arise. Several of these regional kibbutz factories rely heavily on hired labor, a violation of the kibbutz prohibition against paying wages, which is synonymous with exploitation in kibbutz ideology.

Even when confined to an individual kibbutz, however, the factory presents problems. Although the technology and economics of agriculture can be extremely complicated and sophisticated, the issues an agrarian economy poses for the kibbutz membership as a decision-making body are relatively simple and easy to comprehend. No extensive expertise is needed—an important consideration in a community that stresses maximum member participation on all levels of decision making. With industrialization, however, the kibbutz has entered into a new constellation of decisions, many of which are beyond the ability of the individual member to master because of technical knowledge necessary to comprehend the issues.

"Once upon a time," a kibbutz member recounted, "everything was simple. Everybody could understand the budget. We didn't have much money anyhow. It wasn't sophisticated. Any second man could be the treasurer. When you came to the assembly, you could argue: 'Do we need a tractor? Do we need a building? Or do we need this?' Because everybody was involved in things that were not complicated even for somebody who didn't learn economics. Now, today, it's very hard. So then it was real democracy. But now it's very hard. What happens in the assembly is that when it comes time to decide on the heavy millions, only a few people understand about it. Of course, there are more things to decide—for example, whether eight people go abroad this year or ten people go abroad, which is peanuts. Those are the arguments that go hot and heavy. But those are peanuts. Because the real arguments are now to divide between the investment and what we eat.

"Comes forward the treasurer and says, 'I've got to pay back this year seven million to the bank.' Comes the fellow who was treasurer last year and says, 'You don't have to pay it back. I can show you a way.' What the bloody hell can all these four hundred people (the membership) understand about all this maneuvering of money and know about it? There was an argument about seventy millions [Israeli pounds] and nobody could find his hands and feet about it. And only the very sophisticated—about three or four people—understood what was going on. And everyone was trying to convince the assembly that he is right, but who understood about it? So the main questions go back to the committee, to the people who know about it. So I ask you, what is democracy?"

In many ways the kibbutz is ideally suited to industry. It has a literate, skilled, and stable labor force that is highly motivated and capable of meeting high-performance standards. Since salaries are not paid, the problem of filling relatively low-paying jobs does not present itself. Older, semiretired members of the kibbutz who work a reduced number of hours perform many of the light, if somewhat boring but still necessary factory jobs. The problems of elderly citizens, incidentally, has not been completely "solved" on the kibbutz, but older members continue to live and work on the kibbutz, often near their children and grandchildren, leading useful and productive lives according to their abilities.

Since salaries are not paid, however, the kibbutz has to pay more attention than the average factory to worker satisfaction. Although the factory manager has decision-making authority, he or she is not a "boss" in the conventional sense. Decisions are made democratically, with the factory employees (like the agricultural workers) discussing problems and coming to a consensus. "There are certain functions that it's agreed by everyone that I should perform—administrative things," a kibbutz factory manager said, "but I wouldn't take it upon myself to do other things without bringing it before the others."

Since work is stressed as a value, the problem on some kibbutzim is not getting members to work, but restraining them from overwork. On one kibbutz I visited, members show up at the factory on Saturday, the Sabbath, even though the factory is not officially functioning. At another kibbutz a younger member complained to me that although the kibbutz has been extremely successful financially, the older members resist suggestions that income be diverted from investment to increased leisure for the members. "They just can't stop working," he said.

"The feeling here is," his father explained, "that as long as you're busy, you keep evil and mischief away."

Given this inherent high level of motivation, the problem for the intelligent kibbutz factory manager is not salary but satisfaction, seeing to it that the workers in his factory enjoy their work. "It's no great secret," a factory manager said. "If they're happy, they'll produce more and our profits will increase."

Profitability, though, is not the only consideration for a kibbutz in choosing industry. Since the people choosing the kind of factory are the same people who will go to work in it and who benefit from its success or suffer from its failure, they have a real incentive to choose a factory that will provide profitable *and* enjoyable work.

The trend evident fifteen years ago toward industrial enterprises that require hired labor has been reversed. Approximately 70 percent of workers in all kibbutz industries (some of them are joint enterprises) are kibbutz members. The remaining 30 percent are hired workers. Some kibbutz movements have been stricter about hiring labor than others. In the Kibbutz Ha'Artzi movement, affiliated with the left-wing Mapam party, roughly 87 percent of factory workers are kibbutz members. In the Ihud HaKvutzot ve HaKibbutzim movement, affiliated with the Mapai party, 43 percent of the factory workers are members of kibbutzim. In the past five years, however, new kibbutz industries have employed virtually no hired labor.

The question of hired labor on a kibbutz illustrates one of the dilemmas confronting kibbutzim as they try to meet their responsibilities to the rest of society in Israel. No one contends that kibbutzim do not pull their own weight. Kibbutzniks constitute a disproportionate number of the officers and pilots of the Israeli army. Kibbutzniks are well represented in the all-volunteer, special units of the army. Despite right-wing criticisms of kibbutzim in Israel prior to 1977 for allegedly paying insufficient income taxes to the Israeli government, a study made after the Likud party formed the government found that kibbutzim were actually *overpaying* their taxes.

In a formal sense, then, Israel's kibbutzim are full and active partners in the life of the country. At the same time, though, for ideological and social reasons, the kibbutz has remained aloof from the rest of Israeli society. One of the first issues that arose between the kibbutz movement and the new State of Israel centered on the question of hired labor. Ben-Gurion, anxious to find as many jobs as possible for new immigrants in the early 1950s, implored the kibbutzim not only to provide volunteers to help establish newly formed cooperative settlements but also to hire workers. The kibbutzim reluctantly complied with the urgent request.

Yet kibbutzim resist becoming too intimately involved with the rest of Israeli society. Kibbutz children attend primary school on their own kibbutz and then usually go to a regional kibbutz high school where the other students also are from kibbutzim. Kibbutzim arrange social affairs with other kibbutzim so that single members have an opportunity to find a mate within the movement. Much of the financing for kibbutz enterprises is arranged through the offices of whatever movement a kibbutz belongs to.

As self-contained, socialist communities, kibbutzim are not anxious to expose themselves to what they see as the corrupting influences of the larger society. Although drug use is not unknown on kibbutzim, even the use of a relatively mild drug like marijuana produces an extremely stern reaction from the kibbutz. Users may be warned once to stop using the drug altogether. If they persist, they are expelled.

Some kibbutzim, wishing to maintain total control and influence over their children, provide for their education all the way through until they finish high school and go off to the army at age seventeen or eighteen.

Kibbutzim, of course, are not citadels of socialist virtue in the midst of capitalist decadence, or islands of tranquillity in a sea of turmoil. Human drama and conflict are no strangers to the kibbutz. If anything, the close quarters of kibbutz life intensifies some of life's less-pleasant experiences. A divorce, for example, can be an experience that shatters not only a marriage and friendships, but causes deep rifts within the community. As Amos Oz's novel about kibbutz life, *Elsewhere, Perhaps,* makes clear, human behavior on the kibbutz can be as mean and petty as in any large city. Even children born and raised on a kibbutz often find the atmosphere close and oppressive. Privacy, for those who wish it, is a scarce commodity in a community where one works, eats, and relaxes with the same people every day of the year.

Then, too, success has brought changes in the lifestyle of the kibbutz—new opportunities and new problems. One obvious, immediately noticeable change is in the comfort of kibbutzniks. Kibbutz housing is built more or less according to a standard plan: simple, one-story buildings—usually divided into two or three apartment groupings with standard units. The houses of veteran kibbutz members show signs of expansion as prosperity allowed the addition of space beyond the usual single room that kibbutzim built originally. Furniture, although not lavish, tends to be modern and stylish. A television set is usually found in the living room, and it is not unusual to find a stereo set as well. Items like furniture and clothing are usually bought by the kibbutzniks themselves, using the allowance for the purpose given them by the kibbutz. (It is a matter of some ideological difference from one kibbutz to another as to how individuals' funds can be spent. For example, some kibbutzim insist that the annual clothing allowance be spent on nothing but clothing and, if not spent, that it revert to the kibbutz treasury rather than being allowed to accumulate in the member's account and used for discretionary purchases. Kibbutz members ordinarily are not permitted to have their own private bank accounts, although members of one kibbutz recounted—with expressions of shock, dismay, and outrage—that they had heard that members of another kibbutz had been allowed to open private bank accounts. Although this change may seem innocuous to someone used to having a private bank account, in kibbutz society it represents a significant and potentially damaging shift.)

Kibbutzim now often can afford to send their members abroad for vacations on a rotating basis. The kibbutz members, as a group, frequently take trips around Israel to see the country, and kibbutz families often take trips inside Israel—at kibbutz expense—during their annual vacations.

A second major result of prosperity is that individual wants and desires have come to play a much larger role in kibbutz life. Prosperity means, among other things, increased opportunities and alternatives. Kibbutzniks no longer are scratching the soil for mere subsistence. They now have the luxury of choice. One kibbutz member decided in his late thirties, after working hard on the kibbutz all his life, that he wanted to go back to school to get a master's degree in social work. This wish represented a mid-life career change, but the kibbutz agreed not only to allow the member to stop working so that he could go back to school, but to pay his tuition. This kibbutznik expected to work as a social worker within the kibbutz network, counseling adults and teenagers who had problems, once he finished his schooling.

Yehiel Shemi, a member of Kibbutz Cabri in the north of Israel and one of Israel's foremost artists, struggled for several years to win the right to work as an artist full-time, establishing the principle that a kibbutznik did not necessarily have to be a farmer or a factory worker to be a responsible, productive member of the kibbutz. Shemi now works in a substantial building on the grounds of his kibbutz, traveling frequently to Tel Aviv, Jerusalem, and more or less annually to the United States where he also exhibits his work. The income from Shemi's work goes to the kibbutz.

Shemi's career illustrates the classic conflict between the individual and society, the responsibility and obligation of one to the other. Since a kibbutz is a society that has grown with the stress on group effort and collective well-being, this tension is felt keenly, especially since too doctrinaire an attitude on the part of the members will mean a loss of membership and even, perhaps, a weakening of the movement in the long run. Kibbutz members now pursue a variety of careers outside the kibbutz—education, scientific research, military, politics. Some kibbutzim are more rigid in their approach to the question than others. During my stay in Israel one kibbutz insisted that one of its members— serving in the Knesset—resign his position and return to the kibbutz. It was a decision made by the membership and the Knesset member complied, stating publicly that his kibbutz was correct in requiring him to return to his community. Kibbutz members who spend too much time outside the kibbutz pursuing their own careers lose contact with the communities of which they are nominally a part.

Still, it is clear that a basic trend is under way that sees kibbutz members looking for greater self-expression within the framework of the kibbutz. How far certain institutions and customs associated with kibbutz life can bend without destroying the essence of the kibbutz is unknown and a matter of concern to kibbutz traditionalists. "I think," one kibbutz member said, "we are going more and more from concern about the common life to concern about privacy, family, personal needs, and so on. People are much more concerned about their own small surroundings."

Where kibbutzniks all dressed more or less alike and had furniture in their homes that was the same, the use of allowances to permit individual members to purchase goods to suit their own tastes has introduced variety into kibbutz life on a rather mundane level. The movement toward individualism has expressed itself in ways more fundamentally at variance with traditional kibbutz practices, however. Collective child rearing, a practice once thought to be synonymous with kibbutz life and an essential part of the ideology, has come under increasing attack from younger mothers on some kibbutzim who want to have their children living at home.

The basic complaint about kibbutzim within Israeli society is that the kibbutz, for all its past contributions and the heroic participation of its members in the army and politics, has become a prosperous, insulated subculture within Israeli society, indifferent to the problems of less fortunate Israelis living on the other side of the fence.

It is a charge that many kibbutzniks acknowledge. Historically, the kibbutz was not successful in taking in the Oriental Jews who came to Israel in the 1950s and 1960s. Oriental Jews were not familiar or comfortable with the socialist and predominantly antireligious or areligious attitudes of the kibbutz. Coming out of traditional societies where the family was the basic unit of organization, the social organization of the kibbutz—with its diminished role for the family—did not appeal to many Oriental Jews. Those who sought a life in farming were more comfortable in moshavim, where the family unit could remain intact and the economic arrangement was not so radically new as on a kibbutz.

With the ebbing of nationalist fervor in Israel, kibbutzim have come to see themselves as socialist enterprises in competition with nonsocialist businesses in Israel. From the kibbutz perspective, the world tends to be divided between those who are inside the movement and those who are not. One businessman, who had no kibbutz experience but who was active in public affairs, described the kibbutz of the 1980s as a "burnt-out rocket." "They did the job," he added, "but now they're spent."

Kibbutzim, it is true, provide young leaders for the Histadrut's youth movement, the Working and Studying Youth. But the movement itself loses much of its membership in the mid– and late– teen-age level when ideological content is inserted into the program.

Individual kibbutzim have attempted, with varying degrees of success, to confront the question of their responsibility to the rest of Israeli society. One very prosperous kibbutz decided to use 10 to 15 percent of its annual net profits to establish a youth village for nonkibbutz problem children. Teen-agers from the kibbutz also volunteered to work in the village, which was planned to have an initial capacity of sixty youths.

Members of another kibbutz in the north described an abortive experience they had had in trying to give assistance to a nearby development town. The kibbutz membership was overwhelmingly Ashkenazic, while the development town's population was almost entirely Oriental. After their efforts received a chilly reception from the townspeople, the kibbutz broke off contact. The problem, one member said in a post mortem discussion of the experience, was that the kibbutz members had entered the town "like missionaries," intent on showing people living an inferior life how they could improve themselves. The townspeople resented the kibbutzniks' attitude and spurned their attention.

"It's not very healthy for our society, kibbutz society, to talk all the time about the impact on our nation," one member said. "Because I think the justification for the kibbutz should be both reasons—from the missionary point of view it should be a society that has a mission in the country, but also it is a way of life that justifies itself. I think if you always think about the impact on the society—what is your mission and what do you do about this and that problem—you become a missionary. I wouldn't like it. I don't think of myself and many other people here as missionaries."

"Thirty years ago," said a member of the same kibbutz, expressing an opposite point of view, "we were much more concerned with political affairs. I had the feeling thirty years ago that the kibbutz had a greater task in building the country, in security. Now I ask what are the tasks of the kibbutz in the eighties?"

As an economic enterprise the kibbutz undoubtedly is a success. As an alternative social system based on equality and social justice, providing security and support for its members, the kibbutz must also be judged successful. But kibbutz life is a radical choice, suitable for only a minority of Israelis.

During the period of mass immigration, the kibbutz was an important means of settling large numbers of immigrants. Yet the kibbutz has not contributed to integrating the various ethnic groups in Israel. Kibbutzim remain overwhelmingly Ashkenazic institutions in a country whose Oriental population already is the majority.

Political Zionism set as its goal the establishment of a Jewish homeland in the ancient Land of Israel. In the 1920s, 1930s and 1940s the kibbutz played a key role in establishing a Jewish presence on land purchased in Palestine for Jewish settlement. These settlements were Jewish "facts" in the face of Arab opposition to the Jewish presence and British efforts to limit Jewish settlement. The harshest judgment of the kibbutz as an institution of national importance to Israel is that it "has fulfilled its objective—it implemented the form of settlement which made possible the conquest of the country under conditions of an Arab majority and foreign rule. It makes no difference whether or not this was the conscious and original intention of the kibbutz's creators" (Yeshayahy Leibowitz, in *Unease in Zion*). According to this view the kibbutz no longer has a contribution to make to Israeli society outside of its own membership.

Considering their relatively small numbers, the fact that they live in isolated, self-contained communities, and the changed circumstances and values in society, kibbutz members no longer can be regarded as the vanguard of Israel. The sense of community and order that is so strong in kibbutz life is but dimly reflected in Israeli society today.

Also the nature and character of the kibbutz member has changed in recent years. The pioneering kibbutznik is a dwindling breed. The modern kibbutznik is a farmer, an industrialist, an administrator, a consumer—and only occasionally a pioneer.

The pioneering tradition—rather than the utopian example—
has become the enduring legacy of the kibbutz movement. As a
romantic, even heroic image, the picture of the pioneering kibbutznik has great appeal and attraction for Israelis. It has the stuff
of legend about it. It draws upon a revered tradition of Zionism.
Within Israel's pre-1967 borders, Israelis find diminishing opportunities for pioneering in the old style—for establishing new settlements and planting the Jewish flag in the soil. The Negev was
once seen as a likely area for pioneering, but lack of water has
inhibited agricultural development there, and more recently the
peace treaty with Egypt—which will require setting aside large
areas of the Negev for army training—make the south an unlikely
area for extensive settlement. In the north the Israeli government
is trying, with mixed results, to encourage small, self-sufficient
industrial settlements in the Galilee.

A strong claim to continuation of the pioneering tradition is
coming from a new, historically unlikely, source—from religious-
nationalist groups, which see pioneering not only as a means of
extending national sovereignty but as the acting-out of the divine
will. It is one of history's ironies that the vehemently antireligious
kibbutzniks of fifty and sixty years ago should find religious zealots
describing themselves, in their effort to settle the West Bank, as
the logical heirs to the pioneering tradition of the kibbutz movement.

9/RELIGION

The street where we lived in Jerusalem was within a stone's throw of several synagogues. The typical synagogue in Israel is a small, rather modest building with room enough for thirty or forty male worshipers and a small, separate section or balcony for women. Altogether, Israel has about six thousand synagogues. The ones in our neighborhood included a very small structure, used primarily by Jews from Turkey, and two larger buildings around the corner —one for Sephardic Jews and the other for Ashkenazim.

Prayer services were held every morning and evening. On Saturday mornings, the Sabbath, the synagogues were especially full. From our bedroom on a Saturday morning it was possible to hear the sound of the services being conducted in one, two, or even all three.

Speaking one day to the eleven-year-old son of a neighbor who had recently returned from a year in Boston, I asked him how he liked being back home. He answered that he enjoyed it generally, except that he did not like being awakened on Saturday morning, the only day he could sleep late, "by all those Jews praying."

A little surprised by this reference to "Jews" as though they were a breed apart, I asked the boy what religion he was. "I'm not anything," he said. "I'm an Israeli."

Although hardly the norm in Israel, the attitude my young neighbor was expressing is not unusual, either. Many Israelis who are fiercely proud of being Jewish, who would contemplate living nowhere else in the world but Israel, are just as fiercely antireligious in their sentiment, eschewing religious observance and chafing under the strictures imposed upon their lives by religious interests in Israel. Leaving a kibbutz once after a short visit, I was somewhat startled when a kibbutz member blurted out: "You're going to Jerusalem? I can't stand it there with all those religious bastards!"

Another Israeli described filling out a form for a security clearance required before he could undertake some work for the Israel Aircraft Industry. He returned the form to the security official, who checked it over and noticed an omission.

"You forgot to fill in your religion," the official said. "I'll just write in Jewish."

"I left it blank on purpose," the other Israeli said. "Don't write in anything. I don't have any religion."

"You're Jewish!" the security official said.

"I'm not anything," the other insisted. "Just leave it blank."

The struggle between nationalism and religion, between the profane and sacred, that revived one hundred years ago with the rise of Zionism goes on in Israel. That struggle is as old as the Bible. It goes back to the time when the Jewish people found themselves living as a nation, practicing a common religion, in the ancient Land of Israel. The dispersion of Jews from Israel that began two thousand years ago muted the national character of the people. Zionism, which must be seen at least in part as a rejection of strict religious doctrine, revived Jewish national sentiment and provided a new source of controversy—as if one were needed—for Jews.

Rather than merely providing a sanctuary where Jews could practice their religion without fear of prosecution, the establishment of Israel has precipitated conflict among Jews over the proper role of religion. Religious factionalism contributed to the defeat of Israel by the Romans two thousand years ago and, as we shall see, religious political differences today present a serious threat to the stability of the modern State of Israel.

Thoughtful Israelis worry periodically about *kulturkampf,* a term borrowed from the German, meaning "culture struggle." The struggle in Israel reflects the split personality of the Jewish state, a continuing conflict to establish a new Jewish identity.

In Judaism, religion and nationality are tightly interwoven, to the point where identifying the separate strands is extremely difficult, if not impossible. God's covenant was made with the Jewish *people.* The exhortations of the prophets invariably were addressed to the collective—to the people of Israel, to the Jewish nation. This emphasis on the group and on the cohesiveness of the collective extends to prayer, where traditionally a *minyan,* or quorum, or ten adult males is required for conducting a service. The concept of *am Yisrael,* "the people of Israel," is central in Judaism—not that the individual is insignificant, but that the individual has an obligation to the people, to the group, as well as establishing his or her own relationship with God.

From the destruction of the Second Temple in A.D. 70 until the nineteenth century, the national aspects of the Jewish people were expressed largely through religious observances. Jewish communities throughout the Diaspora centered on the synagogue, and the rabbi became not only spiritual guide but community leader as well. Without a country of their own, expressions of nationalism could go no further than the community, the sense of unity with other Jewish communities, and the liturgically expressed desire to return to Zion.

The emancipation in Europe of the early nineteenth century offered Jews the choice of integrating into the life of the countries where they were living—thus losing their national character altogether—or remaining isolated and apart, cut off from the mainstream of economic, political, and social development and at the continuing mercy of the foreign powers that allowed Jews to live together.

The ultrareligious solution was to remain within the community, to continue to hold strictly to the laws of the Torah as interpreted down through the centuries by the rabbis, and to ward off the developments of modern science and philosophy. In this way, at least, the integrity of the Jewish community was preserved against what the ultrareligious saw as the contaminating influences of the goyim, the non-Jews. Thus, many of the ultrareligious—especially in eastern Europe, continued to interpret literally the commandments of the Bible. Men did not shave their beards, did not trim their sideburns, strictly observed the Sabbath and the dietary laws (*kashruth*), maintained a style of dress that was distinctive, and disparaged worldly wealth and possessions in preference for a life of learning and study. Learning and study did not mean, however, broad areas of intellectual investigation but rather pursuit of the laws and wisdom of the Torah and the rabbinical commentaries on it. Barred in many countries from taking a full part in the commerce of the community, many Jews buried themselves in *Talmud Torah* ("study of the Torah"), elevating their isolation to a virtue.

The Zionist solution emphasized the unnatural aspects of Jewish existence in the Diaspora and the threat to the Jewish community, especially in eastern Europe. The early Zionist thinkers, men like Moses Hess, Pinsker, and Herzl, recognized that rapid changes in the larger society of Europe were making the life of the Jewish community increasingly tenuous. Herzl summed up the dilemma of European Jewry in his visionary novel, *Old-New Land:*

> In former times they had known the communal identity created by the persecution and oppression in the Ghetto. Then they had known freedom, liberty and equality presented to them as a gift by the civilized world. But here was the dilemma: in the Ghetto they were without honor, without rights, without justice, without defense—but when they left the Ghetto, they ceased to be Jews.

The solution advocated by the Zionists—revived nationalism—was vigorously opposed by the ultrareligious leadership, which recognized the threat to its authority and to strict observance of Jewish law posed by emphasizing the national, rather than the religious, character of the Jewish people.

"We can see," the ultrareligious Rabbi of Lubavitch wrote,

> precisely what emerges from all the articles of the Zionists, that their whole aim and purpose is to make it, as they are making, a supposition amongst the people of Israel, that everything to do with the Law and the Commandments is merely a device for preserving the group and is not a personal duty. This concept will be easily accepted by our youth, who are ready vessels for such a concept. And with this concept established among them, they see themselves as completely exempt from the Law and the Commandments, thinking that there is no need for them, especially when they have another device for preserving the group . . . and now nationalism takes the place of religion in preserving the society. After this supposition, he who enters the society of the Zionists does not consider himself at all obliged to maintain the Law and the Commandments, and moreover one cannot hope that even someday he will return to the Law and the Commandments and even if you crush him in a mortar with a pestle, he will not repent because in his own reckoning he is a pure Jew once he is a loyal nationalist.

The criticism was more than a little accurate. The nonreligious and antireligious Zionists, to the extent that they paid attention to religion, did so out of nostalgia or because they recognized that Jewish nationalism was affected by Jewish culture and that in turn meant paying some homage to Jewish tradition. But as little as possible. In their view religion was, if not the opiate of the Jewish masses, certainly a principal source of their abnormality—of their passivity, docility, and indolence. Religion continued to foster the idea that learning was preferable to physical work and thus perpetuated the dependence on charity that was humiliating and demeaning. Chaim Weizmann described Jerusalem, in the years before the First World War, as "a city living on charity, on begging letters, on collections." With ill-disguised distaste Weizmann also wrote about his attempts to enlist able-bodied Jewish men from the religious community of the Old Yishuv to work in the labor battalions formed during World War I, after the Balfour Declaration:

> The wages paid them were, of course, far above the meager dole they received from charity. But neither this fact, nor our careful arrangements to provide for their comfort and satisfy their scruples, could persuade them to stay in the settlements for more than a very short time. It must be admitted that they were quite unfit for agricultural labor, physically as well as mentally. Mostly they regarded it as a "worldly" occupation, liable to distract a man from the proper purposes of existence, which were prayer and Talmudic study. As to the financial side of it, one of them very seriously explained to me that physical exertion entailed the consumption of more food, as well as greater wear and tear of clothes, so that he preferred less money and a sedentary life.

The Jews of the Old Yishuv, Weizmann said, "lived immured behind the walls of a medieval ghetto—but a ghetto of their own making, and stronger than any which an enemy could have erected around them." The separation between these pious Jews and the Zionists arriving to begin in earnest the work of reestablishing a Jewish homeland was brought home to Weizmann when the British chief censor of Palestine asked Weizmann to assist in censoring the Hebrew-language letters the Jews of the Old Yishuv had written (the war was still being fought). Most of the letters, from the pious Jews of the Old Yishuv, Weizmann found, were written to Jewish contributors in the United States and other countries. Some ninety percent of the letters, according to Weizmann, complained about the Zionist Commission established by the British,

LAWRENCE MEYER

suggesting that funds were being maladministered and that the Old Yishuv was undergoing hardships as a result. Weizmann notes that he saw the letters as another device by the residents of the Old Yishuv to extract money from Jews abroad.

Herzl had promised in *The Jewish State* that it would not be a theocracy. "We shall keep our priests within the confines of their temples in the same way as we shall keep our professional army within the confines of their barracks," Herzl wrote. "Army and priesthood shall receive honors high as their valuable functions deserve. But they must not interfere in the administration of the state which confers distinction upon them, else they will conjure up difficulties without and within."

In his autobiography, written on the eve of the establishment of the State of Israel, Weizmann suggested that religious interests had to be put in their place at the outset. "There are powerful religious communities in Palestine, which now, under a democratic regime, will rightly demand to assert themselves," he wrote.

> I think it is our duty to make it clear to them from the very beginning that whereas the state will treat with the highest respect the true religious feelings of the community, it cannot put the clock back by making religion the cardinal principle in the conduct of the state. Religion should be relegated to the synagogue and the homes of those families that want it; it should occupy a special position in the schools; but it shall not control the ministries of state.

The crisis conditions prevailing when the state was created, however, did not allow a no-holds-barred debate within the Jewish community about what the relationship would be between state and religion. That debate, along with the writing of a formal constitution, was deferred for a more appropriate, peaceful moment. Herzl's blueprint and Weizmann's warning were disregarded. Circumstances may have left no choice, but religious interests now are deeply embedded in the State of Israel, adding one more factor to an already complicated equation.

Arthur Koestler, the journalist and author, predicted in the late

1940s that the religious parties might develop a "stranglehold" on Israel, so that marriage, divorce, and inheritance might "temporarily fall under the exclusive and medieval jurisdiction of rabbinical courts." Koestler's prediction was right on target, but his gift of prophecy was limited. "This state of affairs, one can safely predict," he continued,

> will last some five or, at most, ten years. Then the young native generation, which has no memory of ghettos and is developing a national tradition of its own, will carry out a vociferous but bloodless secular revolution and achieve a clean division between church and state.

Secular Israelis have yet to launch their "bloodless revolution."

When we first arrived in Israel in early summer, I was surprised by the time of the sunsets. It was dark in Jerusalem by 7:00 P.M. even though it should have been light—I thought—until 8:30 or 9:00 P.M. By contrast, the sun rose at about 5:00 A.M., which meant that for the vast bulk of the population two hours of daylight were being wasted. Israel had no daylight savings time or "summer time" as the United States does. The concept was not unknown in Israel. It was simply not used. Why? Because religious interests feared, among other things, that allowing daylight to continue until 9:00 P.M. would lead to mass desecration of the Sabbath, which—by Jewish law—begins and ends at sunset. If people had to wait until 9:00 P.M. for the Sabbath to end, they might demand that movie theaters, for example, which ordinarily show films at 7:00 P.M. and 9:00 P.M., disregard the Sabbath and start "early."

Ultimately, an Israeli engineer went to court and forced the government to institute daylight savings time. Economists calculated that the change would bring a modest savings in energy consumption. Undaunted, religious interests pushed a law through the Knesset to make sure that Israeli clocks would not be put back during summer in the future.

Among nonobservant Israeli Jews, attitudes toward the religious range from respect and tolerance to amusement, indifference, and even outright hostility. The attitude of religious Jews toward the nonobservant covers the same spectrum. During dinner with two religious couples one night, I heard a description of a current flap that had stirred up the parents at the nursery school where they sent their children. Their school, which was for religious children, shared a building with a regular, nonreligious nursery school. Several of the religious parents, they said, wanted to seal all the doors connecting the two halves of the building and to institute strict measures to ensure that their children would not come into contact with the nonreligious children of the other school.

Roughly half of the Jewish Israeli public favors some kind of relationship between state and religion, with about 15 percent of the population in favor of Israeli law being tailored after Jewish law. The other half of the population supports—more or less militantly—a separation of state and religion. The 15 percent favoring a close relationship between state and religion are more than balanced by about 35 percent who are outspoken in their opposition to religious influence. For many religious Jews, religious observance remains a private affair, a matter of arranging their lives in order to worship and observe Jewish ritual and tradition as they see fit. Religious schools, supported by the state, are available for parents who want their children to receive a religious education. (Secular schools study the Bible as *history*.) Religious Jews who serve in the army are assured that the food they eat will be kosher.* Since the most important religious holidays are also national holidays, observance by religious persons involves no major inconvenience or financial sacrifice.

---

* Technically, all males, whether religious or not, must serve in the army. But in practice ultrareligious men are generally exempted from service if they prefer not to serve. By law, women who object to serving in the army or to performing alternative national service on religious grounds are exempted. This exemption causes considerable resentment among nonreligious women, who must serve in the army for two years.

Friction between religious and nonreligious Jews, though not a constant factor in Israeli life, is not infrequent, either. There have been heavily-publicized incidents of rock throwing by some of the ultra-Orthodox Jews of Jerusalem's religious neighborhoods who were objecting to traffic on roads going by their neighborhoods on the Sabbath, advertisements on public buses, the indecent attire of women walking through their neighborhoods, or the construction of a public swimming pool in Jerusalem where coed swimming would be permitted on Saturday. These are extreme reactions, to be sure, but they are not lightly brushed off by secular authority. Although religious extremists were not able to prevent the construction of a public swimming pool in Jerusalem, they did force the municipal government to relocate the soccer stadium and to build a new road to carry the offensive Sabbath traffic along a more remote route.

The conflict is not limited to Jerusalem. Sharp conflicts have developed in remote Israeli towns where religious groups, constituting a majority, enforced sexually segregated swimming in the municipal swimming pool.

The movement of ultrareligious persons into a previously nonreligious neighborhood is a cause for concern among the area's inhabitants. One Israeli complained that his neighborhood was being "invaded" by religious families, who were objecting to music being played too loud in private homes on the Sabbath and also to automobile traffic. This Israeli was concerned that the next step would be an attempt by the religious residents to have the neighborhood sealed off to automobile traffic on the Sabbath.

Despite the significant impact that Reform and Conservative Judaism have had in the United States, the influence of these two movements in Israel is negligible. Most practicing Reform or Conservative Jews in Israel come from the United States. Israelis tend to adopt an all-or-nothing attitude toward religion. One Reform rabbi, an American working in Israel, observed that Israelis see Orthodoxy as the traditional and, therefore, the only acceptable form of religious observance. "And then they say to themselves: 'Well, I can never be that. That's not for me.' And so, they don't make any effort at all," he said. "Reform Judaism is perceived as not being genuine Judaism. The attitude here is 'If you're going to do it, do it right. I'm not going to mess around with anything but the real McCoy.' "

But the "real McCoy" is unacceptable practically and ideologically for the vast bulk of Israelis. Even though the laws of *kashruth* are easier to observe in a country where most of the food available is kosher, observing those laws requires a certain amount of discipline that strikes many as a nuisance. For an active, mobile population the prohibition against public transportation on the Sabbath is a further inconvenience. For the poorer elements of Israeli society the ban is immobilizing.

Yet the question of a "Jewish identity" without any observance of the Jewish religion is a troublesome one for any Israeli who gives thought to the problem. Judaism has not traditionally recognized a difference between religion and nation. The idea of a Christian Jew is a contradiction in terms in Judaism. One may be a nonobservant Jew, a Jew who fails to keep the laws and commandments, but one cannot take up another religion without also renouncing Jewish nationality. Judaism does not recognize a way to separate the two. The nonreligious or antireligious solution in Israel is to incorporate the religious holidays into a secular observance. Thus, kibbutzim, which are often, but not always, antireligious, observe Passover—the celebration of the Jewish escape from Egypt—with a secular seder rather than a religious seder (a combination meal and religious observance in which the story of the Jewish flight from Egypt is retold, using food, song, and prayers as part of the ritual). As a celebration of freedom and an opportunity for recalling the travails of the Jewish people, Passover is eminently observable as a nonreligious event. Similarly Hanukkah—the celebration of the triumph of Judah Maccabee over the Assyrian Greeks in 165 B.C. is a minor religious holiday but a significant national holiday, used to dramatize the Jewish struggle for survival and independence against seemingly superior forces.

But what happens to tradition when a religious event is transformed so radically and the original spiritual rationale is wrenched from it? In the United States the closest—though not entirely similar—analogy is the secularization and commercialization of Christmas, which has led to annual complaints that the spiritual meaning of the holiday has been drowned in an orgy of consumption. In Israel the secularization of the holidays means that on the Jewish New Year—Rosh Hashanah—it will be almost impossible to find a hotel room in a resort area in Israel or a beach not packed with sun worshipers. Hundreds of thousands of Israelis do attend services on the Day of Atonement—Yom Kippur—and almost no one drives the entire day, a concession to the holiest day of the year and to the convictions of religious Jews. Even among the nonreligious, some vestigial remnant of religiosity, perhaps an atavistic "fear of God," prevents them from behaving in a normal way this one day of the year.

Yet hundreds of thousands of Israelis, finding the rigidity of traditional Orthodox Judaism too inflexible and too at variance with modern life, reject any form of religious content in their lives —or in their children's lives. Does this mean, as some religious Israeli Jews assert, the eventual extinction of Judaism in Israel, or at least a profound separation between religious and nonreligious Israeli Jews? According to Yeshayahu Leibowitz, a biochemist, religious intellectual, and gadfly, it does. "Behind the pseudo-Jewish facade of the State of Israel," Leibowitz asserts,

> a process is in motion, eradicating the historical character of the Jewish people, i.e., transforming it into a different nation: a member of this nation will not be defined by his Jewishness (Judaism) but only by an identity card signed by an official of the Israeli Ministry of the Interior. Since there is no copyright barring the use of the name "Jew," it may be that this nation will be called "Jewish" (though it will probably prefer to be called "Israeli" or "Hebrew"). However, it is clear that this nation will not be the continuation of the historical Jewish people, just as the Greek nation of our days is not the historical descendant of Ancient

Greece. Since a minority of Jews will continue to maintain the historical continuity, a point may be reached where it will be divided into two nations, whose members wouldn't be able to eat at the same table (*kashruth*), nor to intermarry, nor to work together (the Sabbath).

The solution seized upon by the Orthodox establishment of Israel is to try to guard the faith to the maximum extent possible using the coercive power of the state. Despite the overwhelming dominance of Jews in the country, Israel is not a religious state. It is a secular state. The primary reason why religion is an issue in Israel is because religious and nonreligious Jews (not to mention Israeli Arabs) do not agree on the appropriate role of religion in the Jewish state, which is to say whether "church" and state should be entirely separate or not. In other words, the issue in Israel centers on the use of state authority to enforce religious beliefs and practices.

Israel's lack of a written constitution is directly attributable to this lack of agreement over the proper relationship between church and state. In order to draft a formal charter the role of religion would have to be defined, and moderate forces on both sides recognize that the debate would be fearsome. As a result, the whole subject of religion in the Jewish state is one of those sleeping dogs that has been left to slumber lest a discussion result in the utter disruption of the state.

Still, the subject does come up periodically. It is unavoidable, since roughly 10 percent of the Israeli population (Arab voters included) vote for the National Religious Party and another 3 or 4 percent annually vote for the ultrareligious Agudat Yisrael party. With roughly 15 percent of the vote these two parties— which make it their business to safeguard religious interests— would not be anything more than a small minority in most governmental systems. In Israel, however, with its multiple-party system, the religious parties have traditionally provided the votes for the dominant party to form a majority in the Knesset and grasp ruling power. The price of religious support within the government coalition in the first twenty-nine years of the state was concessions on matters relating to Sabbath observance, *kashruth,* and personal status. Were it not for this involvement in secular matters—using the coercive authority of the state to enforce religious doctrine—much of the resentment harbored by Israelis toward the religious community probably would evaporate.

As it is, under existing Israeli law it is not possible to obtain a civil marriage or divorce in Israel. Christians, Muslims, and Jews—believers or not—must go to their respective religious institutions to be married or divorced. The state has ceded its authority over marriage and divorce to the religious establishment in Israel.

For the dominant Jewish society an elaborate and extensive structure has been established under the control of the Ministry of Religion and Chief Rabbinate, presided over by Israel's two chief rabbis—one for Ashkenazic Jews and the other for Sephardim. The two chief rabbis sit as presidents of the Rabbinical Council, which has ten other members, and is reponsible for authorization and training of judges for religious courts, licensing marriages and divorces, supervising *kashruth,* and perhaps most important, interpreting Jewish law and applying it to modern circumstances.

Each locality in Israel has its own religious council, and the country's larger cities also have their own chief rabbis.

Control of *kashruth* is a source of enormous power for the chief rabbis, since the lack of a certificate by a hotel, restaurant, or butcher means that religious customers will not patronize the establishment. Jewish law, like any other body of rules that is subject to interpretation, can be construed liberally or strictly, depending upon the outlook and philosophy of the person or persons providing the interpretation. Over the centuries rituals and practices in Judaism were modified to meet new circumstances or to reflect new beliefs. But these changes were not always universally accepted. Thus, to speak of food as being kosher, or acceptable according to the laws of *kashruth,* leaves the impression that the matter of judging whether something is or is not kosher is fairly cut-and-dried. It can be—pork, mollusks, and crustaceans are absolutely not kosher and forbidden by the laws of *kashruth.* Beef, depending upon how it is slaughtered and what part of the animal it comes from, may or may not be kosher. Then, too, one person's standards may be more flexible than another's, since every person in Judaism must decide where to draw the line in his or her observance of the laws and ritual, or how to interpret them.

As a result of this need for subjective judgment in interpreting *kashruth,* the authority granting the license (*hechsher*) has tremendous power over a firm or business. The opportunity for mischief or graft is clear. A business cannot pick and choose who will grant the *hechsher* since it is under the control of the local rabbinical authority. The chief rabbis of the various cities of Israel, as well as the chief rabbis of the state are elected by an electoral assembly. Winning election involves campaigning, forming alliances, and making promises just as in any other political process. Patronage is a clear part of the process, and one of the positions at the disposal of chief rabbis to award is the supervision of *kashruth.*

One of Jerusalem's most exclusive restaurants lost its *hechsher* after the city's chief rabbi charged that it had been buying meat that was not kosher. The restaurant's owner replied that his meat had been supervised by a rabbi and certified as kosher. The chief rabbi responded that the rabbi who had inspected the meat was not acceptable to him and therefore that his approval was of no legal value. The restaurant's owner then revealed that the rabbi who had been approved by the chief rabbi of Jerusalem to inspect his establishment had tried to extort money from him in return for granting a *hechsher.* Ultimately, the matter was turned over to the Israeli police for investigation.

An executive of a major hotel in Jerusalem recalled that his hotel had conducted extensive negotiations with the chief rabbi of the city in order to have its *hechsher* renewed. As it so happened, the hotels of Jerusalem had been operating under *hechsherim* granted by the Ashkenazic chief rabbi of Israel because the position of chief rabbi for the city had been vacant. When a chief rabbi for the city was chosen, he moved to assert his authority by insisting on stricter procedures than those demanded by the chief rabbi of Israel. Among the demands made by the city's chief rabbi was an insistence that hotels not employ Jews to work on the Sabbath. Failure to comply, the chief rabbi warned, would mean that a *hechsher* would not be granted, which would put the hotel off limits to religious Jews.

The demand that Jews not be employed on the Sabbath put the city's hotel in a tight position, since they were hard-pressed to find non-Jews capable of performing certain key jobs only one day a week. "So," the hotel executive said, "once we established that this was a real demand and not an attempt to shake us down for money, we entered into negotiations to work out some kind of arrangement. One of the agreements we came to involved serving guests in the restaurant on Friday night. We can't close down completely because it's the Sabbath. But we're not supposed to handle money. Besides that, we agreed that we wouldn't even have anyone out in the open *appearing* to handle money. What was the agreement? We had a Jewish woman sitting in the kitchen with a cash register. The customers' tabs would be brought in to her and she would punch up each individual item, but she wasn't allowed to punch the total button. When it came time to punch the total button, an Arab waiter standing behind her would push it. That arrangement was acceptable to the chief rabbi and we got our *hechsher*."

On another occasion the same hotel received a call from the chief rabbi's office asking who the house doctor was. The caller was given the name of the doctor, a physician in private practice in Jerusalem and a nonreligious Jew. "A few days later," the hotel executive recalled, "we got another call from the chief rabbi's office. They told us that we would have to have a religious doctor instead. We asked if they had someone specific they could recommend. The caller gave us the name of a doctor. We were a little suspicious, so we called the doctor we had been using and asked him if he had had any similar experiences with the chief rabbi's office. He said he had been the house doctor for another Jerusalem hotel as well, that they had gotten a call from the chief rabbi's office with the same demand and that the same doctor was recommended as a replacement. Our doctor had been forced out as house physician for that hotel. Well, obviously this was just a case of the chief rabbi trying to muscle us around in order to provide patronage for a supporter. We weren't going to give in, but we didn't want to confront them head on, either. The next time the chief rabbi's office called, we said we would consider using the physician they recommended instead, but he would have to try out on the next four Sabbaths, Rosh Hashanah, and Yom Kippur. Then we would decide. Things cooled off after that."

Although Jerusalem's hotels have many guests who are not Jewish, the city's chief rabbi does not necessarily make allowances for their preferences and tastes in issuing demands to the hotels. A Jewish women's organization was having its monthly dinner meeting at a major Jerusalem hotel on December 31. Although wine was ordinarily served with the meal, the women noticed that it was not that evening. When they asked to have it served, they were told it could not be. "It turned out," one of the women told me afterward when I met her at a New Year's Eve party, "that the hotels had been warned that if they permitted any celebration of New Year's Eve—which the Orthodox consider a Christian holiday —they would lose their *hechsher*. So to avoid anyone's making a toast, the hotel took no chances and served no wine." The loss was a minor one for the women at the dinner, but Christian guests in hotels throughout the Jewish part of Jerusalem found that their hotels were especially somber and forbidding on a night that many of them wished to celebrate.

Although Israel's Declaration of Independence guarantees freedom of religion, and Christians and Muslims are free to worship without fear of intimidation or persecution, Jews in Israel have only one officially sanctioned and supported trend—the traditional, Orthodox branch of Judaism. Reform and Conservative Judaism in Israel, to the extent that they exist, operate outside the umbrella of official recognition—supported by neither the state nor the various religious authorities of the country. Reform and Conservative Judaism are movements that trace their roots back to the nineteenth century when Jews in Europe and the United

States attempted to find a way of adapting religious practice to a changing world. The response of the Orthodox establishment was to view the attempts of Reform and later Conservative Jews to modernize and liberalize ritual and practices as heresy, a dangerous departure from tradition that ultimately would undermine the Jewish religion. Right or wrong, Reform and Conservative Judaism have made significant inroads in the United States where the bulk of the Jewish community has moved away from Orthodox Judaism to the more modern, more flexible mode of religious observance.

In Israel, however, the country's religious authority remains firmly in the grasp of the Orthodox establishment. Reform and Conservative rabbis, who come primarily from the United States, may not perform marriages or perform any other legal function entrusted to religious authority. In the Israeli army Reform and Conservative rabbis are not recognized as clergymen, but rather as laymen. At times the Orthodox establishment has tried to prevent the issuing of permits for the construction of Reform and Conservative synagogues and has tried to bar religious observance in those synagogues. The first year we were in Jerusalem, the city's two chief rabbis inserted an advertisement in the English-language *Jerusalem Post* shortly before the Jewish New Year of Rosh Hashanah advising Jews that they could not fulfill their obligation under Jewish law to hear the shofar (ram's horn) blown if they heard it in a Reform or Conservative synagogue. The advertisement caused a minor uproar, but the rabbis made no move to back down from their ruling (which readers could follow or ignore as they saw fit).

Attempts to modify Israeli law in order to give equal status to Reform and Conservative Judaism in Israel have been consistently rejected in the Knesset, where even the Labor Alignment and before it the Mapai party failed to support efforts to change the law. Periodically, the Orthodox establishment in Israel attempts to tighten its grasp by expanding its authority beyond the borders of Israel. Under existing Israeli law, anyone born a Jew or converted to Judaism is automatically eligible for Israeli citizenship under the Israeli basic law, the Law of Return. Within Israel, obviously, only Orthodox rabbis may convert non-Jews to Judaism, according to procedures established by Jewish law. Outside of Israel, Reform and Conservative rabbis also perform conversions. These conversions, however, are often not acceptable as valid by Orthodox rabbis. Nevertheless, the State of Israel has recognized as valid conversions performed by non-Orthodox rabbis outside of Israel. The Orthodox establishment in Israel has consistently tried to amend Israeli law to recognize *only* Orthodox conversions, regardless of where they are performed.

The question of "who is a Jew?" is one of the most sensitive, most explosive issues in Israel, a nation whose people have kept their identity for three thousand years by strict observance of the laws and commandments laid down in the Bible. In the late 1950s a left-wing minister of interior, who was charged by law with the responsibility of certifying citizenship, separated the question of Jewish nationality from Jewish religious identity. This decision, reflecting the antireligious nature of left-wing Zionism, created an immediate furor in religious circles, where it was argued that in Judaism, religion and nationality could not be separated. The minister of interior's ruling was that a person born a Jew who claimed to be a Jew was Jewish, even if he or she chose to practice some other religion. The religious position was that the state could determine who was a citizen of Israel, but not who was a Jew. Jewish law, according to the Orthodox rabbis, dictated that a Jew was a person born of a Jewish mother, and if a male, he must have been ritually circumcised. Alternatively, a person could become Jewish, according to the Orthodox rabbis, by undergoing conversion according to Jewish law.

The government almost fell during a protracted crisis over the issue. The matter was finally resolved, with the Orthodox establishment victorious. Henceforth, Jewish identity was defined according to the prescription of Jewish law, which is to say religious, rather than secular, law.

Subsequently, an Israeli Jew with a Gentile wife (they had been married outside the country) sought to register his two children as

Israeli citizens. The children had been born in Israel and were, therefore, qualified for citizenship. The parents were both atheists, however, and they declared on the application papers that the children were Jewish by nationality, but when asked to state the children's religion, they responded, "None." The registrar handling the application refused to acknowledge the children's Jewish identity and entered "No registration" under the nationality category. The parents took the matter to court and in 1970, by a five to four majority, the Israeli Supreme Court—taking pains to say it was not ruling on the question of "who is a Jew?"—ruled that the two children should be listed as Jewish nationals on their identity cards.

The religious parties again threatened a crisis over the issue and the Labor Alignment government quickly enacted a law forbidding children of Gentile mothers from being listed as Jewish nationals. The Law of Return was eased in other respects as a concession to antireligious forces, but the Orthodox establishment again forced the issue to be resolved to its general satisfaction.

Not only is the Orthodox establishment vigilant in making sure that the only official religious view is the strict Orthodox one, but the Israeli Orthodox establishment is also careful to prevent rabbis from outside the country—even if they are acceptably Orthodox —from having any authority inside Israel. Orthodox rabbis from abroad may not perform marriages in Israel, officiate at ritual circumcisions, or perform any of the other religious-legal functions of local rabbis. Israel, in this sense, is a "closed shop," where even an Orthodox rabbi may not function in an official capacity without a "union card." For Israel's Orthodox rabbis, performing marriages, granting *hechsherim*, and fulfilling the other official functions is a source of income that they refuse to jeopardize by opening up the field to foreign competition.

In fact, a rabbi granted authority by a religious council in one area of Israel has no authority to function in another area governed by a different religious council. A council's authority is strictly limited to the geographical area of its jurisdiction.

This state of affairs may appear unseemly and even corrupt in the eyes of those who like to think of religious authority as devoting itself to spiritual matters and leaving worldly matters to secular authority. The direct involvement of the Orthodox establishment in politics, through the National Religious Party and the ultrareligious Agudat Yisrael and Poalei Agudat Yisrael parties is designed to safeguard religious interests in Israel, especially the religious-school system.

The National Religious Party has lent its support to every governing coalition since the founding of the state. In return for its support the NRP has been awarded—at one time or another—control of the ministries of religion, health, post office, infrastructure, interior, police and education. Each of these ministries provided the NRP, as a political party, with significant opportunities to create jobs and to fill them with political supporters. Since the NRP regularly polls only about 10 to 12 percent of the vote, some Israelis charge that its real constituency is really little more than government employees and their families who depend upon the NRP's participation in the government for their jobs. The NRP, like other political parties, also has had the opportunity to channel substantial amounts of funds from the government treasury to institutions within the various religious movements supporting the NRP, without being limited by official regulations or guidelines governing the distribution.

Although the NRP's behavior as a party is not much different from the behavior of other Israeli political parties, the fact of its participation contributes to the cynical, hostile attitude many Israelis have about religion in general. It is, after all, difficult for religious interests to present themselves as concerned with spiritual matters and disdainful of the profane world when its agents are seen elbow deep in the political muck of Israeli life, trading votes and making deals in order to accomplish its own purposes. Political wheeling and dealing, even if done in the name of religion, hardly creates the sort of atmosphere where Israelis can look on the Orthodox establishment as maintaining a higher standard of morality. When Minister of Religious Affairs Aharon Abuhatzeira became the first minister to be put on trial while in office, charged with a crime committed in his official capacity, thousands of Israelis made no effort to hide their delight. Abuhatzeira, scion of a proud, old Sephardic family of rabbis and scholars, was a member of the NRP. Although ultimately acquitted, his indictment and prosecution on charges of bribery and corruption was taken by many Israelis as proof of the essential hypocrisy of religious participation in politics.

Indeed, Israel's religious leadership is notable for its silence on secular matters that do not touch on religious interests. Despite all the agonizing that Israelis do about moral values, materialism, treatment of Arabs, civil rights, and similar issues, the voice of Israel's spiritual leadership is almost never heard. Unlike the United States, where clergymen of the Catholic, Protestant, and Jewish religions were heavily involved in the civil rights movement and the antiwar movement of the 1960s and 1970s, the clergy in Israel takes almost no interest in such matters. The only time that Israel's two chief rabbis chose to speak on a secular matter during my stay in Israel was to announce that the granting of immunity to a state's witness in return for his testimony against another person was contrary to religious law. The practice of granting immunity to witnesses in criminal cases is well-established in Israel and had been used for years without the chief rabbis' ever protesting or even commenting on the practice. What made the situation different in this instance was the target of the investigation—Minister of Religious Affairs Aharon Abuhatzeira.

Criticism of state involvement in religion and religious involvement in the state is not limited to antireligious forces in Israel. Any visitor to the ultrareligious quarter of Mea Shearim quickly discovers that the authority of the Jewish state is not universally accepted by all Jews living in Israel. Mea Shearim, whose inhabitants often can trace their ancestry in Israel back for generations and even hundreds of years, is a bastion of anti-Zionism. The few hundred members of the ultrareligious Hasidic Neturei Karta sect are adamant (and occasionally violent) in their opposition to the state. Inscribed on the wall of a synagogue within the sprawling compound that constitutes Mea Shearim are the words (in English block letters): JUDAISM AND ZIONISM ARE DIAMETRI-CALLY OPPOSED.

Neturei Karta and other ultrareligious sects in Mea Shearim and elsewhere in the country, though a small minority, oppose the state as a violation of God's supposed admonition to Jews to remain obedient to the governments of the countries to which they had been dispersed after the destruction of the Second Temple. The attempt to create a state, in the view of these fundamentalists, contravenes the prophecy that Jewish sovereignty would be restored in Israel with the return of the Messiah, not before. Israeli state holidays are an occasion for ritual mourning among these fundamentalist groups. According to a Neturei Karta publication: "The zionists [sic] said, 'Who is G–d? We will roll up our sleeves and take the Land back by ourselves.'" Zionists, according to Neturei Karta, "view the Torah and the Jewish faith as an impediment to their nationalistic and materialist ends. The leaders of the state do not represent the Jewish people."

The antistate religious fundamentalists also refuse to recognize the authority of the Chief Rabbinate, the institution established during the British Mandate and continued under the state to formalize supervision and enforcement of the functions ceded to religious authority by secular authority. As an extension of the state, the Chief Rabbinate is seen by religious fundamentalists as a symbol of corruption.

Neturei Karta and other religious fundamentalists are obviously at the extreme end of the spectrum in their opposition to the Jewish state. More moderate voices also can be heard in Israel from religious sources supporting the state. Professor Yeshayahu Leibowitz, who served as editor of the *Hebrew Encyclopedia* and is a religious Jew, has been a persistent critic of the melding of secular and religious affairs in Israel. In Leibowitz's view Israel would do well to emulate the United States—keeping the state out of religious affairs and religious interests out of the state's business. The maintenance of religion "by an irreligious government" leads to perversion and corruption, according to Leibowitz.

The demand for the separation of religion from the existing secular state derives from the vital religious need of preventing religion from becoming a means for satisfying political-social needs, preventing religion from becoming the ministry of a secular authority, a function of the governmental bureaucracy and administration. The government "maintains" religion and religious institutions not for religious reasons but because of political interests.

Leibowitz refers acidly to organized religion in Israel as "a kept woman of the secular power." The religious institutions that promote their interests with the state, in Leibowitz's words, "are the pimps of this whore."

While the conventional wisdom holds that secular authority in Israel has caved in to religious interests in order to gain political support within government coalitions, Leibowitz turns the argument on its head, asserting that secular authority in Israel adopts only enough of the religious program "to arouse anger, and sometimes even rage, against religion." Contrary to the prevailing view that the state—to some extent—has become a prisoner of religious interests, Leibowitz maintains that in Israel the state has neutralized religion as a source of potential opposition by giving religious institutions a vested, financial interest in the state through large-scale subsidies. In return, Leibowitz argues, religious authorities maintain a hands-off policy in matters of secular interest, providing no moral guidance or criticism. The prophets have been silenced.

Leibowitz's view is hardly the conventional interpretation of the relationship between secular and religious authority in Israel. Leibowitz himself, though generally considered to be a brilliant man with far-ranging interests, is considered something of a maverick in Israel, the kind of "character" that Israelis find amusing—and even attractive—in small doses. I have introduced him into this discussion precisely because he does go against the grain of the conventional wisdom in Israel, a country no less prone than any other to modish analysis and stilted thinking that enshrines pat explanations long after they cease to reflect reality.

Leibowitz is certainly unrepresentative in his vociferous criticism of Israeli fixation with the Western Wall.

For Jews the world over probably no greater symbol of Judaism exists than the Western Wall, the only remaining edifice from the structure of the Second Temple. After the Romans destroyed the Second Temple in A.D. 70, the remaining western wall upon which the Temple Mount had been constructed became the famed "Wailing Wall," at which devout Jewish men and women came to pray and to weep at the tragedy that had overcome the Jewish people.

For Leibowitz, however, this fixation with the wall and the Temple Mount

> has become idolatry. Holy place is a totally idolatrous concept. The Western Wall is vile. It is a religious discotheque. It is not even holy. It is nothing. It is a few stones remaining from the wall of the Temple Mount that arouses sincere sentiment. That's the way it was when it was in a narrow alley. [After the Old City of Jerusalem came under Israeli control in 1967, the buildings built next to the wall were torn down and an elaborate plaza was constructed.] Today the wall, with half a football field, has become a showplace for tourists and military parades. There are even people who think it is the Lord's post office—and that is really the Golden Calf. [Prayers written on scraps of paper are traditionally inserted between the stones in the wall.] In all Israel's history there was no religious phenomenon like the calf. But the calf need not be made of gold. It can be a country, a state, a people or a person.

Although some nonreligious Israelis may share Leibowitz's views toward the Western Wall and his willingness to give up Israeli control over it in order to remove what he calls the source of "conflict between us and six hundred million Muslims," most Israelis would disagree. The maintenance of Israeli control over

Jerusalem remains the one question that united the overwhelming majority of Israelis—religious or not, hawk or dove, Ashkenazim or Sephardim. Any Israeli government that willingly negotiated an end to a unified Jerusalem under Israeli sovereignty would not be able to survive a vote of confidence in the Knesset. One of the first acts of the Knesset after the 1967 war was to take steps to annex the eastern half of Jerusalem, including the Old City and the holy places, which, since 1948, had been under Jordanian control and completely inaccessible to Israelis.

Israel has spent hundreds of millions of dollars ringing Jerusalem with new communities in order to ensure that the city cannot again be divided. All of this effort reflects the deep-seated belief in Jerusalem as a religious and national symbol of unparalleled importance for Israelis, and Jews all over the world.

As we have already seen, Zionism was hardly welcomed by the Orthodox leadership, especially in eastern Europe. "We are in the *Golus* [the Diaspora] for our sins," one ultrareligious opponent of Zionism said. "We have been elected by Divine Providence and must lovingly accept our sentence."

Yet not all religious Jews were ready to oppose or to turn their backs on Zionism. A religious party, the Mizrachi, took its place within the Zionist movement with the avowed intention of establishing a religious majority in Palestine. Far from prominent in Zionism, these early members of the movement did provide a link with the Orthodox community.

The reconciliation of Zionism and religious Judaism is a process that still is not complete. From a theoretical and a practical point of view, one of the most important supporters of Zionism was the first chief rabbi in Palestine, Abraham Isaac Hacohen Kook. Kook also founded a Jewish academy, the Yeshivat Mercaz HaRav (Central Rabbinical Seminary), an institution that has become the spiritual fountain for the Gush Emunim movement in Israel.

Kook, a philosopher and theologian, provided the exposition that synthesized religious Judaism and Zionist nationalism. According to Kook modern Zionism was a sign that the process of redemption foretold in the Bible had begun. The Balfour Declaration and the other political progress made by Jews in reconstituting a homeland in Palestine were all tangible symbols of this process. The Messianic era was being hastened by the work of the Zionists, even though they might not be aware of their role, Kook told his followers. That this process might seem strange or that secular and even profane Zionists might be unusual instruments for inaugurating the Messianic era did not trouble Kook. Man, according to Kook, could not fully comprehend the workings of God's plan.*

Kook died in 1935, but his work was carried on by his son, Rabbi Zvi Yehuda Kook, who continued to lecture and teach at the academy his father had founded in Jerusalem. Israel's achievement of independence and her later victory in the Six Day War were taken as further evidence that Zionism was a fulfillment of God's promise for Jewish dominion over the Land of Israel and the advent of the Messianic era.

Rabbi Zvi Kook's work produced a nucleus of young, militant Orthodox Jews who were passionate supporters of the Jewish state as a secular instrument of God's will. This nucleus provided the foundation for the group that became Gush Emunim. Deeply religious, but also involved in contemporary affairs, the members of Gush Emunim have proved to be zealous and purposeful in pursuit of their program. "Imbued with the belief that the age we are living in is of Divine imminence, they are convinced that He who saw to it that the War of Liberation and the Six Day War would take place will also see to it that the process continues, when the ordained time comes," Sprinzhak has written of Gush Emunim. The members of Gush Emunim see themselves as actors in a divine historical process. The need of the hour is to be bold, in the view of Gush Emunim.

Once the Divine moment has occurred, it would be unthinkable to allow feebleness, cowardice or the "now people" to

---

* I am substantially indebted to Dr. Ehud Sprinzhak for this analysis of Gush Emunim.

dictate the pace of events or for the [Israeli] government to give up what has been attained. It is a sacred duty to stand firm, to resist pressures from the U.S. and other nations, to prevent the establishment of any new Arab settlements within the boundaries of Eretz Yisrael and to help with the great process of redemption.

The importance of Gush Emunim for Israel is not as a formal organization. From the outset Gush Emunim avoided formalizing itself and establishing a bureaucratic structure. The significance of Gush Emunim lies in its embodiment of a frame of mind and attitudes deeply engrained and widely held in Israel. The institution of Gush Emunim is less important than the force that it represents in Israel. The institution itself may come and go, or may appear in other guises, but the force behind it is constant.

In its only comprehensive published articulation of its ideology, Gush Emunim presented this statement of its program:

> Its aim is to lead to a great movement of reawakening among the people of Israel, for the realization of the Zionist vision in its full scope, out of the realization that the sources of that vision lies in the heritage of Israel and in the roots of Judaism, and that its objective is the complete redemption of the people of Israel and of the whole world.

But Gush Emunim, Sprinzhak notes, is not a universal movement. To the contrary, "its thinking is nationalist and particularist, and its interest is not in humanity as a whole but in the people of Israel."

In the development of Gush Emunim and the formation of its program, one event stands out in a way that may be taken—if one is so inclined—as divine intervention in the world. For religious Jews, who take literally the biblical statement that the Land of Israel was promised to the Jewish people, further evidence of God's plan was provided by the reunification of Jerusalem after nineteen years of separation during which Jewish holy sites were totally inaccessible to Jews, and by the restoration—after two thousand years—of Jewish sovereignty over the city as well as over Judea and Samaria. Indeed, graduates of Rabbi Kook's academy had been witnesses only a few weeks before the war at what must have seemed in retrospect a moment of prophecy:

> On the eve of Independence Day 1967, most of the group met for an Old Boys' get-together at the Yeshivat Mercaz HaRav. As was his wont, the venerable Rabbi Kook gave a festive sermon, in the course of which he suddenly dropped the quiet tones to which his listeners were accustomed and began to lament loudly the division of the historic Land of Israel. He conveyed to his loyal students the message that this situation was intolerable and could not last much longer. It is hardly surprising then that when, only three weeks later, his former students found themselves to be citizens of the expanded state of Israel, they were convinced that their Rabbi had, that Independence Day, been inspired by the genuine spirit of prophecy. Rabbi Kook himself is a man of great charisma and his loyal students became his emissaries, imbued with a sense of duty and of unshakable self-confidence in the rightness of their mission and in the existence of Divine backing for their actions.

In 1968 seventy-three young religious men and women formed a settlement in a hotel in the city of Hebron, contrary to the Israeli government's policy at the time, which forbade settlement on the West Bank near large population centers. Ultimately, after considerable tension between the settlers and the Arab community and between the settlers and the government, the settlement was permitted to move to the outskirts of Hebron where temporary, and later permanent, structures were built for the settlers and for those who joined them. The settlement was given the biblical name Kiryat Arba (Town of the Four), after its proximity to Hebron where Abraham, Sarah, Isaac, and Jacob are buried.

Among the settlers in Kiryat Arba were Israelis who later provided the nucleus of Gush Emunim, which was formally constituted in 1974. The precipitating event in the formation of Gush Emunim apparently was the separation-of-forces negotiations between Israel and Egypt following the 1973 war. Demoralized by the war and entering the talks under pressure to make territorial concessions, the Labor Alignment government was weak and divided. The National Religious Party had again entered the government coalition and appeared to be taking a conciliatory position regarding the negotiations. Taking its place as a group within the NRP, Gush Emunim's purpose was to counterbalance sentiment within Israel sympathetic to making territorial concessions in the approaching negotiations.

Although Gush Emunim left the NRP to become an independent organization after a short period, the Gush has remained close to the NRP. Prominent among the organizers of Gush Emunim were several graduates of Rabbi Zvi Kook's seminary. Consistent with the interpretation of Zionism offered by Rabbi Kook, Gush Emunim favored more settlement on the West Bank and formal extension of Israeli sovereignty to the West Bank, which they referred to by the biblical names of Judea and Samaria.

Working within the interlocking network of Israel's religious communities, Gush Emunim's leadership met with other Israelis in private homes, in religious high schools, in yeshivas, and in other places to explain its outlook and program. Settlement groups were formed and demonstrations organized to protest the government's concessions in the negotiations. Gush Emunim gave support in its demonstrations to protests organized by the Movement for a Greater Land of Israel, another ultranationalist group that opposed returning any territory captured in the Six Day War. Gush Emunim also organized demonstrations to dramatize its support for more settlements in Judea and Samaria.

The official position of the Israeli government, until 1977, was to view settlement on the West Bank from the pragmatic view of security. The only settlements sanctioned by the government, with the exception of Kiryat Arba and Kfar Etzion, between Jerusalem and Hebron, were those regarded as increasing the security of Israel proper. Using public and private pressure, Gush Emunim succeeded in establishing four small settlements on the Golan Heights and the West Bank.

The most dramatic breakthrough came from a zealous group from Kiryat Arba that attempted eight times to start a settlement outside the Arab city of Nablus in Samaria. The first seven times the group attempted to settle, the Israeli army stopped the settlers and destroyed whatever foundations they had established for a settlement. On the eighth attempt, after a dramatic confrontation between the settlers and the army, a compromise was worked out with the government and the settlers were allowed to move into a nearby army camp. Following this success, which exploited devisions within the Labor Alignment, Gush Emunim was able to establish contact with members of Labor-supported settlements and to win their backing.

Following the victory of Menachem Begin and the Likud party in May 1977, Gush Emunim moved forward vigorously with its program of "creating facts" on the West Bank. Although friction ultimately developed between Begin and Gush Emunim over Begin's proposal to grant autonomy to West Bank Arabs as part of the peace agreement with Egypt, the overall policy of the Israeli government was strongly supportive of settlements on the West Bank. No firm figure can be given for the Israeli government's investment on the West Bank during the Begin government's tenure, but it is generally agreed that the total expenditure on settlements and the infrastructure to support them has run into hundreds of millions of dollars.

Gush Emunim was able to draw heavily for support from the expanding religious community in Israel. Higher birth rates and immigration, especially by religious Jews from the United States, had substantially increased the position of religious Zionism in Israel by the late 1970s. Although only a fraction of these religious Zionists were willing to leave the warmth and comfort of Jerusalem, Tel Aviv, and the other established areas where they lived to endure the relative isolation and inconvenience required to establish a new settlement on the West Bank, thousands were sympathetic to what Gush Emunim was doing. Gush Emunim was part and parcel of the "knitted skullcap" subculture of Israel, so named for the knitted caps worn by young religious Israelis. The knitted caps, in addition to being tokens of their observance of the commandment that men must keep their heads covered, also signified the wearer's participation in the life of the community as a full and active member.

After the establishment of the state, the separate school systems or "trends" maintained by the various movements within Palestine's Jewish community were merged into a single, state-operated system—with the exception of religious schools, which were permitted to remain separate from the secular system. Using the schools and the religious youth movement, B'nei Akiva, as a base, the religious Zionists were able to fashion a strong, broadly based, ideologically committed movement. Whereas ideology has waned in the secular society, the importance of ideology has grown under the guidance of the graduates of Rabbi Kook's academy, who have spread out through the religious community and have maintained their ties to Rabbi Kook and his teachings.

According to Dr. Sprinzhak:

At a time when the general educational system in Israel underwent a general eclipse of inspiration, the national-religious public was spared this process, and emerged instead strengthened and consolidated. Around this powerful educational system, patterns of behavior and life emerged for an entire public which preserves its religiosity not only in the homes and in the synagogue, but also for the future. It has been at the greatest pains to see to it that the sons and daughters of its adherents perpetuate its way of life. For this purpose, it has mapped out a route from the neighborhood kindergarten through to college or yeshiva. The main indication of the success of this great step may be discerned in the prestige that is attributed to the teaching profession. In secular education in Israel today, teaching has lost much of the prestige that attached to it at the time of the prestate Yishuv . . . and has today become a woman's profession, while where religious education is concerned, teaching has lost none of its value and prestige in the scale of social status. The cream of the school students and the sons went on to attend *yeshivot* or study to become rabbis and did not hesitate to come back to teach at all levels of the system. They meet with each other, form marriage links, belong to the same organizations.

Coming from a strongly unified subculture, with shared values and a shared outlook on secular as well as religious matters, this younger generation of religious Zionists is in a strong position to challenge the still larger, but less unified Israeli society. "If Israeli society, with its characteristic scale of values as it was in the forties and fifties, had preserved its spiritual and Zionist movement-imbued characteristic in later years as well," Sprinzhak asserts,

> the "knitted skullcaps" would have by now overcome the equation of historic Zionist inferiority that was attributed to them [a Jew in a skullcap equaled a Diaspora Jew] and taken an honorable place in our present-day society. But against the background of the "end of ideologies," Israeli version, their victorious emergence as a spiritual community and a group of unique cultural and social characteristics is particularly striking.

Israelis have been accustomed to seeing Gush Emunim as a radical, extreme fringe group divorced from the larger religious community. Though more pronounced in its views than the rest of the religious Zionist community, Gush Emunim draws considerable support from it.

Understood simply as a movement of religious fanatics, Gush Emunim is hardly comprehensible. Seen as a movement that grows out of Israeli society, that speaks the vocabulary of the Zionist movement and uses many of the same techniques that Zionists used in the prestate era, Gush Emunim comes into focus. Up close, its members hardly seem fanatical at all. Gentle, soft-spoken, and thoughtful, they present a reasonable, moderate appearance. Visited in their homes—especially in the cramped quarters of the mobile homes used to house them temporarily on the various West Bank settlements until permanent structures are built—one cannot help but be impressed by the sacrifices they are making to carry out their beliefs. They freely concede that they may be out of step with public opinion, but they are motivated by a sense of historical and divine destiny and believe that in the long run they will be vindicated.

In an era marked by hesitation and drift in Israeli life, Gush Emunim members see themselves as the logical heirs of a spirit and philosophy that sustained the earliest Jewish pioneers in Israel in their drive to settle the land and later to establish the state. From this perspective, opinion outside of Israel—and even inside Israel—is less important than action. What counts, David Ben-Gurion once said, "is not what the Gentiles say, but what the Jews do." When the issue arose in the prestate era of Jewish right to settle on land in the Negev owned by the Jewish National Fund, Ben-Gurion's solution was to encourage settlement groups to "create facts." These groups, in the span of a single day, established walled stockades to house the settlers and protect themselves from Arab attack. They went to work in the fields carrying rifles, which were always at the ready. In much the same way, Gush Emunim has pressed for settlements in order to "create facts" that would be difficult for any future Israeli government to ignore or circumvent in negotiating a peace agreement.

As the last frontiers have been conquered and Israel has changed from a pioneering society to a modern industrial country the prestate years and the early years after independence have taken on a romantic allure in the minds of many Israelis. Nostalgia grips older Israelis as they remember the sense of dedication and commitment they once felt. The problems of the past seem simpler than those confronting Israel today. Whether or not problems actually *were* simpler in those days is beside the point. Israelis profoundly miss that sense of dedication, that drive to overcome seemingly insurmountable obstacles that they believe they once had. The weakening of ideology in Israel creates a profound sense of loss among Israelis who come from what they describe as "a strong Zionist upbringing." Part of the problem is the enormous emphasis that Zionism placed on the return to the land and the settling of it. Once the return was accomplished and the settlement was achieved, what mission remained for those who longed to be foot soldiers in the crusade? What heroic tasks remained to be performed in the streets of Tel Aviv and Jerusalem, in the increasingly prosperous kibbutzim and moshavim of the coastal plain and Israel's lush valleys, in the factories of Haifa?

The Israeli malady is twofold. First, Israeli life today lacks a general sense of purpose. The same aimlessness that pervades Western society can be found in Israel, but in Israel the void is felt more acutely among people who so recently grew up believing that they had a mission to perform for the Jews of the Diaspora and that their experience would be a moral example to the rest of the world. Industrialization, a population explosion, a series of wars, easy money, and the unavoidable influence of the outside world have transformed Israeli society.

Second, the Zionist dream has been realized with the establishment of the Jewish state. For revolutionaries and visionaries, the achievement of their goal is always a trauma. The reality in which we find ourselves living never quite measures up to the utopia we pictured in our minds. The basic thrust of Zionism's main concern was establishing a Jewish state, not debating the particulars of what that state would be.

Once the state was established, Zionism had little to offer about what direction matters should take. Unlike Communism, Zionism had no central body of dogma to fall back on to construct a program. The Mapai party, to be sure, continued to pursue its own program of pragmatic socialism, but eventually Mapai moved away from strict socialist ideology to compete for votes in a population that was increasingly nonsocialist. Ben-Gurion *had* thought about what direction the state should take, but Ben-Gurion was sixty-two when the state was established and had already led an exhausting life.

When Ben-Gurion finally stepped down as prime minister, he

was succeeded by the shrewd Levi Eshkol, a man competent to preside but not capable of inspiring Israelis to any great cause. Eshkol and his successors in the Labor Alignment—Golda Meir and Yitzhak Rabin—were pragmatic doers rather than visionaries. The heroic days of Ben-Gurion were over. Indeed, as Amos Elon points out in *The Israelis,* the new generation of sabras—Jews born in Israel—who came of age in the early 1950s, were not interested in theoretical formulations or *talking,* but in *doing.*

Yet this pragmatic, expedient attitude carries only so far. It sums up a temperament rather than expressing a philosophy. Ultimately, the question becomes, For what? Despite unprecedented prosperity and the most secure strategic position that Israel has enjoyed since the state's establishment, a malaise has settled over the country. "You see," an Israeli academic said, "we thought we could get along without ideology. People stopped talking about Zionism. It wasn't fashionable to talk—just to do. But now we are finding out that we can't live simply with action, without ideology. Without ideology, we've discovered, our society deteriorates."

Gush Emunim has appeared on the Israeli scene as the old spirit and drive has lost its force. Reality, tarnishing the visionary ideology of the early pioneers, has left the present generation disillusioned and despondent. As a nation Israel seems to have lost its sense of mission and direction. Materially, Israelis have never had it so good, yet they seem ill at ease with their comforts, sometimes embarrassed and almost apologetic that they should be violating the old ascetic ethic by living in relative luxury.

By contrast, Gush Emunim—despite its detractors and critics in Israel—seems motivated by a sincere and profound spiritual principle. The members of Gush Emunim do not surround themselves with material possessions or consider personal comfort to be a priority. Living in a cold, damp mobile home with five children on the top of a rocky hill reachable only by a muddy road is hardly soft living. What Gush Emunim possesses, however wrong-headed it may seem to Israelis who oppose it, is a vision of the future and a sense of how to get from here to there. And therein lies its success in Israel.

A poignant example of how many Israelis, totally in opposition to Gush Emunim's program and methods, nevertheless find themselves admiring the group's members for their seemingly selfless dedication was contained in an article in *Ha'aretz*, the moderately liberal independent morning newspaper of Israel. The article presented a lengthy portrait of Beit-El, a new settlement on the West Bank not far from Jerusalem. One after another of the settlers was given the opportunity to explain his or her views toward the Israeli government, the Arabs, Israeli society, the future—the whole range of issues confronting contemporary Israel. The author, reporter Dan Margalit, describes the sense of community and purpose that exists among the settlers, and the quiet, reasonable, and democratic way that they go about reaching decisions on the problems confronting them.

"In every conversation," Margalit wrote,

> I was asked what my point of view was. I agreed that all Zionist education required an understanding of the Jewish heritage, that the Jews' right to the Land of Israel is eternal, that the PLO is not interested in dividing the land but plans to undermine the State of Israel, that anti-Semitism is rampant in the world, that the West is weak (like it was in the thirties). Do they not have the slightest doubts, I asked? Do they not feel that they are making the conflict worse? Are they not responsible for splitting the nation? Did not the Jewish sages state that a war among brothers was the worst of all? Why should they not make do meanwhile with settling the Galilee [inside Israel proper], the sovereignty of which is also being threatened? Is there no price they feel is worth paying to slow down the deterioration in relations with the United States or with their political opponents inside Israel? I asked also whether they should not make concessions with regard to their plans. In the same way the true mother was prepared to give up her child when King Solomon judged that it should be cut in half.
>
> They were adamant in their views. . . . Samaria, they repeated, would not wait for them under [Israeli army] rule for

another decade. Political needs were decisive. The danger of withdrawal had to be prevented.

At the article's end, after presenting the issues and profiles of several settlers, Margalit focuses on one settler, a woman, summing up not only the settlers' sense of their own mission, but the author's own ambivalence in the face of what he perceives to be the settlers' selfless sincerity and his own sense of lost mission:

> "There have been more evenings when I've wanted to leave, than there have been mornings when I've wanted to stay," confessed Edith Ehrlichman to her colleagues. "With me it was not even a matter of historical link to the biblical period. Certainly I did not participate in the demonstrations or take part in any of the ruckus made by Gush Emunim. That isn't for me. But my grandfather was one of the founders of Tel Hai [an early settlement in the Galilee whose members were killed by the Arabs]. Recently I had a look at some documents from that period. I saw how they were told that they were a burden, were causing trouble for the entire Yishuv, and that they should stop their settlement activity because they were endangering the public peace. Now we know that the settlers of the Galilee were right and their critics were mistaken. For me to remain here means that history will repeat itself and that in time everyone will know that we were right. Just like my grandfather was. The scorn will be replaced by a settlement effort."

"This is Edith's prediction," the author concludes. "A new ladder which leads to the heavens is now situated in Beit-El [see Genesis 28:10–22]. I departed from her doubtful as before. But in my heart I envy her."

When I spoke with the author of the article some weeks after it had been published, I mentioned to him that I sensed his ambivalence toward the settlers. "I don't agree with them at all," he told me. "But I love them."

Nonetheless, the phenomenon that Gush Emunim represents is a serious threat to the stability of Israeli democracy. That repossession of all of the Land of Israel—including land occupied by more than one million Palestinian Arabs—may mean the end of democracy in the State of Israel is not a matter that causes much concern among members of Gush Emunim. Given a choice between territory and democracy, the members of Gush Emunim—and thousands of other Israelis—will choose territory. For one thing, some Israelis believe that many Arabs will choose to leave rather than to live under Israeli rule. Even though the annual census of the territories does not reflect any mass emigration of Arabs—just the opposite—the prospect of Jews in Israel eventually being outnumbered by Arabs is not worrisome for Gush Emunim members.

"Democracy," a Gush Emunim member said, explaining the group's philosophy, "is supposed to serve the interests of the people, not undermine their interests. That's why it's conceived as a positive political system that has been adopted in the West, because it's good for the people, not disadvantageous for the people. When it becomes disadvantageous for the people, as in wartime, they close up democracy and put people in camps, as they did to the Japanese in America. Or they declare national emergency measures. If democracy becomes inimical to the fundamental interests of the State of Israel, then it has to be reconsidered and analyzed and maybe eliminated."

Given Israel's present political system and the power that the National Religious party has been able to wield despite its minority status, it is unlikely that any Israeli government will have a free hand in negotiating a peace treaty with other Arab states besides Egypt if dismantling the roughly eighty Jewish settlements on the West Bank is necessary for an agreement. Gush Emunim and its supporters are a crucial part of the NRP's constituency. For these religious Jews possession of a unified Land of Israel is a task of the highest order, a fulfillment of a divine promise and therefore something that no mere government—even a Jewish government—can change. As Sprinzhak put it:

384

The NRP . . . could not in the past, cannot today and will not be able in the future to alienate itself entirely from Gush Emunim because that would mean ideological alienation from the cream of its members, who adhere if not to the practice of Gush Emunim, then at least to its world philosophy. That is why any government in Israel that gets into a sharp confrontation with Gush Emunim will face the danger of a coalition crisis. Gush Emunim is not merely a movement deeply rooted in present-day Israeli political culture, but it has also created a new reality of existence for thousands of people, of links with Judea and Samaria and of readiness to protect these links at virtually any price. . . . Democracy, seen from their viewpoint, is an acceptable regime, provided it functions in the framework of Zionism as conceived by Gush Emunim. In case the two should clash, Zionism—Gush-style— must prevail. And if the majority—as represented by the government of Israel—should decide otherwise, then this is only a temporary political majority. It'. . . must be combated at any price.

As part of its settlement program the Begin government reorganized the defense of the West Bank, excusing settlers there from reserve duty so that they could participate in a regional defense system. Although Israeli officials are reluctant to provide details, it is generally understood that the settlers have been well-armed, not only with light weapons, including automatic rifles, but with artillery and antitank weapons. The settlers have been trained and many have served in combat with the Israeli army. The strictures within Judaism generally, and among these settlers in particular, against one Jew's taking up arms against another are very strong. And the likelihood that Jewish settlers would resort to violence to resist being moved out of their settlements is extremely remote—but not beyond the realm of possibility. What is certain is that these settlers would not, to meet the requirements of any peace agreement, willingly leave their homes at the request of the Israeli government. Monetary incentives might convince some, perhaps even many. But many more would remain and would have to be removed physically, perhaps even forcefully.

Alternatively, Israeli officials speak about Jewish settlers "remaining behind, on the other side of the border," to live in the ancient Land of Israel after a peace settlement. This prospect seems just as unlikely since living in the Land of Israel for these settlers is only half the idea. The other half is Jewish sovereignty over the land. Yet assuming for a moment that a peace agreement were reached, that the settlers remained, their presence *across* the border, their physical security, their continued contact with forces inside Israel who had resisted return of any territory to Arab control—all these factors would be a constant irredentist stimulant in Israeli politics.

In the absence of a clear, assertive majority willing to support strong measures and concessions to negotiate a peace treaty with Israel's remaining Arab adversaries, the opportunity for the small, vocal minority that Gush Emunim represents to rally more significant support among Israelis may postpone indefinitely the peace settlement Western countries are prodding Israel to accept.

10 / CONCLUSION

More than thirty years now have passed since the establishment of
the State of Israel. The novelty of a Jewish state has long since
worn off. The world has become accustomed to its existence and
the memory of the reasons for its creation are fading. A generation
later, the world is a far different place with different problems and
different concerns from those with which it was preoccupied immediately following World War II.

It is hardly an exaggeration to say that Israel has achieved
enormous accomplishments in the relatively brief span of her
existence. In one sense, Israel's accomplishments work against her,
raising expectations she cannot yet meet. Israel's accomplishments
also obscure her vulnerabilities.

For purposes of comparison and perspective it is useful to
remember that Israel is roughly at that point in her history where
the United States was when Andrew Jackson occupied the White
House. Lincoln and the Civil War, Ulysses Grant and the Robber
Barons, McKinley and the Spanish-American War, Teddy Roose-

velt and the Progressive Era, Woodrow Wilson and a world made safe for democracy, the Great Depression and the New Deal, World War II, the Atom Bomb, the Kennedy and King assassinations, Watergate—all of that was far into the future.

Familiarity has dimmed the impact of what Israel has achieved. In slightly more than a generation, a people literally scattered around the world has been united. They have revived a language that had been all but dead one hundred years ago and formed a nation capable of feeding itself, created a modern industrial state, and fielded an army fully able to defend the country and the people. The early Zionists dreamed of a utopia. Israel obviously falls short of the mark. But always we confront the question of perspective and standards. "Considering where we were in 1948, the diversity of the population and what *has* been accomplished," Israeli intellectual Yehoshua Arieli said, "Israel *is* a utopia."

Herzl believed that a Jewish state would end the anomalous position of Jews in the world. The wonder and elation that Jews once felt at seeing Jewish policemen, farmers, laborers, soldiers, pilots, porters, and waiters working in their own country has faded. In this respect, Israel has fulfilled Herzl's dream of making the Jews a "normal" people. Israel has Jewish scientists and criminals, Jewish professors and prostitutes, Jewish soldiers and statesmen, Jewish tax collectors, Jewish football, soccer, and movie stars. A whole generation of Israelis has grown up without experiencing the humiliation of anti-Semitism. "When I hear the phrase 'dirty Jew,'" one Israeli said, "my first impulse is to think I need a shower."

Israel is a country still in the throes of development, attempting to come to grips with very serious, although not necessarily insoluble, problems. Socially, economically, and politically, Israel is still grappling with problems that have confronted the state since its establishment.

These problems, though serious, are relatively minor when viewed against the malaise of the spirit and lost sense of purpose that has afflicted Israelis in the last decade. The most vital struggle going on in Israel today concerns neither territory nor security but the soul of the country. It is a struggle to determine what sort of nation Israel—despite all of her problems—is going to be.

Israelis' self-perception has changed from seeing themselves as bold pioneers. The idealism and sense of self-sacrifice fostered in the years immediately after the state was founded have given way to a generation out for themselves, challenging the values of a society conditioned to think in terms of the group's welfare. Most important, the vision of Israel as a just and humane society is challenged by a perception of Israel—at home as well as abroad—as an occupier and oppressor, denying to Palestinian Arabs what Israeli Jews so passionately sought for themselves.

The Jewish state was created, among other reasons, to permit the Jewish people to rejoin history as a nation. In the past decade, Israel has become more and more isolated in the world community. Israelis, sensing their isolation, have begun to view themselves as pariahs, concluding that whatever good they do will have no effect in convincing a hostile world of the justice of their cause. According to this view, the wrongs done to Israel go unnoticed while Israel's virtues and righteous acts go unheralded. Were Israel to meet the demands of the hostile world that many Israelis see, would it make any difference?

"Beyond any doubt," Shmuel Schnitzer, editor of the mass circulation afternoon paper, *Ma'ariv,* wrote in the summer of 1979 when criticism of his country was reaching new heights, "we are bound to discover after we prove to the world that we are so sensitive to its criticism and ready to accept its advice, that it has in store another bundle of expectations and another list of good advice to give us before it will agree to remove the moral boycott imposed on us."

The Israelis' perceptions that much of the world is at best indifferent and at worst hostile to their fate may well be correct. Much of the world *is* indifferent or hostile. In that sense, the creation of Israel has not normalized the Jewish people. Herzl's idea that restoring the Jewish people to the family of nations and permitting the Jewish nation to reenter history would eradicate anti-Semitism has proved wrong.

Far from being an integrated member of the world community, Israel is isolated. Far from being independent and self-sufficient, she is increasingly reliant on the largesse and support of a single benefactor—the United States. Israel's response in the face of growing hostility has not been to moderate her course, but to redouble her efforts. In spite of—perhaps because of—the opposition to her policy of consolidating control of territories captured in 1967, Israel has hardened her position, assuming a pugnacious stance in world forums. The mood of chauvinism is growing within Israel. The rhetoric of Israel's leaders, once characterized by proclamations of peaceful intentions and visions of a just, new society, now refers to dark forces threatening not only Israel but the entire Western world and stresses the need for brute strength and the resort to force.

Without a doubt, the world Israel finds itself in today is far different from that hopeful and expectant era following World War II when the state was established. The changes of outlook in Israel, however, are more than the simple shift from a benign view of the world that comes with the end of innocence. For all of the fresh-faced, optimistic imagery of Israel in its early years, Israelis already had learned first-hand in a bitter war of independence—which followed the greatest slaughter of a single people in the history of the world—what sort of a world they lived in. They could not have been unaffected by their baptism by fire.

Still, despite the problems and the contradictions, Israel held out the promise that it would find the middle course that would bring it stability, security, and peace because Israel was determined to make the effort.

The question that arises today is whether Israel still is determined to find that middle course. Although not fully appreciated by the world outside, Israel has paid a considerable price—economically and psychologically, if not strategically—to secure peace with Egypt. In their own minds, Israelis see themselves taking a large calculated risk in order to accomplish their ultimate goal to live in peace with their neighbors.

Yet, the sense of a transcending higher purpose that once motivated Israel seems to be succumbing to a simple urge for territorial possession dressed up in historical, religious verbiage that cannot disguise Israel's apparent intention to impose her will and rule on more than one million unwilling subjects. A generation of Israelis is now growing to maturity believing that it is only right and natural that they should control the lives of this disfranchised minority. Whether Israelis have fully reckoned the cost of this enterprise is not clear. "When the white man turns tyrant," George Orwell wrote of his own experience with colonialism, "it is his own freedom he destroys. He becomes a sort of hollow, posing dummy, the conventionalized figure of a sahib. For it is the condition of his rule that he shall spend his life in trying to impress the 'natives,' and so in every crisis he has got to do what the 'natives' expect of him. He wears a mask, and his face grows to fit it."

The question confronting Israel is not so much what the world thinks of her or what the world expects of her, but what Israel thinks and expects of herself. Israel stands in danger today not only of estranging herself from the democratic civilizations which were present at her creation, but more important, from her own moral and spiritual aspirations.

Other Middle Eastern countries, to be sure, indulge in rhetoric and actions far more severe and extreme than what Israel says or does. But Israel alone among the nations of the Middle East is considered one of the family of Western democracies. As her isolation in the world community grows and her pugnacious stance in the world forums reflects a growing mood of chauvinism, a bunker mentality is beginning to set in among a broad section of Israelis. In place of the humane values that the Zionist leaders of the pre-state and early poststate era proclaimed, a narrowly nationalistic vision of Israel and her place in the world is being articulated.

This current thrust is taking Israel down a far different road from the vision of Israel as a "light unto the nations" held out by Ben-Gurion.

"Against this vision of a 'light unto the nations,'" wrote Israeli kibbutz member Allan E. Shapiro, "stands the current cult of darkness, proclaiming the national mission as survival in a world that will be hostile forever. It preaches a new tribalism, a togetherness that emphasizes both how embattled we are and how alone we are. Forget the old secular faiths we are told. After all, they assume that there are universal values, that humanity does exist as a normative concept. Religious nationalism, a synonym for the new tribalism, includes just us."

Other Israelis perceived the same dark forces at work within Israel. Amos Oz, the Israeli writer, said on the eve of the 1981 election, that Israel was dividing itself into two camps. "On one side," Oz said, "the emotional world of siege and war, of glory and of race, of brutality and 'masculine' adventure, of blood and fire and delight in death.

"On the other side, the emotional world rooted in building and agriculture, in the fields of the valley (Jezreel), in the life of purity, the life of liberty."

To read the Bible is to read how human weakness and folly time and again brought the Jewish people to tragedy and ruin. In biblical times, the prophets warned the people against their excesses. Today in Israel, as in those times, secular prophets have raised their voices in warning. It is characteristically Israeli, as we have seen, to look at the bright side of things, to insist on seeing silver linings where others see only clouds, to point to more than thirty years of accomplishments—undeniably impressive—as proof that skepticism is misplaced. Yet thirty, forty, or even fifty years in the life of a nation is but a moment, however eventful those years might be. Drawing eternal principles from less than four decades of experience may be inviting disaster. As Israel grows more isolated, it begins to find satisfaction—even a certain superiority—in its isolation rather than seeking ways to reverse the trend.

The notion of a fortress Israel, though appealing to chauvinists, raises the specter of siege and isolation, a dead end whose final chapter is obliteration. That specter, of course, is not without historical precedent. Once in their history, the Jewish people in Israel—badly divided—found their country in the hands of the Romans. Fleeing Jerusalem after its fall and the destruction of the Second Temple, almost one thousand religious zealots made their way to the mountaintop fortress of Masada where they managed to keep the Roman army at bay for more than a year. Finally, faced with defeat, capture, and slavery or death, they elected to commit mass suicide rather than fall to the Romans. In all, 960 men, women, and children perished by their own hands.

As an inspiration to an infant country fighting for its very life, the legend of Masada served Israel well in encouraging its citizens to be willing to make the supreme sacrifice. Different times call for different responses. There is also virtue in survival, in distinguishing between the essential and the desirable, in rejoining history rather than seeking to re-create it. The essence of Israeli existence is a dynamic tension between two diametrically opposite poles. Moving too close to either invites destruction. The middle course, the way of restraint and self-denial that Israelis knew and practiced so well in the early years of the state, now seems excessively timid to the new Israeli leadership and to the younger generation, which has grown up in a country no longer the underdog but the dominant power in the region.

Although constantly under threat and embattled, an Israel true to her moral and spiritual heritage is more than capable of surviving and prospering in a dangerous world. It is when Israel wanders from the path of her own principles that she runs the greatest risks. In the final analysis, the greatest danger to Israel lies not outside her borders, but in her own soul and spirit.

Chaim Weizmann, Israel's first president, addressed himself on his deathbed to the contradictory nature of the Jewish people: "We are a small people," he said, "but a great people. An ugly and yet a beautiful people. A creative and a destructive people. A people in whom genius and folly are equally commingled. We are an impetuous people who time and again repudiated and wrecked what our ancestors built. For God's sake, let us not allow the breach in the wall to swallow us."

BIBLIOGRAPHY

Abramov, S. Zalman. *Perpetual Dilemma: Jewish Religion in the Jewish State*. Crambury, N.J.: Associated University Presses, 1976.

Allon, Yigal. *The Making of Israel's Army*. New York: Bantam, 1971.

Anderson, Elliott, ed. *Contemporary Israeli Literature*. Philadelphia: The Jewish Publication Society, 1977.

Antonius, George. *The Arab Awakening*. New York: Capricorn Books, 1965.

Arendt, Hannah. *Eichmann in Jerusalem*. New York: Viking Compass, 1965.

Baker, Henry E. *The Legal System of Israel*. London: Sweet and Maxwell, Ltd., 1961.

Bank of Israel. Annual Report.

Bar Zohar, Michael. *Ben Gurion*. New York: Delacorte Press, 1978.

Bartov, Hanoch. *Dado: 48 Years and 20 Days*. Tel Aviv: Ma'ariv Book Guild, 1981.

Begin, Menachem. *The Revolt*. New York: Nash, 1981.

Bellow, Saul. *To Jerusalem and Back*. New York: Viking, 1976.

Ben Ezer, Ehud, ed. *Unease in Zion*. New York: Quadrangle, 1974.

Ben-Gurion, David. *Israel: A Personal History*. Tel Aviv: Sabra Books, 1972.

———. *My Talks with Arab Leaders*. Jerusalem: Keter, 1972.

———. *Rebirth and Destiny of Israel*. New York: Philosophical Library, 1954.

Benvenisti, Meron. *The Torn City*. Jerusalem: Isratypeset, Ltd., 1976.

Bettelheim, Bruno. *The Children of the Dream*. New York: Avon, 1970.

Bevan, E. R., and Charles Singer, eds. *The Legacy of Israel*. London: Oxford University Press, 1965.

Bondy, Ruth. *The Israelis*. Tel Aviv: Sabra Books, Funk & Wagnalls, 1969.

———, et al, eds. *Mission Survival*. New York: Sabra Books, 1968.

Buber, Martin. *Israel and the World*. New York: Schocken, 1948.

Collins, Larry, and Dominique Lapierre. *O Jerusalem!* London: Pan Books, Ltd., 1972.

Curtis, Michael, and Mordecai Chertoff. *Israel: Social Structure and Change*. New Brunswick, N.J.: Transaction Books, 1973.

Dawidowicz, Lucy S. *The War Against the Jews*. New York: Bantam, 1976.

Dayan, Moshe. *Story of My Life*. New York: Morrow, 1976.

———. *Diary of the Sinai Campaign*. New York: Schocken, 1967.

Deshen, Shlomo, and Moshe Shokeid. *The Predicament of Homecoming*. Ithaca, N.Y.: Cornell University Press, 1974.

Duverger, Maurice. *Political Parties*. Cambridge: Methuen & Co., 1964.

Eban, Abba. *Autobiography*. New York: Random House, 1977.

Eisenberg, Dennis, Uri Dan, and Eli Landau. *The Mossad*. New York: Paddington Press, Ltd., 1978.

Eisenstadt, S. N. *Israeli Society*. London: Weidenfeld & Nicolson, 1967.

Elizur, Yuval, and Eliahu Salpeter. *Who Rules Israel?* New York: Harper & Row, 1973.

Elon, Amos. *Herzl*. New York: Holt, Rinehart & Winston, 1975.

———. *The Israelis: Founders and Sons*. New York: Holt, Rinehart & Winston, 1971.

———, and Sana Hassan. *Between Enemies*. New York: Random House, 1974.

Facts About Israel. Jerusalem: Israel Information Center, 1979.

Fein, Leonard J. *Israel: Politics and People*. Boston: Little, Brown & Co., 1967.

Friedlander, Saul. *When Memory Comes*. New York: Farrar, Straus and Giroux, 1979.

Friedman, Abraham. "Union Structure and Rank and File Revolt: The Israeli Experience." *Industrial Relations Industrielles*, Vol. XXXI, No. 2.

Gilbert, Martin. *The Jews of Arab Lands: Their History in Maps*. London: Furnival Press, 1975.

————. *Jerusalem: Illustrated History Atlas*. London: Macmillan, 1977.

————. *The Arab-Israeli Conflict: Its History in Maps*. London: Weidenfeld & Nicolson, 1974.

Golan, Matti. *The Secret Conversations of Henry Kissinger*. New York: Bantam, 1976.

Golden, Harry. *The Israelis*. New York: Pyramid Books, 1972.

Gordon, A. D. *Selected Essays*. New York: Arno, 1938. (Reprint)

Grayzel, Solomon. *A History of the Jews*. Philadelphia: The Jewish Publication Society, 1963.

Haber, Eitan. *Menachem Begin: The Legend and the Man*. New York: Delacorte Press, 1978.

Halkin, Hillel. *Letters to an American Jewish Friend*. Philadelphia: The Jewish Publication Society, 1977.

Harel, Isser. *The House on Garibaldi Street*. New York: Viking, 1976.

Harkabi, Yehoshafat. *Arab Strategies and Israel's Response*. New York: The Free Press, 1977.

Hasdai, Ya'acov. *Truth in the Shadow of War*. Tel Aviv: Zmora, Bitan, Modan, 1979.

Hazleton, Lesley. *Israeli Women*. New York: Simon and Schuster, 1977.

Heikal, Mohamed. *The Road to Ramadan*. New York: Quadrangle Books, 1975.

Herman, Simon. *Israelis and Jews*. Philadelphia: The Jewish Publication Society, 1971.

Herzl, Theodor. *The Jewish State*. London: H. Pordes, 1972.

Herzog, Chaim. *The War of Atonement*. Boston: Little, Brown & Co., 1975.

Hoffer, Eric. *The True Believer*. New York: Perennial Library, Harper & Row, 1966.

Hurewitz, J. C. *The Struggle for Palestine*. New York: Schocken, 1976.

Isaacs, Rael Jean. *Israel Divided: Ideological Politics in the Jewish State*. Baltimore: Johns Hopkins University Press, 1976.

Israel Pocket Library. Jerusalem: Keter, 1973.

Jiryis, Sabri. *The Arabs in Israel*. New York: Monthly Review Press, 1976.

Josephus. *The Jewish War*. London: Penguin Books, 1959.

Katz, Shmuel. *Battleground: Fact and Fantasy in Palestine*. New York: Bantam, 1977.

Khouri, Fred J. *The Arab-Israeli Dilemma*. Syracuse, N.Y.: Syracuse University Press, 1968.

Koestler, Arthur. *Promise and Fulfillment 1917–1949, Palestine*. London: Macmillan & Co., 1949.

Kollek, Teddy, and Amos Kollek. *For Jerusalem: A Life*. New York: Random House, 1978.

Kook, Abraham I. *Lights of Return*. New York: Yeshiva University Press, 1978.

Kraines, Oscar. *Government and Politics in Israel*. Boston: Houghton Mifflin, 1961.

Kurian, George Thomas. *The Book of World Rankings*. New York: Facts on File, 1979.

Laqueur, Walter. *A History of Zionism*. New York: Schocken, 1976.

———. *The Israel-Arab Reader*. New York: Bantam, 1970.

Levin, Harry. *Jerusalem Embattled: A Diary of the City Under Siege, March 25, 1948 to July 18, 1948*. London: Victor Gollancz Ltd., 1950.

Lewis, Bernard. *The Middle East and the West*. New York: Harper Torchbooks, 1966.

———. *The Arabs in History*. New York: Harper & Row, 1966.

Lieblich, Amia. *Tin Soldiers on Jerusalem Beach*. New York: Pantheon Books, 1978.

Lorch, Netanel. *One Long War*. Jerusalem: Keter, 1976.

Luttwak, Edward, and Dan Horowitz. *The Israeli Army*. New York: Harper & Row, 1975.

Marx, A., and M. L. Margolis. *A History of the Jewish People*. Cleveland and New York: Meridian Books (The World Publishing Co.), 1958.

Medding, Peter Y. *Mapai in Israel*. Cambridge: Cambridge University Press, 1972.

Meir, Golda. *My Life*. New York: Dell, 1978.

Melville, Herman. *Journal of a Visit to Europe and the Levant, 1856–57*. Princeton, N.J.: Princeton University Press, 1955.

Moorehead, Alan. *The Blue Nile*. New York: Harper & Row, 1980.

―――. *White Nile*. New York: Harper & Row, 1971.

Olami, Ihud, ed. *Israel Today*. Tel Aviv: Hamenora, 1967.

Oz, Amos. *Unto Death (Late Love and Crusade)*. New York: Harcourt Brace Jovanovich, 1978.

―――. *Elsewhere, Perhaps*. New York: Bantam, 1974.

―――. *My Michael*. New York: Alfred A. Knopf, 1972.

Pearlman, Moshe. *Ben Gurion Looks Back*. New York: Simon and Schuster, 1965.

Penniman, Howard R., ed. *Israel at the Polls*. Washington, D.C.: American Enterprise Institute, 1979.

Peres, Shimon. *David's Sling: The Arming of Israel*. London: Weidenfeld & Nicolson, 1970.

Rabin, Yitzhak. *The Rabin Memoirs*. Boston: Little, Brown & Co., 1979.

Rubenstein, Murray, and Richard Goldman. *Shield of David*. Englewood Cliffs, N. J.: Prentice-Hall, 1978.

Sachar, Howard M. *A History of Israel*. New York: Alfred A. Knopf, 1976.

Safran, Nadav. *Israel: The Embattled Ally*. Boston: Belknap Press, 1978.

Schama, Simon. *Two Rothschilds and the Land of Israel*. New York: Alfred A. Knopf, 1978.

Schiff, Ze'ev. *October Earthquake: Yom Kippur 1973*. Tel Aviv: University Publishing Projects, 1974.

―――. *A History of the Israeli Army*. New York: Straight Arrow Books, 1974.

Shapira Avraham, et al, eds. *The Seventh Day*. London: Penguin Books, 1971.

Shuval, Hillel, ed. *Water Quality Management Under Conditions of Scarcity*. New York: Academic Press, 1980.

Singer, Isaac Bashevis. *The Manor*. London: Penguin Books, 1968.

Sprinzhak, Ehud. *Gush Emunim: The Iceberg Model of Political Extremism*. Unpublished.

Statistical Abstract of Israel. Central Bureau of Statistics, Jerusalem: 1978, 1979, 1980.

Sykes, Christopher. *Crossroads to Israel*. Bloomington, Ind.: Indiana University Press. Paper, 1973.

Teveth, Shabtai. *The Cursed Blessing*. New York: Random House, 1969.

————. *The Tanks of Tammuz.* London: Sphere Books Ltd., 1970.

————. *Moshe Dayan: The Soldier, the Man, the Legend.* Boston: Houghton Mifflin, 1973.

Turki, Fawaz. *The Disinherited.* New York: Modern Reader Paperback, 1972.

Twain, Mark. *Innocents Abroad.* New York: Harper & Row, 1869.

Uris, Leon. *Exodus.* New York: Bantam, 1959.

Vigo, Avigdor. "A propos du terme 'Palestine,' " *Pouvoirs, Revue d'Étude Constitutionelles et Politiques,* Number 7: 1978.

Vilnay, Ze'ev. *Israel Guide.* Jerusalem: Daf-Chen Press, 1978.

Wallach, Y. D., and Moshe Lissak. *Carta Atlas History of Israel.* Tel Aviv: Carta, 1978. (in Hebrew)

Weisgal, Meyer W., and Joel Carmichael, eds. *Chaim Weizmann: A Biography by Several Hands.* New York: Atheneum, 1963.

Weizman, Ezer. *On Eagles Wings.* New York: Berkley, 1979.

Weizmann, Chaim. *Trial and Error.* New York: Schocken, 1966.

INDEX

Abimelech, 6
Abraham, 3, 190
Abuhatzeira, Aharon, 153, 231–232, 366–367
Achdut Ha'Avoda, 185, 186
Achtar, Muhammad, 246
Agranat, Shimon, 203
Agriculture, 4, 98–99, 146, 327–328, 332, 333–334
Agudat Yisrael party, 66, 206, 210, 215, 358, 366
Air force, 297, 302, 303–304, 315, 316
Alami, Musa, 248–249
Allon, Yigal, 278, 281
Altalena, 196–197, 224
Amit, Meir, 150, 321
Antonius, George, *The Arab Awakening*, 238, 246–247
Arab-Israeli conflict, 25–26, 237–239, 244–247, 252–253, 288
Arabs, Israeli, 61–62; army and, 299; attitudes towards, 264–268, 269; education of, 264, 272–273; in politics, 261–262, 271–272; population, 258, 291; refugees, 254–256, 276; rights of, 234, 258; work of, 258–261, 273
Arieli, Yehoshua, 235, 388
Arlosoroff, Chaim, 221
Army, 296–326; between 1967 and 1973, 306–309, 312–313; leadership, 321; problems of, 300, 317–318; public attitude toward after wars, 311, 314–315; reputation of, 320, 323–324; serving in, 113–115, 299, 318–319, 324; and Six Day War, 305–306; women in, 64, 66–67 and Yom Kippur War, 299, 304–305, 308–310; *see also* Israel Defense Forces
Ashkenazi Jews, 153, 193; *see also* European Jews
Avineri, Shlomo, 256

Bader, Yohanan, 198
Balfour, Arthur James, 18–19
Balfour Declaration, 19–20, 103, 372
Bank Leumi, 115–116
Bar Lev, Haim, 321
Bar Yohai, Rabbi Shimeon, 167–168
Bedouins, 285, 299
Begin, Menachem, 30, 32, 153–154, 176, 195–198, 209, 211, 222, 282, 283, 286, 290, 292, 385
Bellow, Saul, 38
Ben-Gurion, David, 15, 38, 41, 52, 56, 60, 70, 89, 102–103, 161, 182–183, 188–189, 197–198, 199–200, 213, 221, 224, 243, 247–248, 260, 296, 380–381
Ben-Yehuda, Eliezer, 17
Bialik, Chaim, Nachman, 12
Bilu, 102
Black money, 140, 141, 142, 143, 148
B'nei Akiva, 377
Brit Shalom, 247, 249, 250
British Mandate, 24–25, 103
British Zionist Federation, 18–19

Canaan, 3
Censorship, 228
Children, 3, 5, 70, 328, 331–332
Citizenship, 363–365
Conservative Judaism, 355, 362–363, 364
Corruption, 207, 231–232
Crime, 67–68, 69, 84, 165
Crossman, R.H.S., 23

Dakar, 54–55
David, King, 3, 43
Dayan, Moshe, 56, 57, 82, 210, 213, 228, 276, 278, 303, 305–306, 321; *Diary of the Sinai Campaign*, 306
Dayan, Ruth, 56
Declaration of Independence, 26
Defense, *see* Army

Deir Yassin massacre, 254, 255
Democratic Movement for Change (DMC), 208, 217
Diamond, Stanley, 331
Dinitz, Simcha, 54
Dreyfus, Alfred, 7, 8
Duverger, Maurice, 199

Eban, Abba, 86–87
Economy, 97, 98, 113, 120–123, 148–150
Education, 71, 87, 155, 160, 371, 377–378
Egypt 26, 27, 29, 30, 60, 300, 301, 303–304, 307–308, 315, 317, 390
Ehrlichman, Edith, 383
Eichmann, Adolf, 37
Eisenstadt, S.N., 80
Eitan, Rafael, 225, 228–229
El Al, 108–109, 229
El-Khaldi, Yussef Ziah, 241–242
Elazar, David, 204, 305–306
Elon, Amos, *The Israelis: Founders and Sons*, 156, 256, 381
Emerson, Ralph Waldo, 387
Emigration of Israelis, 73
Employment, 110–111, 126–129
Emunim, Gush, 79
Eshkol, Levi, 147, 200, 213, 217, 381
Ethnic conflict, 152–154, 170–172
Etzel, 24; *see also* Irgun
European Jews, 50–51, 69, 153, 155, 156, 157, 166–167; *see also* Ashkenazi Jews
Exports, 146
Ezekiel, 1
Ezrahi, Yaron, 89

Factories, 107–108, 109–110; *see also* Kibbutzim
Farming, 146, 328, 332
Fein, Leonard, *Israel: Politics and People*, 198
Foreign aid, 120–125, 133–134, 149–150
Frankfurter, Felix, 245
Friedman, Abraham, 108, 118

Gafny, Arnon, 149
Gahal party, 172
Galilee, 263, 269–270, 274–275, 292
Gaza Strip, 189–190, 278, 279
General Federation of Jewish Labor, *see* Histadrut
Germany, 7, 20, 120, 122
Ginsburg, Asher, 12

Golan Heights, 27, 28, 189–190, 278, 305–306
Gordon, A.D., 12, 13, 96, 101
Griever, Gad, 81
Gur, Mordechai, 50, 307
Gush Emunim, 209, 210, 281, 371, 372–373, 374–379, 381–382, 384, 385, 386
Gush Etzion, 280

Ha'am, Achad, 12
Haganah, 24, 194–195
Halevi, Nadav, 125
Halutzim, 101
Hanukkah, 356
HaPoel HaZair, 13, 186
Harkabi, Yehoshafat, 42–43, 294–295
HaShomer HaZair, 186
Hasid, 170
Hebron, 279–280, 374
Herut party, 32, 172, 194, 196–198, 211
Herzl, Theodor, 1, 47, 242–243, 296, 346; *Altneuland (Old-New Land)*, 220, 349; *The Jewish State*, 8–10, 11, 16–17, 18, 352, 388, 389
Hess, Moses, 12, 349
Hevrat Ovdim, 104
Histadrut, 30, 63, 80, 103–107, 116–117, 212
Hobhouse, Leonard, 327
Hoffer, Eric, *The True Believer*, 39, 72
Holidays, 356–357
Holocaust, 21–22, 251
Hourani, Albert, 40
Housing, 136–138
Hovevei Zion, 8
Hussein, King, 287

Immigration of Jews, 21, 31, 102, 111–112, 157–159
Independence Day, 51
Inflation, 133, 144, 145, 146, 147–148
Iraq, 301, 317
Irgun Z'vai Le'umi (Irgun), 24, 187, 194–195, 254
Isaac, 3, 190
Israel Aircraft Industry (IAI), 131–133, 322–323
Israel Broadcasting Authority, 226
Israel Defense Forces (IDF), 26, 44, 263, 297, 298–301, 306–309, 317–319

Jabotinsky, Vladimir (Ze'ev), 16, 194, 195
Jacob, 3, 190

INDEX

Jerusalem, 25, 189–190, 283–284, 351, 360–362, 371, 373
Jewish Agency, 26, 255, 262
Jewish-Arab state, 247–248
"Jewish identity," 356, 364–365
Jewish law, 359, 364
Jewish National Fund, 249
Jordan, 26, 27, 42, 256, 270, 275, 277, 300, 301, 317
Joseph, 3
Joshua, 3
Journalism, 228–231; see also Press
Judae, see West Bank

Kahane, Rabbi Meir, 232, 265
Kahn, Zadok, 241
Kashruth, 349, 356, 359–360
Kfir, 322, 323
Kibbutz, 65, 101, 103, 327–345
Kibbutz Degania, 328
Kibbutz Ha'Artzi, 338
Kiryat Arba, 278, 280, 374, 376
Knesset, 62, 63, 83, 177–179, 204, 208, 215, 261
Koestler, Arthur, 196, 352–353
Kollek, Teddy, 54
Kook, Rabbi Abraham Isaac Hacohen, 371–372, 374
Kook, Rabbi Zvi Yehuda, 372
Kosher, 349, 356, 359–360

Labor Alignment, 30, 31–32, 116, 118, 172, 173, 175–176, 185, 198–199, 202, 204, 205, 206–207, 212–213, 215–216
Labor Zionism, 16, 173, 327
L'ag B'omer, 167–168
Language, 16–18, 161
Lavon, Pinchas, 199
Law of Return, 364, 365
Lebanon, 2, 26
Leibowitz, Yeshayahu, 357–358, 368–370; *Unease in Zion*, 344
Levin, Harry, 93–94
Liberal Party, 32, 208–209, 210
Libya, 301, 317
Lieblich, Amia, 58; *Tin Soldiers on Jerusalem Beach*, 49
Likud party, 32, 172, 176, 208–209, 215, 216
Litani, Yehuda, 289–290

Ma'Arach, 186
Mamluks, 5, 240

Mapai party, 116, 185–189, 204, 380
Mapam party, 186
Margalit, Dan, 382–383
Masada, 59, 93, 393
Matcote, 51
Mea Shearim, 367–368
Media, 224–227
Meir, Golda, 46, 62–63, 70, 200–201, 202, 203, 204, 213, 381
Melville, Herman, 5, 99–100
Memorial Day, 51, 324–325
Military, 33–34, 44, 232–233; see also Army
Mitla Pass, 305, 306
Mizrachi party, 371
Moroccan Jews, 158–159, 165
Moses, 1, 3
Moshavim, 103, 334
Movement for a Greater Land of Israel, 375

National Religious Party (NRP), 180–181, 184, 189, 205, 206, 215, 358, 366, 375, 385, 394
Navon, Yitzhak, 51
Nawi, Eliahu, 168–169
Nayon, Yitzhak, 154
Negev, 292, 315, 345
Neturei Karta sect, 367, 368
Newspapers, 224–226
Nuclear weapons, 228

Ofer, Avraham, 207
Oil, 134, 146; boycott, 277
Oriental Jews, 31–32, 50–51, 69, 153–160, 165–166, 169, 172–173, 192–193, 194, 212, 215
Orthodox Judaism, 355–356, 357, 362–365
Oruze, 299
Orwell, George, 391
Oz, Amos, 59, 92, 393; *Elsewhere, Perhaps*, 339

Palestine, 5–6, 13–14, 19–20, 24–26, 102–103, 239, 240, 243–247, 249, 251–253, 292–293, 327, 344
Palestinian Liberation Organization (PLO), 257, 271, 277, 288–289
Palmach, 187
Passover, 356
Peace Now Movement, 219
Peres, Shimon, 96, 169, 203, 204–205, 214, 221

Perlman, Eliezer, 17
Pinsker, Leo, 10–11, 12, 349; *Auto-Emancipation,* 8
Pinto, Daniel, 225
Poalei Agudat Yisrael, 366
Political parties, 179–183, 218; *see also* specific party
Politicians, 86, 88–89
Politics, 217–219, 221–223, 233–234
Population, 31, 58, 291, 329
Press, 224–226; *see also* Journalism
Productivity, 126–129, 130
Proteksia, 76, 78

Rabin, Yitzhak, 43–44, 83, 93, 174–175, 204–205, 206, 207, 213–214, 221, 305–306, 321, 381
Rakah party, 262, 271, 272
Reform Judaism, 355, 356, 362–363, 364
Religion, 346–359, 366–369
Revisionists, 16, 194, 195
Rosh HaNiqra, 1, 2
Rosh Hashanah, 357, 363
Rothschild, Lord, 18–19
Rubenstein, Amnon, *To Be a Free People,* 133
Rubenstein, Danny, 287–288, 289
Ruppin, Arthur, 249–251

Sachar, Howard M., *A History of Israel,* 254
Samaria, *see* West Bank
Sapir, Pinchas, 204
Sartre, Jean-Paul, 35–36
Saudi Arabia, 301, 317
Schnitzer, Shmuel, 389
Sephardic Jews, 153; *see also* Oriental Jews
Shamir, Yitzhak, 228
Shapiro, Allan E., 391–392
Sharon, Ariel, 82, 87, 209, 222, 282–283, 284, 285, 321
Sheli party, 265
Shemi, Yehiel, 340–341
Shimshi, Siona, 94–95
Shuval, Hillel, 333
Sinai Peninsula, 1, 7, 28, 189–190, 305
Six Day War (1967), 27–28, 42–43, 54, 275–276, 300, 303–304, 307, 324; territories, 32–33, 189–192, 279
Solomon, 3

Sprinzhak, Ehud, 372, 373, 377–378, 384–385
Sprinzhak, Yosef, 247
Suez Canal, 19, 307–308
Synagogue, 346
Syria, 26, 27, 29, 300, 301, 304–305, 307, 308, 317
Syrkin, Nahman, 16

Tal, Israel, 301
Talmon, Jacob, 33, 293–294
Taxes, 135, 297; evasion of, 140, 142, 143
Torah, 7, 100, 349
Twain, Mark, 5–6, 45

United Nations partition plan, 25–26, 252–253
United States, 120–121, 134

Vusvusim, 161

Wadi Salib riots, 160
"Wailing Wall," 370
War of Independence (1948), 26–27, 253–254, 324
Water, scarcity of, 332–333
Weapons, manufacturing, 322–323
Weizman, Ezer, 82, 92, 240, 298, 302, 321
Weizmann, Chaim, 19, 52, 61–62, 211, 221, 222, 236, 346, 351–352, 393
West Bank, 27, 28, 33, 190–192, 198, 276, 278, 279–292, 375, 376, 385–386
Western Wall, 370
Wiesel, Elie, 50
Women, 62–67, 69–71, 139, 258, 299
Work ethic, 101, 126, 127–129
Work force, 126, 139–140; productivity of, 126–129, 130; wages, 110–111, 135–136, 138

Ya'ariv, Aharon, 321
Yadin, Yigael, 150, 208, 222–223, 299
Yadlin, Asher, 207
Yeshivat Mercaz HaRav, 371
Yishuv, 13, 24, 104; Old, 33, 351–352
Yom Kippur, 357
Yom Kippur War (1973), 29–30, 41, 97–98, 277, 300, 301, 304–305, 308–310, 324

Zionism, 8–11, 14–16, 18, 33–35, 36–37, 38–39, 71–72, 181, 220, 240–241, 244, 245, 251–252, 327, 344, 350, 371, 380